THE MASS OF ALL TIME

THE MASS OF ALL TIME

ARCHBISHOP MARCEL LEFEBVRE

EDITED BY FR. PATRICK TROADEC
TRANSLATED BY ANGELUS PRESS

Angelus Press

PO Box 217 | Saint Marys, KS 66536

Originally published in French as *La Messe de Toujours* by Clovis © 2005.

English version by A. M. Stinnett, except for the passage of "The Three Against the Other," a poem by Jacques Debout, which was translated anonymously for Angelus Press.

Cover photo: Readers may wonder about the scar on Archbishop Lefebvre's right cheek. According to his sister Mother Marie-Christiane ("My Brother Archbishop Marcel," *The Angelus*, July 1996), he got it from an accident with barbed wire during his military service.

Library of Congress Cataloging-in-Publication Data

Lefebvre, Marcel, 1905-1991.
  [Messe de toujours. English]
  The Mass of all time : the hidden treasure / Marcel Lefebvre ; edited by Fr. Patrick Troadec.
     p. cm.
  Includes index.
  ISBN 978-1-892331-46-5 (trade softcover)
  1. Mass. 2. Catholic Church–Doctrines. I. Troadec, Patrick, 1960- II. Title.
  BX2230.3.L4413 2007
  264'.02036--dc22
                                                                  2007038167

©2007 by Angelus Press
All rights reserved. No part of this book may be reproduced or transmitted in any form or by any means, electronic or mechanical, including photocopying, recording, or by any information storage and retrieval systems without permission in writing from the publisher, except by a reviewer, who may quote brief passages in a review.

ANGELUS PRESS
PO BOX 217
ST. MARYS, KANSAS 66536-0217
PHONE (816) 753-3150
FAX (816) 753-3557
ORDER LINE 1-800-966-7337
www.angeluspress.org

ISBN 978-1-892331-46-5
FIRST PRINTING–January 2008
SECOND PRINTING–October 2022

Printed in the United States of America

For the glory of the most Blessed Trinity, for the love of Our Lord Jesus Christ, for the devotion to the Blessed Virgin Mary, for the love of the Church, for the love of the Pope, for the love of bishops, of priests, of all the faithful, for the salvation of the world, for the salvation of souls, keep this testament of Our Lord Jesus Christ! Keep the sacrifice of Our Lord Jesus Christ! Keep the Mass of All Time!

–Archbishop Lefebvre, Golden Jubilee Sermon

Contents

Acknowledgments ix
Foreword xi
Preface xv
The Heart of the Mass xvii

PART ONE: The Holy Sacrifice
    I. The Mass of the Catechumens 3
    II. The Sacrifice, or Mass of the Faithful 51
    III. The Communion 125

PART TWO: The *Novus Ordo Missae*
    I. What Was the Liturgical Reform? 177
    II. Luther's Mass 235
    III. The Consequences of the Novus Ordo Missae 244
    IV. Judgment of the Reform 261
    V. The Authority of the Traditional Rite 286
        General Conclusion 299

Appendices
    The Indult Mass 305

Lexicon of a Few Difficult Words 309
Brief Biographies 313
Index 319

Acknowledgments

This book was Fr. Gregory Celier's idea. I warmly thank him for having suggested that I collect the writings and remarks of Archbishop Lefebvre on the Mass with the help of the seminarians and Brothers at Flavigny.

I thank Ecône's Audio Department for having allowed me access to numerous unedited transcripts. I equally thank the Sisters of the Priestly Society of Saint Pius X, the Capuchins of Morgon, the Little Sisters of St. Francis of Lanorgard, and the Dominicans of Avrillé for the homilies and talks they sent me.

I must also especially thank the seminarians who listened to the recordings and patiently transcribed them during their stay at Flavigny during the summers of 2001 through 2004. I thank in particular Brother Alphonse-Marie, Fr. Christophe Callier, and Brother Jean-François for having successively overseen the work with tireless zeal.

I express my thanks also to those who helped me improve the work in its final stages by their precious advice. I thank especially my fellow priests: Fathers Delagneau, Joly, Laroche, La Rocque, Portail, and Simoulin.

I address my thanks equally to the numerous proofreaders, notably Father Bruno of Bellaigue, the Sisters of the Society of Saint Pius X, Mr. Vergeau (seminarian), Mr. François Triomphe, Madame Pages, and Miss Ferrard.

I wish to express my gratitude to His Excellency Bishop Bernard Tissier de Mallerais for his encouragement.

I equally thank Clovis Publications, which arranged the design and publication of the book.

Finally, I address my warm thanks to all those whom I have not named but who, in one way or another, collaborated in the publication of this work.

Fr. Patrick Troadec

Foreword

It is very often the altar that exercises a great power of attraction on the young man who longs to become a priest. The prospect of one day celebrating the holy sacrifice of the Mass, of holding the Sacred Host in his hands and communicating It to others, is the dream that inspires him. It was no different for the young Marcel Lefebvre when for the first time, on October 25, 1923, he crossed the threshold of the major seminary. Fifty years later, he would recount the place held, during the years of his formation, by the altar and the Mass: "As a young seminarian at Santa Chiara, at the French Seminary in Rome, they used to teach us attachment to liturgical ceremonies.... We loved to prepare the altar, we loved to prepare the ceremonies, and we were already imbued with the spirit of the feast the evening before a great ceremony was to take place upon our altars. We understood therefore, as young seminarians, how to love the altar."[1]

Thus the counsel he would give one day to his seminarians is undoubtedly the echo of his own experience lived daily at the French Seminary in Rome: "Never separate the Mass from your studies. Your studies have no purpose outside the Mass. All of theology revolves around Our Lord Jesus Christ, His Mass and His Cross. The synthesis of what has been taught to you in the seminary is the altar; it is the sacrifice of the Mass."[2]

His whole life long, Archbishop Lefebvre never stopped savoring the inexhaustible riches bequeathed to His Church by Our Lord when He said to His Apostles: "Do this in memory of Me." The tough years of ministry spent in Africa did nothing to estrange him from these profound realities; rather, they made him discover their full worth: "There I began to learn what the Mass truly is. Certainly I knew, by the studies we had done, what this great mystery of our Faith was, but I had not yet understood its entire value, efficacy, and depth. Thus I lived day by day, year by year, in Africa and particularly in Gabon, where I spent thirteen years of my mis-

---

[1] The Golden Jubilee Sermon, Paris, September 23, 1979. [English version: M. Davies, *Apologia pro Marcel Lefebvre* (Angelus Press, 1983), II, 333.]
[2] Spiritual talk, Ecône, May 30, 1971.

sionary life....There I saw–yes, I saw–what the grace of the Holy Mass could do."[3]

At the sight of these numerous pagan villages being transformed under the influence of the holy sacrifice of the Mass, the missionary understood the importance of the great dogmatic truths taught in the seminary. They were the expression of the incredible goodness of God towards us, for "when as yet we were sinners, according to the time, Christ died for us" (Rom. 5:8). This summit of love, renewed daily on our altars, would be henceforth the heart of his life and of his ministry.

Only the profound intimacy existing between Archbishop Lefebvre and the Victim immolating Himself in the holy sacrifice of the Mass can explain the unshakable firmness of his attachment to "the Mass of all time" and his refusal of the rite created by Paul VI. Since the former Archbishop of Dakar believed that the finest way of serving the Roman Church was to defend the endangered Mass, he did not hesitate to decry publicly the serious failings and defects of this liturgical reform, which appeared to him the more clearly as they were seen in the light of the charity consuming his heart. His stand against these novelties, which he rejected because they were destructive to piety, gave rise to the saga of Ecône, the soul of which was expressed many a time by its founder: "Our objective today must be to restore to the holy sacrifice of the Mass its due and rightful place, the place it has held in the Church's history and doctrine."[4]

Convinced from the outset that the Mass is at the heart of the Church, Archbishop Lefebvre never ceased living these great realities and imbuing them in those who, through his work, came to give themselves to the Church. Whether it was for his beloved seminarians or for consecrated souls, he multiplied sermons, retreats, and spiritual conferences, always communicating this love of the holy sacrifice of the Mass.

These different sources, of an unsuspected abundance, are the starting point of this collection. In this Year of the Holy Eucharist, which is also the centenary of Archbishop Lefebvre's birth, the seminarians of Flavigny and Ecône are presenting their Founder's teaching for meditation. Almost spontaneously, these pages di-

---

[3] Golden Jubilee Sermon [*Apologia*, II, 334].
[4] Retreat, Avrillé, October 18, 1989.

vide into two distinct parts. First they lead us to adopt Archbishop Lefebvre's way of looking at the holy sacrifice of the Mass. Much more than a simple doctrinal exposition, these lines constitute an invitation to prayer, following step by step the different prayers of the Ordinary of the Mass in the rite codified by St. Pius V. It is only afterwards that the serious objections Archbishop Lefebvre articulated concerning the new rite and its underlying theology are introduced. These passages, which sometimes speak with considerable firmness, are not meant to voice a spirit of contradiction; they are the fruit of a vital reaction against a poison deemed fatal for souls. They are also marked by his love for the sacrifice of the Cross and the Mass that perpetuates it.

What is revealed in the course of these pages is more than a teaching; it is a soul, the soul of one who was labeled "the Rebel Bishop," but who appears here in his true stature. As a man of God, he lived intimately the great mysteries of our religion. As a man of principle, he refused to relativize the Catholic Faith precisely because the Faith, which reveals God's love for us, is the indispensable foundation of charity. Lastly, as a pastor of souls, he had the sublime intuition of what the Church most needed: to restore the holy sacrifice of the Mass to the heart of the Church and, from there, make it shine upon the whole life of the world through the zeal of holy priests.

May these pages, in which the spoken style has been deliberately conserved, foster the rediscovery of the treasure which is the holy sacrifice of the Mass, a treasure, alas, hidden from very many in this period of liturgical crisis. At a time when Cardinals no longer hesitate to point out the limits of Pope Paul VI's liturgical reform, and when numerous priests, and often young priests, manifest more and more interest in the missal of St. Pius V, this compilation acquires a greater contemporary relevance. It will serve not only to retrace a history of the profound choices of the great twentieth-century figure who was Archbishop Marcel Lefebvre, for his words assume an almost prophetic character; but it will also mark what will become, we hope, the path of a true reform of the Church, beginning with the restoration of the holy Mass.

+ Bernard Fellay
Superior General of the Society of Saint Pius X
Feast of St. Pius X, September 3, 2005

Preface

Archbishop Lefebvre very often spoke and wrote about the Mass because he had made it the soul of his spiritual life. To help us to contemplate the great mystery of the Mass better, we have collected numerous excerpts from his conferences, sermons, and writings that, when organized together, form a very rich commentary on the liturgy of the Mass, be it the prayers themselves, the priest's gestures (Signs of the Cross, bows, genuflections, blessings, incensations, *etc.*), or the requisites for worship (altar, altar stone, relics, crucifix). Each of the prayers from the Ordinary of the Mass is here followed by the selected commentaries.

Since Archbishop Lefebvre did not explicitly comment on each of the prayers, the selected passages are not strictly related to the prayers they follow. The number and length of the citations vary according to the importance of the prayers or Archbishop Lefebvre's didactic focus. For the same reason, the same idea may be developed under several different headings. In short, the extracts are not meant to offer a comprehensive commentary upon the content of each prayer.

Brief introductions have been inserted to mark the transitions between the prayer being commented upon and the selected passages. When several relatively long passages relate to the same prayer, each is preceded by a heading.

THE HEART OF THE MASS

Everything that touches the sacrifice of the Mass touches each and every one of us profoundly and personally because Our Lord's sacrifice is at the heart of the Church, our salvation, and our souls. We must participate in this sacrifice for the salvation of our souls. To save our souls, we must receive the Blood of Jesus by Baptism and all the Sacraments, especially the Sacrament of the Eucharist.[1]

Nothing prepares us to receive the Sacrament of the Eucharist so well as meditating upon the holy sacrifice of the Mass, because the sacrifice of the Mass is a source of suggestions, encouragements, and thoughts that create in us dispositions of charity towards God and our neighbor. Our Lord's sacrifice was indeed the greatest act of charity ever performed in the history of the human race. "Greater love than this no man hath, that a man lay down his life for his friends" (Jn. 15:13).[2]

Our Lord Jesus Christ's goal was to offer Himself on the Cross. He came for no other reason. And the Mass is the continuation of the Cross; Our Lord's goal is then to continue His Cross by the holy sacrifice of the Mass until the end of time. It seems that many souls have forgotten this. They have been looking for the source of grace in little devotions, in the recitation of certain personal prayers, in private devotions to this or that saint... It is good to have devotions, but let us have the essential devotion, the chief and fundamental devotion of the Church and of all the saints: the one brought us by Our Lord. Nothing can replace the sacrifice of the Cross. No devotion, not even to the Blessed Virgin, can replace the holy sacrifice of the Mass. Indeed, the Blessed Virgin encourages us to come to the cross; she is always present there.[3]

Archbishop Lefebvre discerned in the Mass a whole way of life, for the faithful as well as for the priest.

What is the Mass? What does it represent? The Mass is a living catechism. What the catechism teaches us–the Creed, the

---

[1] Homily, Ecône, June 29, 1982.
[2] Easter retreat, Ecône, April 6, 1980.
[3] Retreat to the Sisters, Albano, September 1976.

Commandments of God, the Sacraments, the Christian virtues, the Our Father–all that is admirably accomplished point by point during each Mass.

The first part of the Mass is the teaching part. It sets forth the different truths of the *Credo*. It leads us slowly but surely to our profession of faith. And if the Creed is the song of God's love for us, the second part of the Mass is its accomplishment. As Our Lord said, all the Law and the Prophets are contained in these two Commandments: the love of God and the love of neighbor. Now, everything that happens from the Offertory and the Consecration to the *Pater* is the accomplishment of God's love for us, and the love of Our Lord Jesus Christ for His Father. Consequently, the two essential commandments, which sum up the Decalogue, are realized in this part of the Mass. For can there be an act of love for God greater than the act accomplished by Our Lord Jesus Christ on Calvary? Jesus Christ, by dying on the Cross, manifested His infinite love for His Father, and this is accomplished again on our altars.

The Second Great Commandment, which consists in loving our neighbor as ourselves, is also exactly carried out in the holy sacrifice of the Mass. It is Our Lord Jesus Christ who has said it: Can there be any act of love greater than laying down one's life for those one loves?[4] Now, Our Lord Jesus Christ gave His life for those He loves, that is to say, for us; and this is also accomplished in the holy sacrifice of the Mass. The death of Our Lord Jesus Christ is the greatest act of charity that He could perform for the redemption of men, His brothers. He gave all His Blood as well as His Soul; He gave His life for those He loved. And this same Divine Blood purifies and sanctifies us during the Mass.

Thus the Decalogue is lived. It is not only inscribed on the pages of our catechism, in dead letters, but it is also lived. Every day, every time the holy sacrifice of the Mass is offered, the Decalogue is accomplished by Our Lord Jesus Christ Himself. What an example for us! That is why we desire to participate in the life of Our Lord Jesus Christ, so that we too may have this desire within us,

---

[4] Following Jn. 15:13.

we too may have this need, in some sense, to love God and to love our neighbor.[5]

The sacrifice of the Mass is an entire program. It is a jewel. The Mass has three parts: instruction; the Consecration, in which Our Lord comes upon the altar; and, finally, the Communion. The priest finds there all that he must do. These three parts express the priest's ministry in its three powers: the *potestas docendi*–the power to teach; the *potestas sanctificandi*–the power to sanctify; and the *potestas regendi*–the power to govern the faithful.

The first part of the Mass corresponds to the power of teaching given to the priest. The second, to sanctification: the priest sanctifies the faithful by his prayer. The third, to the power to direct souls, for, by giving the Body, Blood, Soul and Divinity of Our Lord to the faithful, by that very act the priest communicates to them the Commandment of charity. It is truly the act of charity that enables the faithful to steer a safe course in the Christian life. By transmitting to them the living Law which is Our Lord, the priest exercises his power of direction.

For the faithful, the different parts of the Mass correspond to faith, hope, and charity: faith in the teaching, hope in the cross. Transubstantiation signifies the cross of Jesus, which is our hope. "*O Crux, ave, spes unica*–Hail, O Cross, our only hope."[6] The Communion, which is union in love with Our Lord, is charity. Our Lord could not give us a greater proof of His love than to give Himself to us as food for our souls.[7]

---

[5] Homily, Lausanne, July 9, 1978.
[6] From the Passiontide hymn "*Vexilla Regis.*"
[7] Retreat, Avrillé, October 18, 1989.

PART ONE

THE HOLY SACRIFICE

I. The Mass of the Catechumens

If we are to approach the great mystery of the Cross of Our Lord, it is essential that we should prepare ourselves. That is why, during the first part of the Mass, the Church joins to her praise prayers of a nature to excite humility and interior contrition; then she nourishes our faith by the passages she offers for our meditation.

The first part of the Mass, called the Mass of the Catechumens, is consecrated to praise and to compunction,[1] but especially to teaching, a teaching that is summarized in the *Credo*.[2]

It was fitting that the holy Mass be an occasion for teaching, for a communication of the Word of God, Who "enlightens every man that comes into this world" (Jn. 1:9). ...The first part of the Mass should increase our faith in Our Lord Jesus Christ, and this faith must be in its turn a source of zeal that manifests Our Lord to souls.[3]

The Sign of the Cross

The Celebrant:

In nómine Patris, et Fílii, ✠ et Spíritus Sancti. Amen.

In the name of the Father, and of the Son, ✠ and of the Holy Ghost. Amen.

The Sign of the Cross, symbol of Our Lord's sacrifice, calls to mind the means by which the order established by God in the beginning and then destroyed by sin has been re-established.

We believe that in God there are three Persons: the Father, the Son, and the Holy Ghost. We were baptized in the name of these three Persons, and whenever we make the Sign of the Cross we

---

[1] Compunction is the attitude of a soul filled with both humility and contrition. Archbishop Lefebvre speaks about it while commenting on the *Confiteor*.
[2] Retreat, Le Barroux, August 1985.
[3] Notes for a priests' retreat, no date; Ecône Seminary archives, *O Mysterium Christi*, p.11.

say, "In the name of the Father, and of the Son, and of the Holy Ghost." It is thus a belief that has entered our daily life and which is a fundamental principle of the Christian life.[4]

The Cross makes us think of the Trinity, for it is the Son who is attached to the Cross; He is there out of love for His Father; and thus He is filled with the Holy Ghost. The three Persons of the Blessed Trinity encompass the Cross.[5]

The Cross is the deepest and most admirable expression of what Our Lord Jesus Christ, true God and true Man, has done for us.[6] Order was restored by the Cross. It was at the moment Our Lord died that order was re-established, the devil was vanquished, and God served as He should be.[7]

All graces come from the Cross, from Calvary, from the pierced heart whence flowed blood and water. The blood represents the sacrifice of the Mass and the water represents Baptism, which washes away our sins. Consequently, it is by Our Lord's sacrifice that we have acquired redemption from our sins. We must keep this reality constantly in mind.[8]

THE ANTIPHON *INTROIBO AD ALTARE DEI*

ANT. Introíbo ad altáre Dei.

℟. Ad Deum qui lætíficat juventútem meam.

ANT. I will go in unto the altar of God.

℟. To God Who giveth joy to my youth.

The Mass brings us close to Our Lord Jesus Christ. It is a source of joy and real happiness for those who choose to follow Him in His sacrifice and to abide with Him.

1. I will go in unto the altar of God

Where will we find Our Lord Jesus Christ? Must we go to Palestine to the mount of the Transfiguration? No, we will find Him on our altars, for henceforth Our Lord Jesus Christ is on our altars. It is there that we shall find Him in all His splendor...and

---

[4] Retreat, Morgon, October 1988.
[5] Homily, Chatillon-sur-Chalaronne, April 16, 1989.
[6] Ordination retreat, Flavigny, June 23, 1976.
[7] Spiritual conference, Ecône, December 3, 1974.
[8] Spiritual conference, Ecône, December 2, 1975.

we will have the same sentiments as the Apostles on the mountain of the Transfiguration. That is why we cannot abandon our altars.[9] Our altar is Sinai; our altar is Tabor; Our Lord is there in all His glory. If we could see the altar as well as the angels and saints do, our faces would also be always radiant, beaming with joy, with the glory of Our Lord. It is at the foot of our altars that we will find Our Lord's light. This light is the emanation of Divine charity and of this Divine life that must fill our souls.[10]

2. Unto God, who giveth joy to my youth

May the holy sacrifice of the Mass be for you the very source of your spirituality, the source of your joy, the source of your happiness. May you find your greatest happiness in the holy Mass and in your daily Communion.[11] May the Mass procure for you also, beyond joy, an inalterable peace. If your faith, your doctrine, and your spirituality are founded on the holy sacrifice of the Mass, you abide in the truth. You cannot be mistaken when you have established your faith on the holy sacrifice of the Mass.[12]

THE PSALM *JUDICA ME*

Judica me, Deus, et discérne causam meam de gente non sancta: ab hómine iníquo et dolóso érue me.

℟. Quia tu es Deus, fortitúdo mea: quare me repulísti, et quare tristis incédo, dum afflígit me inimícus?

℣. Emítte lucem tuam et veritátem tuam; ipsa me deduxérunt et adduxérunt in montem sanctum tuum, et in tabernácula tua.

℟. Et introíbo ad altáre Dei: ad Deum qui lætíficat juventútem meam.

Judge me, O God, and distinguish my cause from the nation that is not holy; deliver me from the unjust and deceitful man.

℟. For Thou, O God, art my strength: why hast Thou cast me off, and why do I go sorrowful whilst the enemy afflicteth me?

℣. Send forth Thy light and Thy truth; they have conducted me and brought me unto Thy holy hill, and into Thy tabernacles.

℟. And I will go unto the altar of God; to God Who giveth joy to my youth.

---

[9] Homily, Munich, March 6, 1977.
[10] Homily, Ecône, March 15, 1975.
[11] Clothing ceremony, Weissbad, March 17, 1978.
[12] Homily, Ecône, March 15, 1975.

℣. Confitébor tibi in cíthara, Deus, Deus meus: quare tristis es, ánima mea, et quare contúrbas me?

℟. Spera in Deo, quóniam adhuc confitébor illi: salutáre vultus mei, et Deus meus.

℣. To Thee, O God, my God, I will give praise upon the harp; why art thou sad, O my soul, and why dost thou disquiet me?

℟. Hope in God, for I will still give praise to Him; the salvation of my countenance, and my God.

Our Lord, a sign of contradiction, was very much loved, but also hated so much that He was persecuted and put to death. His life He offered out of love for His Father and love for souls. In this psalm, Our Lord can be seen imploring His Father's help in the midst of the trials that will lead Him to the altar of sacrifice. The priest, another Christ, must in his turn draw strength from God to carry generously his own cross, following Him.

1. Our Lord, a sign of contradiction

When we say at the beginning of the Mass "*Judica me, Deus, et discerne causam meam de gente non sancta*–Judge me, O God, and distinguish my cause from the nation that is not holy," we seem to be saying that we are the pure ones and that the others are impure, but that is the truth! We cannot deny that there are those who want nothing to do with Jesus Christ. In the hymn of the Feast of Christ the King "...evil crowds cry once again with frenzied will, Christ shall not reign." Yes, indeed, that crowd exists. It is everywhere in the world still. Now more than ever the refrain is to be heard: "Christ shall not reign!" Well, as for us, on the contrary, we must always affirm this desire, this will to seek Our Lord's reign.[13]

A conflict broke out at the beginning of time when our first parents sinned, and it is still raging in our day. We are the witnesses of the titanic struggle between Our Lord Jesus Christ and Satan, and between the devil's disciples and the disciples of the Cross of Our Lord Jesus Christ. We see this war waged in the Old Testament by those who became the people of Israel, the tribe chosen by God from which would come forth the one who would vanquish the devil, the world, and sin–Our Lord Jesus Christ. The people of Israel, a figure of the the Church, had to fight hard against those who sought their destruction–against Satan. They went out from

---

[13] Homily, Ecône, April 3, 1976.

Egypt, leaving Pharaoh's entire army behind them engulfed in the waters, and wandered in the desert for forty years. Does that not represent a conflict? And this struggle continued at the time of Our Lord. Our Lord will be its victim, but a triumphant victim....

Henceforth, the history of the Church will be nothing less than a combat between Satan and the faithful of the Cross of Our Lord Jesus Christ. His Cross will be the sign of Constantine's victory over his enemies. The Church will henceforth triumph over those who want her destruction.

The history of France in particular is an extraordinary image of this struggle to stay Catholic. France, the eldest daughter of the Church, must remain Catholic. Today, she is in danger of becoming Protestant, atheistic, pagan, apostate. She is in danger of abandoning Our Lord Jesus Christ and of having no religion but the religion of luxury, pleasure, money, and lust. That is why, at the moment, when she is engaged in discussing the murder of children with a law permitting abortion, and soon the murder of the elderly by euthanasia, we must be the defenders of our holy religion; we must fight against those who want to reduce us to the worst kind of paganism.... We want to take the oath today to keep the Law of God, to keep the love of the Cross of Our Lord Jesus Christ, to be the faithful of the Cross of Our Lord Jesus Christ.[14]

2. A sacrifice for the love of the Father and for the love of souls

Our Lord gave His life, first of all, out of love for His Father and to re-establish His Father's glory. We sense that Our Lord on the Cross is completely oriented towards His Father. He addresses Him at the beginning of His Passion. All His sentiments are directed towards His Father. Undoubtedly, He sheds His Blood to redeem us, for the redemption of the sins of the world, but His thoughts are turned towards the immense love that He has for the Father. He wants to do His Father's will, to re-establish His glory. Never has a creature been able to sing the praises of the Father as

---

[14] Homily, Orleans, April 9, 1978.

His own Incarnate Son. Obviously, no creature could ever do as much.[15]

To form an idea of what Our Lord Jesus Christ was thinking while He was on the Cross, can we not put upon His lips the words of the great prayer He uttered going from the Cenacle, before ascending the Cross? This admirable prayer includes the most beautiful words ever spoken by Our Lord Jesus Christ: "And now glorify thou me, O Father, with thyself, with the glory which I had, before the world was, with thee" (Jn. 17:5). This elevates us to a heavenly atmosphere, divine with the very eternity of God. "With the glory which I had, before the world was." No one here below, not even the Blessed Virgin, could pronounce words like those. They were reserved to the Man-God, to God. Our Lord asks His Father to glorify Him again, and by that He will glorify His Father.[16] And while He asks for this glorification, Our Lord cannot but stoop in mercy towards men.

When on the Cross He says, "It is consummated" (Jn. 19:30), He repeats the word He spoke before His Passion, "I have finished the work which thou gavest me to do" (Jn. 17:4). And what was this work? It was to choose and to guide the elect: "Those whom thou gavest me have I kept" (Jn. 17:12). I have kept the souls You gave Me: the Apostles, the disciples, the faithful who followed them, and all those who have believed in the mission that You had given Me and which I accomplished. All those have I kept, and I ask that one day You glorify them also[17]: "That they may be one as we also are one" (Jn. 17:22-23). "...I have chosen you out of the world" (Jn. 15:19), Our Lord says, "because they are not of the world; as I also am not of the world" (Jn. 17:14); and "I pray not for the world" (Jn. 17:9).

Why does Our Lord pronounce all these words? He pronounces them because of those who refuse to believe in His Divinity and who oppose Him. Our Lord asks the good God to protect the faithful from the world, "Keep them from evil,"[18] so that they

---

[15] Easter retreat, Ecône, April 6, 1980.
[16] Cf. "Father, the hour is come, glorify thy Son, that thy Son may glorify thee" (Jn. 17:1).
[17] "Father, I will that where I am, they also whom thou hast given me may be with me" (Jn. 17:24).
[18] Paraphrase of Jn. 17:11.

can be faithful by their perseverance in the choice that He made of them. All this is indeed serious and mysterious. These words were certainly reiterated by Our Lord while on the Cross. They would have been in His mind since they were the last words He addressed to His Father while contemplating the work He had accomplished during the course of the years He had spent on earth.[19]

THE INCLINATION AT THE *GLORIA PATRI*

℣. Glória Patri, et Fílio, et Spirítui Sancto.
℟. Sicut erat in princípio, et nunc, et semper: et in sǽcula sæculórum. Amen.
ANT. Introíbo ad altáre Dei.
℟. Ad Deum, qui lætíficat juventútem meam.
℣. Adjutórium nostrum ✠ in nómine Dómini.
℟. Qui fecit cælum et terram.

℣. Glory be to the Father, and to the Son, and to the Holy Ghost.
℟. As it was in the beginning, is now, and ever shall be, world without end. Amen.
ANT. I will go in unto the altar of God.
℟. Unto God Who giveth joy to my youth.
℣. Our help ✠ is in the name of the Lord.
℟. Who made heaven and earth.

At the end of the psalms you say: "*Gloria Patri et Filio et Spiritui Sancto...in sæcula sæculorum. Amen.*" That is the most beautiful prayer that you make–don't forget! It is prayed as the conclusion of the psalms. If the Church wishes to place this prayer at the end of the psalms, it is because it is, as it were, the conclusion and the crown of every prayer. We can pray no better than to say "*Gloria Patri et Filio et Spiritui Sancto...in sæcula sæculorum. Amen.*" It is the most beautiful prayer we can make. And if, while reciting this prayer, the head is bowed before the Most Holy Trinity, it is to adore Him, for there is nothing grander or more sublime or more beautiful than the Most Holy Trinity.

The Faith reveals to us that God the Father produces a Person like unto Himself: the Word. To discover this is marvelous, extraordinary! God the Father is not alone. In His love He produces the Word of God, a Person absolutely equal to Himself. And the Word

---

[19] Homily, St-Michel-en-Brenne, March 17, 1989.

loves His Father with a love equal to Himself. And the love by which the Father and the Son love each other mutually produces a third Person, which is the Holy Ghost. It is a revelation that makes us understand the intimate life of God throughout eternity, before the beginning of the world, and which makes us grasp how God has communicated His love to creatures.

The good God has always had this intense life of love which surpasses everything that we can conceive or imagine. If the Word is absolutely equal to the Father, it is because the Father holds back nothing of His love; He gives everything to the Word: His own life and all His being, while remaining Himself, of course. The only difference between the Father and the Son is that the one begets and the other is begotten. Outside this relationship of paternity and sonship, they are exactly equal. There are no more qualities, or power, or intelligence in the Father than in the Son, and it has been so for all eternity. From all eternity, God the Father begets His Son, and the love of the Father and of the Son produces the Third Person who is the Holy Ghost. The Father and the Son are co-principles of the Holy Ghost. The Holy Ghost is the love with which they love each other. This is the great mystery. The mystery of the Incarnation and the mystery of the Redemption are certainly great mysteries that show the love of the good God for us, but they only exist because of the Blessed Trinity. If there had not been the Blessed Trinity, there would not have been the Incarnation or the Redemption. Thus the great myst ery that shall delight us for all eternity is especially the mystery of the Trinity.[20]

The *Confiteor*

CONFITEOR Deo omnipoténti, beátæ Maríæ semper Vírgini, beáto Micháeli Archángelo, beáto Joánni Baptístæ, sanctis Apóstolis Petro et Paulo, ómnibus Sanctis, et tibi, pater: quia peccávi nimis cogitatióne, verbo et ópere: mea culpa, mea culpa, mea máxima culpa. Ideo precor beátam Maríam semper Vírgi-

I CONFESS to almighty God, to blessed Mary ever Virgin, to blessed Michael the Archangel, to blessed John the Baptist, to the holy Apostles Peter and Paul, to all the Saints, and to thee, Father, that I have sinned exceedingly in thought, word, and deed: through my fault, through my fault, through my most

---

[20] Retreat, Morgon, October, 1988.

The Mass of the Catechumens

nem, beátum Micháelem Archángelum, beátum Joánnem Baptístam, sanctos Apóstolos Petrum et Paulum, omnes Sanctos, et te, pater, oráre pro me ad Dóminum Deum nostrum.

℣. Misereátur vestri omnípotens Deus, et, dimíssis peccátis vestris, perdúcat vos ad vitam ætérnam.
℟. Amen.

℣. Indulgéntiam, ✠ absolutiónem et remissiónem peccatórum nostrórum tríbuat nobis omnípotens et miséricors Dóminus.
℟. Amen.

℣. Deus, tu convérsus vivificábis nos.
℟. Et plebs tua lætábitur in te.

℣. Osténde nobis, Dómine, misericórdiam tuam.
℟. Et salutáre tuum da nobis.
℣. Dómine, exáudi oratiónem meam.
℟. Et clamor meus ad te véniat.
℣. Dóminus vobíscum.
℟. Et cum spíritu tuo.

grievous fault. Therefore I beseech blessed Mary ever Virgin, blessed Michael the Archangel, blessed John the Baptist, the holy Apostles Peter and Paul, all the Saints, and thee, Father, to pray to the Lord our God for me.

℣. May almighty God have mercy upon you, forgive you your sins, and bring you to life everlasting.
℟. Amen.

℣. May the ✠ almighty and merciful Lord grant us pardon, absolution, and remission of our sins.
℟. Amen.

℣. Thou shalt turn again, O God, and quicken us.
℟. And Thy people shall rejoice in Thee.
℣. Show unto us, O Lord, Thy mercy.
℟. And grant us Thy salvation.
℣. O Lord, hear my prayer.
℟. And let my cry come unto Thee.
℣. The Lord be with you.
℟. And with thy spirit.

Every man is a sinner and must admit it.

The traditional liturgy, such as the Church has bequeathed it to us down the centuries, is an admirable school of humility. We can see it in the gestures and the actions: the prostrations, genuflections, bows–these are so many manifestations of our humility, our reverence above all before God....For example, it is a custom in the liturgy that at the beginning of the Mass the priest bows down for the recitation of the *Confiteor*. He bows like the publican, his eyes lowered to the ground, saying: "O God, be merciful to me, a sinner" (Lk. 18:13). We too are sinners.[21]

The first Epistle of St. John is very clear on this point:

> If we say that we have no sin, we deceive ourselves, and the truth is not in us. If we confess our sins, he is faithful and just, to forgive us our sins, and to cleanse us from all iniquity. If we say that we have not sinned, we make him a liar, and his word is not in us.
>
> My little children, these things I write to you, that you may not sin. But if any man sin, we have an advocate with the Father, Jesus Christ the just: And he is the propitiation for our sins: and not for ours only, but also for those of the whole world. (I Jn. 1:8-2:2)[22]

St. Thomas wonders whether we should recall the fact that we are sinners. Why do we have to remember that we are sinners? Is it not better to forget it? St. Thomas answers: We do not have to remember the sins individually and concretely, but we must remember our state as sinners.

We must remind ourselves of it always, and even the most perfect souls have always remembered that they were sinners. They felt within their own nature all the consequences of sin. They suffered from it, and this was always a reason for them to be more fervent, more mindful of Our Lord's Passion, more attached to the Cross of Our Lord in order to become more perfect. This appears in all the lives of the saints. The saints have always considered themselves to be sinners.

"Come now, that's an exaggeration. They were not such sinners as that!"

On the contrary, they were so close to God that their petty faults and failings seemed enormous to them. They regretted them infinitely. They felt that spending their whole life sorrowing for even the slight offenses they had committed against God's goodness and Our Lord's love for them could never be enough. It is a little like approaching a well-lit painting: all the defects are very visible up close, whereas if you move away, they are no longer as

---

[21] Retreat, St-Michel-en-Brenne, September 1984.
[22] Spiritual conference, Ecône, November 22, 1977.

clearly visible. When our souls draw closer to the Lord God, our faults appear much greater.[23]

Throughout the Mass, the prayers remind us that we are sinners as they implore God's grace and mercy towards us. One virtue that we must seek, which is highly recommended by the prayers of the holy Mass, is interior contrition, which the ancient spiritual writers called *compunction*. Compunction is that habitual contrition which consists in having our sins always before us. "My sin is always before me" (Ps. 50:5)....

This does not make us downcast. Do not think that it is to humiliate us that the Church requires these virtues of us. No, it is for our sanctification and to place us in the reality of the spiritual life. Dom Marmion says it very well, following St. Thomas: someone living in a state of habitual compunction would avoid very many sins[24] because this continual regret for sins committed, this interior attitude in reaction to the state of being a sinner which is ours, obviously separates us from sin. If we are sorry for sin, if we have true contrition for it, we hold it in horror; and thus we have this sentiment, or rather an instinct of contempt for and rejection of sin. I think that these are interior dispositions that are very favorable to our spiritual life and which favor the practice of charity. For we do not do penance for penance's sake: penance is required by God and by the Church to make us practice charity, to destroy in us every vestige of selfishness and pride, and of all the vices that constrict our heart in some way, locking up our heart in a little ivory tower.[25]

---

[23] Retreat, Brignoles, July 27, 1984.
[24] *Christ, the Ideal of the Monk*, 2nd. edition (Maredsous, 1947), pp.197-228. [English version (reprint): Roger A. McCaffrey Publishing, n.d., pp.148-171.]
[25] Spiritual conference, Ecône, March 13, 1981.

The Prayer *Aufer a nobis*

Aufer a nobis, quǽsumus, Dómine, iniquitátes nostras: ut ad Sancta sanctórum puris mereámur méntibus introíre. Per Christum Dóminum nostrum. Amen.

Take away from us our iniquities, we beseech Thee, O Lord, that we may be worthy to enter with pure minds into the Holy of Holies. Through Christ our Lord. Amen.

It is fitting to approach the altar with profound sentiments of humility and a great desire for holiness.

Throughout the Mass, the Church invites the priest to clothe himself with dispositions of humility. This is clear in the prayers the priest says in a low voice while going up to the altar: "Take away from us our iniquities, we beseech Thee, O Lord....We beseech Thee, O Lord, that Thou wouldst vouchsafe to forgive me all my sins."[26]

The virtue of humility, so essential to the Christian, is in fact the foundation of all the virtues, because it inclines us to adoration and is the result of adoration. This is what St. Thomas very clearly says.[27] The humble man is humble because he finds himself in the presence of God. He strives to be always in God's presence, and this life in the presence of God makes him humble and continually aware of his nothingness–that he is nothing and God is all. The virtue of humility corresponds perfectly with the adoration we must have before God.[28]

St. Paul aptly says that if we believe ourselves to be something, when we are nothing, then we are deluded: "...whereas he is nothing, he deceiveth himself" (Gal. 6:3). Everything is in God's hands. If God wanted, if Our Lord were to say, "I abandon this or that person," we would vanish into nothingness. We would exist no longer. Immediately, instantaneously, we would disappear. We would no longer be in the world. So, insofar as we conduct ourselves without reference to Our Lord, we are living in an illusion; likewise, if we believe ourselves to be something by ourselves. If

---

[26] Notes for spiritual conferences, p.42; cf. *Rule of St. Benedict*, Ch. 7.
[27] *Summa Theologica*, II-II, Q. 84, Art. 2; II-II, Q. 161, Art. 3, ad 1, and Art. 4, ad 1.
[28] Spiritual conference, Ecône, March 13, 1981.

we were something by ourselves, we would be God, because if we could give ourselves even an iota of our existence, we would give it forever, we would have always had it, and thus we would be God. The simple fact that we cannot give ourselves existence proves that it does not come from us, that it is given by someone else–by Our Lord, by God.[29] The virtue of humility is not a necessary virtue solely from the fact that we are sinners. Every creature must be humble. Our Lord was humble: "Learn of me," says Our Lord, "for I am meek, and humble of heart" (Mt. 11:29). It is not simply because we are sinners that we must try to acquire the virtue of humility. Undoubtedly, being sinners is another reason, and a very important reason, for us to humble ourselves even more, but the simple fact of our being creatures requires us to place ourselves *as creatures* before the One who created us, before God.[30]

Here below we cannot see the place held by God. In heaven, we shall realize that nothing, absolutely nothing, subsists without God. Consequently, creatures are nothing compared to God; they are absolutely nothing without God. God could make millions upon millions and billions of worlds like the one He made. Not an insect, nor a leaf, nor a flower, nor anything develops without His being present. It is He who makes all the wonders we know. All that we are we owe to the good God.[31]

Moreover, humility is not a virtue destined merely to abase or diminish us somehow. It is not meant to suffocate or crush us–not at all. Here is how humility might be defined: "Humility is a moral virtue that inclines us, by reverence towards God–and this is important, it is St. Thomas's definition[32]–to abase ourselves and to remain in the place that we perceive to be our due." We must abase ourselves in the sense that we must put ourselves in our proper place. Insofar as we lack humility, we are not in our proper place. It is important to realize that we are constantly living in a certain illusion....

---

[29] *Ibid.*, September 20, 1976.
[30] Spiritual conference, Ecône, January 28, 1975.
[31] *Ibid.*, January 25, 1982.
[32] Cf. *Summa Theologica*, II-II, Q. 161.

Let us meditate upon these words: "to remain in the place that we perceive to be our due." Our due place is the place of a creature, and a creature redeemed by the Blood of Our Lord Jesus Christ. Thus we have two profound bonds with God: that of a creature, and that of a redeemed creature, which presupposes that we are sinners.

We are creatures. Insofar as we deepen our understanding of the notion of what it means to be a creature, in the same measure shall we put ourselves in our proper place before God. And we must also deepen our understanding of the benefit of the grace God gives us by redeeming us and by making us His children by the Blood of Our Lord Jesus Christ. We must meditate upon our state as sinners and upon God's great mercy towards us. This will also help us to put ourselves in our proper place before Our Lord Jesus Christ. Is there anything more important here below than to put ourselves in our proper place before God? We have no right not to be in our place.[33]

Finally, humility necessarily goes hand in hand with charity: the higher our degree of humility, the nearer we shall be to perfect charity.[34] The highest degree of humility is charity. We pursue humility so as finally to attain charity, to be in the state of charity. We do not pursue the warfare against sin for the sake of the fight itself; we pursue it so as at last to attain true charity towards God and towards our neighbor. The goal is charity, union with God, union with Our Lord.[35]

Kissing the Altar

Oramus te, Dómine, per mérita Sanctórum tuórum, quorum relíquiæ hic sunt, et ómnium Sanctórum: ut indulgére dignéris ómnia peccáta mea. Amen.

We beseech Thee, O Lord, by the merits of Thy Saints whose relics are here and of all the Saints, that Thou wouldst vouchsafe to forgive me all my sins. Amen.

---

[33] Spiritual conference, Ecône, November 15, 1977.
[34] Notes for spiritual conferences, p.42; cf. the *Rule of St. Benedict*, Ch. 7.
[35] Spiritual conference, Ecône, November 22, 1977.

The Mass of the Catechumens

While reciting the prayer *Oramus te*, the priest kisses the altar, which contains a stone encasing relics of some martyrs.

From the fourth century, the popes have required that altars be consecrated. The consecrated altar stones are the image of Jesus Christ Himself. The five crosses carved in the altar stone represent Our Lord's five wounds, since Jesus Christ Himself is the Altar of sacrifice. Moreover, the recess in the altar stone encloses the relics of some holy martyrs, saints who shed their blood for Our Lord. This souvenir of the blood shed by the martyrs united to Our Lord's blood shed upon our altars reminds us of the Passion of Our Lord and of His sacrifice.

The symbolism is magnificent, isn't it? It attaches us to Our Lord's sacrifice and to our altars. Our altars must be the heart of our virtue of religion, whose great act is sacrifice.[36] The relics of the martyrs constitute an admirable reminder that encourages us to offer our lives with that of Our Lord, as the martyrs did.[37]

The Entrance Antiphon: The Introit

The Introit introduces the theme of the day's Mass in order to dispose souls to draw from it all its benefits.

In her liturgy, the Church wants to be our mother and mistress by teaching us what our sentiments and faith should be concerning Jesus Christ, and the extraordinary action which is the holy sacrifice of the Mass, and the Sacraments which Our Lord instituted. With extraordinary care, the Church, like a diligent mother, magnificently composed these splendid rites. The popes and the councils took such care with the liturgy, because they knew that the liturgy is like our mother, who teaches us to love Our Lord Jesus Christ, to adore Him as we ought, and to receive all the graces we need. That is why it has been said that the rule of prayer determines the rule of faith[38] since we nourish our faith by the way we pray.[39]

We are attached to the traditional liturgy, which truly expresses what we believe in our hearts, what we think in the depths of our

---

[36] Retreat, Avrillé, October 18, 1989.
[37] Conference, Turcoing, January 30, 1974.
[38] *Lex orandi, lex credendi*, DS 3792.
[39] Homily, Lyons, February 8, 1976.

soul; namely, that Jesus is God, our King, and that He is present in the Holy Eucharist.[40] The liturgy marvelously expresses the grandeur and holiness of the Mass, the holiness of the sacrifice of the Cross and of the sacrifice of the altar.[41]

The Kyrie

℣. Kýrie, eléison.
℟. Kýrie, eléison.
℣. Kýrie, eléison.

℟. Christe, eléison.
℣. Christe, eléison.
℟. Christe, eléison.

℣. Kýrie, eléison.
℟. Kýrie, eléison.
℣. Kýrie, eléison.

℣. Lord, have mercy.
℟. Lord, have mercy.
℣. Lord, have mercy.

℟. Christ, have mercy.
℣. Christ, have mercy.
℟. Christ, have mercy.

℣. Lord, have mercy.
℟. Lord, have mercy.
℣. Lord, have mercy.

The *Kyrie*, composed of three groups of invocations in honor of the three Divine Persons, makes manifest that the Mass is offered for the glory of the Holy Trinity.

It is during the holy Mass that we shall draw near to the great mystery of God; there we shall go to the Father; there we shall receive the Holy Spirit; there we shall be in communion with the Son of God. We cannot find anything more beautiful, more grand, or more admirable than the holy sacrifice of the Mass.[42]

The Father, the Son, and the Holy Ghost are active in the sacrifice of the Mass. The prayers of the Mass express this admirably. They call upon the Holy Trinity; they call upon the Holy Ghost; the Son addresses His Father, and the Son is really present there. The whole Blessed Trinity is at work in the holy sacrifice of the Mass to accomplish the sacrifice of the Word Incarnate, the sacrifice of the Cross, the sacrifice of the redemption of our souls.[43]

---

[40] Homily, Ecône, May 17, 1975.
[41] Retreat, Ecône, September 22, 1978.
[42] Homily, Ecône, April 14, 1974.
[43] Ordination sermon, Ecône, August 25, 1977.

The *Gloria*

GLORIA in excélsis Deo et in terra pax homínibus bonæ voluntátis. Laudámus te. Benedícimus te. Adorámus te. Glorificámus te. Grátias ágimus tibi propter magnam glóriam tuam. Dómine Deus, Rex cæléstis, Deus Pater omnípotens. Dómine Fili unigénite, Jesu Christe. Dómine Deus, Agnus Dei, Fílius Patris. Qui tollis peccáta mundi, miserére nobis. Qui tollis peccáta mundi, súscipe deprecatiónem nostram. Qui sedes ad déxteram Patris, miserére nobis. Quóniam tu solus Sanctus. Tu solus Dóminus. Tu solus Altíssimus, Jesu Christe, cum Sancto Spíritu ✠ in glória Dei Patris. Amen.

GLORY be to God on high, and on earth peace to men of good will. We praise Thee; we bless Thee; we adore Thee; we glorify Thee. We give Thee thanks for Thy great glory, O Lord God, heavenly King, God the Father almighty. O Lord Jesus Christ, the only-begotten Son; O Lord God, Lamb of God, Son of the Father, Who takest away the sins of the world, have mercy on us; Who takest away the sins of the world, receive our prayer: Who sittest at the right hand of the Father, have mercy on us. For Thou only art holy: Thou only art the Lord: Thou only, O Jesus Christ, art most high, together with the Holy Ghost, ✠ in the glory of God the Father.

The Church acclaims her Redeemer, Priest, and King.

The *Gloria* is a hymn that extols Our Lord Jesus Christ and attributes to Him all the gifts and qualities that He possesses in reality: He is our Savior, He is our Redeemer. He is now in the glory of the Father; He is truly the only Lord, and only He is the Most High. These are affirmations that it is good for us to repeat often so as to have in mind always the authority and the place that Our Lord must have both in our souls and in society.[44]

Jesus Christ has a right to hymns that are worthy of Him and worthy of heaven–hymns that echo the angels' song.[45]

1. Our only God

Our Lord Jesus Christ is the source of everything; there is nothing outside Our Lord Jesus Christ. He is our God; He is our only God. "For Thou only art holy, Thou only art the Lord; Thou only art most high": such is Our Lord Jesus Christ.[46]

---

[44] Homily, Ecône, June 24, 1976.
[45] *Ibid.*, May 17, 1975.
[46] Homily at St. John Lateran's during the Pilgrimage to Rome, May 24, 1975.

2. Jesus Christ

The very name of Our Lord Jesus Christ contains a salvific power, an extraordinary grace. Read the Office of the Holy Name of Jesus and you will see with what veneration the Name of Jesus is pronounced and explained. The Church's devotion to the Name of Jesus is unlike that for the name of any of the saints which might be made on their feast days. No, it is much more profound. In the Church's doctrine, the Name of Jesus contains within itself all the attributes and virtues of Our Lord Jesus Christ. This is why the Church asks us to bow our heads when it is named in the liturgy. The simple utterance of Our Lord Jesus Christ's name carries with it the obligation for all men to be subject to His reign and to believe in the truths He proposes.[47]

3. Savior, Priest, and King

"[Thou] who takest away the sins of the world, who sittest at the right hand of the Father, have mercy on us." Jesus Christ is Savior, Priest, and King: these are the three essential attributes of Our Lord Jesus Christ by the fact of His hypostatic union, that is to say, His union to God Himself in a single Person. Where are these three attributes realized, and where do we encounter them? In the holy Mass.

In the holy Mass, Our Lord Jesus Christ is the Redeemer—who could deny it? The sacrifice of the Cross is His redemptive act. Consequently, by offering the holy sacrifice of the Mass, you contribute to the redemption accomplished by Our Lord Jesus Christ.

Our Lord is Priest. Where is He more Priest than in the holy sacrifice of the Mass? He is the Priest; you are only His ministers; you only act in the person of Christ, who is the real Priest. Consequently, your holy sacrifice of the Mass is still Our Lord Jesus Christ in one of His essential attributes.

Finally, Our Lord is King: "*Regnavit a ligno Deus.*"[48] Our Lord has reigned from the tree of the Cross: it is His throne; it is His crown. By it He conquered the world, and He has a right to that

---

[47] Spiritual conference, Ecône, June 3, 1980.
[48] "God reigned from the wood," a line from the "*Vexilla Regis*," the hymn for Vespers during Passiontide.

kingship. It is also in the sacrifice of the Mass that His supreme royalty manifests itself.[49] Jesus Christ reigned from the wood of the Cross, for He vanquished sin, the devil, and death by His Cross. These are, then, the three magnificent victories of Our Lord Jesus Christ. If this is triumphalism, then we readily admit that we are for it–the triumphalism of Our Lord Jesus Christ. That is why our ancestors built such magnificent cathedrals. Why did these people, who were much poorer than we, spend so much money and time to build the splendid cathedrals that we, and even nonbelievers, still admire today? Because of the altar, because of Our Lord Jesus Christ, to commemorate Our Lord Jesus Christ's triumph on the Cross. Indeed, we want to profess the triumph of Our Lord Jesus Christ in our Mass. That is why we kneel, and why we love to kneel before the Blessed Sacrament.[50]

4. Mediator

Our Lord Jesus Christ is essentially Priest because He is essentially Mediator: "mediator of God and men" (I Tim. 2:5). As soon as He was united to a human soul and a human body in the womb of the Virgin Mary, Our Lord was the Mediator, the Savior, the Priest. For us, these are very beautiful and consoling realities. This is what St. Paul also expresses profoundly when he speaks of Our Lord's priesthood and of His being the Victim for our sins, especially in his Epistle to the Romans and the Epistle to the Hebrews. These are the two Epistles in which are to be found St. Paul's most beautiful statements on these great mysteries.[51]

There is only one Mediator between God and men: Our Lord Jesus Christ crucified, and this mediation He exercised by His Cross. One God, one Mediator, one pope, one bishop with whom we celebrate, and one priest who celebrates the holy Mass; whence there is only one religion. There cannot be two of them, or else the sacrifice of the Mass no longer makes any sense, and Our Lord's sacrifice no longer has any value. "Thou having overcome the sting of death, didst open to believers the kingdom of heaven."[52] Yes, by

---

[49] Homily, Ecône, June 27, 1980.
[50] Homily, Lille, August 29, 1976.
[51] Easter retreat, Ecône, April 17, 1984. Among the passages Archbishop Lefebvre refers to, cf. especially Heb. 5:1-10 and 8:1-2.
[52] Quote from the *Te Deum*.

ascending the Cross to be crucified, Our Lord opened for us the gates of Paradise. No one else has opened the gates of Paradise! No matter where we look, the human inventions represented by the false religions are worthless because there is only one Mediator: the one who opened the gates of heaven, Our Lord Jesus Christ with His Cross. We have no choice; those who do not go in by the way of Our Lord's Cross do not enter by the door to the sheepfold, as Our Lord Himself said: "I am the door" (Jn. 10:7). We are thus obliged to go through this door in order to enter heaven. Thus there is only one religion, only one way to go to heaven.[53]

The social reign of Our Lord Jesus Christ has been rejected under the pretext that it is no longer possible. But it is one thing for a thing to be no longer possible in fact, and another to accept that impossibility as a principle and consequently no longer to seek the social reign of Our Lord Jesus Christ. But what do we say every day in the Our Father? "Thy kingdom come, Thy will be done on earth as it is in heaven." What is this reign? A little while ago you sang in the *Gloria*: "You alone are the Lord, You alone are the Most High, Jesus Christ." And are we to sing these words and then go out and say, "No, Jesus Christ must not reign over us any longer." Are we living illogically? Are we Catholics or not? There will be no peace on earth except in the reign of Our Lord Jesus Christ.[54]

The Collect

Collects are the liturgical prayers that implore the particular grace the Church is asking for us during Mass. This grace is related to the mystery being celebrated or the particular virtues of the saint being honored.

So that we might participate more in the graces of the holy sacrifice of the Mass, the Church has set the Mass in a context of feasts and remembrances of the life of Our Lord and of the saints, because each feast and each event in Our Lord's life brings with it a particular grace. We need this liturgical year of feasts and seasons because we are incapable of comprehending what is the breadth,

---

[53] Homily, Rouen, May 1, 1990.
[54] Homily, Lille, August 29, 1976.

and length, and height, and depth of the mystery of Christ.[55] The Church alone puts it at our disposition in a very maternal way. She distributes these graces all year long, especially during the two great cycles of the year: namely, Christmas and Easter. This is what Fr. Pius Parsch explains in the *Guide to the Liturgical Year*:
"What should we expect from the liturgical year? Divine life, life in abundance. The divine life, the germ of which is deposited in our soul by baptism, must develop during the liturgical year and tend towards its perfection by means of liturgical prayer. The liturgy is like a precious ring, the diamond of which is the Holy Eucharist and the Eucharistic sacrifice, and the setting of which is formed by the feasts and ecclesiastical seasons....The liturgy is a school of faith. During the year, the truths of the Faith are recalled and presented to us. The liturgical year is a zealous educator; it wants not only to communicate to us the truths of the Faith, it wants to make us better, to educate us for heaven."[56]

And obviously, if we really want to penetrate the mystery of Our Lord, if we really want to love Him as we ought to love Him and become attached to Him and receive His graces, it is absolutely necessary that we know, appreciate, and study the liturgy. This is certainly a great means of sanctification. The difference between Catholics and Protestants is that, for the latter, the liturgy (if it can even be called that) is a mere reminder, a history that is recounted but which has no vital significance, nor is it considered to be a capital source of life.[57]

The holy sacrifice of the Mass is at the heart of our sacred liturgy and is even its synthesis. One might say that it summarizes the liturgy of the entire year. The preparation of the liturgy from Advent, Christmas, the Epiphany, and Lent lead us to Our Lord's sacrifice and His resurrection, the heart of the liturgy. Then the effect of the liturgy is expressed by the time after Easter and Pentecost in which the Holy Spirit is communicated to us.[58]

---

[55] Cf. Eph. 3:18.
[56] Vol. I, *Christmastide* (Mulhouse: Ed. Salvator, 1954), pp.23-25.
[57] Spiritual conference, Ecône, January 17, 1978.
[58] Homily, Ecône, April 14, 1974.

The Epistle

In the Missal, a hundred and six different Epistles are by St. Paul, and some of these are repeated several times. While listening to extracts from these Epistles, let us not forget that he was miraculously prepared for his ministry by Our Lord Himself.

By his letters, St. Paul appears as the model of the ministry inaugurated by Our Lord's Apostles and disciples just after His Ascension and Pentecost. But St. Paul's case is extraordinary, for he was not formed by Our Lord in the same way as the others were; he received his preparation for the ministry miraculously. His election, his baptism, his sojourn in the desert: everything contrasts with the election of the Apostles. And yet St. Paul will become the model Apostle, especially of missionaries.

At a time when the very ends of the ministry are being questioned, and when the methods also seem to have changed radically, it is useful to refer to what is essential in the ministry whose source is Our Lord. The essential will be those things accomplished by those who learned it from Our Lord. Thus it is of paramount importance to place oneself in the school of St. Paul....

What exactly does Jesus desire of St. Paul? "For to this end I have appeared to thee" (Acts 26:16): clearly, Our Lord is preparing to tell him the precise motive for His visit. "I have appeared to thee, that I may make thee a minister, and a witness of those things which thou hast seen, and of those things wherein I will appear to thee" (*ibid.*). It is indeed Our Lord who constitutes him Apostle, that is to say, His representative, His witness of the things that he has seen and that Our Lord will show him again. Thus it is obvious that Paul's knowledge was infused, like that which the Apostles received on Pentecost, but without the long preparation they had received. Our Lord will appear to him again to complete his knowledge. St. Paul will narrate the extraordinary visions that transported him to heaven, things it is impossible for a man to express.[59]

What is the reason for these extraordinary graces from Our Lord to St. Paul? "Delivering thee from the people, and from the nations, unto which now I send thee" (Acts 26:17). It is a curi-

---

[59] Cf. II Cor. 12:2ff., the Epistle for Sexagesima Sunday.

ous sentence, which seems contradictory and yet characterizes the Apostle ever after. Our Lord takes Paul from the midst of the Hebrew people, undoubtedly, and from other peoples. He withdraws him from this milieu to send him back again. One cannot help thinking of the light set upon the candlestick to enlighten everything around it. He will appear henceforth before the people, marked by this election, by this divine function.

Our Lord sends St. Paul "to open their eyes, that they may be converted from darkness to light, and from the power of Satan to God, that they may receive forgiveness of sins, and a lot among the saints, by the faith that is in [him]" (Acts 26:18). This is the magnificent goal that Paul must strive to attain. Conversion is indeed the issue–passage from death to life, for the darkness resists [is opposed to] the light, the power of the devil resists the power of God, and the works of sin resist the works of faith in Our Lord. Such is the purpose indicated by Jesus Himself to St. Paul's ministry.[60]

St. Paul's descriptions of Our Lord are marvelous, and incite us to make of Jesus Christ our life–"For to me, to live is Christ" (Phil. 1:21)–and always to become more Christian, for Jesus Christ "is the image of the invisible God, the firstborn of every creature: For in Him were all things created in heaven and on earth, visible and invisible, whether thrones, or dominations, or principalities, or powers: all things were created by Him and in Him. And He is before all, and by Him all things consist" (Col. 1:15-17).[61]

The Gradual and the Alleluia, or the Tract

The Church meditates on the teachings received, and prays that souls be disposed to garner the grace offered therein.

The essence of prayer is the elevation of the soul to God. It is an error to think that paying attention at Mass means reading all the prayers in the Missal. It is a very good thing to unite oneself with the feast being celebrated. The liturgical movement really took off over the last fifty or sixty years. Everyone had beautiful Missals, but they made of them an almost essential element. Anyone not open-

---

[60] Pastoral letter, January-February 1967.
[61] *Spiritual Journey* (Angelus Press, 1991), pp.30-31.

ing his Missal during Mass and reading the prayers would have scandalized his neighbor. Yet it is possible that such a person would have been praying better than the person reading his missal. If that person, understanding the different parts of the Mass, united himself with all the prayers of the priest as the priest advanced towards the Consecration; if he prepared himself well for Communion and united himself lovingly to Our Lord in Holy Communion, such a person would have been following the Mass admirably. God's blessings perhaps descended upon him more than upon someone who followed the Mass closely in his missal but who was perhaps distracted by trying to understand all the words and by attaching himself to the letter while forgetting the spirit of the Mass. We make errors like that nowadays. The New Mass has been conceived so that everyone can understand everything. Everyone must follow everything; that is why the priest speaks aloud. Everyone must follow everything, and the faithful must talk all the time. In reality, the faithful certainly pray less during modern ceremonies than they did before. It is not without reason that the Council of Trent affirmed that if anyone says that the prayers during the Canon of the Mass must not be spoken in a low tone, let him be anathema.[62] This is one of the canons of the Council of Trent concerning the holy sacrifice of the Mass. Nowadays some people are completely deluded. It is necessary to come back to the definition of prayer: the elevation of the soul to God;[63] this is what matters. Now, it is certain that the holy sacrifice of the Mass and the entire traditional liturgy help us very much to lift up our souls to God.[64]

---

[62] Cf. Council of Trent, Session 22, DS 1759.
[63] Cf. *The Catechism of St. Pius X*, Part II, Ch. 1, and the Introit of the First Sunday of Advent.
[64] Retreat, Le Barroux, August 25, 1987.

The Prayer *Munda cor meum*

MUNDA cor meum ac lábia mea, omnípotens Deus, qui lábia Isaíæ prophétæ cálculo mundásti igníto: ita me tua grata miseratióne dignáre mundáre, ut sanctum Evangélium tuum digne váleam nuntiáre. Per Christum Dóminum nostrum. Amen.

Cleanse my heart and my lips, O God almighty, Who didst cleanse the lips of the Prophet Isaias with a burning coal; and vouchsafe through Thy gracious mercy, so to purify me that I may worthily proclaim Thy holy Gospel. Through Christ our Lord. Amen.

Sacred Scripture is the word of God. It must be announced with a pure heart and received with faith in order for the soul to be nourished.

Even though the Scripture passages are often the same—we repeat them often throughout the year—one never tires of hearing them. Let us not forget that it really is the Word of God, the Word of the Holy Ghost, and that in these words there is something infinite. One can always find nourishment in the passages of Scripture even though one has read them over and over again. There are always aspects that escaped us or that did us good and enlightened us and lifted up our hearts to the good God. Repeating them helps us recover the sentiments that we had when, for the first time, we discovered the depth of the thoughts that God wanted to communicate to us.

The preaching of the Scripture that the holy Church places on our lips is a lesson for us....God cannot be mistaken. Since He taught us these truths, since He told us that the Sacred Scripture is His word, we must accept this word. This word is certain. The teaching and the faith transmitted to us by the Apostles are certain. If our reason experiences obscurity and raises objections to the enunciation of these truths, it must always first approach them with an attitude of faith.[65]

Our faith is not the result of reasoning, but rather it is the adherence of our minds to revealed truth because of God's authority—not because of our reason, not because of the arguments we can find by our human intelligence, but because of the authority

---

[65] Priestly ordination retreat, Flavigny, June 24, 1976.

of God who reveals: *"propter auctoritatem Dei revelantis."*[66] This is what the anti-modernist oath says, and it is the definition of our faith. God has revealed it; He has total authority over our minds and wills. We must accept the word of God as He gives it to us and as it is given to us infallibly by the Church.

Our faith pertains to realities that are obscure for us. St. Paul says that "at present we are looking at a confused reflection in a mirror" (I Cor. 13:12).[67] We do not know directly the divine realities, but faith is not meant to last forever. Our faith is a stage: one must think about this often. The virtue of faith will not last eternally. Faith will disappear before the vision of God; when we see God, faith will cease. We will no longer need to believe; we will no longer need the testimony of eye-witnesses; we shall be face to face with the reality.

When one reads the lives of the saints or the lives of persons who have received extraordinary graces in the domain of faith, especially the people who have had the privilege of beholding an apparition from heaven, something visible, it seems to me that one better understands the grandeur, and beauty, and richness, and sublimity of our faith. Our faith is a life. It is not a simple belief, a simple narration, a history that someone tells us; no, it is a life! Our faith is living: "The just man liveth by faith" (Rom. 1:17; Gal. 3:11). Why? Because this faith puts us in contact with God. Faith really allows the most intimate contact we can have with God. And we hope to reach before long this beatific vision, the vision of God!

The privileged people who received particular graces became strangers to everything on earth. For instance, little Bernadette and the children of Fatima were able to discover a little corner of Heaven. The veil was lifted a little. If it had been raised completely, they would have died; they couldn't have survived. Our body would disappear or somehow disintegrate before the splendor of Heaven. The children who had a heavenly vision fell into a kind of ecstasy, admiring what they saw. Think of Bernadette: while she was looking upon the Blessed Virgin, a lighted candle was placed under her fingers to see if she could still feel. Well, she no longer

---

[66] Cf. The Anti-Modernist Oath by St. Pius X; *Summa Theologica*, II-II, Q. 2, Art. 9, ad 3.

[67] English translation: Knox version.

felt anything. It was if she had left her body, engrossed as she was by what she was seeing. We are all destined to have not just this glimpse of heaven, which these privileged children had, but heaven itself, God Himself, Our Lord Jesus Christ in His splendor and glory.[68] The saints were able to know the Blessed Trinity in a certain measure; oh! in a very little measure. For if the good God had revealed to them what He is, His Holy Trinity, they would not have been able to remain upon earth; they would have died of contemplating the most Blessed Trinity. One cannot be in a body of flesh like ours and have the vision of the most Holy Trinity. If just the slight lifting of a corner of the veil can send the saints who have had this grace into ecstasy, then we must certainly believe in the existence of the Holy Trinity and consider that this will be our happiness and our joy for all eternity.[69]

It seems to me that when we die, it will be this discovery of the place God holds that will really amaze us. Then, instead of knowing Him, as St. Paul puts it, *in ænigmate,* "in a dark manner" (I Cor. 13:12), we shall know Him by vision. Today, there is a veil that prevents us from seeing God, but this veil will be rent; and at that moment, we shall have this incredible vision of God. The Divine omnipotence will appear to us in a way that surpasses us.[70]

So, let us understand better what our faith is. Our faith is replete with the vision of heaven. That is what we should be meditating on as we assist at this first part of the Mass that concludes with our *Credo.*[71]

The Gospel

The Gospel reports the episodes and teachings of the life of Jesus. The attentive reading of Sacred Scripture is an invitation to follow Our Lord.

1. Meditation on the life of Jesus

The meditation on the life of Jesus in all its details puts us little by little in an atmosphere of supernatural reality and delivers us

---

[68] Homily, reception of the habit, Flavigny, July 5, 1977.
[69] Homily, reception of the habit, Ecône, June 5, 1977.
[70] Spiritual conference, Ecône, January 25, 1982.
[71] Homily, reception of the habit, July 5, 1977.

from the customary way in which men live, so deceived as to take no account of this great reality. Sin, and the results of sin, have succeeded in creating a world of mirages, illusions, and errors. This has developed to such an extent that men end up by becoming accustomed to this sensitized, sensualized, humanized world, no longer being able to see that all this is vain and ephemeral in relation to the true spiritual, supernatural, and eternal life.

The holy and admirable life of Jesus is a constant reminder of the spiritual and divine realities which alone are valuable and eternal. Everything in Jesus returns to God, to the truth, to reality, to wisdom, and to sanctity. Would that we might always be more convinced of the necessity of following Jesus, as He tells His disciples: "He who follows me does not walk in darkness" (Jn. 8:12). "If someone wishes to be My disciple, let him carry his cross and follow Me" (Mt. 16:24). For there is no other choice: either follow Jesus or follow Satan.

It is not at all surprising if Jesus suffers to see men prefer the darkness to the Light–and what Light! It is the Light which created the world, which supports it in existence, which enlightens every man who comes into this world, which brings to them the Light of salvation and eternal glory. But they prefer the darkness of the world, a world which is against Our Lord, a world of the flesh, money, selfishness, pride–the threshold to hell!

Before leaving the person of Jesus Christ, let us concentrate on understanding His redeeming work of salvation and on meditating on the means instituted by Jesus to communicate anew the grace of salvation. In this way we shall mark indelibly in our souls the real, living image of Jesus, Who should illuminate and direct all of our lives.[72] "Be careful to reproduce in your conduct the gospel you announce, so that it can be said of you: 'How beautiful are the feet of him that bringeth good tidings, and that preacheth peace: of him that sheweth forth good'[73] (Is. 52:7). Follow the examples of the saints so that you can preach fruitfully the gospel of peace. That is where peace is to be found" [the Roman Pontifical]. Order cannot exist without God, without Our Lord Jesus Christ.[74]

---

[72] *Spiritual Journey*, pp.39-40.
[73] Cf. Rom. 10:15.
[74] Spiritual conference, Ecône, October 28, 1978.

2. The unique Gospel

St. Paul gave the Galatians a precious piece of advice for staying faithful to the unique Gospel of Christ.

It is very useful to read the first chapter of St. Paul's Epistle to the Galatians, for it gives an extraordinary lesson applicable to our time and situation. What does St. Paul say? "*O insensati Galatæ*"; he is not afraid to call them "senseless Galatians!" (Gal. 3:1). Why, what did the Galatians do? "I am astounded that you have gone over to another gospel"[75] (Gal. 1:6): How can it be? I had just taught you the gospel and went away for a year and a half or two, and there you are going back to your old observances.

What was this gospel? They wanted to resume the practices of the Old Testament, whereas he had said: The Old Testament is finished. Now there is Baptism, the Eucharist, the practice of faith, hope, and charity; there is certainly no more need of circumcision or the observances of the Old Testament; there are no more sacrifices. How could they have gone over to another gospel? It is because they had prophets and doctors who led them into error. St. Paul says: If what you are doing now is just, then it was not worth the Lord's while to be crucified and rise from the dead, since He was crucified and rose to begin a new era in the sanctification of souls. We have wasted our time. At this point he utters the beautiful words we quote so often: "But though we, or an angel from heaven, preach a gospel to you besides that which we have preached to you, let him be anathema" (Gal. 1:8); let him be excommunicated! Magnificent! And he repeats: "As we have said before, so now I say again: If any one preach to you a gospel, besides that which you have received, let him be anathema" (Gal. 1:9).

Such is the first chapter of the Epistle to the Galatians; it explains our situation perfectly. Since the Second Vatican Council, they have gone over to another gospel: the Gospel of the Rights of Man, the Gospel of Religious Freedom, the Gospel of Ecumenism. And this new gospel is incarnated in new Sacraments, a new Mass, new teaching, a new catechism. Everything is new in accordance with new principles, principles which belong to another gospel, which is not the gospel of the Catholic Church. And they would

---

[75] "*Transferimini in aliud evangelium.*" [English from the Knox version.]

like to drag us along with them. We are considered dissidents because we refuse to follow in their footsteps, along their adulterous path. Once again, we say no. We will not change our faith for another gospel. We only know the gospel of Our Lord Jesus Christ and of the the Church of all time, the gospel the Church has taught for twenty centuries.[76]

Preaching

> The sermon, which prolongs the Word of God, is a function reserved to the ministers of the sacrifice. It must have a sacred character in order to dispose souls to live the gospel and to unite themselves to Our Lord's sacrifice.

1. A ministry conferred upon the deacon

[Note: The Archbishop is speaking to subdeacons on their retreat before receiving the diaconate.] Ordination to the diaconate confers a power not only over the real, physical Body of Our Lord in the Holy Eucharist, but also over His Mystical Body. For, insofar as a consecrated person advances nearer to Our Lord Jesus Christ, from the tonsure to the diaconate and finally ascending to the priesthood, he enjoys a proportionally greater power over the Eucharist and equally over the Mystical Body of Our Lord Jesus Christ. That is why the Church already grants you a certain number of powers. You will eventually be able to give Our Lord Himself in the Blessed Sacrament to souls. By reason of this authorization and power, you have the duty to prepare souls to receive the Blessed Sacrament well, and that is what you will do by preaching. Preaching is, then, a very important thing.[77]

2. The principal object of the sermon

One of the chief manifestations of the presence of the Holy Ghost in a soul is his preaching. When the Holy Ghost enlightens a soul about the work of Our Lord and His Passion, at the same time He imparts the desire to speak. The Acts of the Apostles relate

---

[76] Conference to the Sisters of the Society of St. Pius X, St-Michel-en-Brenne, April 6, 1988.
[77] Retreat to future deacons, Ecône, May 12, 1989.

that, after St. Peter's discourse before the Sanhedrin, the Christians gathered together, and they prayed. And "when they had prayed, the place was moved wherein they were assembled; and they were all filled with the Holy Ghost, and they spoke the word of God with confidence" (4:31). At a time when no one believes any longer in Our Lord Jesus Christ, when no one believes any longer in the power of the Holy Ghost, nor in the supernatural gifts and the virtues, we must show in our words, our preaching, and our whole life, this presence of the Spirit.

"And with great power did the apostles give testimony of the resurrection of Jesus Christ Our Lord; and great grace was in them all" (Acts, 4:33). It is a remarkable fact that the object of the Apostles' and St. Paul's preaching is the person of Jesus. St. Paul has some magnificent expressions on this subject: "I preach Jesus, and Jesus crucified" (cf. I Cor. 2:2)....We must preach Our Lord. A special grace of illumination is given to the faithful concerning all the events of Our Lord's life, and particularly, of course, concerning His crucifixion and resurrection.[78]

A sermon in which Jesus Christ does not figure is useless; either the aim or the means is missing. "For we preach not ourselves," says St. Paul, "but Jesus Christ Our Lord" (II Cor. 4:5). Jesus Christ must always enter into our sermons because everything relates to Him. He is the Way, the Truth, and the Life. Consequently, to ask the faithful to become more perfect or to convert without speaking of Our Lord is to deceive them; it is to fail to show them the way by which they can succeed. "But we preach Jesus crucified" (I Cor. 1:23).[79]

Ardent preaching is mediated by the holy sacrifice of the Mass, that is to say, by the cross and by the most Blessed Virgin Mary. Jesus and Mary are the great sources of grace: Jesus by Mary. Jesus in the holy Sacrament of the Mass represents all the Sacraments, all the sources of salvation; and Mary communicates them. Thus Mary's intercession is necessary because all graces come to us through her hands....We must preach the Cross of Our Lord against the evil spirit of the world, which is the spirit of the devil, which is the spirit of error, the spirit of attachment to earthly goods. What is

---

[78] Spiritual conference, Ecône, March 21, 1988.
[79] Ordination retreat, Montalenghe, 1989.

the most obvious means of detaching oneself from the spirit of the world? It is the spirit of the Cross. It is necessary to preach the Cross so that the people really unite themselves to the Cross of Our Lord Jesus Christ and His sacrifice.[80]

You will preach the doctrine of the Cross. St. Paul preached nothing else: "Jesus Christ, and him crucified" (I Cor. 2:2), as he himself said. That was his preaching; it will be yours, too, I am certain.[81]

In the fifth chapter of the Acts of the Apostles (5:30-33), we read: "The God of our fathers hath raised up Jesus, whom you put to death, hanging him upon a tree. Him hath God exalted with his right hand, to be Prince and Savior, to give repentance to Israel, and remission of sins. And we are witnesses of these things and the Holy Ghost, whom God hath given to all that obey him. When they had heard these things, they were cut to the heart, and they thought to put them to death." This shows another important side of things. Preaching Our Lord Jesus Christ, which is the fruit of the Holy Ghost in the ministry we have to give, leads to persecutions. We mustn't deceive ourselves: we are for Our Lord; the world is against Our Lord. Sinners are against Our Lord. Our Lord, Himself, said it: the world hates me, and it will hate you if you love and serve me (Jn. 15:18-21)....

Remember the magnificent story of St. Stephen. If there is one of the first Christians who manifested the presence of the Holy Ghost within him, it was St. Stephen. We must love to read and re-read the seventh chapter of the Acts of the Apostles, which recounts the story of St. Stephen, because all the manifestations of the Holy Ghost appear in him. His faith is so lively that the good God even allows Stephen to see Him: "But he, being full of the Holy Ghost, looking up steadfastly to heaven, saw the glory of God, and Jesus standing on the right hand of God" (7:55). The good God gave him the grace to see His glory before he died.

The ardor with which he preaches is so extraordinary that his adversaries exhibit an incredible opposition. The terms used in Holy Scripture are clear: not only are they enraged, but "they gnashed with their teeth at him" (7:54). Truly, through them, the

---

[80] Retreat, Avrillé, October 18, 1989.
[81] Homily, Ecône, September 14, 1975.

devil himself acted against St. Stephen. Consider the ardor and effect of his preaching and of his faith, and the persecution they aroused, obviously. He so clearly manifested the Holy Ghost within him that they put him to death, and the good God allowed him to enjoy this blessed vision before his death.[82]

The Apostles St. Peter and St. Andrew died on crosses, and the great missionaries went in the name of the Cross to preach the Gospel. This is what St. Francis Xavier did, and St. Louis-Marie Grignion de Montfort, and so many others. They held up the Cross to impart the Faith or to revive it. The Cross has its own virtue. The good God has willed that the Cross be the salvation for all men. Consequently, one must believe that in every man there is a predisposition to believe in the virtue of the Cross. I have experienced this during the course of my missionary life in pagan villages. When the cross was shown to the villagers and when what it is was explained, an actual grace descended into souls. The souls were touched at the thought that God came upon the earth, suffered for them, and shed His Blood to redeem them from their sins.

Men full of pride and steeped in their knowledge are the hardest to convert. At the idea of adoring Christ, they revolt like the devil, like the bad angels, like the princes of the priests, like the scribes and the Pharisees. But simple souls that are undoubtedly in sin more easily recognize their disorder. They are in a situation that quite often creates in them a certain remorse. So the thought that this degrading situation in which they find themselves has an exit, a way to resurrection, and light attracts them. When they think that God Himself took the trouble to come and sacrifice Himself to get them out of the state of sin into which they have fallen, then souls rise up and thank God, seeing that salvation is possible, resurrection is possible.[83]

THE *CREDO*

CREDO in unum Deum, Patrem omnipoténtem, factórem cæli et terræ, visibílium ómnium et invisibílium. Et in unum Dóminum Jesum Christum, Fílium Dei uni-

I BELIEVE in one God, the Father almighty, maker of heaven and earth, and of all things visible and invisible. And in one Lord, Jesus Christ, the only-begotten Son of

---

[82] Spiritual conference, Ecône, March 21, 1988.
[83] Easter retreat, Ecône, April 17, 1984.

génitum: et ex Patre natum ante ómnia sǽcula, Deum de Deo, lumen de lúmine, Deum verum de Deo vero. Génitum, non factum, consubstantiálem Patri; per quem ómnia facta sunt. Qui propter nos hómines, et propter nostram salútem, descéndit de cælis. Et incarnátus est de Spíritu Sancto ex María Vírgine: et homo factus est. Crucifíxus étiam pro nobis: sub Póntio Piláto passus et sepúltus est. Et resurréxit tértia die, secúndum Scriptúras. Et ascéndit in cælum, sedet ad déxteram Patris. Et íterum ventúrus est cum glória judicáre vivos et mórtuos: cujus regni non erit finis. Et in Spíritum Sanctum Dóminum et vivificántem, qui ex Patre Filióque procédit. Qui cum Patre et Fílio simul adorátur et conglorificátur: qui locútus est per Prophétas. Et unam, sanctam, cathólicam et apostólicam Ecclésiam. Confíteor unum baptísma in remissiónem peccatórum. Et exspécto resurrectiónem mortuórum,✠ et vitam ventúri sǽculi. Amen.

God. Born of the Father before all ages. God of God, Light of Light, true God of true God. Begotten, not made, of one substance with the Father. By Whom all things were made. Who for us men and for our salvation came down from heaven. And He became flesh by the Holy Ghost of the Virgin Mary: and was made man. He was also crucified for us, suffered under Pontius Pilate, and was buried. And on the third day He rose again according to the Scriptures. He ascended into heaven and sits at the right hand of the Father. He will come again in glory to judge the living and the dead. And of His kingdom there will be no end. And I believe in the Holy Ghost, the Lord and Giver of life, Who proceeds from the Father and the Son. Who together with the Father and the Son is adored and glorified; and Who spoke through the Prophets. And one, holy, Catholic, and Apostolic Church. I confess one baptism for the forgiveness of sins. And I await the resurrection of the dead. ✠ And the life of the world to come. Amen.

The *Credo* is the synthesis of our faith. It summarizes all that we believe: We believe in God the Father, in God the Son who became incarnate, taking flesh in the womb of the Virgin Mary, who suffered, was crucified, and gave himself completely for the glory of His Father. We believe in the Holy Ghost, we believe in the Catholic Church, we believe in Baptism for the remission of sins, we believe in eternal life. That is what God has done for us, poor creatures, poor sinners. It is the summary of our faith: the great charity of God for us, the great love of God for us. All this is recounted in the *Credo*; that is why the *Credo* must be the basis of our faith and our spiritual life.[84]

1. I believe in God, the Father almighty, Creator of heaven and earth

The Faith is the most certain knowledge to which we can refer. It teaches us the existence of God: "*Credo in unum Deum, Patrem omnipotentem, factorem cæli et terræ, visibilium et invisibilium.*"

Faith teaches us that God is a Spirit: "*Deus spiritus est.*"[85] It is Our Lord who taught this to the Samaritan woman. He is therefore an omnipotent Spirit who created everything.

There was a time when the world did not exist, when God was alone in eternity, in His sanctity and His perfect and infinite happiness, having no need to create. Our Lord, at the beginning of His sacerdotal prayer, makes reference to this period: "And now glorify thou me, O Father, with thyself, with the glory which I had, before the world was, with thee" (Jn. 17:5).

Faith teaches us that reason can and should lead to the conclusion that God exists, and St. Paul, in his first epistle,[86] reproaches men vehemently for not having known the true God, who declares Himself by His works.

Indeed, everything that is, everything that we are, proclaims the existence of God and sings His divine perfections. All of the Old Testament, and particularly the Psalms and the Wisdom books, sing the glory of the Creator. That is why the Psalms have a central place in liturgical and sacerdotal prayers.

It is good to meditate on the creation "*ex nihilo sui et subjecti*–made of nothing" by the simple decision of the Creator....The more one looks deeper into this reality, the more one is stupefied at the all-powerful nature of God and at our own nothingness and the need of every creature to be constantly sustained in existence under pain of ceasing to be, of returning to nothing. This is exactly what faith and philosophy teach us.

Nothing but this meditation and this realization should plunge us into humility and profound adoration, and establish us immuta-

---

[84] Homily, Lausanne, July 9, 1978.
[85] Cf. Jn. 4:24.
[86] To the Romans, 1:18 ff.

bly in this attitude like to the unchanging God Himself. We should be filled with unbounded trust toward Him Who is all, and Who decided to create us and save us.[87]

2. I believe in God...through Whom all things were made

Our Lord is God, and there is but one God; there are not three Gods, there is only one. God the Father, God the Son, and God the Holy Ghost created the world. The Word created the world: "All things were made by him," hence by Our Lord. For there are not two persons in Our Lord, but one, and this Person is the Person of the Word of God, the Person of God the Son. This thought should be ever-present in our minds.[88]

The Father has created everything by the Son. Why? Because the Son is the Wisdom of God. The Son, being the Word of God, is both the Knowledge and the Wisdom of God. God cannot create without Wisdom or Knowledge. Indeed, God created through His Wisdom and through His Knowledge. The Father created by His Wisdom, which is a divine Person, both distinct from Him and consubstantial with Him, which is God like Himself. Nothing that was made was made without this Wisdom of God, this divine Knowledge of God, without this Word, the Word of God. Everything was made by Him.

We need to reflect and meditate on this great truth because it has considerable consequences for each one of us, because all that we are and all that we possess issued from the Word. Nothing of what we are was made without the Word of God, absolutely nothing. Everything comes to us from the Word of God, from the Wisdom of God.

When one thinks of the idea that men have had and still have of God–even among many Catholics, who have been baptized in the Blood of Our Lord and thus who have been united to Him in their Baptism–how many are there who live by these truths normally and logically? How many are there who are in some way giving thanks to God at all times, singing the praises of God for all that He has done, for all that they can see in the place where they live? This should be usual for the man who knows, especially by

---

[87] *Spiritual Journey*, pp.3-4.
[88] *The Mystery of Jesus* (Angelus Press, 2000), p.16.

Revelation, that everything has come from God. All that he sees, all that he knows, all the wonders that surround him, should make man sing unceasingly the praises of God.

When you think of all the doctors and all the explorers who mine the riches buried in the ground–they create nothing! All they do is look for what God has put there. Where does all the oil everyone is fighting over come from? Who put it there? Among all those who explore or who sell the oil, is there anyone who thinks of thanking God or of singing His praises for this extraordinary matter and incredible source of energy, placed by Him at man's disposition? The same goes for the atom and all the energy sources derived from uranium. These forces discovered in the world were made by the Word of God. All of it is from God and cannot subsist without God; yet do we think of it? Nothing that was made was made without Him. It is wonderful. Indeed, all of that is beyond us because the more one looks, the more one finds oneself before great mysteries.

All of this should lead men to sing a continual hymn of praise for all the grandeurs and beautiful things God has created for mankind. So let us strive not to live like atheists who profit from everything the good God has given us–our health, our eyes, our ears, our bodies–and who, despite that, do not think of Him.[89]

3. Who...for our salvation came down from heaven

Why did Our Lord become truly incarnate? Was it necessary for Our Lord to become flesh in order to save us? To this, St. Thomas replies, to summarize briefly, that the Incarnation and Passion of Our Lord was the most suitable means: *per quod melius*. It was not an indispensable means, but it was the best. By this means, the end was reached in the most perfect manner. The good God could have pardoned us without doing anything in particular. Since He is almighty, even if He was dishonored by man, the good God could eliminate this offense without detriment to His glory, His majesty, or His rights. He does not owe anything to anyone. Nevertheless, God wanted to become man because that was the most adequate means to repair the fault, to make us return to His grace, and to give us back life. It was also the best way to manifest

---

[89] Spiritual conference, Ecône, January 29, 1980.

His charity and to incite us to a greater love for Him. The fact of seeing how much God has loved us calls upon us to love Him in turn with our whole heart.[90]

If one examines the public life of Our Lord, and if one listens especially to His words about His sacrifice, one becomes aware of the real purpose of His coming. Our Lord always speaks of what He refers to as His hour: "My hour[91] has not yet come; my hour comes; my hour has come." He speaks of His sacrifice; He looks forward to His sacrifice. He announces His sacrifice, passion, and death to the Apostles, but they do not understand; they do not want to hear it discussed. Remember the reprimands St. Peter addresses to Our Lord Jesus Christ about this. Our Lord tells the Apostles that He would go up to Jerusalem, suffer many things from the ancients, chief priests, and scribes, be put to death, and rise the third day.[92]

Then St. Peter gets angry and says, "No, it's not possible."

Immediately, Our Lord gets angry too: "You do not have the Spirit of God, you have the spirit of man."

St. Peter does not comprehend that Our Lord can be crucified, sacrificed. Yet Our Lord strives to show His Apostles that all the prophets and the Old Testament foretold and prepared His sacrifice. The lamb immolated before the Hebrews' departure from Egypt prefigured the greatest event that was to occur in the history of mankind: the death of its Creator, the death of the Creator of the whole universe in His Body. Our Lord Jesus Christ always had this as His goal. Why this insistence? Because it is by His sacrifice, His Passion, His Blood, His Cross, that He is will redeem us, that He will open heaven's gates. If the Blood of Our Lord Jesus Christ did not intervene, then the gates of heaven would remain shut to us. For reopening the gates of heaven, Divine Providence willed that there be a Divine Victim, for sin has an infinite dimension: sin is an opposition to God; God is infinite, hence sin is something very bad because it opposes someone who is All, someone who is infinite. A proportionate reparation is necessary. Who will do this? No man is infinite, no man can do an infinite act; only God can. So God resolved to take a human nature and to offer it, to die in or-

---

[90] Easter retreat, Ecône, April 17, 1984.
[91] *Hora mea*; cf. Jn. 2:4; 17:1.
[92] Cf. Mt. 16:21.

der to accomplish an infinite act capable of opening heaven. Such is God's extraordinary plan.[93]

4. He was crucified and suffered His Passion for us

I would like to read to you a few lines from the Catechism of the Council of Trent on the fourth article of the Symbol of the Apostles: "Who suffered under Pontius Pilate, was crucified, died, and was buried." Listen carefully to this important sentence: "For it is on this Article, as on their foundation, that the Christian Faith and religion rest; and if this truth be firmly established, all the rest is secure." I repeat, it is on this Article, which says "who suffered under Pontius Pilate, was crucified, died, and was buried":

> that the Christian faith and religion rest; and if this truth be firmly established, all the rest is secure. Indeed, if one thing more than another presents difficulty to the mind and understanding of man, assuredly it is the mystery of the Cross, which, beyond all doubt, must be considered the most difficult of all; so much so that only with great difficulty can we grasp the fact that our salvation depends on the Cross, and on Him who for us was nailed thereon. In this, however, as the Apostle teaches, we may well admire the wonderful Providence of God; "for seeing that in the wisdom of God the world, by wisdom, knew not God, it pleased God by the foolishness of our preaching, to save them that believe" (I Cor. 1:21). It is no wonder, then, the the Prophets, before the coming of Christ, and the Apostles, after His death and Resurrection, labored so strenuously to convince mankind that He was the Redeemer of the world, and to bring them under the power and obedience of the Crucified.[94]

The good God, in His immense mercy, instead of leaving men, or as St. Augustine refers to the multitude of men, this *massa damnata*, this "multitude of the damned," to their fate, wanted to bring them salvation. And He was to bring this salvation in an unimaginable way: He wanted to offer expiation Himself in order to make reparation for the infinite dimension of the offense men had committed; in some way it was necessary that God Himself personally become Man in order to offer the reparation that was due,

---

[93] Homily, St-Michel-en-Brenne, April 2, 1989.
[94] Easter retreat, Ecône, April 17, 1984; cf. *Catechism of the Council of Trent*, "The Creed: Article IV."

an infinite reparation, to re-establish union between mankind and God. And how did He do it? He could have done it by a simple human word spoken as God; He could have shed a single drop of Blood–*"una stilla,"* as the hymn[95] puts it: a single drop of Our Lord's Blood would have sufficed to redeem all men. But no, He wanted to give all His Blood; He wanted to demonstrate His mercy by going so far as to die on the Cross for us.[96]

Our Lord did not die from the thrust of the lance He received to His heart. He died of love. Our Lord's soul escaped from His body because He willed it. He died of love for His Father first of all, and then of love for us, in order to re-establish the bond between mankind and His Father.[97]

Our Lord, Priest, offered Himself on the Cross. He indeed said: "I offer My life. No one can take it from Me," even those who force Me onto the gibbet of the Cross. It is not they who offer My life; I do.[98] "I lay down my life voluntarily," He says.[99] No one would have been able to take away His life had He not willed it, for He is God. He willed as God-Man to die here below to save us.[100]

The more one reflects and meditates on the extraordinary means that the good God took to save us by His Cross, the more one realizes that for good souls, simple souls, souls that do not try to make their reason prevail over faith, it was the ideal means for enabling souls to best approach all the mysteries of faith. The mystery of God, the mystery of the Incarnation, the mystery of Redemption, the mystery of the Trinity, the mystery of grace, the mystery of the love of God, the mystery of grace, of the life that the good God comes to bring us, all Our Lord's virtues: all that is expressed in the Cross of Our Lord.[101]

Our Lord Himself said before expiring: "All is consummated" (Jn. 19:30). From that moment, Our Lord completed the Redemption, and consequences follow: the Resurrection, the

---

[95] The *Adoro Te*: "Blood whereof one drop for humankind outpoured/ Might from all transgression have the world restored."
[96] Homily, St-Michel-en-Brenne, April 2, 1989.
[97] Homily, receiving of the habit, Weissbad, March 17, 1978.
[98] Cf. Jn. 10:17.
[99] Cf. Lk. 23:45.
[100] Homily, Una Voce, May 20, 1973.
[101] Easter retreat, Ecône, April 17, 1984.

Ascension, and His glorification. Then begins the work of applying the merits of the Cross, redemption, to souls by the holy sacrifice of the Mass and by the Sacraments.

5. He rose again the third day

By His death, Our Lord wanted to deliver us from our sins; and by His Resurrection, to restore our souls to the grace of the good God. The entire Paschal Vigil ceremony expresses it. The ceremony of the blessing of the Easter candle, which symbolizes Our Lord Jesus Christ Himself enlightening the world again, is admirable, as is the blessing of the baptismal water, which signifies the resurrection of our souls in contact with Our Lord Jesus Christ's soul. As St. John says: "And of his fulness we all have received, and grace for grace" (Jn. 1:16). The soul of Jesus was full of grace and truth (Jn. 1:14). The grace in our souls is a participation of the grace present in Our Lord's soul; it is given to us at baptism. Baptism, by which we die to our sins and rise to divine life, is signified by the death of Jesus on His Cross and by His Resurrection. That is why we rejoice today. We rejoice to live anew the divine life. We sing the *Alleluia* and the *Gloria* because He brings us back to life. We have been resurrected, as St. Paul admirably puts it: "For we are buried together with him by baptism into death; that as Christ is risen from the dead by the glory of the Father, so we also may walk in newness of life" (Rom. 6:4). This is the great mystery of our Christian life. But can we say that henceforth we are revived for ever like Our Lord? Alas, no, our body is not resurrected; we know very well that we must die. We have not yet reached the completion of this resurrection. If there is a pledge, a seed of this resurrection by the grace given us in baptism, this grace must germinate, develop, and grow until our death.

Our soul is like a ship on the stormy waves represented by our flesh, this sinful flesh that must die because it still carries sin within it. Yes, despite the grace of baptism, we carry within us a tendency toward sin, a fundamental disorder. The best proof of this is that baptized parents who live wholly in conformity with the law of God, nonetheless communicate original sin to their offspring. The flesh is still infected with the effects of sin, so it must die; and one day it must rise in contact with our sanctified souls, restored to life by the grace of Our Lord Jesus Christ. But even now our souls have arisen if Jesus is truly present in us, and if our souls are purified from sin. That is why we must be firmly resolved to avoid all sin, so as to keep the supernatural life, the life of grace, the life of Our Lord Jesus Christ in our souls, and to reach the port of salvation filled with this grace and assured that one day our bodies will rise from the dead through contact with our living souls. Such is the great mystery of the Christian life.[102]

6. I believe in the Holy Ghost

Sometimes we do not have enough confidence that souls can grow in virtue–with the Lord's grace, obviously. It happens that souls are captivated when someone speaks to them about the gifts of the Holy Ghost, the Beatitudes, and the Fruits of the Holy Ghost which make up part of the spiritual life of all souls once they receive grace by Baptism. When someone preaches to them about these things, how many of the faithful are amazed and say, "But no one ever told us about this! We didn't know that the Holy Ghost acted this way in us."[103]

God wanted to divinize us, to communicate to us the immense charity with which He has burned from all eternity. He wanted to communicate it to us, and He has done this by an extraordinary manifestation, by His Cross, by His Blood poured out.[104] "An effect of the invisible mission of the Holy Ghost and of His presence in us is our deification by grace."[105] One will say, "Come now, it is an exaggeration to use a word like *deification*. We cannot become gods." Of course, we are not gods. Our nature being quite limited, it is only within these limits that we can be deified.[106]

The Christian religion is a religion of the Holy Ghost; it is the religion of love, of charity. It is a religion that has transformed the world. Before, hatred, selfishness, pride, and the pursuit of worldly goods held sway. After Our Lord, the law of charity reigns in hearts; sanctifying grace transforms hearts and souls. Wonderful things developed in Christendom: convents covered all of Christian Europe.

---

[102] Homily, Ecône, April 7, 1985.
[103] Ordination retreat, Montalenghe, 1989.
[104] Homily, Ecône, June 29, 1982.
[105] R. P. Froget, *De l'habitation du Saint-Esprit dans les âmes des justes* (Paris: Lethielleux, 1936), p.268.
[106] Retreat, Brignoles, July 27, 1984.

Everywhere that the Catholic religion took root, convents were built, vocations flourished, Christian families flourished–large families in which charity reigned and from which the vocations sprang that made Christendom. It was a wonderful thing. For thirteen centuries Christendom reigned over the earth, so much so that vestiges of it still remain everywhere: the monasteries and magnificent churches built during the time of Christendom. Well, we must ask the good God to keep us in this same Christian spirit, the spirit of the love of Our Lord.[107]

7. I believe in the Church

The Church has received from Our Lord this magnificent treasure, which is nothing other than His sacrifice and, consequently, His priesthood, for the perpetuation of His sacrifice and the communication of His Spirit to souls by sanctifying grace, this grace that heals and lifts up hearts to God. These are the gifts Our Lord has given us, through His Church.[108]

The Church without the sacrifice of the Mass is unthinkable. It is truly her great work. That is why her children, her most faithful disciples, those who most take to heart her spirit, are to be seen around the altar. All religious congregations put the altar of Our Lord Jesus Christ in the center of their hearts and lives.[109]

The Church Our Lord founded was intended to be priestly; we have no right to change its nature. He wanted all souls to be saved by Himself, through His Humanity and through His Church, which is like the prolongation of His Humanity in time and space. All of this follows an implacable logic. We do not have the right to say: "But no! There are many other souls that can be saved without Our Lord Jesus Christ." Obviously, if the Divinity of Our Lord Jesus Christ is up for discussion, then nothing can stand. If Our Lord is simply an extraordinary man, absolutely dominating mankind by His virtue, wisdom, and knowledge; if He is but a Socrates to the umpteenth degree; if Our Lord is only that, then He is nothing in relation to God! Now there are some who claim that God acts directly on souls by giving them His Spirit when they sim-

---

[107] St-Michel-en-Brenne, January 28, 1990.
[108] Retreat, Le Barroux, August 1985.
[109] Retreat, Avrillé, October 18, 1989.

ply call upon the Spirit of God, as happens in Pentecostalism and many sects of that kind. This is absolutely false and contrary to the will of Our Lord. Our Lord wanted His grace to be mediated by the Church, normally through the sacraments. If it can be communicated outside the normal channels, Our Lord does it to show His omnipotence, but He never disavows what He has established; that would be impossible, it would be to destroy His own work, His creation, that which He has made.[110]

8. I believe in one baptism for the remission of sins

We believe in one God; we believe in one Lord, Jesus Christ, who was born, suffered, and shed His Blood for us. We believe in one Church: *unam, sanctam, catholicam Ecclesiam*. We believe in one Baptism. The term *unum* occurs four times in our Creed: *unum Deum; unum Dominum Jesum Christum; unam, sanctam, catholicam Ecclesiam; unum baptisma*. Four times we say *one*: one God, one Lord, one Church, one baptism. What is the point? The purpose is to define one religion: there are not two, there is only one religion, the Catholic religion; there is no other....And if we believe that our Catholic religion is the unique religion, then we must draw from it the consequences–and the consequences are very simple: all men must adhere to this holy religion if they want to be saved....That is why we must be missionaries.[111]

We do not accept this precious religious freedom invented at the Second Vatican Council, according to which everyone may have a religion following his own conscience. That's false. There is no religion of the conscience; there is only the religion of Our Lord Jesus Christ to which we must adhere. There is the way that Our Lord Jesus Christ opened for us to go to heaven, and there is no other. Our Lord Himself has said: "Narrow is the way" (Mt. 7:14). Take up your cross and follow Me if you want to be My disciples, if you want to enter into heaven.[112]

9. I believe in life everlasting.

I believe in life everlasting: it is the last article of the *Credo*. Eternal life must not be imagined as unending time; otherwise, the

---

[110] Homily, Toulouse, June 19, 1977.
[111] Spiritual conference, Ecône, March 1974.
[112] Homily, Rouen, May 1, 1990.

mere thought of it would be wearisome. Time and eternity cannot be compared. Eternity is not a length of time; it is something else, fortunately for the elect! Time is a fiction: the past no longer exists, the future does not yet exist. Only the present instant exists. But thanks to memory, the past can be remembered and the future foreseen. By the motions of the stars, the hours, days, months, and years can be counted and position on the earth localized. But eternity is something else. Eternity is beyond time. There is no time in eternity. Eternity is like a point, a lasting instant. It is a continual "now." Eternity, says Father Garrigou-Lagrange, is easier to understand than time. Time is more mysterious. God embraces time, so to speak; He embraces the past and the future. He is above it all. That is why time is attached to eternity, and not vice versa.[113]

The Catechism of the Council of Trent describes what eternal life consists in. Here are some passages:

> These words, *life everlasting*, also teach us that, contrary to the false notions of some, happiness once attained can never be lost. Happiness is an accumulation of all good without admixture of evil, which, as it fills up the measure of man's desires, must be eternal....The intensity of the happiness which the just enjoy in their heavenly country, and its utter incomprehensibility to all but themselves alone, are sufficiently conveyed by the very words *blessed life*....
>
> The happiness of eternal life is, as defined by the Fathers, *an exemption from all evil, and an enjoyment of all good*. Concerning (the exemption from all) evil the Scriptures bear witness in the most explicit terms. For it is written in the Apocalypse: *They shall no more hunger nor thirst, neither shall the sun fall on them, nor any heat* (Apoc. 7:16); and again, *God shall wipe away all tears from their eyes: and death shall be no more, nor mourning nor crying, nor sorrow shall be any more, for the former things are passed away* (Apoc. 21:4).
>
> As for the glory of the blessed, it shall be without measure, and the kinds of their solid joys and pleasures without number....
>
> Solid happiness, which we may designate by the common appellation *essential*, consists in the vision of God, and the enjoyment of His beauty who is the source and principle of all goodness and perfection. *This*, says Christ Our Lord, *is eternal life: that they may know thee, the only true God, and Jesus Christ, whom thou hast*

---

[113] Retreat, Morgon, October 1988.

sent (Jn. 17:3)....[B]eatitude consists of two things: that we shall behold God such as He is in His own nature and substance; and that we ourselves shall become, as it were, gods.[114]

Of course, we shall not be gods–that's obvious. Our transformation will happen in heaven by the light of glory. The light of glory, which will be a participation of the light of glory of the good God, will make us, in a certain measure, know God as He truly is. We shall see God directly, but we shall not know Him intimately in full, of course, since that would mean that we ourselves were God. Only the Word, certainly, only the three Persons of the Trinity know themselves perfectly because they are God. It is something truly extraordinary. The Catechism of the Council of Trent continues:

> The only means, then, of arriving at a knowledge of the divine Essence is that God unite Himself in some sort to us, and after an incomprehensible manner elevate our minds to a higher degree of perfection, and thus render us capable of contemplating the beauty of His Nature. This the light of His glory will accomplish. Illumined by its splendor we shall see God, the true light, in His own light (Ps. 35:10).
>
> For the blessed always see God present and by this greatest and most exalted of gifts, being made *partakers of the divine nature* (II Pet. 1:4), they enjoy true and solid happiness....
>
> To enumerate all the delights with which the souls of the blessed shall be filled would be an endless task. We cannot even conceive them in thought....albeit this must be in a manner more exalted than, to use the Apostle's words, eye hath seen, ear heard, or the heart of man conceived (I Cor. 2:9).[115]

What we shall see in God will surpass in beauty, goodness, and splendor all that we can imagine. We shall admire the Church Triumphant and especially Our Lord with all His royal and divine privileges; Mary, Queen of Heaven, adorned with all her gifts; the myriad of archangels and angels, and all the elect with their diversity of glory measured according to their degree of charity. God will truly be all in all, honored and adored as He should be.

---

[114] *Catechism of the Council of Trent*, Article XII [English version: Tr. John A. McHugh, O.P., and Charles J. Callan, O.P. (1923; reprint: Roman Catholic Books, n.d.), pp.133-39 passim.]
[115] Retreat, Morgon, October 1988.

Nothing will be out of place. In the light of the Infinite Being of the Holy Trinity and of His perfections, our souls will be transported in thanksgiving for all that God has deigned to undergo for our salvation. We will be confounded by the mercy that God has exercised on our behalf.

Tradition teaches us that the virgins, martyrs, and doctors will have particular halos that will augment their glory.

Before these prospects, which are the object of our faith and the goal of our existence, how can we not weep, like Our Lord in His agony in the Garden of Olives, at the thought of all the souls separated from Our Lord, despising Him by indifference, forgetfulness, and sin, and taking the broad way that leads to hell?[116]

It is very important, then, to know well what the Creed expresses and to live accordingly. Each time we recite or sing the *Credo*, let us make a deliberate effort to be truly conscious of the fact that the words we pronounce constitute the summary of all that we must believe and love. It is the deepest and dearest reality of our pilgrimage in time, because it expresses all that the Lord God has done to love us. It is the love song of the good God for us. That is what the *Credo* really is: the résumé of the charity of God for us. It is magnificent.

Sic nos amantem quis non redamaret, sings the sacred liturgy in the *Adeste Fideles* of Christmas, following the thought of St. Augustine: "How can we fail to love in return someone who has so loved us?"

Each time we recite or sing the *Credo*, let us remember this appeal to our love, to the charity that we should have towards God. Let us strive to be mindful of this appeal to orient ourselves ever more closely so as to love God truly, to thank Him, to offer thanksgiving, and to do everything in our power to assure that His love for us be not in vain.[117]

If we are not moved by seeing in what manner the good God wanted to resolve the problem of our redemption, by becoming man, by taking flesh like ours, by shedding all His Blood for us, it is because we do not know what God is. If we realized it, we would be dumbfounded to think that He could become one of us. Logically,

---

[116] *Spiritual Journey*, pp.66-67.
[117] *The Mystery of Jesus*, pp.33-34.

one might say, it is utterly inconceivable that God should become a weak creature, that He could have taken a weak, mortal, passible body subject to suffering, hunger, and fatigue. God? No, it is not possible. The mysteries of the Incarnation and the Redemption are great mysteries, of course–mysteries of our faith. The good God has done all that from love of us....Is this for us a matter of continual thanksgiving to God?[118]

We must try to instill in our hearts and souls the sentiment of profound gratitude towards Our Lord for the love He has shown us, because we come forth from Jesus' heart. We are born with the Church, the Church born from the Heart of Jesus. The water that flowed from His Heart represents the grace that heals, and the blood represents the grace that elevates. We also come forth from the Heart of Jesus by Baptism. How grateful we must be to Our Lord![119]

If only we could understand the immense love with which God has loved us! Not only has He created us, He has redeemed us; He has restored to us this divine life that we had lost by original sin, and henceforth, if we truly live as Christians, we can be assured that Our Lord Jesus Christ and His Holy Spirit are present in our hearts and souls. What joy, what hope, what consolation in the midst of trials and difficulties! We must understand that Our Lord is present in us and that we are participants of His Divine Nature. This is what the good God has desired to make of us. What ingrates we would be if we were to live as if we did not know it.[120]

---

[118] Spiritual conference, Ecône, January 25, 1982.
[119] Retreat, Le Barroux, August 1985.
[120] Homily, Ecône, March 30, 1975.

II. The Sacrifice, or Mass of the Faithful

If the first part of the Mass reminds you of the Faith you have to teach, the second part of the Mass, which is in a certain way the most important, is that of the sacrifice. After the Creed, you enter into a mysterious silence. You pray to God and then enter into the great mystery that is God. This is why the Church requires the priest to say these prayers in a low voice. Not that she does not ask the faithful to unite themselves to them, but at that moment the priest in some way disappears from the assembly to find himself face to face with God, like Moses on Mount Sinai, or like the Apostles on Mount Tabor. They went up the mountain; "I will go in unto the altar of God–*Introibo ad altare Dei*." The priest goes up to the altar of God; he now finds himself alone face to face with God. He is going to accomplish a great mystery, the sacrifice of Our Lord, as on Calvary.[1]

The second part of the Mass, which is the sacrifice, represents love of God and love of neighbor. The second part is the main part. Obviously, faith, developed in the first part of the Mass, is a preparation for union with God Our Lord. During the second half of the Mass, the action that renews the sacrifice of Calvary on our altars takes place. It also renews the Lord's contemplation on His Cross, a contemplation that He directs first of all to His Father. Through Our Lord's sacrifice, let us strive to give ourselves without reserve to the Father, to the Holy Trinity. What happens at the moment of the Consecration is truly the summit of the world, the whole Church, and of history.[2]

To accomplish this mystery the priest turns towards the crucifix and towards God, like the high priest of old who passed through the curtain once a year to be alone with God. Then he returned, bringing blessings to the faithful. Today too, after turn-

---

[1] Homily, First Mass, Mantes-la-Jolie, July 2, 1977.
[2] Retreat, Le Barroux, August 1985.

ing towards God, the priest turns back to the faithful to give them Jesus Christ.[3]

THE OFFERTORY

> The sacrifice of the Mass is none other than the sacrifice of Christ. It begins with the oblation, or offering, continues with the Consecration, and concludes with the Communion. The priest, and he alone, has the immense power to offer the Divine Victim to God in the Church's name.

1. Sacrifice, prayer *par excellence*

Sacrifice is the most essential element of normal human life. The most important act of a normal human creature, that is, someone who believes in God and acknowledges God as the Creator of all things, is to express gratitude to Almighty God by sacrifice, by the oblation of a thing signifying the oblation of the man himself to God. And, as St. Thomas says, this gratitude is expressed not only by oblation, but also by immolation.[4] The thing offered is destroyed because it is sacred. The word *sacrificium* means *facere sacrum*, to make sacred, that is to say, to render sacred something given to God. To make manifest the complete gift made of the thing to God, so that it can no longer be used for a profane purpose, the sacred object is destroyed. And this act is essential to man. Sacrifice gives man his true stature, his true place in relation to God.[5]

2. Sacrifice, the principal act of the virtue of religion

In the Encyclical *Caritatis Studium* of July 25, 1898, Leo XIII said: "Now the very essence of Religion implies Sacrifice.... If Sacrifices are abolished, Religion can neither exist nor be conceived." St. Thomas very clearly shows that the virtue of religion, which is a virtue annexed to the virtue of justice, attaches us to God. He continues: "Religion, in the proper sense of the word, implies the notion of sacrifice."[6]

---

[3] Conference, Barcelona, December 29, 1975.
[4] *Summa Theologica*, II-II, Q. 85, Art. 3.
[5] Easter retreat, Ecône, April 17, 1984.
[6] "*Religio proprie importat ordinem ad Deum*" (*ST*, II, II, Q. 81, Art. 1).

We need to exercise our virtue of religion. Even from the standpoint of nature, the virtue of religion pertains to what is most essential in man. The virtue of religion, which is at the center of the virtue of justice, expresses what we are in relation to God and to our neighbor. Fulfilling the duties we owe to God and to our neighbor is to practice the virtue of justice. We have duties to fulfill in relation to God, and the first of these is the virtue of religion, that is to say, adoration of God. Even an infant, if it were conscious of what it is and what it owes God, would adore God in its heart, thanking Him for having been created. And this is simply from the viewpoint of nature. It would be only just that a scarcely created human soul turn towards God in praise: "I am like Our Lord Jesus Christ; I come into the world to do Thy holy will."[7] This should be the first movement of a soul from the first instant of its creation. This is the understanding that parents must inculcate in their children as soon as they are able to understand that they are creatures of God.

The virtue of religion is exercised especially by adoration—not only exterior, but also interior. We need exterior adoration, for if we do not express our adoration of God outwardly in a manner worthy of Him, we risk not having an interior adoration of God, which is nothing else than our submission to Him. By this oblation that we make of ourselves to God, we submit our will, our intellect, and all that we are to the God who created us and who has awaited us for eternity.

Now, if the virtue of religion must be exercised on the merely natural level, all the more must it be exercised on the supernatural level. God desired to come among us. He became flesh, wanting to show us Himself how the religious man, the creature, must conduct himself in relation to God. Our Lord came upon earth; He prayed; He adored His Father. He demonstrated what religion is. He gave Himself totally to his Father on the Cross; He offered Himself totally, completely, for the glory of His Father and the salvation of souls.[8]

---

[7] Cf. Heb. 10:9.
[8] Homily, Lyons, February 8, 1976.

3. A sacrifice can only be offered to God.

As St. Thomas says,[9] sacrifice can only be offered to God because we can only make a complete gift of our person, the sacrifice of what we are, to Him who gave us these things. We can have a certain devotion to creatures, but we cannot offer sacrifice to a creature–that is out of the question. Sacrifice is reserved to God alone.[10]

4. No priest, no sacrifice

The human race has always felt the need to have priests, that is to say, men who, by an official mission confided to them, are mediators between God and mankind and who, wholly consecrated to this mediation, make it the purpose of their life. Priests are thus men chosen to offer official prayers and sacrifices to God in the name of society, which as such also has an obligation to offer God public, civic worship, to acknowledge Him as the supreme Lord and first Principle, to tend towards Him as its last end, and to try to propitiate Him. "In fact, priests are to be found among all peoples whose customs are known, except those compelled by violence to act against the most sacred laws of human nature. They may, indeed, be in the service of false divinities; but wherever religion is professed, wherever altars are built, there also is a priesthood surrounded by particular marks of honor and veneration."[11]

Nothing is so deeply inscribed in human nature as religion and its essential act, sacrifice. Now, to accomplish a sacred act, "*sacrum facere*," there must be consecrated, designated persons capable of drawing near to God and of serving Him. This person will be the priest, *sacerdos*, "giving the sacred." We see how God in His infinite goodness and mercy has arranged everything so that worship worthy of Himself may be offered by men who had strayed far from Him.

5. Christ's sacrifice renewed on our altars

The sacrifice of the Cross, the Catechism of the Council of Trent teaches, was infinitely pleasing to God. Scarcely had Jesus

---

[9] *Summa Theologica*, II, II, Q. 85, Art. 2.
[10] Homily, receiving of the cassock and tonsures, Flavigny, February 2, 1988.
[11] Pius XI, *Ad Catholici Sacerdotii*, December 20, 1935, §8.

Christ offered the sacrifice of the Cross, and the wrath and indignation of His Father were completely appeased. That is why the Apostle is careful to make us understand that the Savior's death was a real sacrifice. "Christ also hath loved us, and hath delivered himself for us, an oblation and a sacrifice to God for an odour of sweetness" (Ephes. 5:2).

The Passion of Our Lord is thus a true sacrifice. This is a truth of faith defined by the Council of Ephesus and the Council of Trent. The Council of Ephesus says: "He...offer[ed] Himself once to God the Father upon the altar of the Cross by the mediation of death, so that He might accomplish an eternal redemption...," and the Council of Trent affirms: "Christ, on the altar of the Cross 'once offered Himself'; ...by His death, He offered Himself to the Father to redeem us, to accomplish the Redemption of all men."[12]

You see, the Passion is a true sacrifice, and the consequences are immense because they affect the entire history of mankind, the history of Creation and all that preceded or followed this sacrifice offered to the praise and glory of God.[13] In a certain way, it can be said that there is only one Sacrifice, one Priest, one Victim, and one Oblation with the faithful, which was accomplished in the sacrifice of the Cross: there are not two sacrifices of the Cross. But the good God wanted this priesthood, this sacrifice, this victim, and this oblation to continue so that the merits earned by His Son might be applied to our souls.[14]

The sacrifice of Calvary becomes on our altars the sacrifice of the Mass, which, as it continues the sacrifice of the Cross, brings about the sacrament of the Eucharist, making us participants in the divine Victim, Jesus Crucified.[15]

THE KISSING OF THE ALTAR

Before starting the sacrifice, the priest again kisses the altar, symbol of Christ. Throughout the Church's history, the altar has occupied the central place in the churches in the midst of our cities.

---

[12] Cf. Dz. 938, 940.
[13] Easter retreat, Ecône, April 17, 1984.
[14] Retreat, Ecône, September 22, 1978.
[15] *Spiritual Journey*, p.44.

The altar is the center of all the basilicas and all the churches, is it not? It is the altar of sacrifice, and not a table for meals or sharing or communion. As soon as the Church found herself at peace, what did Constantine and the Christians do? Right away they built magnificent sanctuaries, churches, and basilicas around the altar–always.

What do the missionaries do in the lands they want to evangelize? The first thing they build is a chapel. They make a place of prayer. And in this place, what do they put in the middle? The altar. And what do they put in the altar? The altar stone, the consecrated stone on which they offer sacrifice.

It is understandable that Christians settled around their bell towers. It is wonderful to see even now in many villages: the bell tower still dominates the scene. The bell tower symbolizes the church with the altar in the center. One could then say that the heart of the village is the altar of sacrifice. The faithful are always gathered around their church; even the cemetery is situated nearby. All this wonderfully expresses the faith of Catholics, the faith of the Church, and shows the importance of the sacrifice of the Mass in the Christian religion.

All the religious, all the founders of orders like Saint Benedict, founded their societies around the altar. They organized the recitation of the Divine Office around the altar. The centerpiece of the Divine Office is the holy sacrifice of the Mass. It is generally celebrated after the hour of Terce, because it was at nine o'clock that Our Lord mounted the Cross and at three o'clock that He came down from the Cross. The religious orders chose that time to celebrate the holy sacrifice in memory of Our Lord's ascent to the altar of the Cross.[16]

The Preparation of the Offering

The bread and wine, chosen by Our Lord Jesus Christ as the matter of the Eucharist, are highly symbolic.

---

[16] Nine o'clock should not be taken to indicate a precise time, but here signifies the third hour of the day, which corresponds to the period between nine o'clock and noon according to the way the Romans told time.

In His Wisdom, Our Lord wanted to use material things, temporal things, to communicate His Holy Ghost to us. He wanted to choose the simplest, most common things: water, bread, wine, oil–things most commonly used as food and in the care of the body.[17]

Our Lord is the Creator of wheat; He is the Creator of the vine. In His eternal decrees, consequently, He wanted to create these foods for the Holy Eucharist, and that is certainly the first reason for which they were created, even before being the nourishment of our natural life.

When people sometimes complain that the Church seems too spiritual and not material enough, it is because they do not understand what God has done. Our Lord uses all these creatures to manifest His love for us and to communicate His life to us. Jesus showed thereby that He was the Creator of all things, and that He could use His creatures to make us partakers of His spiritual life. In His Wisdom, God does all things well.[18]

There is a close link between the Eucharist, the institution of the priesthood, and Our Lord's Passion; between the Last Supper and Gethsemane. Just as Our Lord Jesus Christ chose the fruit of the vine and wheat for His Eucharist, and these elements are crushed in order to become the Body and Blood of Our Lord Jesus Christ–for it is bread and wine that Our Lord chose as the matter of the Sacrament of the Eucharist–so also the olive is crushed to become the sacred chrism used in Holy Orders. Why choose these different fruits, which must be crushed? Our Lord Jesus Christ Himself said: "I have trodden the winepress alone" (Is. 63:3), yet in some way it was He Himself who was in the winepress. It was He who was going to suffer and be crushed, and who was going to shed all His Blood for the redemption of our sins. He wanted therefore to choose for the Sacraments creatures that would also be crushed like Him in order to produce the holy oil, the bread or the wine which would become the instruments of our sanctification. If Jesus wanted to choose the elements and to crush them, it is because we also must become victims with Him; we also must be crushed by penance, trials, and sacrifice, in order to unite ourselves more with

---

[17] Homily, Ecône, March 27, 1975.
[18] Homily, Ecône, April 15, 1976.

Him. For it is to unite ourselves with Him that we eat His Body and drink His Blood and receive the holy chrism.[19]

Why else did Our Lord choose these elements of bread and wine? Surely you know it; it is a comparison that is often made, but always bears repeating. Bread is the fruit of grains of wheat that have been ground together–crushed and blended together. To make bread, it is necessary to grind the individual grains of wheat so that they form a single dough and one bread. The Eucharistic bread is the very image of the union of all the faithful insofar as the species of bread is the fruit of the union of the grains of wheat. The same goes for the wine: all the grapes in the bunch must be united to produce wine. Our Lord thus wanted to choose these elements to show us that we must be united in order to be transformed in Him. If we do not have charity in us, if we are not united among ourselves, Our Lord will not be in us effectively; it would be impossible. Our Lord Jesus Christ cannot enter into a soul that lacks charity. Consequently, we must always strive to keep true charity in our souls.[20]

The Offering of the Host: *Suscipe, Sancte Pater*

The sacrifice properly so-called begins with the Offertory. It is an essential part, because the oblation and the consecration separate the object offered from that which is profane and consecrate it to God. Our Lord, being both Victim and Priest, offered Himself. "He was offered because it was his own will" (Is. 53:7); "No man taketh [my life] away from me: but I lay it down of myself, and I have power to lay it down: and I have power to take it up again" (Jn. 10:18).

While this offering of Our Lord took place formally in His Passion, it is still true to say that Our Lord's entire life was the object of a continual, already present oblation resulting from the hypostatic union, which was nothing else than a consecration and

---

[19] Homily, Ecône, April 16, 1981.
[20] Homily, Ecône, June 17, 1976.

The Mass of the Faithful

separation by which Christ entered into the intimacy of the Trinity as Mediator.[21]

Súscipe, sancte Pater, omnípotens ætérne Deus, hanc immaculátam hóstiam, quam ego indígnus fámulus tuus óffero tibi Deo meo vivo et vero, pro innumerabílibus peccátis, et offensiónibus, et neglegéntiis meis, et pro ómnibus circumstántibus, sed et pro ómnibus fidélibus christiánis vivis atque defúnctis: ut mihi et illis profíciat ad salútem in vitam ætérnam. Amen.

Receive, O holy Father, almighty, eternal God, this spotless host which I, thine unworthy servant, offer unto Thee, my living and true God, for my own countless sins, offenses, and negligences, and for all here present; as also for all faithful Christians, living or dead; that it may avail for my own and for their salvation unto life eternal. Amen.

The holy sacrifice of the Mass atones for sin and purifies souls. The prayers of the Offertory show this clearly, the priest offering the Holy Victim in reparation for his own sins and for the salvation of all the faithful living and dead. The priest concludes this prayer by making a Sign of the Cross with the paten over the corporal, showing by this visible sign that the host is placed upon the Cross on which Jesus Christ offered Himself to His Father for our sins.

All the words of the liturgy express the desire for expiation and the remission of sins. Expiation, the taking away of our sins, is one of the chief goals of the holy Mass.[22]

The Protestants accept the Eucharistic sacrifice, but they deny the propitiatory sacrifice; that is to say, they deny that Mass expiates sins. According to them, the sacrifice of the Mass does not atone for sins, but this is fundamental for us. It is the essential difference that separates us from Protestantism. We believe that the sacrifice of the Mass is a propitiatory sacrifice...even now: the same sacrifice as the one offered on Calvary continues. Consequently, every time a sacrifice of the Mass is offered, sins are remitted and graces of sanctification are spread throughout the whole world. This is why it is really worthwhile to be a priest.

It is consequently good for us to consider what sin is and what its consequences are so that we do everything to avoid it and to

---

[21] Notes for a sacerdotal retreat, undated. Ecône Seminary archives, *O Mysterium Christi*, p.13.
[22] Homily, Ecône, September 14, 1975.

expiate it, and to expiate it for others, also. It is clear that the liturgy helps us very much in this. If we find the aspects of adoration, impetration, and thanksgiving in the liturgy, which obviously are the very fabric of the liturgy, we also find in it everything concerning sin and our appeal to God's mercy, and hence propitiation. Propitiation is expressed in many beautiful prayers of the liturgy, which help place us in the atmosphere of reparation denied by the Protestants. It is indeed necessary to keep in our prayer the propitiatory aspect.

The whole liturgy, in fact, the great prayer of the Church, invites us to consider Jesus on the Cross as Victim, the spotless Lamb immolated because of our sins; the Savior and Redeemer who redeemed us at the cost of His Blood.[23]

Try to unite yourselves to the spirit of the holy sacrifice of the Mass and to acquire it. This will be for you a continual source of particular graces, graces of propitiation and thus of supplication for asking of God the forgiveness of your faults, the healing of your souls from all the evil tendencies that original sin may have left in you, and lastly for asking of Him the grace better to know, love, praise, and live united to the Holy Trinity.[24]

The Blessing of the Water:
Deus, qui humanæ substantiæ

Deus, ✠ qui humánæ substántiæ dignitátem mirabíliter condidísti, et mirabílius reformásti: da nobis, per hujus aquæ et vini mystérium, ejus divinitátis esse consórtes, qui humanitátis nostræ fíeri dignátus est párticeps, Jesus Christus, Fílius tuus, Dóminus noster: Qui tecum vivit et regnat in unitáte Spíritus Sancti, Deus, per ómnia sǽcula sæculórum. Amen.

O God, ✠ Who in creating human nature didst marvelously ennoble it, and hast still more marvelously renewed it: grant that by the mystery of this water and wine, we may be made partakers of His Divinity Who vouchsafed to become partaker of our humanity, Jesus Christ, Thy Son, our Lord, Who liveth and reigneth with Thee, in the unity of the Holy Ghost, one God, world without end. Amen.

---

[23] Retreat, Le Barroux, August 1985.
[24] Homily, diaconate and subdiaconate, Ecône, May 29, 1982.

Every day during the Mass when the priest pours water into the wine, he says this prayer: "Grant that we may be made partakers of His Divinity, who vouchsafed to become partaker of our humanity." Our Lord assumed our human life in order to communicate His Divine Life, to make this magnificent exchange.

"You shall be as gods," (Gen. 3:5) said the ancient serpent, the infernal tempter, to our first parents so as to induce them to pluck the forbidden fruit....Yielding to this foolish pride, they lifted the fatal fruit to their lips, and their eyes were opened immediately, but it was only to contemplate with fright the abyss into which their disobedience had cast them....Ever since that terrible fall, every man is born a sinner even before he can commit a personal fault.... But, wonder of Divine Goodness, the deification, which on Satan's lips was but an alluring lie, is offered to us again, this time by God Himself, not only as something to which we can legitimately aspire, but even as a goal we must attain. It is to make possible for us this supreme exaltation, it is to merit for us this signal benefit, that the Son of God deigned to lower Himself to our level and to clothe Himself with our humanity. "He became man," St. Athanasius says, "to make gods of us."[25] It is what St. Peter says in his second Epistle: "By whom he hath given us most great and precious promises: that by these you may be made partakers of the divine nature" (2 Pet. 1:4). This partaking of the nature and life of God is nothing other than sanctifying grace, such that the gift that justifies us at the same time deifies us, and the justification is a veritable deification.[26]

By grace, we are truly sons of God, and not simply creatures. We are united to God in a very particular way; we possess divine life in ourselves. Now this life, stimulated by our status as adopted children, urges us to a still greater detachment. The total detachment that leads to the priestly or religious vocation is a manifestation of our divine filiation and of supernatural grace. The divine life also pushes us towards the exercise of greater virtue, to the practice of the supernatural moral virtues; it draws us towards the One who is our Father.[27]

---

[25] St. Athanasius, Sermon IV, *Against the Arians*.
[26] Retreat, Brignoles, July 27, 1984.
[27] Spiritual conference, Ecône, December 3, 1974.

The Drop of Water Mixed with the Wine

When the priest pours a drop of water into the wine, the little drop represents the faithful people. This drop of water is united with Our Lord's Blood, since the wine will soon be transformed into the Blood of Our Lord. Thus we participate in the grace of Our Lord; we are a little drop of water in the immense sea of Our Lord's sanctifying grace. His sanctifying grace possesses a certain infinity because it proceeds from the Lord's union with the Divinity. Our Lord could have sanctified worlds upon worlds and generations upon generations more numerous than those that have been sanctified and will be sanctified.[28]

The Offering of the Chalice: *Offerimus Tibi, Domine*

OFFERIMUS tibi, Dómine, cálicem salutáris, tuam deprecántes cleméntiam: ut in conspéctu divínæ majestátis tuæ, pro nostra et totíus mundi salúte, cum odóre suavitátis ascéndat. Amen.

WE offer unto Thee, O Lord, the chalice of salvation, beseeching Thy clemency that, in the sight of Thy Divine Majesty, it may ascend with the savor of sweetness, for our salvation and for that of the whole world. Amen.

The chalice of the sacrifice is also offered for all men. It is the source of all the good that happens here below in souls and in society.

1. The Mass, source of salvation

Our Lord's sacrifice is at the center of human history for the sanctification of mankind, and to lead men to God and to make them sing the praises and the glory of God.[29]

The priest is first and foremost made to offer the redemptive sacrifice so that graces may descend from the Heart of Our Lord Jesus Christ pierced by the lance. The Blood pouring from His Heart was shed for many. Why for "many"? Because many refuse it. It is not because Our Lord did not want to shed His Blood for all, since it says in the Offertory "We offer...the chalice of salva-

---

[28] Retreat, Ecône, September 22, 1978.
[29] *Ibid.*

tion....for the salvation of the whole world." But in reality, how many souls refuse the Blood of Our Lord Jesus Christ! The essential role of the priest lies there: to offer this Blood and to distribute the graces proceeding from it by all the Sacraments.[30]

The most holy Church always sees her mystical Bridegroom in Gethsemane: Jesus prostrate, praying, suffering–suffering so much that His sweat falls as drops of blood because of the anguish He feels! But what is the source of this anguish? Does not Jesus possess the beatific vision? Even here below on earth, yes, Jesus possessed in His holy Soul the beatific vision. Then how could He suffer like this? An angel had to come and console Him as He suffered so. It was because of our sins; it was because of this world that does not want to receive Him: "He came unto His own," says St. John, "and His own received Him not" (Jn. 1:11)! How can this be? It is a great mystery indeed, the mystery of this world that refuses God, that refuses its Redeemer!

God created the world and men, and men have turned away from Him. Even our first parents turned away from Our Lord. He redeemed them by His Cross, by His Blood. He came amongst them. They denied Him: they wanted nothing to do with Him, and they crucified Him. And today still, what a situation! How Jesus suffered then from this vision! How the Virgin Mary suffered a martyrdom at the thought that the Blood of her Divine Son would not be received by the whole human race! That was her martyrdom. This is also the cause of the Church's martyrdom, and must be your martyrdom, too. If you do not understand that, if you are not martyrized by the sight of these souls that refuse Our Lord, then you are not really sons of the Church. And you must be the privileged sons of the Church, so like Our Lord Jesus Christ, you must have the desire to pray, offer yourselves, suffer, and give yourselves entirely to God so that souls might open their hearts and receive the Name of Jesus outside of which there is no salvation. You will be souls of prayer, you will be suffering souls, and you will accept this martyrdom. And you will be missionaries. Seeing the situation of the world, you will be missionaries, but the kind of missionaries that contemplative souls who shut themselves up in monasteries become. You will be missionaries by prayer, and you

---

[30] Homily, ordinations, Ecône, September 20, 1980.

will be missionaries by penance. This is what Our Lord Jesus gave us as an example and what the Church has always desired.[31]

2. The Mass, source of civilization

The virtues that issue from the sacrifice of the Mass, of the Cross, gradually spread in souls. Thus order was re-established in souls little by little, and as it was re-established in individuals it was re-established in families, in villages, and in entire societies....That was how Christian civilization happened.[32]

The history of Christian civilization owes its foundation, development, and vitality to the great public prayer of the Church, which infuses into those who live by it the spirit of love and the spirit of justice. All charitable and godly undertakings have their origin in the spirit infused in us by the Sacraments and the sacrifice of the Altar.[33]

[In Africa] I saw what the grace of the Holy Mass could do. I saw it in the holy souls of some of our catechists. I saw it in those pagans souls transformed by assistance at Holy Mass, and by the Holy Eucharist. These souls understood the mystery of the Sacrifice of the Cross and united themselves to Our Lord Jesus Christ in the sufferings of His Cross, offering their sacrifices and their sufferings with Our Lord Jesus Christ and living as Christians....

I was able to see these pagan villages become Christian–being transformed not only, I would say, spiritually and supernaturally, but also being transformed physically, socially, economically, and politically; because these people, pagans that they were, became cognizant of the necessity of fulfilling their duties, in spite of the trials and the sacrifices of maintaining their commitments, and particularly their commitment in marriage. Then the village began to be transformed, little by little, under the influence of grace, under the influence of the grace of the Holy Sacrifice of the Mass, and soon all the villages were wanting to have one of the Fathers visit them. Oh, the visit of a missionary! They waited impatiently to as-

---

[31] Homily, reception of the cassock and tonsures, Ecône, February 2, 1982.
[32] Spiritual conference, Ecône, December 3, 1974.
[33] *A Bishop Speaks*, "Letter of March 25, 1963...," pp.7-8.

sist at the Holy Mass, in order to confess their sins and then receive Holy Communion.[34]

3. The chapel, sign of Christendom

In mission lands, it is surprising to see how attached the catechumens, the Christians, and the Christian communities are to their chapel, to their place of worship. They all want to have their chapel. As soon as they gather together, they feel this need; they are drawn by the Cross, they are attracted by Our Lord; they are drawn by the offering of themselves. This is a fundamental point of a Christian's life. This reaction is truly inspired by the Holy Ghost. The chapel is the immediate sign of the extension of Christendom. If in a village one sees the chapel, the place of prayer, with its altar and the crucifix above the altar signifying Christ's Calvary, which signifies sacrifice, then one can say that there are Christians in this village. Obviously, that has been the cause of martyrdoms, because the pagans saw their own cult diminishing and their own disciples convert. Some pagan chiefs were so furious that they massacred the missionaries. That is the normal reaction of the devil to the Cross of Our Lord Jesus Christ.[35]

4. Christian civilization is good for all peoples

It is completely contrary to the Faith of the Church to say that Christian civilization is merely a form of Western civilization, a European civilization, and also to say, consequently, that since it is necessary to know how to adapt to all cultures, our Faith must be adapted to other civilizations. That is what Bugnini says in his book on the liturgical reform. He says that the apostolate will have no effect unless the liturgy has been adapted to every civilization and culture, which is what he calls inculturation....In reality, as St. Pius X says very well in his letter on the Sillon movement, there is no need to invent Christian civilization. It has existed and will always exist. It is unchangeable because Christian civilization has as its source all the virtues of Our Lord Jesus Christ, which flow from His Passion and His Divinity by the intermediary of His Sacred

---

[34] Sermon on the occasion of his sacerdotal jubilee [English version: *Apologia pro Marcel Lefebvre*, II, 334-35].
[35] Retreat, Avrillé, October 18, 1989.

Humanity.[36] Its origin is the example of Our Lord, as well as all the Christian virtues He represents and the grace He infuses in us: that is Christian civilization, and that holds good for all men. Indeed, to the extent that all societies are full of vices because of original sin, they all must be purified and sanctified by Our Lord's Passion to become Christian.[37]

The wounds of original sin remain even after Baptism: the wound of ignorance (privation of the virtue of prudence), which blinds us; the wound of malice (privation of the virtue of justice), which prevents us from rendering to each, that is to say to God and our neighbor, his due; the wound of weakness (privation of the virtue of fortitude), characterized by inconstancy; and the wound of concupiscence (loss of the virtue of temperance), which disorders the measure we must exercise in using the goods of this world. These deep wounds can only be closed by sacrifice and renunciation. The return to order requires sacrifice. That is why Our Lord vanquished the devil, destroyed sin, and re-established order by His Cross. And the Cross is the Mass. The Mass reminds Christians every day that they must live a life of sacrifice.[38]

IN A HUMBLE SPIRIT: *IN SPIRITU HUMILITATIS*

IN spíritu humilitátis et in ánimo contríto suscipiámur a te, Dómine: et sic fiat sacrifícium nostrum in conspéctu tuo hódie, ut pláceat tibi, Dómine Deus.

IN an humble spirit, and a contrite heart, may we be received by Thee, O Lord; and may our sacrifice be so offered up in Thy sight this day that it may be pleasing to Thee, O Lord God.

This prayer is adapted from the prayer of the Three Children in captivity at Babylon who, on seeing the fiery furnace in which they were to be cast for refusing to adore the idol, courageously offered themselves as a holocaust to the glory of the true God. It is an invitation to us to offer ourselves, too, and to accept in a Christian spirit the trials of the present life.

---

[36] *Our Apostolic Mandate,* August 25, 1910: "No, civilization is not something yet to be found, nor is the New City to be built on hazy notions; it has been in existence and still is: it is Christian civilization, it is the Catholic city. It has only to be set up and restored continually against the unremitting attacks of insane dreamers, rebels and miscreants. *Omnia instaurare in Christo*" (§11).
[37] Retreat, Ecône, April 17, 1984.
[38] Spiritual conference, Ecône, December 3, 1974.

1. Sacrifice in the Christian life.

The notion of sacrifice is profoundly Christian and profoundly Catholic. Our life cannot be spent without sacrifice since Our Lord Jesus Christ, God Himself, willed to take a body like our own and say to us: "Follow Me. Take up your cross and follow Me if you will be saved."[39] And He gave us the example of His death upon the Cross; He shed His Blood. Would we then dare, we, His poor creatures, sinners that we are, not to follow Our Lord? To follow Our Lord carrying His Cross: such is the mystery of Christian civilization; this is the root of Catholic civilization.[40]

Everyone has problems: personal problems, health problems... We would not be able to understand these trials if we did not think of the holy Victim who offers Himself on the altar.[41]

The whole Catholic religion is founded on the fact that our actions can be meritorious. We repeat it constantly. When you are confined to your sickbed in the hospital and have been suffering for months, you know that if you offer your sufferings with those of Our Lord, you share Calvary; and so doing, you distribute all the merits you earn to the world and yourself for your conversion and redemption. This is what sustains the Catholic. On the contrary, the Protestants do not believe that our actions can be meritorious because they claim that everything was merited by Our Lord on the Cross on Calvary. Consequently, according to the Protestants, we can no longer merit anything. You see the difference: If someone were to tell us, "All your actions are useless for your salvation; they are not meritorious," then of what use would it be to live, suffer, and work?

This is what the father and mother of a family are told: "In your family life you suffer, you have difficulties, you go through hard times. Remember to unite your sufferings to those of Our Lord Jesus Christ on Calvary, to those of Our Lord Jesus Christ in the holy sacrifice of the Mass. Go to Mass; there you will find the mainstay of your life, the help that will give you strength to bear your trials." Then the father and mother of a family who follow this counsel will say to themselves inwardly: "Indeed, Our Lord is

---

[39] Cf. Mt. 10:38.
[40] Golden Jubilee sermon, Paris, September 23, 1979.
[41] Homily, Una Voce, May 20, 1973.

in me by His grace, and I unite myself to His sufferings, so suffering is worthwhile." How many of those who were locked in concentration camps or prisons, or who suffered martyrdom or who are suffering it now, were only able to endure it with that thought in mind? This is what supports them: the thought that they unite their sufferings to those of Our Lord on Calvary.

After that will you then say that the Mass has no power to take away sins, that the Mass is not a meritorious act, or that there are no meritorious works, under the pretext that Our Lord accomplished everything on Calvary, which is completely contrary to what Jesus Christ taught us: "Take up your cross and follow me."[42] Why carry the cross and follow Him if it is not meritorious? Why did Our Lord tell us that? To unite us to His Cross.

"Do penance." Why should we do penance if it is of no use for our salvation? This is what St. Peter said to the crowd that had gathered at Jerusalem and asked him: "What should we do? You tell us that we have crucified Our Lord and that we must make reparation. What must we do?" "Pray, do penance, and be baptized" (Acts 2:37-40), Peter told them. Penance is nothing else than uniting our sufferings to those of Our Lord, without which our life no longer has any meaning. This is what makes the depth and the beauty of our Catholic Faith. As a consequence, even in trials, even in suffering, Catholics have a smile on their lips. They have joy in their hearts because they know that their suffering serves some purpose. Whereas if someone comes and tells you, "That is pointless, you know; you can suffer all you want, but it serves no good purpose whatsoever," it causes you to withdraw into yourself; it puts a void in your life that can destroy you.[43]

When faced with some trial, we know what we must do. If tomorrow we find ourselves bedridden in a hospital, if we go into a clinic, if our parents die or we are abandoned, the Cross of Jesus is always before our eyes. "Bear your sufferings! Carry your cross! Follow Me! Don't let go of your cross! Don't throw away the cross I give you to carry! Carry it on your shoulders! Follow Me! By following Me, you will have everlasting life and you will save the

---

[42] Cf. Mt. 16:24.
[43] Conference, Mantes-la-Jolie, April 22, 1977.

whole world!" Little St. Theresa of the Child Jesus in her Carmel saved millions of souls! How beautiful is our holy Catholic religion! All these generations of holy fathers and mothers of families who suffered in a Christian manner, who accepted their sufferings with joy, who were an example for their children, understood very well what the Christian life is. They endured their sufferings and sorrows with Our Lord Jesus Christ. And these generations of Christian families gave vocations. The vocations were born of the parents' example. They saw their parents live with Our Lord Jesus Christ, suffer with Our Lord Jesus Christ, pray with Our Lord Jesus Christ, assist at the holy sacrifice of the Mass with this faith, with this piety, offering themselves as victims with Our Lord Jesus Christ.[44]

2. Completing the Passion of Our Lord

St. Paul says that we must complete in our flesh the Passion of Our Lord Jesus Christ.[45] We also must desire it. Yes, it is a desire that will cost us dearly, for if we want to fill up the Passion of Our Lord Jesus Christ, it will be necessary to suffer with Him, and to be immolated with Him. It would be too easy to say, "Because I am a Christian, the good God will bless me and exempt me from all suffering. I shall spend my life without suffering, without sacrifice. Because I love the good God well, the good God must love me, and so the good God must not want me to suffer." Such thinking is to understand poorly the mystery of the Passion of Our Lord Jesus Christ. If Our Lord Jesus Christ showed us the example of redemptive sacrifice, we must almost have a desire to suffer with Him, to sacrifice ourselves with Him.[46]

3. Suffering, source of salvation

The understanding of sacrifice in daily life and of Christian suffering are paramount. We must reach the point of no longer considering suffering as an evil, as an unbearable sorrow; we must unite our sufferings and illnesses to the sufferings of Our Lord Jesus Christ, by looking at the crucifix and by assisting at holy Mass, which is the continuation of Our Lord's Passion on Calvary.

---

[44] Homily, Ecône, September 14, 1975.
[45] Cf. Col. 1:24.
[46] Homily, Ecône, September 14, 1975.

When suffering is understood, then it becomes a joy; suffering becomes a treasure. Our sufferings united to those of Our Lord, united to those of all the martyrs, of all the saints, of all the Catholics, of all the faithful who suffer throughout the world united to the Cross of Our Lord become an ineffable treasure. They possess an extraordinary efficacy for the conversion of souls and for the salvation of our own soul. Many holy Christian souls have even desired suffering in order to unite themselves better to the Cross of Our Lord Jesus Christ. That is Christian civilization.[47]

4. Imitate the Blessed Virgin

The Blessed Virgin participated in the sacrifice of the Cross. She suffered a real martyrdom by her compassion, since the old man Simeon told her during the presentation of Jesus in the Temple: "Thy own soul a sword shall pierce" (Lk. 2:35). You too, if you suffer, if you have trials in your life, let the sword pierce your heart out of compassion for Our Lord. Have this desire to suffer with Our Lord and with the Blessed Virgin for your soul and for the salvation of all souls.[48]

COME, O SANCTIFIER

VENI, sanctificátor omnípotens ætérne Deus: et béne✠ dic hoc sacrifícium, tuo sancto nómini præparátum.

COME, O Sanctifier, almighty, eternal God, and bless ✠ this sacrifice prepared for Thy holy Name.

The Holy Ghost, who effects the great miracle of transubstantiation, sanctifies souls during Mass.

Our Lord wanted to give Himself to us in order to communicate to us the fire of love that He had within Himself. Our Lord Jesus Christ, in a certain sense descending from His Cross, comes to us and gives Himself to us to eat, so as to communicate to us the fire of charity He has within Himself, the Holy Ghost that devours Him in some way, that consumes Him with love for His Father and for His neighbor. This fire is communicated to us in the Holy Eucharist. The Holy Eucharist is filled with the Holy Ghost.

---

[47] Golden Jubilee sermon, September 23, 1979.
[48] Homily, Ecône, April 3, 1976.

The Mass of the Faithful

This is what is communicated to us, my dear brethren, by the Holy Eucharist and by the priest. What an admirable invention! How the good God has done beautiful things! How we should appreciate the extraordinary gifts God has given us![49]

At the conclusion of his book on the Holy Ghost, Father Froget says this:

> ...so many Christians in the possession of habitual grace and of the Divine energies which accompany it, remain, nevertheless, so feeble and so sluggish in God's service, so little zealous for their perfection, so inclined to earth, so forgetful of the things of heaven, so easily fascinated by evil. This is why the Apostle exhorts us "to grieve not the Holy Spirit of God: whereby you are sealed unto the day of redemption" (Eph. 4:30), and, above all, "to extinguish not the Spirit" (I Thess. 5:19).

There is another reason which finally explains why a seed so prolific of holiness produces oftentimes so sorry a harvest. It is this: that knowing but very imperfectly the treasure of which they are the guardians, a number of Christians form only a faint estimate of it, and put themselves to little pains to make it yield fruit. Yet what power, what generosity, what respect for self, what watchfulness and what consolation and joy, would not this thought, if constantly held before the mind and piously meditated upon, inspire: *The Holy Ghost dwells in my heart!* He is there, a powerful Protector, always ready to defend me against my enemies, to sustain me in my combats, to assure me the victory. A faithful Friend, He is always disposed to give me a hearing, and, far from being a source of sadness and weariness, His conversation brings gladness and joy; it "hath no bitterness or His company any tediousness, but joy and gladness" (Wisdom 8:16). He is there the ever present witness of my efforts and sacrifices, counting every one of my steps in order to reward them some day, following my whole course, forgetful of nothing that I do for His love and His glory.[50]

Those are indeed encouraging, beautiful words.[51]

---

[49] Homily, Lausanne, July 9, 1978.
[50] Fr. Barthélemy Froget, O.P., *The Indwelling of the Holy Spirit in the Souls of the Just According to the Teaching of St. Thomas Aquinas* (New York: The Paulist Press, 1921), pp.238-39.
[51] Spiritual conference, Ecône, March 21, 1988.

The Incensing

The liturgy is a school of respect. One incenses the others, souls that are temples of the Holy Ghost. This is a mark of respect, which should be our habitual attitude. It is not only while incensing others that one should consider that they have souls made in the image of God and which are temples of the Holy Ghost. This respect should be apparent in our attitudes and our habitual relations with others. It must not be just during the liturgy that we have respect for others. All of this must penetrate our lives and lead us to have this respect and humility in regard to others.[52]

The sacred and the divine inspire respect. One of the Society's characteristics will be respect towards baptized souls and the respectful treatment of all sacred things, especially everything that touches the sacred action *par excellence*, the holy sacrifice of the Mass. We shall thus avoid letting ourselves be dragged along by the current of vulgarity and rudeness, effects of desacralization. Respect for ourselves and for others will be a particular mark of the true spirit of the Church.

The faithful, and even nonbelievers, are very sensitive to this manifestation of the spirit of the Church and of Our Lord. It is the true manifestation of the Christian spirit and of Christian civilization, a civilization of respect based upon faith in the sacred and the divine, that is to say, in Our Lord Jesus Christ, everything that represents Him and everything that emanates from Him.[53]

Psalm 25: *Lavabo*

Lavabo inter innocéntes manus meas: et circúmdabo altáre tuum, Dómine:

Ut áudiam vocem laudis, et enárrem univérsa mirabília tua.

Dómine, diléxi decórem domus tuæ, et locum habitatiónis glóriæ tuæ.

Ne perdas cum ímpiis, Deus,

I will wash my hands among the innocent: and will compass Thine altar, O Lord.a

That I may hear the voice of Thy praise: and tell of all Thy wondrous works.

O Lord, I have loved the beauty of Thy house: and the place where Thy glory dwelleth.

Destroy not my soul with the

---

[52] Spiritual conference, Ecône, January 28, 1975.
[53] June 4, 1981, in *Cor Unum*, p.56.

ánimam meam, et cum viris sánguinum vitam meam:
In quorum mánibus iniquitátes sunt: déxtera eórum repléta est munéribus.
Ego autem in innocéntia mea ingréssus sum: rédime me, et miserére mei.
Pes meus stetit in dirécto: in ecclésiis benedícam te, Dómine.

Glória Patri, et Fílio, et Spirítui Sancto. Sicut erat in princípio, et nunc, et semper: et in sǽcula sæculórum. Amen.

wicked, O God: nor my life with men of blood.
In whose hands are iniquities: their right hand is filled with gifts.
But I have walked in innocence: redeem me, and have mercy on me.

My foot hath stood in the straight way: in the churches I will bless Thee, O Lord.
Glory be to the Father, and to the Son, and to the Holy Ghost. As it was in the beginning, is now, and ever shall be, world without end. Amen.

You must always love the house of God more and more. The priest's house is the church, and what he must love above all is the altar. "O Lord, I have loved the beauty of Thy house: and the place where Thy glory dwelleth" (Ps. 25:8): This is what the priest recites each time he washes his hands. But for this to be true, we must ensure that these places are places the faithful can love and venerate, so that when they enter, they have a sense of the grandeur of God. Let us love to adorn the house of God and to render it worthy of the One who dwells there.[54]

Everything about it must be noble, great, and ordered in the image of God Himself present in the sanctuary, for the temple is not primarily the house of God's people, but first the *Domus Dei* where the people come to find and meet with God, where they may be in communion with Him.[55]

Profoundly convinced that the source of life is to be found in Christ crucified and thus in the sacrifice He has bequeathed us, the members of the Society will discover with an ever increasing joy that the Mystical Spouse of Our Lord, born of the pierced heart

---

[54] Homily for the conferring of the diaconate and subdiaconate, Ecône, March 12, 1978.
[55] Letter to All Members of the Congregation of the Holy Ghost on the First Session of Vatican Council II, *A Bishop Speaks*, p.11.

of Jesus, has had no greater solicitude than to hand down this precious testament with a magnificence inspired by the Holy Ghost. This is the reason for the splendors of the liturgy that sing Jesus crucified and risen. The Church has known how to present to us and to make us live these mysteries in a truly divine way, which captivates hearts and lifts up souls. Everything has been arranged with the love of a faithful spouse and merciful mother. Everything in the holy places–the ceremonies, ornaments, chants, selection of prayers in the missal, breviary, and pontifical–is a source of edification. How could a soul that lives by faith and models its faith on that of the Church afterwards seek to abolish the sacred?[56]

Before beginning the prayer *Suscipe, Sancta Trinitas*, the priest lifts his eyes to the crucifix on the altar. The priest makes this gesture nine times during the Mass in order to show the link between the sacrifice of the Mass and the sacrifice of the Cross.

There is a much more beautiful cross than these stone crosses–they are nothing. They are not living, they are only images or sculptures. Where is the living Cross? It is there on the altar at each Mass after the Consecration, since Our Lord Jesus Christ present on the altar is the same as the one who was crucified.[57]

Catholics have always loved the Mass and have felt the need of this Mass, sometimes without understanding it, telling themselves: I need to go to Mass. Why? Because we need the Cross of Our Lord Jesus Christ, we need to unite ourselves to it in this vale of tears, in this land of exile. We need to feel ourselves supported by the Cross of Our Lord.[58]

"O Cross, our one reliance, hail–*O Crux ave, spes unica nostra!*" The Cross is our hope, because the Cross is but a path. The Cross is a way, the way to eternal life and glory. But one must go by way of the Cross; one must take up the cross and carry it behind Our Lord to reach eternal life. This *via crucis*, this way of the Cross, must be ours during our life in order to arrive at life everlasting.[59]

---

[56] September 26, 1981, published in *Cor Unum*, p.57.
[57] Homily for confirmations, Doué-la-Fontaine, May 19, 1977.
[58] Homily, Massongex, March 20, 1977.
[59] Homily, Ecône, September 14, 1975.

Receive This Offering: *Suscipe, Sancta Trinitas*

Suscipe, sancta Trínitas, hanc oblatiónem, quam tibi offérimus ob memóriam passiónis, resurrectiónis et ascensiónis Jesu Christi Dómini nostri: et in honórem beátæ Maríæ semper Vírginis, et beáti Joánnis Baptístæ, et sanctórum Apostolórum Petri et Pauli, et istórum, et ómnium Sanctórum: ut illis profíciat ad honórem, nobis autem ad salútem: et illi pro nobis intercédere dignéntur in cælis, quorum memóriam ágimus in terris. Per eúmdem Christum Dóminum nostrum. Amen.

Receive, O Holy Trinity, this offering which we make to Thee, in remembrance of the Passion, Resurrection, and Ascension of Our Lord Jesus Christ, and in honor of blessed Mary ever Virgin, of blessed John the Baptist, of the holy Apostles Peter and Paul, of these and of all the Saints; that it may avail to their honor and our salvation: and may they vouchsafe to intercede for us in heaven whose memory we celebrate on earth. Through the same Christ our Lord. Amen.

It is the oblation of Our Lord that glorifies the Blessed Trinity, and the soul united to this offering participates in this glorification, following in the traces of the Apostles and martyrs.

The sacrifice of the Mass is an oblation, and this oblation must be the model of our own. Our life must be an oblation to God by Our Lord Jesus Christ, *per Dominum nostrum Jesum Christum*, always by Our Lord Jesus Christ, in union with the oblation of Our Lord Jesus Christ. There is no other way to attain the beatific vision, to attain beatitude, to attain our last end, which is Our Lord Jesus Christ. Hence the importance of the sacrifice of the Mass, and of true sacrifice.[60]

After Pentecost, the Apostles would assemble to celebrate the holy mysteries, that is, the holy sacrifice of the Mass, "the breaking of bread" (Acts 2:42). All the martyrs received grace, perseverance in the faith, and the courage to endure martyrdom, in the holy mysteries which they celebrated in secret places, where they hid so as not to be pursued by the persecutors. The catacombs are evidence of it. In the catacombs, signs of the sacrifice celebrated by the first Christians are to be seen everywhere.[61]

---

[60] Spiritual conference, Ecône, March 10, 1989.
[61] Retreat, Avrillé, October 18, 1989.

The oblation of the sacrifice of the Mass will continue in heaven. We shall always be victims offered to the glory of the good God. We shall always be under the influence of the Passion and Cross of Jesus; it is to Our Lord that we shall owe the grace of the beatific vision.[62]

Our Lord Jesus Christ will continue in His glorified Mystical Body to offer Himself during eternity, in praise and thanksgiving to the Blessed Trinity. We shall be the little living cells of Our Lord Jesus Christ singing His praises for all eternity.[63]

Invitation to Pray: *Orate, Fratres*

Orate, fratres: ut meum ac vestrum sacrifícium acceptábile fiat apud Deum Patrem omnipoténtem.

℟. Suscípiat Dóminus sacrifícium de mánibus tuis ad laudem et glóriam nóminis sui, ad utilitátem quoque nostram, totiúsque Ecclésiæ suæ sanctæ.

Brethren, pray that my sacrifice and yours may be acceptable to God the Father almighty.

℟. May the Lord receive the sacrifice from thy hands for the praise and glory of His name, for our welfare and that of all His holy Church.

By the Mass, on the altar, Our Lord's sacrifice on Calvary becomes that of the Church, the priest, and the faithful.

Jesus was the model of prayer throughout His earthly life, and He still prays in heaven, where He is always present to make intercession for us (Heb. 7:25).[64] The Church, too, after His example, must be the model of prayer. Faith that does not lead to prayer is a dead faith. Now, what is this prayer that Jesus has handed on to the Church? It is obvious that the great prayer of the Church is the holy sacrifice of the Mass, just as the great prayer of Our Lord Jesus Christ was His Calvary. It is on the Cross that He prayed most, and it is the sacrifice of the Mass that is the great prayer of the Church, to which the Church requires that all the faithful unite themselves intimately, profoundly, adoring God their Creator, adoring Our Lord Jesus Christ, their Redeemer.

---

[62] Spiritual conference, Ecône, March 10, 1989.
[63] Retreat, Le Barroux, August 1985.
[64] *Semper (vivens ad) interpellandum pro nobis.*

What a magnificent prayer Jesus has handed over to the Church! And in this prayer, He has handed over Himself! He wanted us to partake of His Body, Blood, Soul, and Divinity so that we would also become souls of prayer like Him. May our whole life be a prayer, an offering, a chant, a canticle of thanksgiving. That is what Jesus has transmitted to His Church, and that is what you have to do.[65]

The Secret

> **The conclusion of the collects shows our need of Our Lord Jesus Christ's mediation to go to the Father.**

We always pray "through Christ Our Lord"—always! Jesus Christ is God, Jesus Christ is the Word of God made man. He is our God. There is no other way than Our Lord Jesus Christ. He Himself said: "I am the gate of Paradise. I am the gate of the sheepfold. No one can enter heaven without passing by Me."[66] That is why, in the Church, all our prayers end with these words: *Per Christum Dominum nostrum*. Our Lord is, in some way, our prayer. He is our prayer; all our prayers go through Him.[67]

The Church does not pretend to lead us to the Father without the intercession of Our Lord. For her, Our Lord is her all, He is her mystical Bridegroom, and she keeps herself from forgetting it. That is why we always conclude our prayers with "*per Christum Dominum nostrum*." It is inconceivable that grace might be received without reference to Our Lord Jesus Christ. How was it possible that "*per Christum Dominum nostrum*" was suppressed from the new canons? What was in their minds when they erased these words at the end of the prayers of the Canons? One really wonders. The Church, on the contrary, insists on the fact that all graces come to us by Our Lord Jesus Christ and that all must return to God by Our Lord. He is truly the Mediator; there is no other. One must go through Him whether to receive something or to offer our praises, thanksgivings, and oblations.

---

[65] Homily, reception of the cassock and tonsure, Ecône, February 2, 1982.
[66] *Ego sum ostium* (cf. Jn. 10:9).
[67] Conference, Brussels, March 22, 1986.

Our faith is always restored and deepened by the insistence the Church places on the mediation of Our Lord Jesus Christ. He is our only Savior, our only salvation. This truth of faith is paramount. The liturgy accustoms us to ask for everything by Our Lord Jesus Christ, even for those things we need for the State.[68]

We must have faith in the unique mediation and the unique Mediator. It is necessary that the priest have this profound faith, that he know that he is only a minister, that it is not he who is the mediator, and thus he must have confidence in the grace of redemption won by Our Lord Jesus Christ, and that he believe that this grace saves souls, transforms souls, and communicates divine life to souls. Once one no longer believes in the unique Mediator that is Our Lord Jesus Christ, nor in the grace that He came to bring for our salvation, nor in the means by which He communicates this grace to us, then one seeks purely human means, means invented by men purportedly to save men. This is a grave error; these are only apparent means, which are outside the way foreseen by Divine Providence. But if, on the contrary, we truly have faith in this unique Mediator and in all the means that He has provided to save souls, then, whatever the results of our our efforts, whatever the success of our ministry, we know that we are accomplishing the will of the good God, we know that we are continuing the ministry of Our Lord Jesus Christ. This is what consoles priests who have kept the Faith today.[69]

THE CANON OF THE MASS

INTRODUCTION OF THE PREFACE: *SURSUM CORDA*

℣. Dóminus vobíscum.
℟. Et cum spíritu tuo.
℣. Sursum corda.
℟. Habémus ad Dóminum.

℣. Grátias agámus Dómino Deo nostro.
℟. Dignum et justum est.

℣. The Lord be with you.
℟. And with thy spirit.
℣. Lift up your hearts!
℟. We have lifted them up to the Lord.

℣. Let us give thanks to the Lord our God.
℟. It is meet and just.

---

[68] Spiritual conference, Ecône, January 17, 1978.
[69] Homily, priestly ordination, Ecône, December 3, 1988.

The Preface is a prayer of praise that introduces us into the part of the Mass that could be called heavenly. Until then, it was a preparation; afterwards, an action begins. The Church invites the priest, and the assembly with him, to lift himself above all earthly and temporal preoccupations, to find himself somewhat in a moment of eternity. The prayers that follow prepare the words of the Consecration, which produce an immutable effect willed by Our Lord, an effect so important, so capital, for our sanctification, for the sanctification of souls, for the glory of God, for the sanctification of families, and for the sanctification of cities. It is truly the most beautiful, the greatest, the most sublime thing in the history of mankind and in the history of the Church. This instant is so important and so great a manifestation of the love of Our Lord for us that the Church places us in the atmosphere of eternity.

It is a good idea to think often about God's eternity. This is very difficult to do, obviously. For us, there is always a past, present, and future. How then can we conceive of eternity, this moment that always is? It seems inconceivable, and yet it is so.

One is always trying to ascribe time to God, even, for example, in relation to creation. If creation had a beginning, it would seem that something began in God; and yet, that is false. Nothing began in God. He is always the same. We must unceasingly situate our thoughts in relation to the eternity of God, to the eternity of the Word. That deepens in us the sense of God's grandeur, His immensity, His incomprehensibility, because for us, God is incomprehensible. He is far more beautiful, far grander, far more sublime than all that we can imagine. When we know Him better, when we approach Him, it will be something far more beautiful, grander, and more extraordinary. As St. Paul expresses it very well, the happiness that we shall have in heaven outstrips all that we can imagine here below....

The eternity of God and the absence of time in God were already expressed in the Old Testament. When Moses asked God, Yahweh, what His name was, the answer was: "I AM WHO AM"[70] (Ex. 3:14). And God added: "Thus shalt thou say to the children of Israel: HE WHO IS hath sent me to you" (Ex. 3:14). It is extraordinary that the good God defined Himself by these words, which

---

[70] *Ego sum qui sum.*

are not only a description of God, but the most profound description that anyone has ever found for God. The most explicit and the most profound notions that St. Thomas and all the philosophers could find have never been expressed in so simple and so clear a manner. God is all being.[71] He is Being. That is why there is nothing that is outside of God; all being is in God, all being comes from God and subsists in God. There are extraordinary, admirable consequences to this. We are dependent on God; we receive being from God, as do all the material and spiritual creatures that surround us. No man can say that he comes from another principle than God. Consequently, by that very fact, we are all brothers. This brotherhood, this true fraternity, comes to us from our origin, the origin of the Word, hence from God. Not only material creatures, but also spiritual creatures—hence the angels too—cannot say they come from a principle other than God.[72]

The Preface

The Common Preface

Vere dignum et justum est, æquum et salutáre, nos tibi semper, et ubíque grátias ágere: Dómine sancte, Pater omnípotens, ætérne Deus: per Christum Dóminum nostrum. Per quem majestátem tuam laudant Angeli, adórant Dominatiónes, tremunt Potestátes. Cœli, cœlorúmque Virtútes ac beáta Séraphim sócia exsultatióne concélebrant. Cum quibus et nostras voces, ut admítti júbeas, deprecámur, súpplici confessióne dicéntes:

It is truly meet and just, right and for our salvation, that we should at all times and in all places give thanks to Thee, holy Lord, Father almighty, eternal God, through Christ our Lord: through Whom Angels praise Thy Majesty, Dominations worship, Powers stand in awe: the Heavens and the hosts of heaven with blessed Seraphim unite, exult, and celebrate; and we entreat that Thou wouldst bid our voices also to be heard with theirs, singing with lowly praise:

---

[71] God is not identical with the sum of all beings, which is the error of pantheism, but He is Being without limit, without the limitations that one sees even in the most perfect creatures. The creature does not exist by itself; it receives its being from God.

[72] Spiritual conference, Ecône, January 29, 1980.

The Church unites her voice with that of the whole heavenly Court and bows, like the angels, before the throne of the Holy Trinity in order to worthily praise the holiness of God.

1. Imitate the holy angels singing the glory of God

Every day at the Preface of the Holy Mass, the Church invites us to imitate the holy angels, singing the glory of God, *"Sanctus, sanctus, sanctus..."* and also *"Gloria in excelsis Deo...."* Let us strive to penetrate the marvelous world of these spirits filled with the light and the charity of the Holy Ghost, burning with love for God and for one another.

The liturgical offices of the Archangels St. Michael, St. Raphael, and St. Gabriel are marvelous and heavenly indeed. What beautiful lessons they give us by their example and by their words....How encouraging is the Church's faith in the holy angels! Let us preciously guard it....

The thought of the holy angels should be second nature to us, and should thereby prepare us for the heavenly reality. Likewise we should do everything we can to avoid the bad influence of the fallen angels.[73]

St. Thomas says that there are more angels than men. He reasons that the good God usually makes the most perfect things in the greatest number. Angels being more perfect than men, God in His liberality, in His love for what is beautiful and grand, created them in greater profusion than men.[74] Since each of us has a guardian angel, there are already as many angels as men, to which must be added all those of whom God makes use for His Providence and His glory. Consequently, there is a spiritual world perhaps much more significant that we imagine! It will be a discovery when we close our eyes here below and gaze upon heaven's horizon. We shall undoubtedly be amazed at the endless multitude... The Apocalypse makes a reference to it, doesn't it? Thousands upon thousands of angels are mentioned; that makes millions. Then in the Book of Daniel, it speaks of ten thousand times a hundred thousand angels

---

[73] *Spiritual Journey*, pp.15-18 *passim*.
[74] *Summa Theologica*, I, Q. 50, Art. 3.

(Dan. 7:10), or billions. Let us love to live among these great adorers of God.[75]

2. The adoration of angels

The nearer to God one comes, the more one trembles: "*tremunt potestates*–the Powers stand in awe," says the Preface of the Mass. The more you make known to a soul the grandeur and perfection of God, the more this soul becomes desirous of loving and serving God, and finds itself touched by fear: it perceives more and more that to go against the will of God is something terrible.[76]

Consider that all the angels of heaven bow before Our Lord, and that at the mere mention of the name of Jesus, every knee will bend in heaven, on earth, and in hell; and we are afraid to kneel before Him, the mere mention of whose name will bring all mankind to their knees at the moment of the Last Judgment: all the souls in heaven, all the angels, and all those in hell.[77]

3. What our adoration must be

For St. Thomas, it seems that the devotion denotes the interior sentiment, and adoration, the exterior expression of this devotion. Adoration is the profound reverence of our souls before God–before the all of God and the nothingness that we are.[78] The soul humbles itself before God; the soul adores God. This is certainly also the expression and even the action which is most often expressed in our prayers. This is the entire spirit of the Church's prayer: all the bowing, all the inclinations, all the genuflections and

---

[75] Retreat, Morgon, September 29, 1988.
[76] Ordination retreat, Montalenghe, June 1989.
[77] Conference, Tourcoing, January 30, 1974.
[78] St. Thomas distinguishes the two aspects of adoration in the following manner: "As Damascene says, since we are composed of a twofold nature, intellectual and sensible, we offer God a twofold adoration; namely, a spiritual adoration, consisting in the internal devotion of the mind; and a bodily adoration, which consists in an exterior humbling of the body. And since in all acts of latria that which is without is referred to that which is within as being of greater import, it follows that exterior adoration is offered on account of interior adoration, in other words we exhibit signs of humility in our bodies in order to incite our affections to submit to God, since it is connatural to us to proceed from the sensible to the intelligible" (*Summa Theologica*, II-II, Q. 84, Art. 2).

prostrations are directed to the adoration of God, which expresses the total return to God of the spiritual creature. These are definitive dispositions that will remain after our death. Death will change nothing. The soul that has devoted itself to God, the soul that has given itself to God, the soul that adores God will pass from earth to heaven while keeping its devotion and its adoration. It will keep this attitude with a much greater plenitude and perfection in the vision of God. That is why these are fundamental dispositions for every human soul, not just for monks and nuns. It is an exigency of human nature itself. As soon as they become aware of their own existence and of the existence of the good God, all men should possess these fundamental dispositions. Thus it undoubtedly was for the Blessed Virgin Mary. This was also the disposition of Our Lord's human soul towards His Father. But He had the beatific vision; His adoration was more perfect than we can imagine. The soul of Jesus is the model of what our souls should be.[79]

THE *SANCTUS*

SANCTUS, Sanctus, Sanctus Dóminus Deus Sábaoth. Pleni sunt cæli et terra glória tua: Hosánna in excélsis. Benedíctus qui venit in nómine Dómini: Hosánna in excélsis.

HOLY, holy, holy, Lord God of hosts. Heaven and earth are full of Thy glory. Hosanna in the highest. Blessed is He Who cometh in the Name of the Lord. Hosanna in the highest.

What is substantial holiness, if not the Word of God Himself. *Verbum Dei*: it is the Lamb in the Apocalypse surrounded by the twenty-four ancients and an innumerable crowd of angels and elect who sing: "Holy, holy, holy, Lord God Almighty." It is indeed the Word, and the Word Incarnate, who is meant.[80]

If God is sanctity itself, if we sing of Our Lord that He alone is holy, *"Tu solus sanctus,"* it is that God is the source of all sanctity, and that it is inasmuch as we are united with God and Our Lord that we will be saints. But this union with God can only be con-

---

[79] Retreat, Le Barroux, August 25, 1987.
[80] Homily, Ecône, November 1, 1990.

cretely realized under the influence of the grace of the Holy Ghost. This union has a name: prayer, *oratio*.

In studying deeply both the nature of prayer and its extension in our human and Christian existence, we become convinced that the profound life of the created spirit must be one of continual prayer. Every angelic or human spirit is ordered to God by its spiritual nature–by its intelligence, by its will–and gratuitously elevated by grace to enter and participate in the eternal beatitude of the Holy Trinity. Therefore every spirit is first religious, and its religious life manifests itself in prayer: vocal, mental and spiritual.[81]

The exterior acts of the virtue of religion like vocal prayer are made for the sake of the interior acts....We recite prayers to express what we think, to produce in ourselves what we say. What matters is the interior virtue of religion (contrary to the Pharisees' outward show). One of our resolutions must be to live the prayer we make. Let us not be unconscious, perpetually distracted, or robots.[82]

The Canon, Recited Silently

A profound motive is attached to the rubric to say the prayers of the Canon in a low voice.[83] It is because of the grandeur of the mystery that is to be accomplished. It is not by any external manifestation, but by the action of the Holy Ghost that the bread will be transformed into the Body, Blood, Soul, and Divinity of Our Lord. All this must make us very attached to the prayers of the Canon, and truly make of it the center–the heart–of our spiritual life. Let us therefore approach this most important moment of our days with great respect. Imagine that the Church allowed us to say one Mass during our life as priests: how carefully we would prepare this moment of our life; with what respect, adoration, and humility we would pronounce the words of the Consecration! Whether it is done one time or a thousand, the grandeur of this act is un-

---

[81] *Spiritual Journey*, p.26.
[82] Notes for a retreat for the Brothers, Senegal, September 11-17, 1960.
[83] The Council of Trent states: "And since such is the nature of man that he cannot easily without external means be raised to meditation on divine things, on that account holy mother Church has instituted certain rites, namely, that certain things be pronounced in a subdued tone [canon 9]," and gives as examples a part of the Canon and the words of consecration (Session 22, Ch. 5, and canon 9; Dz. 943, 956).

changed! The fact that the good God grants us the signal grace to do it often, every day, must not diminish our fervor or adoration, for its importance is always the same. Let us ask the Blessed Virgin Mary to help us better understand the great action produced by our sacerdotal ministry.[84]

The sacrifice of the Mass is truly the sacrifice of the Cross. Now, the Blessed Virgin was present at the sacrifice of the Cross. And how did she attend? She attended in silence. Is it not for this reason that, when the priest has recited the beautiful prefaces that lead to the heart of the sacrifice of the Mass and that convey him in some way to Sinai like Moses, and he finds himself in the cloud wherein dwells the Divine Presence, the people keep silent? While the priest offers the sacrifice and pronounces the sublime words of the Canon of the Mass–this holy Canon that goes back in large part to the very origins of Christendom, and for the essential to Our Lord Himself in the words of the Consecration–the people remain in silence. Mary remains in silence. What does this silence mean? Is it a silence of indifference? Certainly not; not for the Virgin Mary in any case. It is well said of the Virgin Mary that she kept in her heart all the words spoken by Our Lord: "But Mary kept all these words, pondering them in her heart" (Lk. 2:19 and 51). And so, hearing the words spoken by Our Lord on the Cross, she adored in silence the great design of the Redemption. She adored in silence the design that was being accomplished before her eyes, and she certainly shared the sentiments of her divine Son.

I think that there is a lesson there for you, dear faithful, who attend the holy sacrifice of the Mass: share the sentiments that are expressed in the Canon of the Mass and which lift us to heaven, which really link earth to heaven and heaven to earth.[85]

You may notice that in the Canon the parts that precede and follow the Consecration have an ascending and descending structure, in the sense of going from the particular to the general and then returning to the particular. You have the particular oblation, the *Memento* of the living, then the *Communicantes* in which we are united to the Church triumphant. Then comes the oblation. This

---

[84] Ordination retreat, Flavigny, June 26, 1976.
[85] Homily, St-Michel-en-Brenne, March 17, 1989.

prayer is so beautiful that I thought it good to choose it for the act of oblation in the Society, because it seemed to me that the summit of the liturgy of the Mass is the *Hanc Igitur*.

Then follow the words of the Consecration; then the oblation of Our Lord present, an oblation prefigured by the sacrifice of Abel and of Melchisedech; then comes the remembrance of the dead in parallel to the memento of the living; then the prayer for fellowship with all those in heaven, by asking in a more personal prayer that despite our sins and not on account of our merits, we may obtain the pardon of our faults and be with them one day–"not considering our merits, but of Thine own free pardon."

Partem aliquam[86]: It is very beautiful. The little word *aliquam* is particularly touching. The priest does not ask much, just "some" part, a very little place with the martyrs in heaven, with all the blessed. *Da nobis partem aliquam*: give us a little place. The priest does not ask more: may a small place be afforded him with the enumerated martyrs.

Then the *Pater*, which follows the Consecration, corresponds to the Preface which precedes it, just as the Communion corresponds to the Offertory.[87]

The Prayer to God the Father: *Te igitur*

Te ígitur, clementíssime Pater, per Jesum Christum, Fílium tuum, Dóminum nostrum, súpplices rogámus ac pétimus, uti accépta hábeas et benedícas hæc ✠ dona, hæc ✠ múnera, hæc ✠ sancta sacrifícia illibáta, in primis, quæ tibi offérimus pro Ecclésia tua sancta cathólica: quam pacificáre, custodíre, adunáre et régere dignéris toto orbe terrárum: una cum fámulo tuo Papa nostro N. et Antístite nostro N. et

Wherefore, O most merciful Father, we humbly pray and beseech Thee through Jesus Christ, Thy Son, our Lord, that Thou wouldst vouchsafe to receive and bless these ✠ gifts, these ✠ presents, these ✠ holy and unspotted sacrifices, which in the first place we offer Thee for Thy holy Catholic Church, that it may please Thee to grant her peace; as also to protect, unite, and govern her throughout

---

[86] "*Nobis quoque peccatoribus...partem aliquam et societatem donare digneris*–To us sinners also...vouchsafe to grant some part and fellowship...."
[87] Retreat, Ecône, September 1978.

ómnibus orthodóxis atque cathólicæ et apostólicæ fídei cultóribus.

the world, together with Thy servant N., our Pope; N., our bishop; as also all orthodox believers and professors of the Catholic and Apostolic Faith.

It is around the altar that the Church, one and hierarchical, as Our Lord instituted it, is built up.

The Mass is essentially hierarchical, and that is why the priest turns towards God, towards the crucifix, and not towards the assembly. To turn towards the assembly would give the impression that it is the essential thing in the sacrifice of the Mass or in Communion. But this is an error, for it is not the assembly that counts, but God to whom we offer the sacrifice. What counts is the sacrifice of the Cross; it is Our Lord Jesus Christ. That is why the priest turns towards the cross; he offers sacrifice to God, followed by the faithful, for the pastor walks before his flock to lead it towards Our Lord Jesus Christ, towards God, and towards heaven.

In the sacrifice of the Mass there is a hierarchy; it is not a collegial Mass. There is no collegiality in the Church. In the Mass, one does not say that the Mass is offered in union with the college of bishops. At the beginning of the Canon, the priest says that he offers the sacrifice of the Mass together with him who fills the function of pope and with him who fills the function of bishop. Whether he does it well or badly is something else, and it is the good God who will judge him. But it is a fact, the hierarchy comes first, then the priest, then the faithful; and not just some individuals or families, but the whole society of the faithful. For all society must be represented at the sacrifice of the Cross: kings, princes, magistrates, military men, the trades and professions–all must unite with Our Lord Jesus Christ because He is the only way to go to heaven.

This is what sanctified society, and that is why the church is placed in the heart of the village and at the center of our cities, representing the house of God in which the entire Christian population assembles to ascend to heaven. All this has a wonderful signification, and it is the signification of the true sacrifice of the Mass.[88]

---

[88] Homily, Rouen, May 1, 1990.

Memento of the Living

Memento, Dómine, famulórum famularúmque tuárum N. et N. et ómnium circumstántium, quorum tibi fides cógnita est et nota devótio, pro quibus tibi offérimus: vel qui tibi ófferunt hoc sacrifícium laudis, pro se suísque ómnibus: pro redemptióne animárum suárum, pro spe salútis et incolumitátis suæ: tibíque reddunt vota sua ætérno Deo, vivo et vero.

Be mindful, O Lord, of Thy servants and handmaids, N. and N. and of all here present, whose faith and devotion are known to Thee: for whom we offer, or who offer up to Thee, this sacrifice of praise for themselves and all their own, for the redemption of their souls, for the hope of their safety and salvation, and who now pay their vows to Thee, the eternal, living, and true God.

> The holy sacrifice of the Mass is the unique source of grace for all the faithful, and the source that feeds all the Sacraments. It is thus, for example, that at every Mass, Christian spouses renew the grace of their marriage.

1. The Mass, application of the merits of the Cross

The renewal of the sacrifice of Calvary enables the merits of the Cross to be applied to the faithful present; it perpetuates this source of grace in time and space. St. Matthew's Gospel concludes with these words: "And behold I am with you all days, even to the consummation of the world" (28:20). We must not forget that if the presence of Our Lord among us is the source of our sanctification, it is also the source of sanctification for society as a whole. This also has a very great importance: we must not limit the influence of the Mass and the Consecration to our own sanctification, but extend it, not only to the sanctification of the assembly present, but also to the whole of society, for it is from the Eucharist that all the graces of the Sacraments emanate.

2. The Mass, source of graces for Christian spouses

Too often we forget that the Sacrament of marriage derives its signification and symbolism from the Sacrament of the Cross. God wanted to create woman while Adam slept, taking from his side what was necessary for her creation....When Our Lord bowed His head and died, His heart was pierced, and it is from His heart that His mystical Bride, the Church, was born. What a beautiful comparison! The birth of woman is the symbol of the birth of the Church from Our Lord's side pierced by the lance. And that is the meaning of marriage. The grace of marriage is a grace that proceeds from the heart of Our Lord Jesus Christ and is symbolized by His sacrifice. Thus, marriage is associated in a very particular way with the sacrifice of Calvary. This is why the Church has always wanted the Sacrament of marriage to take place in the context of the sacrifice of the Mass. All of this has a remarkable, extraordinary signification, and must encourage those in the bonds of marriage during their difficulties and trials.[89]

The fecundity of the marriage between Our Lord and His Church is signified by His Passion, by His Blood that flowed to bring into being the Christian family. It is indeed this meaning that is applied to the Sacrament of marriage.[90] Consequently, it can truthfully be said that couples that attend frequently the renewal of the sacrifice of the Cross, and hence the renewal of the espousal of Our Lord with His Church, revive the grace of their marriage and increase the particular grace they need in order to worthily accomplish, as true Christians, what marriage requires of them. They must assist at holy Mass. The holy Mass is truly the foundation stone of the Christian family. The Church wanted it to be so.[91]

Just as the union between Our Lord Jesus Christ and His mystical Bride has produced countless children and has been extraordinarily fruitful, so also the spouses must love each other, give their life for each other if need be, to bring forth natural life and supernatural life....That is the sign of the grace of marriage.

---

[89] Homily, Unieux, Feast of the Precious Blood, July 1, 1979.
[90] St. Paul describes marriage as the symbol of the union between Christ and the Church (Eph. 5:21-33). The magisterium has often commented on this teaching; in this discourse Archbishop Lefebvre echoes the allocution of Pope Pius XII to newlyweds on April 22, 1942: "Marriage is not only an act of nature, but for Christian souls it is a great Sacrament, a great sign of grace and of the sacred espousal of Christ with His Church, which He made His own, conquered by His Blood in order to regenerate to a new life of the spirit the children of men who believe in His Name, and who were born not of blood, nor of the will of the flesh nor of the will of man, but of God (Jn. 1:12-13)." [English version: *Dear Newlyweds: Pope Pius XII Speaks to Married Couples* (Kansas City: Sarto House, n.d.), p.86.]
[91] Easter retreat, Ecône, April 6, 1980.

Consequently, when the spouses hear Mass, the sacramental grace[92] of their marriage is renewed and strengthened by the example of Calvary, by the Eucharist they receive, by the Victim who is in them. They must love each other and give themselves to each other, unto death if need be, in order to populate heaven with the elect. That's what marriage is. We must not forget it. Thus everything is met with again in the Holy Eucharist, everything is met with in the Blood of Our Lord Jesus Christ.[93]

Marriage is at the origin of the Christian family and of future vocations, children who will consecrate themselves to God. It is really the origin of the Church. The sanctification of the family by the Cross, by the holy sacrifice of the Mass, is very important. Family virtues arise from it. Since society is nothing else than the union of families, if the families strive for holiness, then society is holy. Thus the source of Christian civilization is the holy sacrifice of the Mass. The Catholic societies that existed before were built around the altar.[94]

United to the Church Triumphant: The *Communicantes*

The Canon is not a story. Look at old missals. Above the "*Communicantes*" you will see "*Infra actionem.*" Out of curiosity, look at your missals. "*Infra actionem*–during the action." What does that mean? It means that the priest performs an act, a sacrificial act.[95]

The priest tells the story of the Passion, but a telling that is efficacious. It is not only a narration, but an act that produces what Our Lord asked of the Apostles when He told them: "Do this in memory of Me" (Lk. 22:19). The "memorial" is the story; the "do this" is the act. By retelling the story, the priest redoes the sacrificial

---

[92] A particular form of habitual grace. Certain actions, certain special supernatural effects needed to attain the end of the Sacrament proceed from this sacramental grace. For example, the sacramental grace received in the Sacrament of marriage enables the couple to acquit themselves of their marital duties (rearing of children, mutual support, *etc.*).
[93] Homily, first Mass, Fanjeaux, July 7, 1979.
[94] Spiritual conference, Zaitzkofen, February 7, 1980.
[95] "Crisis of the Church or Crisis of the Priesthood," *A Bishop Speaks*, p.174.

act of Our Lord Jesus Christ. Then transubstantiation occurs by the consecration of bread and wine: that is the reality of our Faith.[96]

COMMUNICANTES, et memóriam venerántes, in primis gloriósæ semper Vírginis Maríæ, Genetrícis Dei et Dómini nostri Jesu Christi: sed et beáti Joseph, ejúsdem Vírginis Sponsi, et beatórum Apostolórum ac Mártyrum tuórum, Petri et Pauli, Andréæ, Jacóbi, Joánnis, Thomæ, Jacóbi, Philíppi, Bartholomǽi, Matthǽi, Simónis et Thaddǽi: Lini, Cleti, Cleméntis, Xysti, Cornélii, Cypriáni, Lauréntii, Chrysógoni, Joánnis et Pauli, Cosmæ et Damiáni: et ómnium Sanctórum tuórum; quorum méritis precibúsque concédas, ut in ómnibus protectiónis tuæ muniámur auxílio. *He joins his hands.* Per eúmdem Christum Dóminum nostrum. Amen.

IN communion with and honoring the memory, first of the glorious, ever Virgin Mary, Mother of our God and Lord Jesus Christ: as also of blessed Joseph, her Spouse, and of Thy blessed Apostles and Martyrs, Peter and Paul, Andrew, James, John, Thomas, James, Philip, Bartholomew, Matthew, Simon, and Thaddeus; Linus, Cletus, Clement, Sixtus, Cornelius, Cyprian, Lawrence, Chrysogonus, John and Paul, Cosmas and Damian, and of all Thy saints; by whose merits and prayers grant that we may in all things be defended by the aid of Thy protection. Through the same Christ our Lord. Amen.

At the hour of the sacrifice by which her Redemption will again be effected, the Church on earth unites with the Church Triumphant gathered around the most Blessed Virgin Mary.

1. United to the saints in heaven

The holy sacrifice of the Mass places us in the presence of God, in the presence of heaven. It puts us in communion with heaven, with all the elect already there, whom one names during the course of holy Mass: the Virgin Mary, the martyrs, and the holy angels. We must follow the path they trod to arrive there in our turn.[97]

2. The Blessed Virgin united to her Son at the foot of the Cross

The most Blessed Virgin Mary is first and foremost the mother of the eternal Priest. Our Lord Jesus Christ is essentially a Priest for eternity, a Priest according to the order of Melchisedech. Our

---

[96] Easter retreat, Ecône, April 17, 1984.
[97] Homily, Rouen, May 1, 1990.

Lord Jesus Christ's whole life, His entire reason for being, was to offer Himself on the Cross. That was the goal of Our Lord's life. His whole life long, Our Lord Jesus Christ was haunted by the desire to ascend the Cross. That is why He came, and that is what the most Blessed Virgin Mary teaches us, for the Virgin Mary is the mirror of Our Lord Jesus Christ. In her heart there is no other name inscribed than the name of Jesus, and Jesus Crucified. The most Blessed Virgin Mary accompanied Him everywhere, even to the sacrifice of the Cross. She was present there as if to teach us that what was dearest to her was to accompany Our Lord on Calvary at the sacrifice of the Cross.

How did God, the Creator of all things, Immutable, Infinite, Perfect, Holy, Eternal, take a body like ours and be attached to the Cross? Of whom shall we ask the solution? Of whom shall we ask what happened in Our Lord's heart, mind, and soul during the Passion from the Garden of Olives through all the sufferings to the way of the Cross which led Him to Calvary and onto the Cross, if not of the most Blessed Virgin Mary?

If it is true that, even in nature, it is the mother who fathoms her son's heart and guesses his thoughts even without his needing to speak, how much more did the most Blessed Virgin Mary, who was near the Cross of her Divine Son Our Lord, try to scrutinize the thoughts, desires, joys, and sufferings of Jesus. It is a great mystery, the mystery of God Himself! Jesus is God. Then how could the most Blessed Virgin Mary, who is only a creature, even if she is filled with the Holy Ghost, measure the sentiments and the thoughts of God? As Scripture says: "For the Spirit searcheth all things, yea, the deep things of God" (I Cor. 2:10). Since the most blessed Virgin Mary was filled with the Holy Ghost, the good God surely gave her very particular graces to understand why this God was attached thus to the Cross. She who had followed Him, to whom she had given birth, for these three and thirty years, was the most apt to understand all that happened in Jesus' soul.[98]

3. United to the Holy Virgin at the holy altar

The Blessed Virgin Mary, who participated the most perfectly, the most profoundly, in the sacrifice of the Cross, and thus in the

---

[98] Conference to the SSPX Sisters, St-Michel-en-Brenne, April 10, 1987.

sacrifice of the Mass, is the person who best truly understood the holy sacrifice of the Mass, after Our Lord Himself. She can give you the explication of the mystery of the holy sacrifice of the Mass. It was when she was on Calvary beside the Cross that she participated the most in the great mystery of the sacrifice of the Cross. "Now there stood by the cross of Jesus, his mother" (Jn. 19;25), the Gospel tells us. Her heart was pierced by the sword at that time, seeing the sufferings of her Son. She compassionated Him; she shared the Passion of Our Lord, the sacrifice of the Cross.

Thus, to better participate in the holy sacrifice of the Mass, to be really united for one's entire life to the sacrifice of the Cross, it is good to place oneself under the protection of Our Lady of Compassion, Our Lady of Sorrows.[99]

Remember that the most Blessed Virgin Mary, who was present near Our Lord Jesus Christ on Calvary, will also always be present beside you at the holy altar, for the most Blessed Virgin Mary never leaves her Son.[100]

When we are before the altar during the sacrifice of the Mass, we can tell ourselves that we are really present as if we were beside the Blessed Virgin, St. John and St. Mary Magdalen at the foot of the Cross. It is absolutely the same thing. In the Eucharistic miracles, the blood flows from the host; the blood is really present in the host.[101]

When you hear the holy sacrifice of the Mass, you can tell yourself: I am with the Virgin Mary, I am with St. John, I am with Mary Magdalen near the Cross of Our Lord Jesus Christ; and you can ask that the Blood of Jesus flow upon your soul in order to be saved.[102]

It seems to me that the Virgin Mary who is to be found near the Cross, Our Lady of Compassion, Our Lady Co-Redemptrix, invites each one of us and every human creature who will be born in this world. She takes us by that hand as it were to lead us to Calvary, to make us participate in the merits of Our Lord Jesus Christ.[103]

---

[99] Conference to the Sisters, Ecône, November 19, 1974.
[100] Homily for a priest's first Mass, Besançon, September 5, 1976.
[101] Spiritual conference, Ecône, December 2, 1974.
[102] Homily, Bordeaux, May 24, 1981.
[103] Pilgrimage, Mariazell, September 8, 1975.

The Prayer of Oblation: *Hanc Igitur*

Hanc ígitur oblatiónem servitútis nostræ, sed et cunctæ famíliæ tuæ, quǽsumus, Dómine, ut placátus accípias: diésque nostros in tua pace dispónas, atque ab ætérna damnatióne nos éripi, et in electórum tuórum júbeas grege numerári. *He joins his hands.* Per Christum Dóminum nostrum. Amen.

We therefore beseech Thee, O Lord, graciously to accept this oblation of our service, as also of Thy whole family; dispose our days in Thy peace, command us to be delivered from eternal damnation and to be numbered in the flock of Thine elect. Through Christ our Lord. Amen.

With hands extended over the host and chalice, the priest asks God to accept the offering of the members of the Mystical Body united to the oblation of Christ, Priest and Victim.

1. Our Lord unites His Mystical Body to the oblation of the Victim

A greater union between the members and the Head of the Mystical Body, between the faithful and Our Lord, cannot be imagined because the members of the Mystical Body are united to Him by a participation of His grace and of His nature. It is Jesus who is in some way extended in the members of His Mystical Body. During Mass, Our Lord both offers the Victim and is offered. We are incorporated in this unity of Our Lord Jesus Christ, and thus we are already at the same time, a little, priests and victims. We offer ourselves with Our Lord, but it is He who is the Priest and the Victim. He draws us as members of His Mystical Body into the oblation of the Victim. One cannot imagine something more beautiful, deeper, or more consoling than this oblation, for a more perfect oblation for us cannot be imagined. This would not be possible if we were not united to Our Lord by sanctifying grace. We could try to offer our souls, our hearts, our bodies to the good God, to offer Him our lives, but you can see what a difference there would be! Being separated from Our Lord, and especially with the stain of original sin, our oblation would not reach God since without grace we are in the state of sin.

But now, henceforth sanctified by the presence of sanctifying grace within us, brothers of Jesus Christ in this participation of the divine nature, it is evident that our oblation assumes the dimension of Our Lord's oblation insofar as we are united to Him.[104]

2. Offering ourselves with Our Lord as victims of love

At the altar we unite ourselves to the great prayer of Our Lord. If we want to really exercise the virtue of religion and really be religious souls, it is by our place at the altar and by uniting ourselves to Our Lord that we will succeed. Offering ourselves with Our Lord at the altar is the most beautiful prayer we can make.[105]

God has made everything for the Cross, for the redemption of souls, for the holy sacrifice of the Mass, and for priests, so that souls can be united to Him particularly as victims in the Holy Eucharist. Our Lord communicates Himself to us as Victim so that we may offer our life with His, and so that we may participate not only in our redemption, but also in the redemption of souls.[106]

For priests, to prepare souls in order to lead them to live and partake in the sacrifice of Our Lord, and to unite themselves to that furnace of charity for the glory of God and the love of neighbor, to live as victims of love in the likeness and in the footsteps of Jesus and Mary, is to live the heavenly, divine reality of the life of grace. It is a life totally oriented to sacrifice, and which comes from the sacrifice of the Cross, from the transfixed hearts of Jesus and Mary.[107]

3. Religious and Christians must offer themselves as victims

What is a religious? A religious is someone who offers himself as a victim on the altar. But if we no longer believe in the holy sacrifice of the Mass, tomorrow there will no longer be religious. And soon there will be no more Christians, because the essence of being a Christian is the offering of oneself as a victim with Our Lord on the altar. That is why it is urgent to return to faith in the holy sacrifice of the Mass.[108]

---

[104] Retreat, Ecône, September 22, 1978.
[105] Spiritual conference, Ecône, December 2, 1975.
[106] Homily, Ecône, June 29, 1982.
[107] Notes for a priests' retreat, September 5-9, 1983. Archives of Ecône Seminary, *O Mysterium Christi*, p.3.
[108] Homily, Garges-lès-Gonesse, February 11, 1973.

The vows of religion are a real application of the sacrifice of Our Lord, of the sacrifice of the Mass. Undoubtedly, not everyone is obliged to make these vows, but persons who vow themselves to the good God must understand that the vows have a supernatural, profound value, that they are as the fruit of Our Lord's sacrifice. Our Lord gave Himself entirely for the glory of His Father and for the salvation of souls, and religious participate in this sacrifice of Our Lord by giving Him their life entirely and without reserve.

There is nothing more beautiful, greater, nobler, more effective than to bind oneself indissolubly by the vows of religion to Our Lord's sacrifice, and consequently to the true holy Mass, the Mass of the sacrifice to which we want to remain faithful because it was the object of God's mercy, because it is the accomplishment here below of Our Lord's sacrifice.[109]

Quam Oblationem

Quam oblatiónem tu, Deus, in ómnibus, quǽsumus bene ✠ díctam, adscríp ✠ tam, ra ✠ tam, rationábilem, acceptabilémque fácere dignéris: ut nobis Cor ✠ pus, et San ✠ guis fiat dilectíssimi Fílii tui Dómini nostri Jesu Christi.

Which oblation do Thou, O God, vouchsafe in all things to make blessed, ✠ approved, ✠ ratified, ✠ reasonable, and acceptable, that it may become for us the Body ✠ and Blood ✠ of Thy most beloved Son, our Lord Jesus Christ.

What was the means chosen by Our Lord to transmit divine life?–the sacrifice of the Cross: the bloody oblation of His human life, signifying the oblation of His soul to His Father, a living and tangible reproduction of the eternal gift of the Son to the Father. This offering He has bequeathed, by an admirable design of His omnipotence, to the Church in an unbloody manner in the Eucharistic sacrifice, which in a real manner perpetuates His sacrifice on the Cross. This oblation is the great prayer of Our Lord. It is necessarily efficacious for the regeneration of souls.[110]

The only difference between the Cross and the sacrifice of the Mass is that one is bloody and the other unbloody. At Mass, the

---

[109] Homily, St-Michel-en-Brenne, April 2, 1989.
[110] Meeting of Superiors, Diocese of Dakar, April 17, 1960, pp.5-6, Ecône Seminary archives.

Blood is there, of course, but obviously we do not see it flow. On Calvary, people saw Jesus' blood flow, but in the sacrifice of the altar we do not see it flow. That is the only difference. It is the same sacrifice, the same Priest who saves, the same Victim as on Calvary.[111] This is what the Council of Trent says quite well about the Eucharist considered as sacrifice:

> We therefore confess that the Sacrifice of the Mass is and ought to be considered one and the same Sacrifice as that of the Cross, for the victim is one and the same, namely, Christ Our Lord, who offered Himself, once only, a bloody Sacrifice on the altar of the Cross. The bloody and unbloody victim are not two, but one victim only, whose Sacrifice is daily renewed in the Eucharist, in obedience to the command of Our Lord: "Do this for a commemoration of me."[112]

A few considerations of Bossuet on the holy Mass seem to me very beautiful as a preface to the holy sacrifice of the Mass:

> God forbid that we forget the holy action of the sacrifice, and the mystery of the consecration.
>
> I see an altar; a sacrifice is about to be offered, the sacrifice of the Christians, the sacrifice and the pure oblation of which it is written: *that it was to be offered from the rising of the sun to the setting* (Malach. 1:11)....
>
> ...I see only some bread on the altar and a little wine in a chalice. And yet, there is no need for more to make this sacrifice the holiest, the most august, the richest that was ever offered.
>
> But, I ask, will there not be any flesh; will there be no blood in this sacrifice? Yes, there will be flesh, but not the flesh of slaughtered animals; there will be blood, but it will be the blood of Jesus Christ, and this flesh and this blood will be mystically separated. And whence will come this flesh; whence will come this blood? They will come from this bread and from this wine: an all-powerful word will be uttered, which will change this bread into the flesh of the Savior, and this wine into His Blood. All of this will take place at the very moment that this word is uttered; it is the same word that created heaven and earth. This word, spoken by the Son of God at the Last Supper, has made of this bread, His body, and of this wine, His Blood. But Jesus said to His Apostles: *Do this;* and His Apostles have taught us that it would be done

---

[111] Retreat, St-Michel-en-Brenne, April 2, 1989.
[112] *Catechism of the Council of Trent*, Roman Catholic Books' edition (Fort Collins, Co., n.d.), p.258; Easter retreat, Ecône, April 17, 1984.

until He came: Donec veniat (I Cor. 11:24-26), until the last day of judgment. Thus the same word, repeated through the ministers of Jesus Christ, will eternally have the same effect. The bread and the wine are changed and become the body and the Blood of Jesus Christ....

...The word does not unite the body and the Blood: if one is present with the other, it is because they have been inseparable since the resurrection of Jesus, for since that time, He dies no more. But the word implants the character of the death, which He really suffered, on this Jesus, Who dies no more. It places the body on one side, the Blood on the other, each one under different signs. Behold Him then assuming the character of His death, this Jesus, formerly our Victim through the shedding of His Blood, and again today our victim in a different manner through the mystical separation of His Blood from His body.[113]

And how did this happen? "For God so loved the world" (Jn. 3:16). It only remains for us to believe and to say with the beloved disciple: "We have believed the charity, which God hath to us" (Jn. 4:16). What a beautiful profession of faith! What a beautiful creed! What do you believe, Christian? I believe the love that God has for me. I believe that He gave me His Son; I believe that He became man; I believe that He made Himself my victim; I believe that He gave Himself to me as my food, and that He gave me His body to eat, and His Blood to drink, and that He took and substantially immolated the one and the other. But how do you believe it? It is because I believe in His love, which can do the impossible for me, which wants it, which does it. To ask Him another "how" is not to believe in His power.[114]

This beautiful page from Bossuet, with his admirable style, tells us what the sacrifice of the Mass is.[115]

There is nothing as great, nothing as beautiful, in the history of the human race, than the last sigh of Our Lord Jesus Christ, as the offering of Our Lord Jesus Christ's soul to His Father. It was at the very moment that He expired that everything was consummated. Our Lord Himself said it: "It is consummated" (Jn. 19:30), as if to say, My love has been perfectly expressed to my Father. "Father,

---

[113] Jacques Bénigne Bossuet, *Selections from Meditations on the Gospel* (Chicago: Henry Regnery Co., 1962), II, 63-65.
[114] *Meditations on the Gospels* [French] (The Last Supper, Part I, 26th day, "Jesus Christ, Our Victim and Our Food").
[115] Retreat, Le Barroux, August 1985.

into thy hands I commend my spirit" (Lk. 23:46). Could Our Lord have done anything greater or more sublime? This act of love, of charity, by the Son of God towards His Father, rendered an infinite glory to God the Blessed Trinity and opened the gates of heaven to us. What an admirable thing! And this act is renewed on our altars; that is what continues on our altars: Our Lord's act of infinite love towards His Father, giving glory to Him. We must associate ourselves with Our Lord Jesus Christ to also give glory to the heavenly Father, to the Holy Trinity, through Our Lord Jesus Christ, with Our Lord Jesus Christ, in Our Lord Jesus Christ.[116]

Inseparably Sacrifice and Sacrament, the Mass makes Our Lord present in His redemptive sacrifice.

It is vital that we contemplate the holy Mass, that is, to contemplate Our Lord Jesus Christ on the Cross..., and to see in this Cross the summit of God's love. Our Lord can be defined as love pushed to the sacrifice of self, to the supreme sacrifice. Our Lord manifested the love of His Father and the love of neighbor unto the supreme sacrifice, unto shedding the last drop of His Blood. That has always been the principal object of contemplation in the Church, but I believe that it was in part lost from sight at the time of the rise of Protestantism, perhaps from a very great emphasis, praiseworthy in itself, on the sacramental aspect of the Eucharist, but leaving somewhat in the shadow its sacrificial aspect. But it is the same reality; both occur by the words of the Consecration: the sacrifice and the sacrament. They wanted to emphasize the sacrament because the Real Presence was denied by very many heretics at that time. But I think that in our time the sacrifice of Our Lord must be restored to honor, with the sacrament, the Real Presence, of course, but the sacrament representing the Victim who immolates Himself on the Cross and in the sacrifice in which we participate.[117]

We must recognize that proper place is not always given, even in the teaching of the Church, in catechisms, to the Sacrifice of the Cross perpetuated on our altars. There is a tendency to give all recognition to the Sacrament of the Eucharist and to make but an

---

[116] Homily, Lausanne, July 9, 1978.
[117] Spiritual conference, Ecône, December 2, 1982.

accidental allusion to the Sacrifice. This is a great danger for the faith of Catholics, especially in face of the violent attacks of the Protestants against the holy Sacrifice. The devil is not mistaken when he is out to make the Sacrifice disappear. He knows that he attacks the work of Our Lord at its vital center, and that any lack of esteem of this Sacrifice brings about the ruin of all Catholicism, in every domain.[118]

The Signs of the Cross over the Host and Chalice

During the prayer *Quam oblationem*, the priest makes three Signs of the Cross over both the chalice and the host, then one over the host and another over the chalice. Thus, the Church always asks for grace through the merits of Our Lord's cross. It is by His merits that transubstantiation will take place. These Signs of the Cross lead us to Calvary, where Our Lord perfectly fulfilled the beatitudes.

It is truly instructive and enlightening to see how Our Lord on the Cross fulfilled all the beatitudes. If we want to share in the beatitudes, which are the crowning effect of the Holy Ghost in souls, beatitudes that prepare for the life of heaven, we must also share in Our Lord's life and in His Cross. At the summit of the spiritual life, above the acts of ordinary virtue and the fruits of the Holy Ghost, are the beatitudes. They are the crowning achievement of the Divine work in us; the last, most sublime effect of the presence of the One whom the Father has vouchsafed to send us for our sanctification, the foretaste of heavenly happiness.

The Lord taught us the beatitudes in the Sermon on the Mount, which opened the period of His public life. "Blessed," He says, "are the poor in spirit, for theirs is the kingdom of heaven. Blessed are the meek, for they shall possess the land. Blessed are they that mourn, for they shall be comforted" (Mt. 5:3-5). Eight times in a row He repeats with variations the same expression: "blessed," proclaiming before the astonished world that which Christian language has named the eight beatitudes. Let us look at these eight be-

---

[118] *Spiritual Journey*, p.43.

atitudes, and try to apply them to the Cross of Christ, to Our Lord Jesus Christ crucified, and we shall see that they apply wonderfully.
- Poverty of spirit. If there is a place where Our Lord is poor, where He manifests His poverty, it is indeed on the Cross. What does He have left? Even His mother He has given to St. John. His disciples have abandoned Him. It is really total abandonment: "Father, into thy hands I commend my spirit" (Lk. 23:46). He practices this spirit of poverty in an extraordinary manner.
- Meekness. Our Lord is the Lamb, the paschal Lamb that is immolated. He is meek like a lamb: "Learn of me, because I am meek, and humble of heart" (Mt. 11:29). He was immolated like a lamb that yields itself, while He had every means of resisting, since He said "If I wanted to, I could summon legions of angels." But no, He really delivered Himself up to His executioners like a lamb.
- Tears. Our Lord wept tears of blood. What more can one ask? "Blessed are those who mourn."
- Hunger and thirst after justice. What else is there besides the Cross to suppress injustice and re-establish justice? To re-establish justice towards His Father and to re-establish love of neighbor: this is perhaps the principal object of Our Lord's desire to go up onto the Cross.
- Mercy. Where do we find Our Lord more merciful than on the Cross? His merciful heart wants to save souls; what more could He do in His desire to come to our aid and save us?
- Purity of heart. If there is a pure heart, it is indeed Our Lord's. His heart is truly turned completely towards His Father, swelled with the love He has for His Father and for all mankind. It is from this pierced heart that all pure hearts will come ever after. His heart will purify souls. He will be the source of all consecrated virginity, and of all chastity.
- Love of peace. What does Our Lord do on the Cross if not make peace? Our Lord came to appease God's wrath and re-establish peace.
- Persecutions suffered for God's sake. What is He on the Cross if not persecuted for God's sake.

We see that the beatitudes are fulfilled with an unsurpassed perfection on the Cross. And if we too want to truly practice the beatitudes, which are the ultimate effects of the presence of the Holy Ghost in souls and which prepare souls for heaven, then let us participate in the Cross of Jesus. Let us not be scared by difficulties, trials, and sufferings of all kind, big or small. That is our lot in life.

As it is well said in *The Imitation of Christ*, everyone has sufferings, but there is a great difference between those who suffer as Christians, in union with Our Lord, to win heaven, save souls, and atone for their sins and those who revolt against suffering. It would be very unfortunate if we who want to consecrate our whole life to the good God were to resemble those who have understood nothing of suffering. Let us willingly accept difficulties, trials, and contradictions in union with Our Lord, and then joy will fill our hearts. The more we practice the beatitudes, the more readily we accept all our crosses in imitation of Our Lord, the happier we shall be and the more joy will fill our souls.

The Priest's Lifting Up His Eyes to Heaven

At the moment of the Consecration, the priest, minister of the universal Mediator, must, like Him, lift up his eyes to heaven with an ardent desire to unite himself with the oblation of Christ, always living, who never ceases to intercede for us nor to offer to the Father together with Himself all the living members of His Mystical Body, especially those who suffer, following His example. Father Garrigou-Lagrange wrote truly moving things on this subject. One gets the feeling that he had a very special devotion to the Consecration: "Devotion to the Eucharistic consecration comprises something essential in Christian life; without it we can have no real interior life. The double consecration, the essence of the Holy Sacrifice, marks the most solemn moment of each day of our lives."[119]

---

[119] *The Love of God and the Cross of Jesus* (St. Louis: B. Herder Book Co., 1951), II, 406. Retreat, Ecône, September, 1978.

The Words of the Consecration

Qui prídie quam paterétur accépit panem in sanctas ac venerábiles manus suas et elevátis óculis in cælum ad te Deum Patrem suum omnipoténtem tibi grátias agens bene ✠ díxit, fregit, dedítque discípulis suis, dicens: Accípite, et manducáte ex hoc omnes.

Who, the day before He suffered, took bread into His holy and venerable hands and with His eyes lifted up to heaven, unto Thee, God, His almighty Father, giving thanks to Thee, He blessed, ✠ broke, and gave It to His disciples, saying: Take all of you and eat of this.

Hoc est enim Corpus Meum.

For this is My Body.

Símili modo postquam cenátum est accípiens et hunc præclárum cálicem in sanctas ac venerábiles manus suas: item tibi grátias agens bene ✠ díxit, dedítque discípulis suis, dicens: Accípite, et bíbite ex eo omnes.

In like manner, after He had supped, taking also this excellent chalice into His holy and venerable hands, also giving thanks to Thee, He blessed ✠ and gave It to His disciples saying: Take and drink ye all of this.

Hic est enim Calix Sanguinis Mei,
novi et æterni testamenti:
mysterium fidei:
qui pro vobis et pro multis effundetur in remissionem peccatorum.

For this is the Chalice of My Blood, of the new and eternal testament:
the mystery of faith:
which shall be shed for you and for many unto the remission of sins.

Hæc quotiescúmque fecéritis, in mei memóriam faciétis.

As often as ye shall do these things, ye shall do them in memory of Me.

1. *Hoc est enim... Hic est enim...*

The words of consecration are brief, certainly, but how weighty with meaning. "This": It is the sacrifice of the Cross continued, perpetuated in its physical and mystical reality; it is the sacrifice of the Cross continued by the bread and wine consecrated to become substantially the Body and Blood of Jesus. "This": It is the unbloody sacrifice of oblation of the living Christ, immolated on the Cross once and for all and continuing to intercede for us. "This": It is the Body and Blood of the risen Jesus becoming the food of His Mystical Body, for from the sacrifice of the Cross flow the graces of resurrection for the souls of the faithful in baptism, penance, extreme unction, and in all the Sacraments. As participants in the priesthood of Jesus Christ, ministers of the divine mysteries, chosen and marked by Our Lord's election as priests for eternity, priests are ordained for the holy sacrifice of the Mass and for the sacrifice of the Cross, the two being substantially one and the same sacrifice of Our Lord. Thus, at the priest's bidding, the Cross of Christ, to which is attached the Priest and Victim *par excellence*, is lifted up. Here is why the Word became flesh, here is what the Redeemer was for. "*Tota via crux et martyrium*—Your whole life was a cross and a martyrdom."[120]

2. *Corpus Meum*

The Catechism of the Council of Trent includes the following statements:

> The priest is also one and the same, Christ the Lord; for the ministers who offer Sacrifice, consecrate the holy mysteries, not in their own person, but in that of Christ, as the words of consecration itself show, for the priest does not say: *this is the body of Christ*, but, *This is my body;* and thus, acting in the Person of Christ the Lord, he changes the substance of the bread and wine into the true substance of His Body and Blood.
>
> This being the case, it must be taught without any hesitation that, as the holy Council (of Trent) has also explained, the sacred and holy Sacrifice of the Mass is not a Sacrifice of praise and thanksgiving only, or a mere commemoration of the Sacrifice performed on the cross, but also truly a propitiatory Sacrifice, by which God is appeased and rendered propitious to us.[121]

This is what our faith teaches us.[122]

3. *Calix Sanguinis Mei*

St. Thomas says that the formula of the consecration of the precious Blood expresses the mystery of our souls' ransom and re-

---

[120] From *The Imitation of Christ*, Book II, Ch. 12.
[121] Catechism of the Council of Trent, p.258.
[122] Easter retreat, Ecône, April 17, 1984.

demption better than does that of the Lord's Body,[123] because the shedding of blood is truly what best expresses our Redemption.[124]

Here below, Our Lord's sacrifice especially has for us the value of an immolation in reparation for sins, for His Blood flows in reparation for our sins. Undoubtedly, He is also rendering great glory and thanksgiving to His Father, but as regards us, it is especially the aspect of reparation that is inscribed on the Cross. It is clear that our eyes can see the blood that flows from the pierced hands, heart, and feet and from the crown of thorns. The blood that flows from every part of Our Lord's body signifies reparation for sin; that is obvious.

Now this reparation must continue so that it can be applied to each of our souls, and this is what happens during the sacrifice of the Mass instituted by Our Lord. Hence the separate consecration of the Body and Blood: this double consecration of the Blood under the species of wine, and of the Body under the species of bread signifies the Lord's death. The separation is a sign of the sacrifice, though in reality the Body and Blood of Our Lord, His Soul and Divinity, are present under both species because now Our Lord can no longer separate His Blood and His Body;[125] He can no longer die. Thus it is a mystical separation, and this separation is willed by Our Lord. Our Lord willed that this separation occur.[126] The sepa-

---

[123] *Summa Theologica*, III, Q. 78, Art. 3, ad 2: "The blood consecrated apart expressly represents Christ's Passion, and therefore mention is made of the fruits of the Passion in the consecration of the blood rather than in that of the body, since the body is the subject of the Passion."
[124] Easter retreat, Ecône, April 16, 1984.
[125] There is only one body of Christ, the one which has been in heaven since the Resurrection. It is this body that is made present sacramentally by the consecration. By the words "This is My body," the body of Christ is made directly present. But since the Resurrection, the body of Christ is united to His blood and His soul; so under the species (that which appears to the senses: color, taste, *etc*.) of bread, the Body, Blood, Soul, and Divinity of Jesus Christ are present (principle of concomitance); likewise, under the species of wine.
[126] This immolation is mysterious, "mystical" in Archbishop Lefebvre's word, for it is indeed real, but not in a bloody manner as on the Cross, but according to the sensible sign we perceive: the separate consecrations of the Body and Blood. It is an immolation that can be called sacramental. The Catechism of St. Pius X teaches us that a Sacrament is an outward sign that causes grace: it signifies and produces grace. For example, for baptism, the ablution with water signifies and produces the ablution of original sin. Just as a Sacrament

ration is mystical, but the sacrifice is real. This sacrifice is the continuation of Our Lord's sacrifice. Our Lord made the consecration of His Body and then of His Blood in order to signify His death for our sins, the fruits of which are abundantly bestowed on our souls.[127]

The form of consecration of the Blood expresses the manner in which we participate in the Passion. The first words, "This is the chalice of My blood," signify the conversion of wine into blood, and the words that follow designate the virtue of the Blood shed in the Passion, the virtue which is at work in this Sacrament. This virtue makes us obtain the eternal heritage. According to the Epistle to the Hebrews, we "hav[e]...a confidence in the entering into the holies by the blood of Christ" (10:19), and to designate that, it is said "of the new and eternal testament." Henceforth, there is an eternal testament.[128] By the blood of Christ we participate in an eternal testament, a testament that shall extend to heaven.

What does this Blood signify? It was not simply to shed blood that Our Lord came on earth. It was because this Blood is charity. The Holy Ghost made the Blood of Our Lord Jesus Christ flow; it is His love. It is the sign of His charity for us. That is what Our Lord's Blood is; the effusion of Blood signifies that Our Lord pours forth His love in us, His Holy Spirit. This Holy Spirit leads us to God, it inclines us to do our duty, to keep the law of God, which is nothing else than the law of charity, a law of love: love God, love your neighbor–that is our law. The Blood of God is nothing other than a source of love.

It is also the sign of penance, the sign of sacrifice. Henceforth, God wanted it so, we can no longer love without self-sacrifice. Indeed, to love, we must efface ourselves, forget ourselves. So long as we still love ourselves with a disordered love, so long as we still seek ourselves, charity is not in us; we are full of egoism, we seek only our selves, our own advantages, our own self-love, and our

---

signifies and produces grace, so also the separate consecration of the species signifies and produces the immolation of Christ sacramentally (by a tangible, efficacious sign). St. Thomas wrote: "The Eucharist is the perfect Sacrament of the Lord's Passion" (*Summa Theological*, III, Q. 73, Art. 5, ad 2).

[127] St-Michel-en-Brenne, April 1989.
[128] [That is, a covenant or alliance. Archbishop Lefebvre uses the word alliance.–*Tr.*]

own pleasure. That is what St. Paul tells us: "Charity seeketh not her own, is patient, beareth all things, believeth all things, hopeth all things" (I Cor. 13:4-7). This is what charity is; this is what Our Lord's Blood gives us, signifies for us, and produces in us.[129]

4. Novi et Aeterni Testamenti

"The blood of the new and eternal Testament." Why is it of the new and eternal Alliance? Is there another Testament, since it is question of a new Testament and an eternal Testament? Yes, there was another Testament. The word *testament* means *heritage*, and there is no testament if there is no inheritance. The first heritage of the first Testament was the promise of the Messias to come, a promise that was concretized in the laws inscribed on the stone tablets enclosed in the ark of the Covenant. But that was not the true Testament, that was not the eternal Testament, the eternal heritage God wanted to give men. It was only a figure, a preparation of the heritage we were to receive, the heritage which is Jesus Christ Himself, present in our tabernacles. It is He who shall give Himself in the sacrifice of the Cross, and who is going to perpetuate the sacrifice of the Cross on our altars by the intermediary of priests. That is the great heritage that the good God wants to give us. This heritage is indeed eternal–*novi et aeterni Testamenti*; an eternal heritage, because Our Lord Jesus Christ, by giving Himself to us, lifts us to Himself and makes us participate in His Divine life. This Divine life in which we participate starting with baptism is already the beginning of eternal life and will be in heaven our joy, our glory, and our happiness. By baptism we already possess this eternal life: *Novi et aeterni Testamenti*.[130]

> **The Mystery of Faith is also the mystery of the charity of God towards us, a mystery of infinite worth for the souls that believe in Jesus Christ, Word of God Incarnate and Redeemer of men.**

5. *Mysterium Fidei*

So beautiful, so great, so immense, so sublime it is to be able to make God Himself descend upon the altar of sacrifice that,

---

[129] Homily, Fanjeaux, July 7, 1979.
[130] *Ibid.*

once he has accomplished so extraordinary an action, he exclaims "*Mysterium fidei*–mystery of faith"! The priest says "Mystery of faith" in the middle of the prayers of consecration of the Blood because he realizes the admirable thing he has just done. Such is our holy religion, and nothing else.[131]

Mystery of faith, *mysterium fidei*: St. Thomas says in his *Summa* that these words certainly come from the Apostolic tradition received from Our Lord Jesus Christ.[132] You see the necessity of these words, which were not put there by chance. The Mass makes us obtain gratuitous justification, which is the fruit of faith, according to the Epistle to the Romans (cf. Rom. 5:1-2, 9).[133]

Even when the priest offers the holy sacrifice of the Mass alone, the result is the same, for the holy sacrifice of the Mass is a public act of the Church. The holy sacrifice of the Mass, offered by genuinely ordained priests who have received the sacerdotal character, always retains its mysterious value, its incommensurable, infinite value, regardless of whether it is solemnly or privately celebrated: the sacrifice of the Mass is the *mysterium fidei*, the mystery of our faith. We are unable here below to understand the grandeur and the sublimity of the sacrifice of the Mass. We shall only understand it in heaven; and even then, will we understand it perfectly? We will understand it in a certain manner as the good God understands it, but only the good God Himself can penetrate the great mystery of our faith.[134]

What is the mystery of our faith? It is the mystery of the love of God for us. It is the mystery of God's charity towards us. We are astounded at what God has done for us: that the good God shed all His Blood for us. As unlikely and inconceivable as it is, we must believe it. It is a mystery of our faith. We do not have the right to hesitate as the Jews did, who withdrew from Our Lord Jesus Christ because He told them: "The man who eats my flesh and drinks my blood has everlasting life" (Jn. 6:55). "Except you eat the flesh of the Son of man and drink his blood, you shall not have life in you" (Jn. 6:54).[135]

---

[131] Homily, Garges-lès-Gonesse, February 11, 1973.
[132] Cf. *Summa Theologica*, III, Q. 78, Art. 3, ad 9.
[133] Spiritual conference, Ecône, March 10, 1989.
[134] Homily, Ecône, June 29, 1975.
[135] Homily Brannay, July 15, 1979.

Our Lord Jesus Christ, true man, represented a genuine mystery for His followers: How is it possible for this man who is like us–who eats like us, who travels like us, who gets tired like us, who takes nourishment like us–to be the Creator of the universe, the one who scattered the stars in the heavens, who created everything, and who holds us all in His hands, each and every one of us? Is it possible, a man like us? Yes, we cannot doubt it. This man, who was born of the Virgin Mary, who grew up at Nazareth, who then trod the roads of Palestine and worked miracles among the men of His nation, was God....

Now, just as Our Lord was a mystery for the Jews when they encountered Him as He went about Palestine, so the Holy Eucharist is a mystery for us, too. To adore Christ under the appearance of bread: Is it possible that the substance of the bread disappeared and left the place for the substance of the Body and Blood of Our Lord Jesus Christ? Is it possible? Unfathomable mystery; yes, an extraordinary mystery–*mysterium fidei*: the mystery of our faith. It is by this that Christians and non-Christians will be judged: those who adore the Holy Eucharist and those who refuse to adore the Holy Eucharist, who snicker before it and mock the Christians because they adore the most Holy Eucharist. That is how those who love Our Lord, who have faith in Him, and those who reject Him will be judged. Consequently, we must submit ourselves, love and adore the most Holy Eucharist.[136]

6. *Qui pro vobis et pro multis effundetur in remissionem peccatorum*

The words of consecration of the Blood are particularly expressive. For, when the priest says that the blood of the New Testament is there and that it is shed for the remission of sins, "shed for you and for many unto the remission of sins," he affirms that the sacrifice of the Mass is made for taking away our sins and, consequently, for infusing in us again the Holy Ghost, the Spirit of love, to re-establish us in the charity we lost by sin. That is why the sacrifice of the Mass is offered.[137]

---

[136] Homily, Ecône, June 6, 1976.
[137] Homily, Brannay, July 15, 1979.

Our Lord is the only High Priest, and the Mass is a personal action of Jesus Christ. The priest is the instrument, and his purity must be in the image of the virgin Christ's.

7. *Haec quotiescumque feceritis*

At the Last Supper, Our Lord conferred the sacerdotal character on those who would be His priests, His instruments, His ministers, for He is always the Priest. He is such yesterday, today, and for eternity. Our Lord is always the High Priest, the only High Priest. The others are only His ministers, His instruments.[138]

What did Our Lord command His priests? He told them: "Do this for a commemoration of Me" (Lk. 22:19). He said to His Apostles: "Do again what I did," that is, reoffer this Sacrament of the Eucharist, by which I give to those who receive Me in Holy Communion My Body, Blood, Soul, and Divinity.[139]

The Protestants say that there is only one sacrifice; afterwards, there must be no other. It is true that it is unique, but it is continued. Our Lord wanted it to be reproduced on the altar every time the words of consecration are pronounced. Our Lord requested this at the Last Supper: "Do this for a commemoration of me."[140]

It is the sacerdotal character that enables you to pronounce the words of consecration of the holy Mass and to oblige God in some way to obey your command. At your words, Jesus Christ comes personally, physically, substantially, under the species of bread and wine. He is present on the altar, and you genuflect to adore Him. That is what the priest is. What an extraordinary reality! We shall have to be in heaven to grasp it; and even in heaven, will we understand what the priest is? Wasn't it the holy Curé of Ars who said, "If I found myself before a priest and an angel, I would greet the priest before the angel."[141]

How beautiful it is for the priest to think that he resembles the Blessed Virgin when he is at the altar and that, poor creature that he is, he pronounces the words of the consecration! At that moment, he, like the Blessed Virgin, has a real power over God, over Our Lord Jesus Christ, since by his words he is capable of mak-

---

[138] Homily, Garges-lès-Gonesse, February 11, 1973.
[139] Homily, Ecône, June 29, 1977.
[140] Retreat, Ecône, 1978.
[141] Homily, first Mass, Geneva, July 4, 1976.

ing Our Lord descend from heaven in His Body, Blood, Soul, and Divinity, as the Blessed Virgin Mary did by her *Fiat*.

There is thus a very great affinity between the priest and Mary, an affinity that is an extraordinary privilege! Never will we understand, perhaps not even in heaven, the incredible mystery of the dignity of Mary and of the priest: that poor creatures should have power over Almighty God, the Creator, the Redeemer, without whom nothing would be, nothing would exist; that these poor creatures should have the power to make Him come down to earth. How admirable it is. And we must believe it![142]

If the good God wanted the Blessed Virgin Mary to have a holiness surpassing that of all creatures, then you, priests of Jesus Christ who make Our Lord come down upon the altar, must also be holy. By her *Fiat*, prepared by her perfect virginity, the Blessed Virgin accepted the Lord's coming. Likewise, your lips, pronouncing the words of consecration, in some way repeat the Virgin Mary's *Fiat* and make Jesus Himself come down upon the altar–the same Jesus to whom you are able to unite yourselves before distributing Him to souls. That is why you also, like Mary, must be holy.[143]

Just as the most blessed Virgin Mary had to be a virgin in order to have such a great and sublime power as to receive Jesus in her womb, so the priest must be a virgin, since he also has a power over the Body, Blood, Soul, and Divinity of Our Lord. This is the reason for priestly celibacy; there is no other real reason. Let us not say that the priest must be celibate because, were he married, he would be too busy: that is a secondary reason. The real reason for the priest's celibacy is that, by the words of the consecration, he has the power to make Our Lord come down upon the altar. It is proper that one who has this power over a God who is Spirit, who is the Master and Creator of the world, should be a virgin, and that he remain celibate. That is the fundamental reason for priestly celibacy.[144]

---

[142] Homily, Garges-lès-Gonesse, February 11, 1973.
[143] Homily, sacerdotal ordinations, Ecône, June 29, 1981.
[144] Homily, Garges-lès-Gonesse, February 11, 1973.

The Offering: *Unde et Memores*

U̲NDE et mémores, Dómine, nos servi tui, sed et plebs tua sancta, ejúsdem Christi Fílii tui, Dómini nostri, tam beátæ passiónis, nec non et ab ínferis resurrectiónis, sed et in cælos gloriósæ ascensiónis: offérimus præcláræ majestáti tuæ de tuis donis ac datis hóstiam ✠ puram, hóstiam ✠ sanctam, hóstiam ✠ immaculátam Panem ✠ sanctum vitæ ætérnæ, et Cálicem ✠ salútis perpétuæ.

W̲HEREFORE, O Lord, we Thy servants, as also Thy holy people, calling to mind the blessed Passion of the same Christ, Thy Son, our Lord, His resurrection from hell, and glorious ascension into heaven, offer unto Thy most excellent majesty of Thine own gifts bestowed upon us, a pure ✠ Victim, a holy ✠ Victim, an immaculate ✠ Victim, the holy Bread ✠ of eternal life and the Chalice ✠ of everlasting salvation.

Let us be conscious of the mystery that has just happened on the altar: the coming of the crucified Victim.[145]

If Our Lord is present on the altar, then imagine what we must do if we have faith. If He is really present and if He offers Himself as Victim, we must kneel. After all, that's not asking too much. Upon the altar is that God who will judge us. He it was who created us; He it is who can cure us if we are sick, who can give us strength if we are weak. He is Almighty.[146]

1. Offer Our Lord to God

What greater offering can there be than Our Lord offering Himself to His Father? The offering of Our Lord Jesus Christ to His Father is the great prayer of the Church. The Church associates herself with this prayer. She is entirely made for this prayer, which she makes during the holy sacrifice of the Mass.[147]

We must thank Our Lord, who substitutes Himself for us by His grace. By sanctifying grace, Our Lord is present in us. He is there as Creator, but He is also there by His grace. Thus in some way it is Our Lord Himself who prays through us, who utilizes us to continue offering the prayer He made on the Cross. This must be a consolation for us, because we feel ourselves to be unworthy

---

[145] *Ibid.*
[146] Conference, Mantes-la-Jolie, April 22, 1977.
[147] Retreat, Avrillé, October 18, 1989.

to pray suitably, to pray as we ought. So let us console ourselves by thinking that the good God, Our Lord, prays with us.[148]

2. The lessons of the Divine Victim of the Cross

Self-sacrifice is for the sake of love. You understand it well: what else do a father and mother of a family do except sacrifice themselves out of love for their family and for each other? Self-sacrifice is necessary, or else there isn't any love. Sacrifice is a condition of love, and Our Lord showed us this very well by His arms outstretched on the Cross, His pierced hands and feet, and His pierced heart. That is Our Lord's sacrifice out of love for God His Father and for His neighbor. It is the great lesson of love by sacrifice![149]

Another lesson Our Lord Jesus Christ gives us on the Cross is that of prayer and penance. His Cross is the great prayer, the prayer He addresses to His Father, the prayer that He makes for the salvation of souls, and it is also that of penance. I think that in order to make this penance practicable for us it is good to designate it under a few particular virtues–virtues that are particularly Catholic, the virtues Our Lord truly taught us in a very particular manner: humility, poverty, and chastity.[150]

THE SIGNS OF THE CROSS OVER THE HOST AND CHALICE

During the prayer *Unde et memores*, the priest makes five Signs of the Cross over the host and chalice.

The Signs of the Cross do not have the same meaning after the consecration as they did before. Before the consecration, they really bless the offerings, whereas afterwards they designate them. It is a designation. The Sign of the Cross designates the Body and Blood. The priest does not bless Our Lord's body. One does not bless God. It is a useful designation that has a signification. It serves

---

[148] Retreat, Le Barroux, August 1985.
[149] Homily, Rouen, May 1, 1990.
[150] Homily, St-Michel-en-Brenne, February 11, 1990.

to clearly manifest faith in the real presence of the Body and Blood of Our Lord.[151]

An Acceptable Offering: *Supra Quae*

Supra quæ propítio ac seréno vultu respícere dignéris: et accépta habére, sícuti accépta habére dignátus es múnera púeri tui justi Abel, et sacrifícium patriárchæ nostri Abrahæ: et quod tibi óbtulit summus sacérdos tuus Melchísedech, sanctum sacrifícium, immaculátam hóstiam.

Upon which do Thou vouchsafe to look with a propitious and serene countenance, and to accept them, as Thou wert graciously pleased to accept the gifts of Thy just servant Abel, and the sacrifice of our patriarch Abraham, and that which Thy high priest Melchisedech offered to Thee, a holy sacrifice, a spotless victim.

We cannot fail to admire how Our Lord united in Himself all the characteristics of the sacrifices of the Old Testament: all that the ancient sacrifices represented, all their elements and their circumstances. Our Lord Himself is the victim; He Himself is the priest; He will give Himself as food to those who will offer the sacrifice. Consequently, it will no longer be necessary to go and look for victims, as did the priests in the Old Testament. The Levites did not really participate in the priesthood of Our Lord Jesus Christ. Afterwards, the priests will participate in the priesthood of Our Lord Jesus Christ because Our Lord Jesus Christ is the only Priest, the Pontiff.[152]

The sacrifice of Abraham prefigured Our Lord's sacrifice. The lamb immolated before the departure from Egypt, whose blood was used to mark the door posts: all that was a symbol of the greatest event that could happen in the history of the human race: the death of the Creator of the universe.[153]

Each year, during the Feast of Atonement, the high-priest entered into the Holy of Holies, and, as Scripture says, he did not enter without the blood of victims (Heb. 9:7). That, as St. Paul says,[154] is an image of what in future was to be the true sacrifice, the

---

[151] Retreat, Avrillé, October 18, 1989.
[152] Spiritual conference, Zaitzkofen, February 7, 1980.
[153] Conference to the SSPX Sisters, St-Michel-en-Brenne, April 2, 1989.
[154] Cf. Heb. 10.

sacrifice of Our Lord Himself. Neither would He, the Holy *par excellence*, enter into the tabernacle, not made by man's hands, without His precious Blood. And that is what makes the priest...: to reproduce the sacrifice of Our Lord by the Blood of Our Lord, by the Blood which is truly the lood of expiation, the blood of reparation, the blood of redemption. How much greater is the sacrifice the priests offer today, how much more efficacious, how much more sublime, how much more divine than the sacrifice offered before by the high-priest once a year when he entered the Holy of Holies!

The priesthood the good God gives us enables us, with the Blood of Our Lord Jesus Christ, to associate our blood with His and to enter into the eternal tabernacle in heaven. With the Victim that is Our Lord Jesus Christ, by the Victim which is Our Lord Jesus Christ, we enter into heaven. And with us, we draw the faithful who unite themselves to Our Lord's sacrifice; those who, baptized in the Blood of Our Lord, can participate in this sacrifice and can by that very fact receive the extraordinary graces that sacrifice gives: graces of redemption, the grace of being associated with the repast of the Victim who offered Himself, grace of the Holy Eucharist. That is the holy sacrifice of the Mass.[155]

An Ardent Supplication: *Supplices*

SUPPLICES te rogámus, omnípotens Deus: jube hæc perférri per manus sancti Angeli tui in sublíme altáre tuum, in conspéctu divínæ majestátis tuæ: ut quotquot ex hac altáris participatióne sacrosánctum Fílii tui Cor ✠ pus et Sán ✠ guinem sumpsérimus omni benedictióne cælésti et grátia repleámur. Per eúmdem Christum Dóminum nostrum. Amen.

WE most humbly beseech Thee, Almighty God, to command that these offerings be borne by the hands of Thy holy Angel to Thine altar on high in the sight of Thy Divine Majesty, that as many of us as at this altar shall partake of and receive the most holy Body ✠ and Blood ✠ of Thy Son, ✠ may be filled with every heavenly blessing and grace. Through the same Christ our Lord. Amen.

---

[155] Homily, Ecône, September 27, 1986.

> **These offerings are borne to the altar of God by the hands of His holy angel. This angel is Our Lord Jesus Christ Himself. At the Mass, He makes Himself our messenger to His Father, so that the Father will pour forth His graces upon us.**

Once Our Lord is present on the altar after the words of consecration, He cannot do otherwise than pray to His Father to give us all the blessings we need. He is not there for His own sake. He is quite content in heaven; it is not in His own interest that He comes upon our altars. He comes for us. He is the great supplicant. He is the one who addresses our supplications to the good God, to open the gates of heaven to us. Consequently, we must profit from His presence near to us and love to attend the holy sacrifice of the Mass, convinced that we receive very many graces even if we do not receive Holy Communion, but even more so if we do receive, of course. That is why the Church requires us to attend holy Mass at least every Sunday.[156]

The Third Commandment and the first precept of the Church oblige the faithful to attend the holy sacrifice of the Mass once a week under pain of mortal sin, while the Church obliges us to receive Holy Communion and to go to confession just once a year under pain of serious sin. She is thus much more exigent for the holy sacrifice of the Mass. All Christians must attend the holy sacrifice of the Mass once a week in order to participate in Our Lord's sacrifice, in Our Lord's oblation, and to offer their days, their week, their lives, to Our Lord.[157]

Prayer on Behalf of the Church Suffering: The *Memento* of the Dead

Memento étiam, Dómine, famulórum famularúmque tuárum N. et N., qui nos præcessérunt cum signo fídei, et dórmiunt in somno pacis.
Ipsis, Dómine, et ómnibus in Christo quiescéntibus, locum refrigérii, lucis et pacis, ut indúlgeas,

Be mindful, O Lord, of Thy servants and handmaids N. and N., who are gone before us with the sign of faith and sleep in the sleep of peace.
To these, O Lord, and to all that rest in Christ, we beseech Thee, grant a place of refreshment, light,

---

[156] Homily, Ecône, April 20, 1975.
[157] Retreat, Avrillé, October 18, 1989.

deprecámur. Per eúmdem Christum Dóminum nostrum. Amen. and peace. Through the same Christ our Lord. Amen.

The holy Mass is the continuation of Our Lord's sacrifice for the application of His merits to the souls of the living and the dead. The Protestants do not believe this, and the Protestant idea of the Mass has unfortunately penetrated into Catholic circles and affected Catholic priests. According to Catholic theology, the sacrifice is especially propitiatory. The Council of Trent particularly emphasizes this point: "And since in this divine sacrifice, which is celebrated in the Mass, that same Christ is contained and immolated in an unbloody manner, who on the altar of the Cross 'once offered Himself' in a bloody manner [Heb. 9:27], the holy Synod teaches that this is truly propitiatory."[158] The most characteristic end of the Mass is "propitiatory." ...The Mass purifies the souls in purgatory, and as they can no longer merit for themselves, they await our prayers and in particular the great prayer which is the holy sacrifice of the Mass.[159]

The victory assured by Christ for all the souls of the faithful departed inaugurates a combat that will not end for each of us until death, and for mankind until the Last Judgment. The prayer of Our Lord on the altar under the appearances of the immolated victim sets before us the reality of this bitter strife between the forces of good and evil.[160]

If we wish to conform ourselves to the spirit of the Church, we must have true devotion towards the souls in purgatory, where very probably we will spend a longer or shorter time–let us hope so, for this will be the sign of our election. If we could know the holiness and incomparable purity of God, we would not be surprised that He discovers in us imperfections which are discordant with the sanctity of the Holy Trinity.[161]

---

[158] The Council continues: "Therefore, it is offered rightly according to the tradition of the apostles, not only for the sins of the faithful living, for their punishments and other necessities, but also for the dead in Christ not yet fully purged" (Dz. 940).
[159] Retreat, Ecône, September 22, 1978.
[160] Notes for a priests' retreat, n.d., Ecône Seminary archives, *O Mysterium Christi*, p.15.
[161] *Spiritual Journey*, p.61.

The Bow at the End of the Prayer for the Dead

While saying "Per eumdem Christum Dominum nostrum" at the end of the prayer for the dead, the priest nods his head in memory of Christ, who bowed His head as He breathed His last sigh. The architecture of some churches incorporates this gesture of Christ's.

Churches generally form a cross with the nave and the transept. There are even ancient churches like that of Fontgombault, for example, in which chapels are to be found that are slightly pitched to the left, hence slightly to the right of the cross. The little chapels are slightly angled toward the sanctuary; they are not along the axis. Why?–They symbolize Our Lord's head bowed on the Cross. One can say that the entire architecture of these churches recalls the mystery of the Cross of Our Lord Jesus Christ, Our Lord's sacrifice. All that has a great meaning, doesn't it? The Church, having understood that sacrifice is the essential act of the virtue of religion, has inscribed it in the architecture of churches and cathedrals.[162]

Prayer for the Church Militant: *Nobis Quoque Peccatoribus*

Nobis quoque peccatóribus, fámulis tuis, de multitúdine miseratiónum tuárum sperántibus, partem áliquam et societátem donáre dignéris, cum tuis sanctis Apóstolis et Martýribus: cum Joánne, Stéphano, Matthía, Bárnaba, Ignátio, Alexándro, Marcellíno, Petro, Felicitáte, Perpétua, Agatha, Lúcia, Agnéte, Cæcília, Anastásia, et ómnibus Sanctis tuis: intra quorum nos consórtium, non æstimátor mériti, sed véniæ, quǽsumus, largítor admítte.

To us sinners also, Thy servants, hoping in the multitude of Thy mercies, vouchsafe to grant some part and fellowship with Thy holy Apostles and Martyrs: with John, Stephen, Matthias, Barnabas, Ignatius, Alexander, Marcellinus, Peter, Felicitas, Perpetua, Agatha, Lucy, Agnes, Cecilia, Anastasia, and with all Thy saints, into whose company we pray Thee to admit us, not considering our merits, but of Thine own free pardon.

---

[162] Retreat, Avrillé, October 18, 1989.

Throughout the Mass, the Church invites the priest to manifest his sentiments of profound humility. It is thus that he strikes his breast while saying "To us sinners also."

Poor creatures that we are! What a responsibility it is to participate in what is essential to Jesus Christ: His Redemption, His priesthood, His royalty! What a responsibility the priest has before all the faithful! With what humility you must accomplish these holy mysteries![163]

A deep faith in Our Lord necessarily makes us humble; it is a consequence of adoring Our Lord. And that is why our Mass is so beautiful, because it is a constant manifestation of our adoration of the Lord.[164]

The result of contact with the good God in prayer..., and in the Mass, must be an increase of humility. If vanity or a little pride results because we have the feeling that the good God gives us particular graces, more than to others, then it is our imagination that is working; it is not the reality, it is not really the light of the good God or of the Holy Ghost that is enlightening us. The nearer we draw to God, as St. Thomas says, the more we are convinced that we know Him less: "The more someone knows God, the more he is convinced that he knows Him less." These are golden words. Everything that can make us approach God must have humility as the result. If it isn't humility, then something is not right.

Someone who doesn't know God thinks that when he pronounces the name of God he knows Him. It is a complete illusion. The most spiritual souls who draw near to God, who begin to perceive the great mysteries of God, the mysteries of the Creator, the Savior, the Redeemer, the Sanctifier, the Glorifier, discover with amazement that God is an ever greater mystery...: an immense ocean. The reaction of a spiritual soul, a soul that begins to understand that, must be humility. "My God, what am I in relation to this great mystery? I did not know that the good God was so great, so infinite, so powerful, so good, so merciful. I begin to discover it a little. Before this tiny discovery, I fall awe-struck." It is good to listen to St. Thomas, who tells us "The more someone knows God, the more he is convinced that he knows Him less," to keep us also

---

[163] Homily, sacerdotal ordinations, Ecône, June 27, 1980.
[164] Spiritual conference, Ecône, June 8, 1978.

humble should we be tempted to tell ourselves, Ah! now I know the good God well. I've reached the summit. I'm sure to know the good God well.[165]

> In the prayer *Nobis quoque peccatoribus*, the priest implores the intercession of several saints, including St. Cecilia, a young Roman martyr.

It would have been easy for the martyrs to say that our religion is more beautiful than the others, but that it is only one among others. Look at St. Cecilia. This great saint converted her brother-in-law Tiburtius and her executioner, Maximus. She was from a very noble Roman family. She could have aspired to the greatest honors in the city of Rome. So how might one go after someone like her to try her perseverance in her Catholic Faith?

To make it easier for her, the Roman prefect told her: "Return home. We shall send you some food that was sacrificed to idols, but no one will know it. Everything will be done in secret. If you partake of this food, you will not be put to death. We shall let you go free."

You know St. Cecilia's response: "I will never agree to eat the least morsel of food that has been offered to your devils, to your idols. Never, never! I would rather die!"

And so she received three sword strokes, which did not manage to decapitate her. She remained alive like that for three days, still preaching the gospel and dying like a great saint. Such is the example of the martyrs. It would have been easy for Cecilia. By secretly eating the food offered to idols, her life would have been spared. But no, she preferred to keep the holy Christian religion and her attachment to Our Lord Jesus Christ.[166]

Conclusion of the Canon

Per quem hæc ómnia, Dómine, semper bona creas, sanctí ✠ ficas, viví ✠ ficas, bene ✠ dícis et præstas nobis.

Through Whom, O Lord, Thou dost create, hallow, ✠ quicken, ✠ and bless ✠ all these good things and give them to us.

---

[165] Retreat to Carmelites, Quiévrain, July 23, 1986.
[166] Homily, Châtillon-sur-Chalaronne, April 16, 1989.

P er ip ✠ sum, et cum ip ✠ so, et in ip ✠ so,

Est tibi Deo Patri ✠ omnipotenti, in unitate Spiritus ✠ Sancti,

Omnis honor, et gloria, Per omnia sæcula sæculorum.
℞. Amen.

T hrough ✠ Him and with ✠ Him and in ✠ Him,

Be to Thee, God the Father ✠ Almighty, in the unity of the Holy ✠ Ghost,

All honor and glory, For ever and ever.
℞. Amen.

Everything is done by Our Lord, in Him, and with Him. Without being incorporated into His Mystical Body, no man can be agreeable to God and glorify the Holy Trinity. This is the admirable plan of God.

Everything was made for Our Lord and in Our Lord, for the good God could never receive greater glory from any creature than from Our Lord Jesus Christ, who is God Himself.[167]

There were not two moments in God's plan, there was only one. This one moment comprehended sin, foreseen by God from all eternity, and already comprehended the Incarnation of Our Lord Jesus Christ. From this moment, everything was ordered to the Incarnation of Our Lord Jesus Christ, to the Incarnation of the Word, to the existence of the Man-God. "The firstborn of every creature" (Col. 1:15), He is the model of all creatures. Consequently, God's plan is Our Lord Jesus Christ. Nothing that was done, nothing that the good God created, nothing that the good God foresaw, was done outside Our Lord Jesus Christ. That is normal. How can it be imagined that the coming of God amongst us, the Incarnation of the Word, which is the most extraordinary event in all of human history, was not for God the summit of His creation? For God could not receive greater glory, praise, love, or more ardent charity than by His own incarnate Son. What are our small praises–the small measure of glory that we can bring to God by offering Him what we have, which He has given us–next to what the very Word of God, His Son, who lives in Him from all eternity, gives Him? He is the very Word of God.... God's great thought is the Incarnation of His Son, the model of every crea-

---

[167] Spiritual conference, Ecône, January 26, 1982.

ture and the synthesis of all creation. If man is to a certain extent the synthesis of all creation because he is both spiritual and material, there is one that is the synthesis of all things: Our Lord Jesus Christ.[168]

Our Lord's sacrifice is the perfect sacrifice that joins the four ends of prayer: praise, thanksgiving, supplication, and reparation; and which allows us to accomplish these four ends. It is necessary to participate in His sacrifice. We can no longer pray otherwise than by Our Lord Jesus Christ. Our religion can no longer be anything but Christian. It cannot be otherwise. A religion that is not Christian is no longer a religion. Since God Himself came on earth to give us our holy religion and to die for us on the Cross, there is no other religion than the Christian religion.…This is a fundamental principle. The entire Gospel of St. John shows it. Our Lord repeats it constantly: "Without me, you can do nothing" (Jn. 15:5). He is the Shepherd: "No one enters the sheepfold save by Me," Our Lord tells us. He is the gate of the sheepfold: "I am the gate" (Jn. 10:7). Likewise in the parable of the vine, Our Lord affirms that the branch that is not attached to the vine will be pruned and burned; it is worthless.[169] Our Lord does not stop saying this.

"When I shall be lifted up from the earth, I shall draw all things to myself" (Jn. 12:32). Why does He say "all"?–Because all must pass through Him; all religion must pass through His Cross. There is no other religion because the Cross is the great prayer of Our Lord; it is the principal act of His life. His whole life was made for this hour. His "great hour" is His Cross. It is the religion He gave us.[170]

We can no longer choose our religion and the acts of our religion; they have been marked for us ever since. None of us can say, "I want to express my religion in such and such a way"; nor another: "But I don't like that way; I prefer another." That time is past, if it ever existed. Even in the Old Testament, God gave rules and laws for religion in very precise detail. The Jews could no longer choose

---

[168] Retreat, Ecône July 15, 1981.
[169] Cf. Jn. 15:6.
[170] Retreat, Le Barroux, August 25, 1987.

their way of rendering their worship to God and of practicing the virtue of religion. The same holds true for the Christian religion.[171]

The Church, gathering up the extraordinary heritage that Our Lord Jesus Christ entrusted to her, made this liturgy, a liturgy that can be diverse according to place: Eastern liturgy, Latin liturgy. This liturgy is codified in the rites and ceremonies that have been fixed with love and devotion in order to magnify Our Lord Jesus Christ, to glorify Him, and to be a school of religion for all the faithful.[172]

There is only one name on earth that can transform souls, civilization, and even bodies, society, and the economy: it is the name of Our Lord Jesus Christ. There is no point in looking elsewhere. People want to transform society, to make it livable and virtuous; people want to make it economically and politically sound: the means is Our Lord Jesus Christ. I left Africa with the conviction that there is only one way to save souls and at the same time to give them a Christian civilization here below, to let them participate somewhat here below in the happiness of heaven through the happiness that grace gives: it is the reign of Our Lord Jesus Christ.[173]

For every creature, the measure by which God will judge us—what we are, what we have of value, the "esteem" God may have for us—will henceforth be our union with Our Lord Jesus Christ. In such measure as a creature is near to Our Lord Jesus Christ, it is of value to God. In such measure as it is far from Him, or, *a fortiori*, if it rejects Him completely, it can only have God's contempt. Everyone will be judged in relation to Our Lord Jesus Christ, even the angels. All creation will be seen and judged by God in relation to His incarnate Divine Son. Consequently, let's not hold the idea that God wanted to add something to us, by supernature or by grace, as if He had thought about it twice. From all eternity, God prepared, foresaw this human nature completed by grace, by the supernatural, so that it might share in His inmost reality.

---

[171] Homily, Blessing of a chapel, Nantes, April 11, 1987.
[172] Homily, Lyons, February 8, 1976.
[173] Homily, Zaitzkofen, February 15, 1987.

III. The Communion

The third part of the Mass, the Holy Communion, the partaking of the Body and Blood of Our Lord Jesus Christ, at the same time represents all the Sacraments. Holy Communion is the center of all the Sacraments. We unite ourselves in this communion with the Victim that is Our Lord Jesus Christ Himself. It is also a perfect rule of life. We must become with Our Lord victims for our sins, for the sins of the world, and at the same time sing the glory of the good God.[1]

The *Pater Noster*

Oremus.
Præcéptis salutáribus móniti, et divína institutióne formáti, audémus dícere:

Pater noster, qui es in cælis: Sanctificétur nomen tuum: Advéniat regnum tuum: Fiat volúntas tua, sicut in cælo, et in terra. Panem nostrum quotidiánum da nobis hódie: Et dimítte nobis débita nostra, sicut et nos dimíttimus debitóribus nostris. Et ne nos indúcas in tentatiónem.
℟. Sed líbera nos a malo.
Amen.

Let us pray.
Taught by the precepts of salvation, and following the Divine commandment, we make bold to say:

Our Father, Who art in heaven, hallowed be Thy name. Thy kingdom come. Thy will be done on earth, as it is in heaven. Give us this day our daily bread. And forgive us our trespasses, as we forgive those who trespass against us. And lead us not into temptation.
℟. But deliver us from evil.
Amen.

> **The *Pater* is the perfect prayer. At the moment of receiving the Holy Eucharist, it orders the desires of our soul by expressing all that Our Lord taught us to desire and to request all that He Himself obtained for us.**

In the holy Mass, the *Pater* fits in its place like a gem. In it we find the four parts of the Catechism of the Council of Trent: the Creed, the Commandments of God and the precepts of the Church,

---

[1] Retreat, Le Barroux, August 1985.

the Sacraments, and prayer. The four parts of the Catechism are vitally present in the Mass; everything is united in the holy Church. We always find the fundamentals, that is to say, all the love God has shown to us.[2]

More than ever, we need to pray. Prayer is the respiration of our souls; prayer is the life of our souls. Prayer is the impulse the good God put in the spiritual, rational creatures that we are in order to lift us towards the One who is our Creator and our Redeemer, the One to whom we owe everything, Our Lord Jesus Christ.[3]

All the saints...had a very elevated notion of the life of prayer. Penetrating both the will and the heart, it enables us to attain the end for which God has created and redeemed us: namely, to adore Him in a total offering of ourselves, following the example of Our Lord coming into this world and saying to His Father: "*Ecce venio ut faciam voluntatem tuam*–Behold, I come to do thy will, O God" (Heb. 10:9)....

The conception that reduces prayer to vocal prayer or mental prayer is a disastrous one, for prayer should involve our whole being, like the prayer of the angels and the elect in heaven. The requests of the *Pater* cannot be separated. The first three requests are indissolubly linked. Likewise, the First Commandment of God cannot be separated from the other commandments.

"*Ignem veni mittere in terram et quid volo nisi ut accendatur*–I am come to cast fire on the earth: and what will I, but that it be kindled?" (Lk. 12:49). The fire is the Holy Ghost, the Spirit of Charity which fills the Holy Trinity and which created spiritual beings to set them afire with this charity.

This burning fire is the prayer of every soul adoring his Creator and Redeemer, surrendering itself to His holy will, following Jesus Crucified, who offered His life in a great transport of charity towards His Father and to save souls. Whence the "*oportet semper orare*–we must always pray" (Lk. 18:1). If that prayer ended, that would signify that the Holy Ghost had abandoned us![4]

---

[2] Retreat, Ecône, September 22, 1978.
[3] Homily, pilgrimage to Rome, St. John Lateran, May 24, 1975.
[4] *Spiritual Journey*, pp.27-28.

1. Our Father

"God is called *Father* for more reasons than one," the Catechism of Trent tells us.[5]

"Even some on whose darkness the light of faith never shone conceived God to be an eternal substance from whom all things have their beginning, and by whose Providence they are governed and preserved in their order and state of existence. Since, therefore, he to whom a family owes its origin and by whose wishes and authority it is governed is called *father*, so by an analogy derived from human things these persons gave the name Father to God, whom they acknowledge to be Creator and Governor of the universe. The Sacred Scriptures also, when they wish to show that to God must be ascribed the creation of all things, supreme power, and admirable Providence, make use of the same name. Thus we read: "Is not he thy Father, that hath possessed thee, and made thee and created thee?" (Deut. 32:6). But God, particularly in the New Testament, is much more frequently, and in some sense peculiarly, called the Father of Christians....

"Hence, when we say that the Father is the First Person, we are not to be understood to mean that in the Trinity there is anything first or last, greater or less. Let none of the faithful be guilty of such impiety, for the Christian religion proclaims the same eternity, the same majesty of glory in the Three Persons. But since the Father is the Beginning without a beginning, we truly and unhesitatingly affirm that He is the First Person, and as He is distinct from the Others by His peculiar relation of paternity, so of Him alone is it true that He begot the Son from eternity."[6]

2. Who art in heaven

It is good to think that God is everywhere. To think that God is with us, near us, in us, should be a source of love. We ought not think that the good God is far from us by misunderstanding the words of the Our Father: "Our Father, who art in heaven." It is a formula. The good God is particularly in heaven, of course, but He is always present near us. In our difficulties, our trials, our moments of weariness, it is a consolation to be able to say, "The good

---

[5] *Catechism of the Council of Trent*, pp.189-90.
[6] Retreat, Morgon, October 1988.

God is with me at my side." Being able to call upon Him at any moment, saying "My God, have mercy on me," is a consolation for us. God is always ready to help us. He always has the same desire for our sanctification. We can be tired of loving God because of our disordered attachments to creatures, but the good God never tires of loving us. This continual presence of God should be for us a great consolation. If we have this conviction, then in difficult moments we can rely upon Him with the certitude of being heard. It is not the good God who refuses us His graces; it is we who refuse to be with Him by negligence or discouragement.

3. Hallowed be Thy name

God is both unnameable and all-nameable; that is to say that there is no name that perfectly expresses what He is, and yet He must be given all the names that signify something positive, beautiful, great, or infinite. Unnameable is the most just of all the names, because it places Him from the outset above all that one could try to say. God is unnameable because a name would reduce Him; it would set limits to Him, but God has no limits. God cannot be grasped by our intellect. We know Him here below by grace, and we shall know Him in heaven by the light of glory, but our knowledge will remain imperfect. We shall not fully know the Divine essence, otherwise we would be God. St. Justin says: "These terms *Father, God, Creator, Lord,* are not Divine names; they are appellations taken from His benefits and works."[7] Let us piously admit our ignorance rather than proudly boast our knowledge. Only the Persons of the Trinity can know God perfectly and infinitely. As for us, we shall always be created beings, even with the light of glory by which we shall resemble God in a certain manner; but we shall never be God. And our happiness will be to find ourselves face to face with the infinite....

Even though God is infinitely above us, we can still try to meditate on what is said about Him by the authors who teach the knowledge of God. Since this will be our happiness in heaven, we might increase our happiness here on earth a little by knowing God better. Father Lessius, a Jesuit and professor at Louvain at the beginning of the eighteenth century wrote a book on the Divine names.

---

[7] *Apologia,* II, 6.

He has some very beautiful reflections on the Divine perfections. He says this: "That the knowledge of God is the rule of virtue, reason shows. The perfection of man consists in union with God, his origin and his last end. Now this union originates in knowledge, which is the foundation of all union with God. The first union is made by the understanding; from this union follows that of the heart by hope and love. The blessed in heaven themselves have no other law. All their affections and movements are formed according to the unique and most perfect rule of the knowledge of God. From this rule as from their source emanate all the teachings and examples of the saints."[8] This is a very precious little book that helps us to lift ourselves up towards God and to better understand who God is.[9]

How do you speak about the unnameable? We have seen that *unnameable* is the name that best fits God. However, if you want to give Him another name, you must open the Scriptures. In Exodus there is a passage in which God tells Moses His name: "Moses said to God: Lo, I shall go to the children of Israel, and say to them: The God of your fathers hath sent me to you. If they should say to me: What is his name? what shall I say to them? God said to Moses: I AM WHO AM. He said: Thus shalt thou say to the children of Israel: HE WHO IS, hath sent me to you" (Ex. 3: 13-14). So God Himself has taken care to give us His name: "HE WHO IS." It is not a very extensive explanation; nothing could be simpler. God is. And why precisely did God not add something to the verb *to be*? Precisely because whatever would have been added would have limited Him, whereas "HE WHO IS" possesses all being. St. Thomas says about this name: "HE WHO IS is before all other terms the proper name of God.[10] Since God's being is His essence, the name in question is His proper name *par excellence*. Secondly, this name is the most adequate by its universality. All the other Divine names present a less general signification. And thirdly, "HE WHO IS" signifies not only being, but being whose existence has neither past nor future.[11]

---

[8] [The Venerable Leonard Lessius, S.J., *The Names of God and Meditative Summaries of the Divine Perfections* (New York: The America Press, 1912).]
[9] Retreat, Morgon, October 1988.
[10] *Summa Theologica*, I, Q. 13, Art. 11.
[11] Retreat, Morgon, October 1988.

Natural theology gives us many little phrases which can be meditated on for a long time, I assure you: *Deus est ens a se*–God is being by His own power. But we exist by someone else; we exist by God: *Homo est ens ab alio*. One who is being by Himself has no cause. He always was. God has existed for ever. Our Lord says this several times in His discourses: "And now glorify thou me, O Father, with thyself, with the glory which I had, before the world was" (Jn. 17:5). "Before Abraham was, I AM" (Jn. 8:58). God cannot define Himself otherwise than "HE WHO IS," who exists, who has always existed and who possesses all that being can contain. All the qualities of being can be ascribed to God. God is infinite; He is good; He is almighty; He is eternal.

As for us, we exist by Him. Consequently, we depend upon Him continuously. This is fundamental. These affirmations are the basis of every philosophy, spirituality, and our moral life. The Catholic is someone who affirms his complete, total, continual dependence on God–whence his humility, his adoration, his profound reverence towards God, and his thanksgiving. In heaven, the discovery of all the divine attributes will be the cause of our happiness when we definitively close our eyes here below, provided that we die a happy death and our soul goes to heaven. Then we will tell ourselves: "I am with the good God for all eternity. I am with God, who possesses every quality, all possible and imaginable riches, all love!" We shall see the Persons of the Blessed Trinity like a sun. Contrariwise, the poor people who have spent their lives against God are appalled when they depart this world. They tell themselves: "How could I be against the good God?" But then it is over. It is too late. They are fixed in their bad will and their disobedience.[12]

Which of the Church's acts really places us in dependence on God, Our Lord Jesus Christ? It is the holy sacrifice of the Mass. The Mass is the heart of the Church; the Mass is the most beautiful, most profound, and most real expression of our dependence on God.[13]

---

[12] *Ibid.*
[13] Priests' retreat, Paris, December 13, 1984.

4. Thy kingdom come

The holy sacrifice of the Mass, my dear brethren, is nothing else than the proclamation of the reign of Our Lord Jesus Christ. "*Regnavit a ligno Deus*–God has reigned by the wood"[14] of the Cross. He vanquished the devil and sin by the wood of the Cross. Thus, by renewing the holy sacrifice of Our Lord and His Calvary on the altar, we uphold the kingship of Our Lord Jesus Christ; we affirm His Divinity.[15]

Do we not say in our daily prayer, the Our Father: "Thy kingdom come, Thy will be done on earth as it is in heaven"? But do we want that to happen? We know very well that it is difficult. We know that we must suffer very much. And in spite of that, we must have the lively desire that Our Lord Jesus Christ reign over ourselves, our family, and our society. That is why we want to conserve the holy sacrifice of the Mass, for, do not forget, Our Lord reigns by the Cross. Our Lord vanquished by His Cross, and He is King by His Cross. And His Cross is our Mass. The Cross is the Catholic Mass.[16]

By destroying, in a certain sense, our holy sacrifice of the Mass, they destroyed the affirmation of Our Lord Jesus Christ's Kingship and of His Divinity. And that is why adoration of the Blessed Sacrament has diminished in our time; or rather let us say that sacrileges have multiplied endlessly. Since the Council, it must be said– it's plain and clear–Our Lord Jesus Christ in the Blessed Sacrament has been relegated from our altars. He is no longer adored; people no longer want to genuflect before the Blessed Sacrament. And yet, that is the reign of Our Lord Jesus Christ: acknowledging that He is God, that He is our King, and consequently manifesting this love of Our Lord and the existence of His Divinity. As proof of this refusal of Our Lord's reign I need only point to the public event that just took place: In the United States, at the Eucharistic Congress of Philadelphia, was there a procession of the Blessed Sacrament? No, there was not–no more than there was four years ago at the Eucharistic Congress at Melbourne.[17]

---

[14] Cf. The *Vexilla Regis*, hymn for Vespers during Passiontide.
[15] Homily, Ecône, August 22, 1976.
[16] Homily, Friedrichshafen, October 24, 1976.
[17] Homily, Ecône, August 22, 1976.

You know what Cardinal Pie, Bishop of Poitiers, said to the Chamber deputies: One day someone told him: "But today it is no longer possible for Jesus Christ to reign over society." He replied: "If today it is no longer the time for Our Lord Jesus Christ to reign over societies, then it is no longer the time for societies to last."[18] He was perfectly right. We could give the same answer to the bishops who say the same thing. Now it is no longer Masonic or radical deputies but bishops who say: "It is no longer the time for Our Lord Jesus Christ to reign over the State." Well, we shall always say: Our Lord Jesus Christ must reign over the State, even if it is humanly impossible, even if those who rule no longer want it. We shall continue to affirm that Jesus must reign; we shall sing it, for Our Lord Jesus Christ must be King.[19]

5. Thy will be done on earth as it is in heaven

His reign must be established on earth as in heaven. It is He himself who said so in the prayer that He taught us, the Our Father: "Thy kingdom come, thy will be done on earth as it is in heaven." And this must be the object of our prayers, the intention of our sufferings, and the purpose of our life. We must have no rest until Our Lord's reign is established. A Catholic whose heart is not animated by this profound desire is not a Catholic. He is not one of the faithful of Our Lord Jesus Christ. It suffices to reread these lines: "Now at last in these times He has spoken to us, with a Son to speak for Him; a Son, whom He has appointed to inherit all things, just as it was through Him that He created this world of time" (Heb. 1:2).[20]

Our Lord Jesus Christ is King now. All power has been given to Him in heaven and on earth. "Thy will be done on earth as it is in heaven," says Our Lord. If, then, Our Lord's will must be done on earth, it means that His law, the Decalogue, must be applied on earth as it is in heaven. We must profess this even if churchmen want no more of it. This is what is dividing the Church at present. As for us, we want Our Lord's honor and the social kingship of Our

---

[18] Cf. Théotime de Saint-Just, *La royauté sociale de Notre Seigneur Jésus-Christ d'après le Cardinal Pie* (Ed. de Chiré, 1988), pp.76-79.
[19] Confirmations sermon, Doué-la-Fontaine, May 19, 1977.
[20] *The Mystery of Jesus*, p.25.

Lord Jesus Christ, which must be applied universally. We will fight for this, and we will do our utmost to crown Jesus Christ King.[21]

Because we speak of the social reign of Our Lord, we are accused of engaging in politics. If this is engaging in politics, then we want to do so, because we want Our Lord Jesus Christ to rule over us. We do not want to be governed by men who are not subject to Our Lord. If only all our rulers understood that they must be subject to Our Lord Jesus Christ, who is the King of kings, the Lord of lords! He is the King. He could have been the king on earth and continue to govern us. But He will be one day, when He descends upon the clouds in the heavens. Everyone will have to render an account to this King and Judge.

Meanwhile, today we want authorities, leaders, who know that they will render an account to God for the exercise of their power and their government. For we love to be subject to persons who do not believe themselves to be the authors of all power. Even if they have been elected by the people, the people do not have power; the people are not God. The people can designate the one who will exercise authority, but it does not give the authority; authority comes from God: "There is no power but from God," says St. Paul (Rom. 13:1).

This is the greatness of authority. This is the true foundation of the power of authority, whether civil or paternal. Paternal authority comes from God. Children know that when they are subject to their parents, they are at the same time subject to God. How beautiful this is; how well God has made things! But how men destroy them!

The Communists say that religion is a form of alienation. Yes, religion is an alienation in the sense that we convey our body, our soul, our understanding, and our will into God's hands. We alienate ourselves to give ourselves entirely to God, to the One who created us, who saved us, and who shed all His Blood for us. Love for love, we desire to alienate ourselves in order to give ourselves entirely to Our Lord Jesus Christ. So on this point we are in full agreement with what the Communists say about our holy religion. And I would say to these friends, who are in error: "You alienate yourselves for a party, for men; you place your nature, your strength,

---

[21] Homily, Fanjeaux, June 18, 1977.

and all that you have in the hands of men: that is a bad alienation. And that is not at all the order willed by God."

We do not want to be subject uniquely to men who will do with us what they will. We would not be allowed to think except as these men think. We would not be allowed to act except as these men want to make us act. No, we want to be subject to God and not to such men; but to men who are subject to God, yes, we are willing to be subject. That is what we think and what we want. We want to belong to Our Lord Jesus Christ, who is our King.[22]

6. Give us this day our daily bread

The special, sacramental grace of the sacrament of the Holy Eucharist is sustenance for our souls. Our Lord instituted the Blessed Sacrament to help us live. That is why this food should be taken daily. The Catechism of the Council of Trent emphasizes daily Communion, and St. Pius X thought it necessary to remind the people of the need for daily Communion, and the need to give Communion to young children and not to wait until they reach the age of ten or twelve, but to give it to them as soon as they reach the age of reason...: "It will therefore be the duty of the pastor frequently to admonish the faithful that, as they deem it necessary to afford daily nutriment to the body, they should also feel solicitous to feed and nourish the soul every day with this heavenly food. It is clear that the soul stands not less in need of spiritual, than the body of corporal food. Here it will be found most useful to recall the inestimable and divine advantages which, as we have already shown, flow from sacramental Communion."[23] As one of the characteristics of the Sacrament of the Eucharist is to be our nourishment, we need to receive it as often as possible, and every day if possible.[24]

7. Forgive us our trespasses as we forgive those who trespass against us

What was the sentiment that impelled Our Lord to effect this absolutely incredible, unimaginable, inconceivable work, namely, to give Himself as food for our souls? Undoubtedly, it was His charity–that's obvious. Our Lord can only act from charity. Can

---

[22] Homily, Besançon, September 5, 1976.
[23] *Catechism of the Council of Trent*, p.249.
[24] Easter retreat, Ecône, April 1, 1980.

there be anything even greater than the charity which is God? Yes, mercy; mercy is the plenitude of charity, because it is poured out on someone who has lost charity. In reality, charity should be repelled by someone who does not have charity; it should draw back from someone lacking charity. Now, we had lost charity, but Our Lord took care of us in our misery. He really wants to restore charity in us, on condition that we are disposed to receive it.

The priest too must have these sentiments in his heart. He must not spurn souls in their misery, sufferings, and difficulties; rather he should go to those who are in error in order to bring them the light of truth, to those in sin to try to restore to them supernatural life, the life of charity. The heart of the priest should be a merciful heart.

"Forgive us our trespasses, as we forgive those who trespass against us." Is this not what Our Lord says in the Our Father? "Blessed are the merciful, for they shall obtain mercy" (Mt. 5:7). It is the sentiment of mercy that dictated the most beautiful parables spoken by Our Lord, like that of the prodigal son or of the good Samaritan, and which guided His attitude towards the woman taken in adultery and all poor sinners. Let our heart too be merciful!

Our Lord did not want to reject us for ever. He took care of us; He dressed our wounds and healed us. He wants to heal us. So let the priest's heart also be always welcoming–not for compromises, not for watering down truth or diminishing God's grace, but for the sake of drawing souls to the truth and attracting them to the good God's grace. Let the heart of the priest be always sensitive to the miseries of the world: miseries of mind, will, and body. Let him carry out the works of mercy!

May the Mother of mercy, the most blessed Virgin Mary, make priests understand Our Lord's mercy in the sense that He Himself understood it so as not to deviate from it either by being too hard or too soft. May God pour forth into the hearts of our priests graces to be merciful.[25]

8. And lead us not into temptation

So many Catholics do not think of receiving Communion; they do not think of receiving Our Lord! Afterwards, they find that

---

[25] Sermon for ordinations, Ecône, August 25, 1977.

they prove to be weak under temptation, and they often sin. It is no wonder why. It is because they do not fortify themselves with Holy Communion; it is because they do not want to have Our Lord Jesus Christ in their heart to fight with them. Our Lord is there for that; He made Himself ours, and He remains with us until the end of time to help us.[26]

9. But deliver us from evil

It is a terrible thing to think that one can spend almost one's whole life–sometimes one's whole life, alas, for many–in a complete illusion, in a way of thinking completely out of touch with reality. People dispose of themselves, of what they are, their intellectual faculties, their will, their body, their goods–of all that they have–as if they were made for themselves, as if they had given themselves existence, as if they were masters of their destiny. A total illusion! It is unimaginable to think that millions of men, perhaps billions of men, live like that, without reference to God.[27]

We should strive every day to fight against this illusion and a false estimation of things. We live in blindness and error because we do not succeed in putting God in His right place in relation to the world and ourselves, and consequently we do not succeed in judging things by their just measure. This just measure is the wisdom the good God endeavors to give us by grace, by the gift of wisdom, by the gifts of the Holy Ghost, and by prudence. By all the virtues and the supernatural gifts, the good God endeavors to make us see things as He sees them Himself....That is what St. Thomas says: "Wisdom consists in seeing things according to the eternal reasons."[28] Now, if we were to consider our spiritual life according to the eternal reasons of God, I do not say that we would be right to tremble every day, but we would maintain the attitude which Our Lord often recommended to us: *Vigilate, vigilate, vigilate*–Watch, watch, watch!" Don't fall asleep. The end is coming. This end will lead you to an eternity either happy or unhappy! Consequently: Watch![29]

---

[26] Homily, Confirmations, Ecône, April 20, 1975.
[27] Spiritual conference, Ecône, September 20, 1976.
[28] *In rationibus aeternis* (a phrase reprised from St. Augustine) or also the "Divine reasons," *Summa Theologica*, II-II, Q. 19, Art. 6; Q. 45, Art. 2.
[29] Spiritual conference, Ecône, January 25, 1982.

Deliverance from Every Evil: *Libera Nos*

Líbera nos, quǽsumus, Dómine, ab ómnibus malis, prætéritis, præséntibus et futúris: et intercedénte beáta et gloriósa semper Vírgine Dei Genetríce María, cum beátis Apóstolis tuis Petro et Paulo, atque Andréa, et ómnibus Sanctis, da propítius pacem in diébus nostris: ut, ope misericórdiæ tuæ adjúti, et a peccáto simus semper líberi et ab omni perturbatióne secúri.

Per eúmdem Dóminum nostrum Jesum Christum, Fílium tuum.

Qui tecum vivit et regnat in unitáte Spíritus Sancti Deus.

Per ómnia sǽcula sæculórum.
℟. Amen.

Deliver us, we beseech Thee, O Lord, from all evils, past, present, and to come; and by the intercession of the blessed and glorious Mary ever Virgin, Mother of God, together with Thy blessed Apostles Peter and Paul, and Andrew, and all the saints, mercifully grant peace in our days: that through the help of Thy mercy we may always be free from sin and safe from all trouble.

Through the same Jesus Christ, Thy Son, our Lord.

Who liveth and reigneth with Thee in the unity of the Holy Ghost, God.

World without end.
℟. Amen.

When the evil to be combatted is particularly deep, like that done by the Freemasons; when it is particularly Satanic, reparation must be made by a spiritual action that is no less deep, under the immediate direction of Mary, terrible to the devil....In every apostle and even in every fervent soul in the Church Militant, there must be a spiritual commitment to the contemplative life and to this holy battle. This commitment consists in a self-offering renewed daily at holy Mass, with increasing devotion at the moment of consecration, the paramount act of the Savior's eternal priesthood. It involves the offering of the day's trials and tribulations by faithfully accomplishing our duty of state, as well as the supernatural acceptance of the daily sufferings Providence sends us. This must be united to a prayer that asks not for crosses, but for the love of the crosses the Lord from all eternity reserves for us to purify us and to make us work for the salvation of our neighbor.

A contemporary poet, Jacques Debout, in his dramatic poem "The Three Against the Other," expresses through the mouth of Satan, railing against Our Lord, the value of a single Mass. The devil of riches addresses Satan, saying: "What can God use against us? What can God do?"

Satan answers: "God stops us dead with the eternal Mass,
"Which crushed my head, and snatches every day
"Souls living and dead from underneath my sway.
"In the true life of nations, hidden from view,
"All Masses said are revolutions true
"Which are, for being unseen, the more profound
"And wreak such change as turns whole worlds around.
"Going far beyond the missal or its priest,
"Worldwide effects are by each Mass released;
"And when a mysterious obstacle stops me dead,
"I know that in some church, or barn, or shed
"A poor weak man held up that sacred sign,
"Of untold dread for me–the host and the wine."

Magnificent! Behold Satan crushed by the Mass. It is by the Cross that Our Lord vanquished the devil. There is no greater exorcism than the sacrifice of the Mass; there cannot be.[30]

A Prayer for Peace:
Pax Domini Sit Semper Vobiscum

Pax ✠ Dómini sit ✠ semper vobís ✠ cum.	May the peace ✠ of the Lord be ✠ always with ✠ you.
℟. Et cum spíritu tuo.	℟. And with thy spirit.

The fruit of the sacrifice of the Cross and of the sacrifice of the Mass is peace: peace in the souls and societies that welcome Our Lord and submit themselves to His law of love.

The prayers that the Church has us say before Holy Communion show that one of the main fruits of Calvary is peace. If anything were ever violent, it was the cruel death inflicted on Our Lord on Calvary: the Blood that flowed, the side pierced, the nails driven into His hands and feet. Yet, during the violence of the crucifixion, Our Lord experienced an unalterable peace, which is one of the fruits of the sacrifice of the Mass and of the Cross.

---

[30] Retreat, Ecône, September 1978.

Peace is the tranquility of order,[31] and order was re-established. The bridge was re-established between God and men by the sacrifice of the Cross, whence the importance of the sacrifice of the Mass, which is its continuation. Indeed, Our Lord re-established order by three victories: over the devil, over sin, and over death. Order was truly re-established.

The victory over the devil: "If the devil was not reduced to powerlessness, nevertheless his defeat is henceforth assured. The proof of this is the Church Triumphant and the Church Suffering in purgatory. There, souls are out of the devil's reach: they have triumphed; it is truly Our Lord's triumph. The devil knows it, but he pitilessly pursues those who have not yet reached heavenly beatitude. That is why we must make the resolution, by and through the strength the holy sacrifice of the Mass gives us, to conquer the devil, to shun all the scandals of the world, and to deliver all those for whom we are responsible from the grip the devil has on them."

The victory over sin: "The elect in heaven are delivered from the anguish that each of us always feels and that prompts us to wonder whether by our weakness, our negligence, our infidelities, we shall not also find ourselves in sin. We must always be vigilant so as to avoid sin and to gain the victory over sin, which is a particular grace of the holy sacrifice of the Mass."

Finally, victory over death: "Undoubtedly, we know that we shall die. But we also know that we have eternal life in us. If we are not defiled by sin, if we have grace within us, we can be convinced that we have eternal life. From this present moment, we have eternal life by the life of grace; we have already vanquished death. But we must maintain this life; we must protect it against all the dangers; we must sustain and nourish it by the Holy Eucharist. This is precisely one of the fruits of the sacrifice of the Mass."

So let us live in this peace. This peace is still relative because we have not personally reached the goal. We still have to march before receiving the crown. Even so, we must have peace of soul, since, by the holy sacrifice of the Mass, which is the continuation of the sacrifice of the Cross, we possess the strength and the grace that will enable us to vanquish the devil, sin, and death.[32]

---

[31] St. Augustine, *The City of God*, XIX, 13.
[32] Priests' retreat, Flavigny, June 27, 1976.

The Prayer *Haec Commixtio*

Hæc commíxtio, et consecrátio Córporis et Sánguinis Dómini nostri Jesu Christi, fiat accipiéntibus nobis in vitam ætérnam. Amen.

May this mingling and consecration of the Body and Blood of our Lord Jesus Christ avail us who receive It unto life everlasting. Amen.

The Eucharist is a pledge of everlasting life.

Why will you offer the holy sacrifice of the Mass, my dear friends? "That they may have life, and may have it more abundantly" (Jn. 10:10). This is also what Our Lord wanted: "That they may have life, and may have it more abundantly," because the sacrifice of the Mass has no other purpose than to give life. And what life? Not the life of this world, not the life of our bodies, but supernatural life, the divine life we had lost. Our Lord wanted to give us His own life, His divine life, to make us enter into the Blessed Trinity, every one of us, however little, however weak we may be. Our Lord wanted us to share in His divine life, and that is why He died on the Cross. Thus you will offer the holy sacrifice of the Mass to give life, and the fruit of the sacrifice of the Mass is the Eucharist, in which are present the Body, Blood, Soul, and Divinity of Our Lord Jesus Christ. How sublime all that is![33]

The Eucharist is the mystery of our hope. It was Our Lord Himself who said: "He that eateth my flesh, and drinketh my blood, hath everlasting life: and I will raise him up in the last day" (Jn. 6:55). He will be our resurrection. The body of Our Lord Jesus Christ present in our poor bodies is a gage of our resurrection. We already possess within ourselves everlasting life; this eternal life will not leave us. Even at the hour of our death, this germ of the resurrection of our bodies for eternity will be in our souls because we have received Holy Communion, because we have been united to Our Lord Jesus Christ in the Eucharist. It is Our Lord Himself who said it, and this Gospel was expressly chosen by the Church for the Mass of the dead.

---

[33] Homily, ordinations, Ecône, June 29, 1975.

The Eucharist is like a seed within us, a seed of our bodily resurrection, because in our Communion we partake of Our Lord Jesus Christ risen. He is in us with His risen body, His glorious body. Thus He is for us like a seed of resurrection. All these thoughts are so beautiful and consoling that we will never thank the good God enough for our being able to receive Holy Communion every day.[34]

Agnus Dei

Agnus Dei, qui tollis peccáta mundi: miserére nobis.

Agnus Dei, qui tollis peccáta mundi: miserére nobis.

Agnus Dei, qui tollis peccáta mundi: dona nobis pacem.

Lamb of God, Who takest away the sins of the world, have mercy on us.

Lamb of God, Who takest away the sins of the world, have mercy on us.

Lamb of God, Who takest away the sins of the world, grant us peace.

Holy souls feel a solidarity with all the souls and with all the sins committed in the world. As a consequence, they carry, in some way, the sins of the world as Our Lord carried them; they feel as if they were burdened with all the sins of the world. They want to imitate Our Lord and even to participate in Our Lord's sufferings, to share ever more closely in His Cross. That is what Our Lord asked of us; that is indeed what St. Paul says[35]: in some way, it is necessary to complete, insofar as it is possible, the Passion of Our Lord Jesus Christ.[36]

The priest in particular carries, in the likeness of His Divine Master, the sins of the world. If there is something at once mysterious, sorrowful, and profoundly heartening for the priest, it is the ministry of confession. In it, souls pour into the priest's heart all their woes, and the priest carries all the sins of the world in the absolute secret of the confessional. He carries them in sorrow and suffering like Our Lord Jesus Christ, but also in the joy of having been able to give Our Lord's Blood and, by the words of absolution, to have washed souls in the Blood of Our Lord Jesus Christ

---

[34] Easter retreat, Ecône, April 6, 1980.
[35] Cf. Col. 1:24.
[36] Retreat [to Dominican Teaching Sisters], Brignoles, July 27, 1984.

so that they might become white as snow and have spiritual life. If indeed the priest suffers from the moral wretchedness he beholds in souls, he thirsts to heal them as Our Lord did. Our Lord went about healing not only bodies but especially souls. This He did during the three years of His public life; this is what the priest does: he heals souls.[37]

We willingly look after the abandoned and the sick, of course, but spiritual misery is even worse, and it is precisely what must constitute the main object of the priest's solicitude. Above all, the priest must have a spirit of mercy towards those who are in a state of spiritual misery or spiritual sickness. The priest must feel within himself a merciful heart and be drawn by souls in a state of sin, so as to bring them life.[38]

Look at the Curé of Ars or St. Padre Pio. These priests spent their lives in the confessional because they knew that there they poured out the blood of Our Lord Jesus Christ by the absolution they gave souls, and because they supported these souls by their counsel. Many souls suffer in their heart things that they can only tell to the priest, that they can only tell to God. The priest carries that in the silence of his heart, since he must keep the secret of confession. He carries the crosses of the world. What a beautiful ministry![39]

New Prayer for Peace after the *Agnus Dei*

The unity of the Mystical Body realized in Holy Communion must be shown by the practice of fraternal charity.

DOMINE Jesu Christe, qui dixísti Apóstolis tuis: Pacem relínquo vobis, pacem meam do vobis: ne respícias peccáta mea, sed fidem Ecclésiæ tuæ; eámque secúndum voluntátem tuam pacificáre et coadunáre dignéris: Qui vivis et regnas Deus per ómnia sǽcula sæculórum. Amen.

O LORD Jesus Christ, Who didst say to Thy Apostles, peace I leave with you, My peace I give unto you: regard not my sins, but the faith of Thy Church, and vouchsafe to her that peace and unity which is agreeable to Thy will. Who livest and reignest, God, forever and ever. Amen.

---

[37] Homily, first Mass, Ecône, June 30, 1979.
[38] Spiritual conference, Ecône, March 26, 1989.
[39] Homily, Mantes-la-Jolie, July 2, 1977.

Communion is also the efficacious sign of the charity that should animate the Mystical Body of Our Lord Jesus Christ, for we are all members of this Mystical Body....It would be unacceptable that souls who partook of the same Body and Blood of Our Lord Jesus Christ should be divided. Charity should reign in the members of Our Lord Jesus Christ more than anywhere else. How can those who have partaken of the same Body and Blood, and of the same victim, Our Lord Jesus Christ, be divided; how can they not love one another? Certainly, the Sacrament of the Eucharist is the paramount cause of unity.[40]

I would like to emphasize the efficacy of the charity produced by the sacrament of the Eucharist. We too need this charity, we who believe, who have the Faith, who want to stay Catholic and Roman until the last moment of our lives. So we must remain in charity. This Sacrament is the sign and symbol of the love that emanates from Our Lord's charity. Yet how painful it is sometimes to think that people who nourish themselves daily with the Eucharist never manage to be completely dominated by the virtue of charity! They need to criticize, to form factions, to make rash judgments, to display antipathy towards persons to whom they should show sympathy. Well, then, let us who want to keep Tradition, this holy faith in the Blessed Eucharist, make the resolution today to also keep the fruit of the Holy Eucharist. It does not suffice to believe in it; it does not suffice to say that we are attached to the tradition of faith and hope in the Eucharist without having within us all its fruits. The fruits of charity are so good, they show so clearly the presence of Our Lord Jesus Christ in our souls![41]

---

[40] *Ibid*. The Magisterium frequently repeats this teaching: Innocent III (1202) speaks of "the power of unity and of love" (DS 782, Dz. 414); the Council of Florence: "The effect of this Sacrament [is that] man is incorporated with Christ and is united with His members" (DS 1322, Dz. 698); the Council of Trent presents the Eucharist as "a symbol of that unity and charity with which He wished all Christians to be mutually bound and united" (DS 1635 Dz. 873a); the effect of the Eucharist is that "we [are] united, as members, by the closest bond of faith, hope, and charity" (DS 1638, Dz. 875).
[41] Homily, Ecône, June 17, 1976.

The Prayer *Domine Jesu Christe*

DOMINE Jesu Christe, Fili Dei vivi, qui ex voluntáte Patris, cooperánte Spíritu Sancto, per mortem tuam mundum vivificásti: líbera me per hoc sacrosánctum Corpus et Sánguinem tuum ab ómnibus iniquitátibus meis, et univérsis malis: et fac me tuis semper inhærére mandátis, et a te numquam separári permíttas: Qui cum eódem Deo Patre et Spíritu Sancto vivis et regnas, Deus, in sǽcula sæculórum. Amen.

O LORD Jesus Christ, Son of the living God, Who according to the will of the Father, through the cooperation of the Holy Ghost, hast by Thy death given life to the world: deliver me by this, Thy most sacred Body and Blood, from all my iniquities and from all evils; and make me always adhere to Thy commandments, and never suffer me to be separated from Thee. Who with the same God the Father and the Holy Ghost, livest and reignest, God, forever and ever. Amen.

By its attachment to God's Commandments, the soul cleaves to Our Lord, Victim of love, and prays for the grace never to be separated from Him.

1. Make me always adhere to Thy Commandments

The union with Our Lord effected by reception of the Holy Eucharist must continue throughout our day by a fundamental disposition to do His will, to carry out our duty, and by a permanent desire to receive Him again as soon as possible in the Blessed Sacrament.[42]

To nourish the desire to follow the law of the good God and to be subject to Him, the Holy Ghost inspired Psalm 18: this psalm is admirable! "Blessed are the undefiled in the way, who walk in the law of the Lord. Blessed are they that search his testimonies: that seek him with their whole heart...." (Ps. 118: 1-16). How wonderful is this zeal to know and to follow the good Lord's law. It would be necessary to read the entire psalm, which is very long; all of it is inspired by the same zeal. We must reawaken this spirit regularly, this genuine desire to follow the law, because it is the only way to understand the necessity of the law; otherwise it can be understood as merely a kind of imposed regimentation, without a purpose....

---

[42] Notes for a sacerdotal retreat. Ecône Seminary archive, *O Mysterium Christi*, p.19.

In the Christian life there is what the spiritual writers call the will signified by the laws and then the will of good pleasure. God's expressed will is found in rules, in written laws. The will of good pleasure is made manifest either by superiors giving you a specific order for something or other not foreseen by the written rules, or by events, and especially by trials....

We priests must accept this will in a spirit of holocaust, in a spirit of oblation, in a spirit of sacrifice. The whole life of us who offer the sacrifice must be a life of sacrifice, of oblation in union with Our Lord's sacrifice. It is in this spirit that we must submit ourselves to the will of God spontaneously, willingly, generously.[43]

The internal law of God is charity. "God is love" (I Jn. 4:8). If God is Love, He can only do charity, and thus His creation was made in love. He cannot do otherwise than require us to love Him and to love our neighbor. Charity is also our law. It is a part of the very essence of creation. God creates us in love and obliges us to love Him in order to merit to be with Him for ever in heaven: that's all. And He asks us to love our neighbor for the good God's sake. We must love our neighbor for the good God. In truth there is only one love, the love of God, because when we love our neighbor, we love him for God's sake. There is only one love: the love of God.[44]

St. Thomas says that the distinction between the precepts of the Decalogue, which is summed up in the two commandments of the love of God and love of neighbor, is given for the sake of the weak. It is given for the weak because, says St. Thomas, everything is contained in the one precept of the love of God.[45] Indeed, we must love all things for God. There is only one end and one formal reason for practicing charity: the love of God, even if this love has several objects. We must love our neighbor for God[46]; we must love ourselves for God[47]; we must love all creatures for God. Hence the formal object of our love is always God, whatever may be the object loved. We must refer all things to God. St. Thomas also says: the very essence of charity consists in that God be loved above all and that man subject himself to Him totally, referring to Him all

---

[43] Spiritual conference, Ecône, September 23, 1977.
[44] Retreat [to Benedictine monks], Le Barroux, August 1985.
[45] *Summa Theologica*, II-II, Q. 44, Art. 2.
[46] *Ibid.*, III, Q. 23, Art. 5, ad 1.
[47] *Ibid.*, III, Q. 25, Art. 4.

that he has.[48] To refer everything to God: in this does our spiritual life consist.[49]

2. Never suffer me to be separated from Thee

The treasure which is the Passion of Our Lord must touch souls. The fear of sin must become the fear of being one of those who are the cause of the Lord's Passion. Having such a dread of paining Our Lord, of being separated from Him, of estranging ourselves from Him, we must act in such a way that we avoid sin at any cost, not only mortal sin, of course, but also venial sin and everything that would estrange us in some way from Our Lord. We pray for this in the beautiful prayer that precedes the Communion: "... never suffer me to be separated from Thee."

Let souls grasp the great mystery of Our Lord, the unfathomable mystery of the love of God for us. It is not only the mystery of creation, it is not only the gift of our existence, but it is the gift of the cross, of Our Lord crucified, an incredible mystery....Souls are made for that. This is not a matter of lofty mysticism, but of merely Christian mysticism: bring souls closer to the Cross of Our Lord Jesus Christ, and consequently to the holy sacrifice of the Mass....

Let us have no longer a mediocre life, telling ourselves, "Oh, I don't commit mortal sins; I try to be charitable, to lead a normal Christian life." That is not enough! Very many souls could take a step forward, and not content themselves with being Christians who merely try to do nothing seriously displeasing to Our Lord. That is one thing; it is something quite different to induce souls to participate in the sacrifice of Our Lord. Let souls truly become oblations, continual victims who offer their whole lives, their trials, all their difficulties and their duty of state (which is often painful to carry out), in marriage or in a profession: such must be our preoccupation.[50]

If only we had the care to render to the good God what He does for us, at least insofar as we can, we would be assured of making rapid progress in virtue, and especially of finding equilibrium in our spiritual life. From the time when I was in Africa as apos-

---

[48] *Omnia sua referendo in ipsum*: cf. *ibid.*, III, Q. 44, Art. 4.
[49] Spiritual conference, Ecône, March 26, 1981.
[50] Ordination retreat, Flavigny, June 1979.

tolic delegate, how often, unfortunately, I had the impression of inconstancy, of an incredible inconstancy, even in the spiritual lives of religious, nuns, and Brothers. One day all is joy, one is happy, everything is fine; the next day, nothing is left.[51]

The Boon of Communion: *Perceptio Corporis Tui*

Perceptio Córporis tui, Dómine Jesu Christe, quod ego indígnus súmere præsúmo, non mihi provéniat in judícium et condemnatiónem: sed pro tua pietáte prosit mihi ad tutaméntum mentis et córporis, et ad medélam percipiéndam: Qui vivis et regnas cum Deo Patre in unitáte Spíritus Sancti, Deus, per ómnia sǽcula sæculórum. Amen.

Let not the partaking of Thy Body, O Lord Jesus Christ, which I, unworthy, presume to receive, turn to my judgment and condemnation; but through Thy goodness may it be to me a safeguard and remedy both of soul and body. Who with God the Father, in the unity of the Holy Ghost, livest and reignest, God, forever and ever. Amen.

1. The Eucharist has a medicinal effect

Catholic doctrine is a doctrine that enlightens souls and compels them to banish sin. It leads them to tell themselves: "I must get rid of my shortcomings and defects and my sins so that my soul will be ready to receive graces from Our Lord and be transformed in Him." This is what the Church has always taught. For this reason she asks missionaries to preach the gospel to the whole world and to carry the grace of Our Lord to souls, and to transform souls in Our Lord. Whence the importance of the holy sacrifice of the Mass, which is the continuation of the sacrifice of the Cross and the application to souls of Our Lord Jesus Christ's Blood, which renews them, which transforms them by the manducation of the Eucharist.

"May the partaking of Thy body be to me a remedy." This we pray to Our Lord in the prayer before receiving Holy Communion: Give me your remedy. It is the propitiatory act of Our Lord renewed every day. We must be convinced of our need of a remedy.[52]

---

[51] Retreat to Sisters, Albano, September 1976.
[52] Priests' recollection, Paris, December 13, 1984.

2. The Eucharist lessens lust

The Eucharist has for effect to keep us pure and unsullied from all sin. It is a heavenly antidote that prevents us from being poisoned and corrupted by the deadly venom of evil passions, especially lust. It is the bread of virgins. That is why it is necessary to highly recommend Communion to people today, and also to couples, who have so many difficulties staying faithful to God's law in the conjugal domain....

The Eucharist is the remedy. People used to receive Holy Communion frequently in olden days. Christians nourished themselves with the Eucharist because it is a specific remedy for reducing our concupiscence. In the Eucharist, we receive the Author of every grace in us, the One who is precisely the opposite of sin, who is the contrary of concupiscence: Our Lord Jesus Christ.[53] Insofar as one receives Our Lord Jesus Christ with the necessary dispositions, the fire of concupiscence abates and souls rest in peace; they are not always tormented by these problems. "The Eucharist restrains and represses the lusts of the flesh, for while it inflames the soul more ardently with the fire of charity, it of necessity extinguishes the ardor of concupiscence."[54] [55]

THE ATTITUDE OF THE CENTURION: *DOMINE, NON SUM DIGNUS*

DOMINE, non sum dignus, *and he continues in a low voice* ut intres sub tectum meum, sed tantum dic verbo, et sanábitur ánima mea.

LORD, I am not worthy that Thou shouldst enter under my roof, but only say the word, and my soul shall be healed.

1. Lord, I am not worthy

We are sick people, and we repeat three times before receiving Holy Communion: "Lord, I am not worthy that Thou shouldst enter under my roof, but only say the word, and my soul shall be

---

[53] Priests' retreat, Ecône, September 1980.
[54] *Catechism of the Council of Trent*, p.244. St. Thomas teaches us that the Eucharist remits our venial sins, a part of the punishment due to sin, and preserves us from future sins (*Summa Theologica*, III, Q. 79, Art. 4-6).
[55] Easter retreat, April 1, 1980.

healed." We need the Physician of our souls. The remedy is Our Lord Jesus Christ, His Cross, His Blood; it is Holy Communion. In Holy Communion we receive Our Lord Jesus Christ immolated on the Cross; He it is who heals our souls. Knowing this, we must accept suffering and penance in reparation for our sins, so that our souls can be restored to the order willed by God.[56]

2. And my soul shall be healed

People no longer want it said that our souls are sick. But if we will not acknowledge our infirmity, then how should we seek penance; how should we look for the remedies of penance, mortification, and self-denial, which attract Our Lord's grace, which attract the remedy which is Our Lord Himself? "Say but the word and my soul shall be healed": We must have this attitude constantly. All of this is an opportunity to maintain our humility. "Say but the word and my soul shall be healed." I can do nothing without Thee; I cannot save myself without Thee. Vouchsafe to save me; be my soul's Physician: This is what we say to Our Lord before receiving Him. When we kneel before the Eucharist, we profess our dependence on God.[57]

While receiving Holy Communion, a loving glance at the Blessed Virgin should express our gratitude to her.

It is impossible to think of the Eucharist without thinking of the most Blessed Virgin Mary, for, after all, if the most Blessed Virgin Mary had not uttered her *Fiat*, we would not have the Holy Eucharist either. It is because she spoke her *Fiat* that today we have the joy, the happiness, to possess Our Lord Jesus Christ in our tabernacles and on our altars. Let us then ask the most Blessed Virgin Mary to give us the charity she knew so well and that she admired in her Son Jesus.[58]

---

[56] December 8, 1984.
[57] Priests' recollection, Paris, December 13, 1984.
[58] Homily, Ecône, June 17, 1976.

The Priest's Communion

PANEM cæléstem accípiam, et nomen Dómini invocábo.

I WILL take the Bread of heaven, and call upon the name of the Lord.

CORPUS Dómini nostri Jesu Christi custódiat áni

MAY the Body of our Lord Jesus Christ preserve my soul unto life everlasting. Amen.

If Our Lord is the bread of life, He was also the bread of life on the Cross; and it is by sharing in His holy Cross that we receive this fruit, which is the parallel of the bad fruit that poisoned our first parents. The fruit that we receive today from the Cross is Our Lord in the Holy Eucharist. He gives us life, whereas the fruit of the tree of good and evil gave death to our first parents.[59]

While the nourishment of the body is transformed into our substance, during Communion the opposite happens. The nourishment we receive transforms us into itself; we truly become members of Our Lord. The body of Our Lord does not become our body or soul, but our entire being truly becomes a member of Our Lord Jesus Christ. The effect is contrary to food's usual effect.

St. Augustine places in Our Lord's mouth these words: "I am the food of strong men; grow, and thou shalt feed upon me; nor shalt thou convert me, like the food of thy flesh, into thee, but thou shalt be converted into me"[60]

The good God has done an admirable thing. "He that eateth me," says the Lord, "the same also shall live by me" (Jn. 6:58). "The bread that I will give, is my flesh, for the life of the world" (Jn. 6:52), transforming us in Our Lord, increasing grace in us. This is an effect of the sacramental grace, the particular grace, of the Eucharist.

---

[59] Homily, Ecône, March 15, 1975.
[60] St. Augustine, *The Confessions*, Book VII, Ch. 10, §16.

The Priest's Thanksgiving

Quid retríbuam Dómino pro ómnibus, quæ retríbuit mihi? Cálicem salutáris accípiam, et nomen Dómini invocábo. Laudans invocábo Dóminum, et ab inimícis meis salvus ero.

What shall I render to the Lord for all He hath rendered unto me? I will take the Chalice of Salvation, and call upon the Name of the Lord. Praising, I will call upon the Lord and I shall be saved from my enemies.

The priest renders thanks to God for the sublime gift that configures him to Jesus crucified. He promises to take the chalice of salvation and call upon the name of the Lord.

I think that a priest, by reason of his sacerdotal character, since he lives with Our Lord at the altar in a quite extraordinary, exceptional, mysterious way, and he follows Our Lord more closely than all other creatures, has a duty to strive to follow Our Lord by carrying his cross, by doing penance with Our Lord, by sacrificing himself with Our Lord. Of course, this is the role of all Christians, especially of religious, but even more especially, it is the role of the priest. Can you imagine a priest who goes up to the altar every morning and pronounces the words of consecration, who is united to Our Lord in an absolutely extraordinary way–who has been especially chosen by the good God–and who would say that he is not a religious and that he is not obliged to practice the virtues of chastity, obedience, and poverty like those who have taken religious vows. Must they follow Our Lord or not?

"*Si quis vult discipulus meus esse*–If any man will come after me, let him deny himself, and take up his cross daily," (Lk. 9:23) says Our Lord. The priest is indeed he who must carry Our Lord's Cross and follow him.[61] "*Tollat crucem suam quotidie*–let him take up his cross daily," says Our Lord. Every day we must carry our cross following Our Lord Jesus Christ if we want to grow in holiness, if we want to have eternal life.[62]

---

[61] Conference to the Sisters, Ecône, November 21, 1974.
[62] Homily, Flavigny, July 5, 1977.

The Priest's Drinking of the Precious Blood

Sanguis Dómini nostri Jesu Christi custódiat ánimam meam in vitam ætérnam. Amen.

May the Blood of our Lord Jesus Christ preserve my soul unto life everlasting. Amen.

The great charity that we must have for Our Lord is ignited by contact with the Lord's Blood, which is the manifestation of His love for us. We need the Blood of Our Lord Jesus Christ in order to love Jesus. That is why He sacrificed Himself: to prove His love for us and so that we would give Him ours in return. "*Sic nos amantem, quis non redamaret*–So true a lover, shall we not requite Him?"[63][64]

It is with respect to the relation which each soul has with Jesus Crucified that the judgment of God will be delivered. If the soul is in a living relation with Jesus crucified, then it prepares itself for eternal life and already participates in Jesus' glory by the presence of the Holy Ghost in it. It is the very life of the Mystical Body of Jesus. "If anyone abide not in Me, he shall be cast forth as a branch, and shall wither, and they shall gather him up, and cast him into the fire, and he burneth" (Jn. 15:6).[65]

All the virtues are expressed in Jesus crucified, and these virtues are roused in us: faith, hope, charity–whence the importance of the holy Mass, which assimilates us to the Divine Crucified.[66]

Confiteor

The prayer of the *Confiteor* recited before Communion disposes souls to receive all the fruits of the Eucharist well.

1. How to prepare ourselves for Holy Communion

We receive Our Lord's grace in the Sacrament of the Eucharist in proportion to our dispositions. Many people observe that since the time they began communicating, they are still the same. But do

---

[63] From the Christmas carol *Adeste, Fideles*.
[64] Homily, Flavigny, July 5, 1977.
[65] *Spiritual Journey*, p.44.
[66] Carmel of Brilon Wald; Ecône Seminary archives.

you go to the trouble to prepare yourself, to have your heart really free of everything? Empty your heart completely so that the good God can fill it! If you always keep the same self-centeredness, the same loves, the same disordered attachments, it is impossible for Our Lord to be Master of the house. This is very important, even for the faithful, because the faithful who come and communicate frequently may be fine folks, but they too can just walk in place because they fail to prepare their souls to receive Our Lord.[67]

It is an extraordinary gift to be able to participate in the Cross of Our Lord every day, to participate in it most intimately by nourishing ourselves with the Body and Blood of Our Lord Himself. All the effects of the Holy Ghost, who is given to us at the same time, are poured forth in our souls. Assuredly, our souls then are souls of desire, souls open to receive Our Lord. How could our souls not grow in perfection; how could our souls not take a little step forward in perfection if they were truly well disposed? For it is important to know that even if the sacraments work *ex opere operato*,[68] as the theologians say, and not only *ex opere operantis*,[69] it is no less true that the virtue of the sacraments is greater in well-disposed souls. If souls are not well prepared, the grace that is given by the sacrament itself will not have the same effects because the soul's disposition is like its capacity to receive the graces the good God wants to give it. If we have a restricted capacity, if we are attached to many things that have nothing to do with Our Lord, if we are not attached to the good God more than to everything else, if we are much more preoccupied by things here below than by the things of God, obviously the graces will be less abundant. That is why it is very important to prepare souls for the sacraments. It would not be worth the trouble to prepare if the reception of a sacrament automatically, invariably gave as many graces.

That is why it is necessary to prepare the souls of children for their First Holy Communion and confession. We too must prepare ourselves for our communion: we must be recollected, pray, ask God for all the graces we need, be sorry for our sins, make an act of contrition–whence the *Confiteor* before receiving Holy

---

[67] Retreat, Le Barroux, August 1985.
[68] The sacraments of themselves impart grace.
[69] According to the dispositions of those receiving the sacraments.

Communion–and ask pardon again for all the faults and failings we may have committed, so that our soul may be as pure as possible for receiving the Divine Guest who comes in us.[70]

Since the good God deemed that the most Blessed Virgin Mary should be immaculate in her conception in order to receive the body of Our Lord Jesus Christ, His soul and His Divinity, we too must make efforts to render our souls immaculate. Let our souls become immaculate by our dispositions, by our efforts, by the good God's grace. Let them conquer the gift which the most Blessed Virgin Mary had as a privilege. We must live on guard against everything that can tarnish our souls, so that it also might be said of our souls: "*Tota pulchra es, et macula non est in te*–Thou art all fair, and there is not a spot in thee" (Cant. 4:7). Thus shall we worthily receive Our Lord Jesus Christ.[71]

2. Imitate the simplicity of children

Imagine, my dear brethren, just try to recall the moments of your life in which you felt the presence of Our Lord Jesus Christ in the Blessed Sacrament. I am sure that on the day of your first Holy Communion–remember the blessed moment of your first Communion–you thanked God for receiving His Body and Blood. How well you were prepared by your parents and by the priests who loved you and who led you to the holy table with an infinite respect for your hearts and souls, which were going to become the temples of the Body and Blood of Our Lord Jesus Christ!

And since that day, how many times have you approached the Blessed Sacrament to ask for the special graces you needed for yourselves, your families, your children, the sick, perhaps for members of your family that were straying away from Our Lord Jesus Christ! Then you made a more fervent Communion and asked Our Lord: "Save souls, do not abandon them! Do this out of love for them! Show Your mercy!"[72]

We must have the dispositions of children towards these mysteries of faith. Children live in the simplicity of their heart, in the simplicity of their mind. They don't make problems for themselves.

---

[70] Retreat, Brignoles, July 27, 1984.
[71] Homily, Ecône, December 8, 1972.
[72] Homily, Ecône, June 17, 1976.

It suffices to tell them, "That's the way things are. It is like that." These children believe their parents. For us, it is God who has revealed these things. Often we are like the Jews to whom Our Lord said: "Except you eat the flesh of the Son of man, and drink his blood, you shall not have life in you" (Jn. 6:54). And the Jews said: "How can this man give us his flesh to eat?" (Jn. 6:53). From that day, many parted company with Our Lord because their reason wanted to look for an explanation of what the Lord was telling them. On the contrary, those who believed followed Our Lord. We also believe that we eat the flesh of Our Lord and drink His blood. If we do it with the simplicity of children who believe what their Father told them, then we receive this flesh and blood in the best dispositions.[73]

Behold the Lamb of God: *Ecce Agnus Dei*

Ecce Agnus Dei, ecce qui tollit peccáta mundi.

Behold the Lamb of God, behold Him Who taketh away the sins of the world.

Domine, non sum dignus, ut intres sub tectum meum, sed tantum dic verbo, et sanábitur ánima mea.

Lord, I am not worthy that Thou shouldst come under my roof. Speak but the word and my soul shall be healed.

Our Lord, the Paschal Lamb, gives Himself as nourishment to the faithful and invites them to participate in His victimhood.

By meditating on the love of Our Lord on the Cross, we will also be more disposed to receive the Victim, to partake of the Victim who offered Himself on the Cross. For we should think that this is what the Eucharist signifies in its reality. It is Our Lord as Victim. In the Sacrament of the Eucharist, there is not just a pure presence, but He is there with a certain character, the character of a victim. The Paschal lamb is the figure of both the sacrifice and the Eucharist. The Jews immolated the Paschal lamb and they ate it afterwards; they partook of the victim. Our Lord is henceforth the Paschal Lamb; He is immolated, offers His sacrifice, and gives Himself to be eaten by us as the Victim, as the Victim of love,

---

[73] Homily, Brannay, July 15, 1979.

Victim of His charity. I think that these considerations inculcate in us an excellent disposition for receiving Our Lord and being ready to make this oblation, which is the essence of sacrifice, a total self-offering unto immolation. We too must make this total offering in receiving the Eucharist. We must produce within ourselves this total offering, this total sacrifice of ourselves to God and to our neighbor with perfect love, with the most ardent love possible.[74]

By communicating, we participate in the Victim who offered Himself. We also participate in the state of victimhood, in the state of a soul that offers itself with Our Lord, that offers its whole life with Our Lord....

Our whole life is a cross that we carry with Our Lord. We are victims with Our Lord....There is not an act that we do, from morning to night, from night to morning—provided that it be in conformity with the law of the good God and that we offer it with Our Lord—that is not meritorious, that does not merit for us eternal life. How this orientation transforms life! How capable one is to bear the difficulties of family life. That is what makes the union and the strength of Catholic homes, and which encourages them to bear their crosses together.[75]

The Communion of the Faithful

In giving Holy Communion, the priest has the unheard-of privilege of realizing his most beautiful dream.

What is the most beautiful dream a priest can have? What is the best thing he can do? He can do nothing greater, richer, more supernatural, or more divine than to give Our Lord Jesus Christ. Now, when does the priest give Our Lord Jesus Christ? When he gives the Holy Eucharist to souls. The priest prepares souls to receive Our Lord Jesus Christ, and he gives Him to them—that is his mission. By giving Our Lord, he gives heaven to souls, he gives them eternal life, he forgives their sins. He gives them all that is

---

[74] Homily, Ecône, April 6, 1980. Pius XII wrote in *Mediator Dei*: "In order that the oblation by which the faithful offer the divine Victim in this sacrifice to the heavenly Father may have its full effect, it is necessary that the people add something else, namely, the offering of themselves as a victim" (§98).

[75] Homily, Massongex, March 20, 1977.

most great, most beautiful. And Our Lord wanted the priest to offer first the sacrifice of the Cross so that souls might be nourished by its fruit. Just as Eve poisoned humanity by the forbidden fruit she ate in the terrestrial Paradise, so the priest communicates life to souls by the fruit of the tree of the Cross which is Our Lord Jesus Christ. The priest gives this Bread of Life, the true fruit of eternal life. Men could no longer take the fruit from the tree of life in the terrestrial Paradise. On the contrary, here is the tree of eternal life again returned to earth, and this tree communicates to us eternal life. It give us the Son of God Himself, the life of God itself: the pledge of our eternal life, the pledge of Paradise. What can a priest do that is more beautiful. What is there more beautiful in the life of a man than to give Our Lord Jesus Christ to others?[76]

Communion Kneeling

We can never show enough reverence, nor ever worship the Eucharist with adequately heartfelt veneration. That is why throughout the ages it has been the custom in the Church to receive the Holy Eucharist kneeling. We should receive the Holy Eucharist prostrate, and not standing. Are we the equals of Our Lord Jesus Christ? Is it not He who will come upon the clouds of heaven to be our Judge? When we see Our Lord Jesus Christ, shall we not do as did the Apostles on Thabor when they prostrated themselves to the ground in terror and wonder at the greatness and splendor of Our Lord Jesus Christ? Let us keep in our hearts and souls that spirit of worship, that spirit of profound reverence for Him who created us, for Him who redeemed us, for Him who died on the Cross for our sins.[77]

> **To receive the Eucharist is to receive Our Lord, our King, and our High Priest who becomes Victim for our salvation. More broadly, communicating is to receive the Blessed Trinity.**

If we really have faith in the Blessed Sacrament, we must think that we are receiving Him who holds all things in His hands, who by nature is King: King of the earth, without whom no one can move his little finger or think a single thought, be he pagan,

---

[76] Homily, sacerdotal ordinations, Ecône, June 29, 1974.
[77] Pilgrimage to Mariazell, Austria, September 8, 1975, *A Bishop Speaks*, p.219.

Freemason, or what have you. No man here below can act or make use of the being God gave him and gives him at every instant without the omnipotence of Our Lord Jesus Christ.[78]

In the Sacraments we receive Our Lord Jesus Christ Himself. But it is not only Our Lord Jesus Christ whom we receive in Holy Communion: we receive the three Persons of the Blessed Trinity.[79]

The Thanksgiving

If any Sacrament should inspire our thanksgiving, it is this one. Reception of Holy Communion is the occasion for us to meditate and consider all that the good God has done for us.[80]

"If thou didst know the gift of God" (Jn. 4:10). What do we know about it, we who are privileged to receive Our Lord Jesus Christ in Holy Communion? Do we know the gift of God; do we know that God is truly in us, and that we are temples of the Holy Ghost? Do we know that God is not simply present in our souls as in all creatures, nor solely in our minds by the knowledge that we have of His existence, nor even by the knowledge that we may have of Him by our faith? No, He is truly physically, really, substantially present in our souls by the gift of grace which makes us His children; and not merely adopted children as in the world, in which the parents who adopt a child cannot give it their substance nor communicate to it their nature. But God, by making us His adopted children, communicates His own nature to the point that He recognizes Himself in us because we truly participate in the Divine nature by the grace the good God gives us.

Behold the gift of God: God gives Himself to us truly, in such wise that little by little, if we are faithful to His grace, the charity God expects to see in us can bloom, a love quite different from that of those who do not know God by grace.[81]

Can there be a religion in which God makes Himself closer to men than He does in the Catholic religion? God does not deem it

---

[78] Spiritual conference, Ecône, March 1974.
[79] March 1980. The Father and the Holy Ghost are inseparable from the Son. Thus they are present, but not by strict concomitance (as is the case for the Divinity, Soul, and Blood under the species of bread). Indeed, the body of Christ is not united substantially to the Father and the Holy Ghost.
[80] Homily, Ecône, Easter 1980.
[81] Homily, St-Michel-en-Brenne, September 22, 1974.

an abasement to come to us and to give Himself to us in His Body and Blood. God does not lower Himself; He remains God. It is we who must manifest our reverence and our adoration of Him. It is not because God acts with simplicity and manifests His charity towards us that we should despise Him. On the contrary, we should thank Him for having this immense charity, this infinite, Divine love to stay near us.[82]

1. The Eucharist is the heart of all the Sacraments

The Catechism of the Council of Trent has this to say on the subject of the virtue and fruits of the Sacrament of the Eucharist:

> But with regard to the admirable virtue and fruits of this Sacrament, there is no class of the faithful to whom a knowledge of them is not most necessary....As, however, no language can convey an adequate idea of its utility and fruits, pastors must be content to treat of one or two points, in order to show what an abundance and profusion of all goods are contained in those sacred mysteries.
>
> This they will in some degree accomplish, if, having explained the efficacy and nature of all the Sacraments, they compare the Eucharist to a fountain, the other Sacraments to rivulets. For the Holy Eucharist is truly and necessarily to be called the fountain of all graces, containing as it does after an admirable manner, the fountain itself of heavenly gifts and graces, and the author of all the Sacraments, Christ Our Lord, from whom, as from its source, is derived whatever of goodness and perfection the other Sacraments possess. From this (comparison), therefore, we may easily infer what most ample gifts of divine grace are bestowed on us by this Sacrament.[83]

A commentator of St. Thomas[84] compares the Eucharist to the sun. The Eucharist is like the center, while the other Sacraments are the rays.[85]

As the doors of the Hebrews were marked with the blood of the lamb so that the exterminating angel would not slay their firstborn, the Blood of Our Lord Jesus Christ must be in us, mark us, which is what is produced by baptism. But as St. Thomas explains,

---

[82] Homily, Ecône, June 17, 1976.
[83] *Catechism of the Council of Trent*, pp.241-42.
[84] Fr. Roguet, *Les Sacraments* (Paris: Ed. Revue des Jeunes, 1945), p.377.
[85] Priests' retreat, Ecône, September 1980.

baptism and the other sacraments revolve around the sacrament of the Eucharist and the sacrifice of the Mass.

The Eucharist is the heart of all the sacraments because in the others, graces come from Our Lord Jesus Christ, while in the Eucharist and in the Mass, it is Our Lord Jesus Christ Himself who comes, the source of all graces. Baptism prepares us and makes us worthy of the worship of God at Mass. Normally, the non-baptized would have to stay at the door of the church. Only the baptized can enter and attend the holy sacrifice. Thus, baptism is ordered to the Eucharist.[86]

2. The Eucharist is heaven

What is the grace you receive in the Sacrament of the Eucharist? It is no more or less than the communication of Our Lord Jesus Christ's divine life to you. Our Lord Jesus Christ came down upon the earth; He took a body like ours in order to communicate to us His Divine life. If today we could see souls as they are, the souls of those in a state of mortal sin would appear to us as leprous, or ulcerous, or afflicted by a dreadful malady. If today the good God revealed what souls in a state of grace look like, we would be amazed; we would think it is impossible for a soul in the state of grace to be so beautiful, so divine, so luminous, so full of charity! Grace is the good God in our souls; it is Jesus in our souls. And Jesus is nothing else than heaven.[87]

God is heaven; Jesus Christ is God; consequently, when we receive God in our hearts, we can truthfully say, "I have heaven in my soul; I have Paradise in my soul." It would behoove us to be united to this Paradise in such a way that we would be prepared for the lasting Paradise, which will consist in being in the glory of Our Lord Jesus Christ for eternity.

Only the true religion can possess such treasures. Only God could have invented such grand and beautiful expressions of His love and His charity for us.[88]

---

[86] Homily, St-Michel-en-Brenne, April 2, 1989.
[87] Homily, Doué-la-Fontaine, May 19, 1977.
[88] Homily, Unieux, July 1, 1979.

3. The Eucharist is our consolation

Imagine a Christian life without the Eucharist! What would we be without Our Lord Jesus Christ, without this extraordinary gift God gave us? What orphans we would be; how alone we would feel, a little abandoned by the good God. But with the Eucharist, when we need to speak to Him, to see Him, to tell Him that we love Him, or when we need special help we can go to our sanctuaries and kneel before Our Lord Jesus Christ, alone perhaps before the Blessed Sacrament. Surely it has happened to you to say to the good God before the Blessed Sacrament: "Come to my help; help me, I have worries and trials. Help my family; help my children." And when you departed, you left the church comforted. And that is what you have felt, I am sure, after every Sunday Mass. How many times it has happened to us as priests to assist the dying. How many times we have had to bring Communion to the sick. What a joy it was for these suffering souls to receive God from the hand of the priest. What a consolation! What a source of courage it was for them. By this Sacrament, Our Lord Jesus Christ worked an extraordinary miracle of His love. Consequently, we too must show Him our love.[89]

4. Communion is the source of civilization

Understand, my dear faithful, that in Holy Communion we unite ourselves to God, to Our Lord Jesus Christ: that is the source of Christian civilization. In Holy Communion, Jesus manifests Himself as our Savior and also as our King: the King of our intellects by giving us the truth; the King of our hearts and wills by giving us His commandments to help us act in accordance with His holy will. Then, going back home, the Christians who nourished themselves with the Body and Blood of Our Lord Jesus Christ understand better what their duty is, how they must conduct themselves in daily life at home and in society. Conversely, to the extent that priests no longer celebrate the holy sacrifice of the Mass, our Christian civilization is reduced to nothing.[90]

---

[89] Homily, Ecône, June 17, 1976.
[90] Homily, First Mass, Besançon, September 5, 1976.

Prayers During the Ablutions

Quod ore súmpsimus, Dómine, pura mente capiámus: et de múnere temporáli fiat nobis remédium sempitérnum.

Grant, O Lord, that what we have taken with our mouth we may receive with a pure mind; and that from a temporal gift it may become for us an eternal remedy.

Corpus tuum, Dómine, quod sumpsi, et Sanguis, quem potávi, adhǽreat viscéribus meis: et præsta; ut in me non remáneat scélerum mácula, quem pura et sancta refecérunt sacraménta: Qui vivis et regnas in sǽcula sæculórum. Amen.

May Thy Body, O Lord, which I have received, and Thy Blood which I have drunk, cleave to my heart; and grant that no stain of sin may remain in me, whom Thy pure and holy sacraments have refreshed; Who livest and reignest world without end. Amen.

After Communion, all the prayers express the desire that our soul remain always united to Our Lord.

It is no longer possible to have the virtue of purity, so they say. But quite simply, they can no longer have it because they no longer avail themselves of the means to keep it. God's gifts and His will remain the same today as a century ago, ten centuries ago, fifteen centuries ago. But some want no part of it or do not profit from it. So they complain that they lack the strength: "In our time, in our time..." But let them avail themselves of the means the good God gave them; they will see that they have the same effects. This is a very important thing that must be kept in mind: family prayer, the Sacrament of Penance, the reception of Holy Communion.

Besides, we still see it; there are still, thanks be to God, Christian homes where the spouses live in continency and live as the good God requires them to live, as Christian parents, desirous of having many children and of bringing them up as good Catholics.[91]

One effect of the Holy Eucharist is the remission of venial sins. There is no doubt that the Eucharist remits–pardons–the slight sins ordinarily called venial. It is like bodily food, which gradually repairs our bodily strength and restores what we lose during the day by the effect of natural heat. This is what St. Ambrose pertinently

---

[91] Homily, Ecône, April 6, 1980.

says on the subject of this heavenly Sacrament: "Our daily bread is a remedy to our daily weaknesses."[92]

Nevertheless, that only applies to sins to which we are no longer attached, for if we remain attached to them, they cannot be remitted. Obviously, souls must be well disposed for their sins to be remitted.[93]

The Postcommunion Collect

The collect that concludes the holy Mass shows once again the Church's desire that the sacrifice offered be a source of fidelity to Our Lord and of everlasting life for the faithful who have taken part.

This nearness of God in His redemptive sacrifice will produce in souls...the same effects, *mutatis mutandis*, experienced by the privileged souls who have received Our Lord's stigmata. The effects are twofold. The first determine the second and are their source. These are the contemplative aspects: an ardent desire for complete oblation as victim in union with the divine Victim, the love of God Our Lord unto the sacrifice of self, complete surrender to the holy will of God, and an ardent union with the pierced heart of Our Lord.

The effects of the Spirit of love, which was manifested on the Cross and continues to be manifested on the altar and in the Eucharist, tend to withdraw the soul from the world, to make it despise fleeting and material things for the sake of eternal and spiritual things. The soul experiences a great horror of sin, profound contrition for its faults, and an immense desire to expiate its own sins and those of others.

We must give thanks to God for communicating to us His Spirit of love and of sacrifice for His Father's glory.[94]

---

[92] Citation from a book of St. Ambrose (*De Sacramentis*, V, 25). This explanation is adopted by St. Thomas Aquinas, *Summa Theologica*, III, Q. 79, Art. 4.
[93] Priests' retreat, Ecône, September 1980.
[94] *Cor Unum*, January 14, 1982, pp.60-61.

The *Ite, Missa Est*

℣. Dóminus vobíscum.
℟. Et cum spíritu tuo.

℣. Ite missa est.
℟. Deo grátias.

℣. The Lord be with you.
℟. And with thy spirit.

℣. Go, the Mass is ended.
℟. Thanks be to God.

At the end of Mass the soul has only one desire: to sing its gratitude to Our Lord and to praise the Blessed Trinity. It carries within a weight of eternity that fills it with the joy, courage, and confidence to make of its life a hymn of praise to the glory of the Blessed Trinity, origin and end of every human life.

1. The Mass has an eternal weight[95]

The more one studies the Mass, the more one perceives that it is truly an extraordinary mystery. It is truly the mystery of our faith. The priest appears as someone who no longer belongs to time, who almost steps into eternity because all of his words have an eternal worth....It is not a simple rite performed today; it is an eternal reality that truly transcends time and redounds to the glory of God and to the salvation of the souls in purgatory and the sanctification of our souls. Every Mass truly has an eternal weight.[96]

2. The Mass, divine praise and a means of ministry

The great reality to contemplate is the holy Mass. The members of the Society should be characterized by their contemplation of Our Lord crucified, seeing therein the summit of God's love, a love pushed to the supreme sacrifice. Such is Our Lord! This is the chief subject of the Church's contemplation. So doing, we shall be missionaries by our desire to pour out the Blood of Our Lord on souls. That is the *mysterium fidei* to contemplate and to effect, the sacerdotal work *par excellence*. The faithful gather around us because of the holy sacrifice of the Mass, not for something else. You cannot be linked to the Cross of Christ without being missionary.[97]

---

[95] Cf. II Cor. 4:17.
[96] Spiritual conference, Ecône, March 23, 1981.
[97] Spiritual conference, Ecône, December 3, 1982.

Nothing is small, nothing is petty in the service of such a Lord and King. Let us always be aware of it. The liturgy is a very effective means of ministry. If the liturgy is first and foremost the praise of the Blessed Trinity, an oblation and sacrifice and source of divine life, it is also the most vivid and effective form of catechesis. We can never do enough to enhance our liturgical ceremonies and to make our faithful and catechumens participate in these mysteries, which are the great means of apostolate, the only means that is really and truly efficacious, because it is the one Christ Himself chose as He chose us, too.[98]

THE INVOCATION OF THE BLESSED TRINITY

PLACEAT tibi, sancta Trínitas, obséquium servitútis meæ: et præsta; ut sacrifícium, quod óculis tuæ majestátis indígnus óbtuli, tibi sit acceptábile, mihíque et ómnibus, pro quibus illud óbtuli, sit, te miseránte, propitiábile. Per Christum Dóminum nostrum. Amen.

MAY the performance of my homage be pleasing to Thee, O Holy Trinity; and grant that the sacrifice which I, though unworthy, have offered up in the sight of Thy Majesty, may be acceptable to Thee, and through Thy mercy be a propitiation for me and for all those for whom it has been offered. Through Christ our Lord. Amen.

The liturgy orientates souls towards the life of the Trinity, origin and end of all God's plans.

One may say in truth that God is Trinity because He is Charity. How could He be Charity if there were only one person in God? God is then a burning furnace of charity in which the Three Divine Persons know and love one another eternally.

The office of the Holy Trinity crowns the entire liturgical year. The Holy Trinity is the great mystery by which all of God's plans are accomplished. Everything proceeds from the Holy Trinity, and everything returns to the Holy Trinity. Nothing is explained, nothing is understood, nothing exists without the Holy Trinity, the inexhaustible and eternal source of Charity, and this both within the mystery itself of the Triune God and outside the Trinity.

---

[98] Superiors' meeting, Diocese of Dakar, April 17, 1960, pp.5-6.

"*Caritas Pater est, gratia Filius, communicatio Spiritus Sanctus, O Beata Trinitas*–The Father is charity, the Son is grace, the Holy Ghost is their communication: O Blessed Trinity!" "*Ex quo omnia, per quem omnia, in quo omnia, ipsi gloria in saecula*–From Whom are all things, by Whom are all things, in Whom are all things, to Him be glory forever" (Antiphons from the Feast of the Holy Trinity). "Now doth the fiery sun decline / Thou, Unity Eternal, shine; Thou, Trinity Thy blessings pour, And make our hearts with love run o'er" (Hymn of Vespers for Trinity Sunday).

How this meditation on the Triune Charity and Charity-Trinity is comforting and encouraging, as it is also a source of unity![99]

The bundle of all the prayers which had their origin in the Church, those formulated, grouped, and harmonized for acts ordained by her, forms that wonderful liturgy which is the expression of the faith, hope, and charity of the Church on earth regarding God through Our Lord Jesus Christ. The thought of this liturgy is first and foremost directed to God, who draws the Church into the life of the Trinity. The Father rejoices in His Church, where He everywhere finds His beloved Son, whose one desire was to inflame the Church with His Spirit of Truth and Love, and thus truly assume it into the life of the Trinity.

But just as all that is born of the Trinity is created to live by and to return to it, so the Church, in the likeness of the Trinity and in its spirit of love, draws all those souls which come to her and hear her call to that new divine life in Jesus through the Holy Ghost. She gives them birth, she gives them food, and transforms them in and through her liturgy. It may be truly said that the liturgy is indeed the bosom of the Church where souls find all for which they hunger, the perfect food for their spiritual life, the teaching of truth, the understanding of true values in their due order, the school of all the virtues.[100]

---

[99] *Spiritual Journey*, pp.9-10.
[100] Letter to All the Members of the Congregation of the Holy Ghost on the First Session of Vatican Council II, *A Bishop Speaks*, p.7.

The Final Benediction

The priest lifts his eyes one last time towards the altar crucifix, then he turns to the faithful to bless them. The Mass concludes as it began: under the sign of the blessed Cross, the source of order restored in charity.

Benedícat vos omnípotens Deus. Pater, et Fílius, ✠ et Spíritus Sanctus. ℟. Amen.	May almighty God bless you. The Father, and the Son, ✠ and the Holy Ghost. ℟. Amen.

Order was restored by the Cross, and life and Christian spirituality are nothing other than the re-establishment of the order that was destroyed by the privation of grace.[101]

Apparently the Cross would signify sacrifice rather than love, yet in truth it signifies love more, which is the cause and finality of sacrifice.[102]

The crucifix is sculpted, living love on the Cross. Thus the desire of all holy souls to have a crucifix before their eyes and to seek in it the mainstay and source of their spiritual life is understandable. How great was the desire of these souls to attend the holy sacrifice of the Mass and to participate in it in order to relive Calvary, to relive what the most Blessed Virgin Mary lived and so to compassionate the sufferings of Our Lord Jesus Christ.[103]

The Last Gospel

The priest finishes the Mass by reading the most beautiful page of St. John's Gospel by way of thanksgiving.

In princípio erat Verbum, et Verbum erat apud Deum, et Deus erat Verbum. Hoc erat in princípio apud Deum. Omnia per ipsum facta sunt: et sine ipso factum est	In the beginning was the Word, and the Word was with God, and the Word was God. The same was in the beginning with God. All things were made by Him, and without

---

[101] Spiritual conference, Ecône, December 3, 1974.
[102] Notes for a priests' retreat, September 5-9, 1983. Ecône Seminary archives, *O Mysterium Christi*, p.3.
[103] Homily, Ecône, September 14, 1975.

nihil quod factum est: in ipso vita erat, et vita erat lux hóminum, et lux in ténebris lucet, et ténebræ eam non comprehendérunt. Fuit homo missus a Deo, cui nomen erat Joánnes. Hic venit in testimónium, ut testimónium perhibéret de lúmine, ut omnes créderent per illum. Non erat ille lux, sed ut testimónium perhibéret de lúmine. Erat lux vera quæ illúminat omnem hóminem veniéntem in hunc mundum. In mundo erat, et mundus per ipsum factus est, et mundus eum non cognóvit. In própria venit, et sui eum non recepérunt; quotquot autem recepérunt eum, dedit eis potestátem fílios Dei fíeri: his, qui credunt in nómine ejus: qui non ex sanguínibus, neque ex voluntáte carnis, neque ex voluntáte viri, sed ex Deo nati sunt. ET VERBUM CARO FACTUM EST, et habitávit in nobis: et vídimus glóriam ejus, glóriam quasi Unigéniti a Patre, plenum grátiæ et veritátis.
℞. Deo grátias.

Him was made nothing that was made. In Him was life, and the life was the light of men; and the light shineth in darkness, and the darkness did not comprehend it. There was a man sent from God, whose name was John. This man came for a witness to give testimony of the light, that all men might believe through him. He was not the light, but was to give testimony of the light. That was the true light that enlighteneth every man that cometh into this world. He was in the world, and the world was made by Him, and the world knew Him not. He came unto His own, and His own received Him not. But as many as received Him, He gave them power to become the sons of God: to them that believe in His Name, who are born not of blood, nor of the will of the flesh, nor of the will of man, but of God. AND THE WORD WAS MADE FLESH, and dwelt among us; and we saw His glory, the glory as it were of the only-begotten of the Father, full of grace and truth.
℞. Thanks be to God.

The best way to place Our Lord Jesus Christ in our spiritual life, in our thoughts, in our minds, in our heart, and in our whole soul, is to reread the most beautiful, most evocative pages of Scripture. In the Gospel and the Epistles, there are pages by St. John and St. Paul that show us what idea these Apostles conceived of the person of Our Lord Jesus Christ. Our life here below as in the hereafter consists in our being united to Our Lord and participating in His Divine life.

In the liturgy, too, there are very beautiful expressions that convey what Our Lord must be for us. The most beautiful page of St. John is the one we read every day at the end of the holy Mass as thanksgiving: the prologue of his Gospel. Doubtless we have read and reread it and know it by heart. But we still need to reread it attentively, peacefully, so as to penetrate our minds with what St. John writes of Our Lord, for it is truly the revelation of Our Lord. The first five verses treat of the person of the Word.

"In the beginning was the Word, and the Word was with God, and the Word was God." As the commentators point out, these words mean that before there was a beginning, the Word was. He existed. The use of the imperfect tense expresses this concept best. One could not use the perfect tense, but only the imperfect tense in order to express the eternity of the Word before all things began.

"And the Word was with God, and the Word was God." In this verse, the consubstantiality of the Word and the Father is discernible. By the very fact that the Word was with God, He was near Him and at the same time He was God; there is at once distinction and unity. One might believe that what was later defined by the Church as consubstantiality is an invention of the Church or the Fathers or the philosophers who taught in the Church and coined this term. Under the pretext that this word is not explicitly found in the Gospel, one might believe that it does not truly represent the reality of revelation in the Gospel. But that is false. The Gospel expresses this truth very clearly, and one cannot conclude otherwise as regards the Holy Trinity than by consubstantiality. Thus, the Word was God.[104]

"In Him was life, and the life was the light of men." The life mentioned here is especially spiritual life. St. John affirms that all intellectual and spiritual life in us comes from the Word. It is like a continual communication of the light that is in God. This light is diffused and comes to us by the intermediary of the Word. It is this light that illuminates our minds. We would be incapable of the least intellectual conception, of formulating an idea or reasoning, without the Word's light.[105] All that our intellect studies, conceives, or produces occurs under the illumination of the Word. It is a marvelous thing!

---

[104] Spiritual conference, Ecône, January 29, 1980.

[105] The light, even natural, of reason is a participation of the Divine light which is the Word.

"And the light shineth in darkness, and the darkness did not comprehend it." What does St. John mean? What is he revealing to us about Our Lord? This light, which is Our Lord, which is the Word, and which is projected in us to make us understand things, shone in the darkness–intellectual darkness, obviously–but the darkness did not comprehend it. Here St. John is revealing the blindness of men. While this light was given to men firstly to make them know God, to make them know the Word, the darkness did not understand it.

Men's blindness has limited, in a certain sense, this light, which was not used for the purpose for which God gave it to them. That is the meaning of *the darkness*, this willful blindness of men who do not want to know the light as the good God sent it to them. Not only does this regard purely intellectual light, but also the light of all spiritual life in man. All that limits this spiritual life in man, all the sins, constitutes what St. John calls *the darkness*.

One might consider that St. John drew close to Our Lord as no other Apostle. He was chosen in a particular way, because it is to him that the Lord confided His mother. St. John is called "the disciple whom Jesus loved."[106] Our Lord had a preference for him, and surely He gave him special graces to know Him better and more deeply than the others. That is why, by imbuing ourselves with his words, we in our turn can try to have an idea like that which he was able to make of Our Lord.[107]

It is terrible to think that all that Our Lord did, that all God does for us, might be in vain. It is terrible to think that, despite all that God has done, there might not be any response to this love. From this realization, we can understand that the justice of God permits and wills that those who refuse this love not enjoy it for all eternity. It is a frightening consideration, about which God Himself can do nothing, for it is man himself who closes the way to the love of God in him; who refuses to recognize Our Lord Jesus Christ, God Creator of all things; who shuts himself up in his self-centeredness and pride, refusing all light.

As St. John wrote: "And the light shineth in darkness: and the darkness did not comprehend it" (Jn. 1:5). God came to His own

---

[106] Cf. Jn. 13:23; 19:26.
[107] Spiritual conference, Ecône, January 29, 1980.

The Communion

family, and His own rejected Him, except those to whom the good God has given the grace to be children of God (cf. Jn. 1:11-12).[108]

"He was in the world, and the world was made by Him, and the world knew Him not" (v. 10) St. John the Evangelist employs a type of repetition. He repeats that the world was created by the Word, but that the world did not know Him. He had already spoken of the darkness that did not receive the light, that resisted the light. "He came unto His own, and His own received Him not" (v. 11). One can surmise that he is speaking particularly of the Jews, but this can also be attributed to the world. It was He who made it, and men did not receive Him.

Through these words, the dogma of original sin and the division that exists in the world between the Light and darkness can be understood. The Word came to His own, but His own did not receive Him. This is the foreshadowing of the conflict between the two cities: the city of the devil and the city of God.

"But as many as received Him, He gave them power to become the sons of God" (v. 12). Meanwhile, some received Him: to those who received Him, He gave the power to become sons of God.[109]

Let us be a part of the "*quotquot autem receperunt eum*–He gave them power to be made sons of God" (Jn 1:12). These words weigh heavily in the history of souls. They are eternally powerful and will separate the just from the unjust. Jesus is not optional. "*Qui non est mecum, contra me est*–He who is not with Me is against Me." To deny this is the fundamental error of religious liberty and ecumenism.[110]

"To them that believe in His name" (v. 12). Those who believed in Our Lord, designated by St. John the Baptist, received the power to become sons of God. This affirmation is extremely important for us. It would seem that we are sons of God by the fact that we are creatures. If God created us, we are already, in some sense, His spiritual sons, since the light that enlightens every man that comes into this world comes from God. But no, there is another, higher filiation. It is one thing to be a creature, another to be a son: the difference is affirmed by this passage. The dogma of

---

[108] *The Mystery of Jesus*, p.34.
[109] Spiritual conference, Ecône, January 29, 1980.
[110] *Spiritual Journey*, p.39.

grace, the dogma of the Divine filiation raises us infinitely higher than the creature's filiation by nature.

"Who are born not of blood, nor of the will of the flesh, nor of the will of man, but of God" (v. 13). St. John emphasizes the fact that the divine filiation does not result from a man's will; it does not come from flesh or blood–it comes from God: *ex Deo nati sunt*.[111]

"And the Word was made Flesh" (v. 14). The consequences of the union of the Word of God, of God Himself, with a human soul and body..., are such that they truly make of this human creature a subject unique in His kind, more divine than human, and more spiritual than corporal. Our Lord's entire life proves it. He lives more in heaven than on earth, for He is heaven. His Person has all power over His soul and His body, even to separate and reunite them as He wishes and when He wishes. His glory, His power, His sanctity, His wisdom, the permanence of the eternal mission which comes from His Father, in the exact realization of His temporal mission of salvation, all these shine forth in His life, in His acts, and in His words.[112]

"And of His fulness we all have received, and grace for grace" (v. 16). Thus we receive no grace that does not come to us through Our Lord Jesus Christ. All these words are of prime importance because they constitute the foundation of our faith and the principles of our daily life.[113] It is extraordinary to find expressed in so few lines almost the whole of our *Credo*, or at least the main outlines of our spiritual life. And with that concludes St. John's vision of the coming of the Word and the divine filiation of all those who receive the light, who receive the truth.[114]

The humility and charity inculcated throughout the Mass communicate to the priest and faithful joy and peace.

How beautiful it is to see the faithful surrounding the priest and singing, as you have just done all together, the praise of the good God![115]

---

[111] Spiritual conference, Ecône, January 29, 1980.
[112] *Spiritual Journey*, p.39.
[113] *The Mystery of Jesus*, p.16.
[114] Spiritual conference, Ecône, January 29, 1980.
[115] Homily, Una Voce, May 20, 1973.

We must leave the holy sacrifice of the Mass conscious that we who are nothing united ourselves with Him who is all. And we must draw from our contact with Our Lord Jesus Christ the feeling that we have spent hours in heaven, in Paradise. How we ought to be filled with humility and the spirit of adoration before Him who is our All![116]

What an admirable act of charity is this offering of Our Lord on the Cross for the honor and glory of His Father and the salvation of our souls! What a lesson! How should we not leave our churches after the holy sacrifice of the Mass more eager to honor God, to give Him glory, and to love our neighbor?[117]

How beautiful Sunday Mass is, with all the faithful gathered around Our Lord Jesus Christ, participating in His Passion, receiving His Body and Blood; and going home with peace in their souls, joy in their hearts, and ready to suffer if need be with Our Lord Jesus Christ and to bear better their trials![118]

I would say that joy seems in some way to erupt at the exit from Mass when faces beam with faith, charity, and the peace of Our Lord Jesus Christ.[119]

Every time, we should leave our altars and these sacred mysteries with our hearts full of a renewed charity for loving God and for singing His glory, for loving our neighbor and for carrying the gospel to the world.[120]

---

[116] Homily, Ordination to the diaconate and minor orders, Ecône, April 3, 1976.
[117] Homily, Châtelperron, August 25, 1977.
[118] Homily, Ecône, June 17, 1976.
[119] Homily, reception of the habit, Flavigny, July 5, 1977.
[120] Homily, Ordination to the subdiaconate and minor orders, Ecône, March 15, 1975.

PART TWO

The *Novus Ordo Missae*[1]

---

[1] The new rite is called the N.O.M., that is, *Novus Ordo Missae*, or the new order of the Mass.

I. What Was the Liturgical Reform?

Introduction

Was a Liturgical Reform Possible and Desirable?

At the time of the Second Vatican Council, Archbishop Lefebvre was not opposed in principle to a reform of the liturgy. He observed that the liturgy is first and foremost the public worship of God for His praise and honor before being a simple means of instructing the faithful. To those who tend to underestimate the traditional liturgy, Archbishop Lefebvre would respond that a lack of appreciation for the liturgy is caused more by spiritual apathy than by the liturgy itself. Consequently, to be effective, liturgical renewal must transform the souls of the faithful inwardly and contribute to the extension of Our Lord's reign within civil society.

1. The basis for a liturgical reform

...[W]e should find deep rejoicing on seeing in our contemporaries a great desire to live by the liturgy and a new reverence for this incomparable source of the Spirit of God. It was the duty of the Council to encourage these holy aspirations by guiding and directing them.

This desire to restore the liturgy to its true place in Christian life is felt today by the whole Church. The early Popes were the first to originate such a renewal, thereby simply expressing a desire deeply felt by many bishops, priests, and laymen. Is it not thus deeply and sweetly that the Holy Ghost acts?

However, the question of what may be called the liturgical renewal poses fundamental problems for the whole Church. What, indeed, is the function of liturgy in the apostolate of the Church? Should any reform of the liturgical entity built up in the course of the centuries relate to liturgical worship or specifically to the liturgy as an instrument of the apostolate? Would it not be to undervalue the liturgy to reduce it to such a function and no longer regard it in the light of public worship and the praise of God? Did this undervaluing of the liturgy arise mainly from the liturgical presentation of acts and teachings which keep an intrinsic living value, or did it, on the contrary, take its origin in the decline of faith and the spirit of religion among believers, and that for reasons remote from the liturgy?

Human activity has again become so foreign to God, so removed from its Creator and His life-giving spirit, that religious souls long to restore the broken links between prayer and action. It would be all too easy, childish even, to lay to the charge of today's liturgy in its forms of action and expression, the decline of belief among the faithful and to regard it as the sole, or at least the principal, cause. Pope Pius XII said to parish priests and Lenten preachers:

> When we look at the humanity about us and wonder whether it is able and willing to receive within itself the reality of this supernatural life, it is clear that for many the answer cannot be yes. The supernatural world has become strange to them and means nothing to them any more. It would seem as though the spiritual organs giving knowledge of such lofty and salutary truths had atrophied or died in them. There has been an attempt to explain such a state of soul by defects in the liturgy of the Church. It has been held that were it purified, reformed and held in respect, those who today have gone astray would find their way back to the road of the sacred mysteries. Whoever reasons thus shows a very superficial conception of such spiritual anemia and apathy. Their roots go deeper.[2]

Let us then admit without hesitation that some liturgical reforms were necessary, and that it is desirable that the Council should continue on that path until it sees fit to draw a halt, for it is unthinkable that missals, breviaries and rituals, *etc.*, should be changed every ten years, just as it is inconceivable that the official texts and translations should continually be amended.

If, however, this liturgical renewal is to be fully effective, it may be necessary to restore the links between liturgical prayer, the praise of God, the natural and supernatural links, with daily activities. This was, and still is, the work of the missionary Church: "*Omnia*

---

[2] Pope Pius XII, Allocution "*In meno di un anno,*" February 17, 1948.

instaurare in Christo." "Omnia," that means "above all" the family, the school, the community, the professions, the city. This work must be done again with the help of Christian families and the cooperation of all organizations for Catholic Action and others dedicated to bringing about the kingdom of Our Lord.

In order to establish the sphere of liturgical reform correctly, one must clearly show that the liturgy, which is primarily the praise of God, is public worship and truly the prayer of society–of the community in all its aspects. The graces of the liturgy descend upon the Christian people and upon the world to sanctify it in all its activities.[3]

Faced with some quite unfortunate liturgical innovations, Archbishop Lefebvre relies upon a speech of Pope Paul VI to show the place and function of the liturgy. As early as 1965, he deplored the suppression of statues in churches and the replacement of Latin hymns with songs of lesser merit in the vernacular. The church has become more a house of men than the house of God. While making this observation, Archbishop Lefebvre nonetheless remained open to certain reforms, especially in the first part of the Mass, on condition that they be in conformity with the purest tradition of the Church, and that they lead souls to a personal union with Our Lord present in the Blessed Sacrament.

2. Principles to uphold in any liturgical reform

The place and function of the liturgy are admirably outlined by the Holy Father in a succinct but vigorous exposition. "In it," said the Pope,[4] "we find homage to the scale of values and duties: God holds first place, prayer is our first duty." Then comes the function of the liturgy, "the chief source of divine life...the chief school of the spiritual life, the chief gift we can offer to a Christian people." In a few lines the Holy Father puts forward an entire program. Finally comes "an invitation to the world to unseal lips once mute–to sing with us the praises of God." It is an ardent appeal to those who do not yet pray with the Christian people.

---

[3] Letter (of March 25, 1963) to All the Members of the Congregation of the Holy Ghost on the First Session of Vatican Council II, *A Bishop Speaks*, pp.8-9.

[4] Paul VI, Allocution at the close of the second session of the Council, December 4, 1963.

Then, in a second paragraph, the Holy Father studies the relationship of the liturgy to the Church, stressing the capital importance of the liturgy in the life of the Church. "The Church is a religious society, it is a community of prayer." He warns urgently that if some simplifications are made, they in no way involve "a diminution in the importance of prayer or its subjection to the other concerns of the sacred ministry and pastoral activities, or weaken its power of expression or its artistic beauty." This must be kept in mind for the right interpretation of all future decrees.

"To achieve this result," ends the Holy Father in a third paragraph, "we do not want any attack on the traditional prayer of the Church by the introduction of private reforms or special rites. We do not wish that anyone should take it on himself arbitrarily to anticipate the application of the constitution. The nobility of the Church's prayer lies in its harmony throughout the world. Let no man trouble it, let no man injure it."

Strong, vigorous words, made necessary, alas, by the incredible experiments witnessed by thousands of the faithful, powerless and deeply grieved. Many indeed are the churches where the rules of liturgy are violated with impunity. Even graver, perhaps, than liturgical innovation itself on the part of the priests concerned is the example of open disobedience by those who have promised obedience and should be a model of that virtue to others.

The official decrees of the Holy See will soon be made public. It is to be hoped that the first result of their publication may be an end to private initiative.[5]

3. A few suggestions for reform

Amidst all the antagonisms, exaggerations, and discussions which have characterized this period of liturgical change, may a few reflections be outlined? In view of the speed, rare in the Church, with which these changes have been carried out in all countries, it is difficult to avoid the fear that some measures may bring unforeseen and unhappy consequences. It is thus with devotion to the Blessed Sacrament and devotion to the Virgin Mary and the saints, whose statues have been banished from many churches, regard-

---

[5] "After the Second Session of the Second Vatican Council" (January 21, 1964), *A Bishop Speaks*, pp.20-21.

less of the simplest pastoral teaching and catechetics; the meet and proper ordering of the house of God, which has become a house of men rather than a house of God; the truly divine beauty of the Latin chants, which are now banned and have not been replaced by other such melodies.

Must we, however, conclude from these considerations that all these things should have been kept unchanged? The Council, with temperance and prudence has answered otherwise. Some reform and renewal was needed.

Despite today's confusion of ideas, may we seek the light of the new dawn that the Council will bring to the world? Such perspectives will doubtless be more easily discoverable in a few years. Is it not devoutly to be wished, however, that those who have lived through the Council should strive, in perfect submission to the Successor of Peter, so to bring them about as to arouse true and generous undertakings sprung from the purest tradition of the Church and born of the Spirit of God yet living in His Spouse?

The first part of the Mass, intended for the instruction of the faithful and as a means of expressing their faith, clearly stood in need of a means of achieving these ends more plainly and, in some way, more intelligibly. In my humble opinion, two of the reforms proposed for this purpose appeared useful: first the rites of this first part and some vernacular translations.

Let the priest draw near the faithful, communicate with them, pray and sing with them, stand at the lectern to give the readings from the Epistle and Gospel in their tongue, sing the *Kyrie*, the *Gloria*, and the *Credo* with the faithful in the traditional divine melodies. All these are happy reforms restoring to this part of the Mass its true purpose. The arrangement of this teaching part of the rite should set, in the sung Masses of Sunday, the pattern to which other Masses should conform. These aspects of renewal seem excellent. Let us add, above all, guiding lines necessary for true, simple, and moving preaching, strong in faith and resolution. That is one of the most important ends to achieve in the liturgical renewal of this part of the Mass.

Where the Sacraments and sacramentals are concerned, the use of the language of the faithful in admonitions may be useful since these concern them more directly and personally, but this is not the case with exorcisms, prayers, and benedictions.

The arguments for keeping Latin in those parts of the Mass which take place at the altar are, however, so strong that it is to be hoped that the days may shortly come when a limit will be set to the invasion by the vernacular tongue of this treasury of unity, of universality, a mystery that no human tongue can express or describe.

How deeply we must long that the souls of the faithful may be united in spirit and in person with Our Lord present in the Eucharist and with His divine spirit, so that all that might be prejudicial to this union, whether by an excess of vocal prayers and ceremonies, by lack of reverence for the Eucharist, or by unseemly vulgarization of the divine mysteries, must be wholly prohibited. Any reform in this domain can be good only if it ensures more fully the essential ends of the divine mysteries established by Our Lord and brought down to us by Tradition.[6]

4. We have never refused certain changes

Catholics who feel that radical transformations are taking place have difficulty in standing up against the relentless propaganda they encounter (and which is common to all revolutions). They are told, "You can't accept change. Yet change is part of life. You're static. What was good fifty years ago isn't suitable to today's mentality or way of life. You're hung up on the past. You can't change your ways!" Many have given in to the reform to avoid this criticism, unable to find an argument against the sneering charge, "You're a reactionary, a dinosaur. You can't move with the times!"...

But we have never refused certain changes, adaptations that bear witness to the vitality of the Church. In the liturgy, people my age have seen some of these. Shortly after I was born, St. Pius X made some improvements, especially in giving more importance to the temporal cycle in the missal, in lowering the age for First Communion for children and in restoring liturgical chant, which had fallen into disuse. Pius XII came along and reduced the length of the Eucharistic fast because of difficulties inherent in modern life. For the same reason he authorized afternoon and evening Masses, put the Office of the Paschal Vigil on the evening of Holy

---

[6] "Between the Third and Fourth Sessions of the Council," *A Bishop Speaks*, pp.37-38.

Saturday and rearranged the services of Holy Week in general. John XXIII, before the Council, added his own touches to the so-called rite of St. Pius V.

But none of this came anywhere near to what happened in 1969, when a new concept of the Mass was introduced.[7]

THE REFORM PRESENTED BY THE REFORMERS

1. The key to *"aggiornamento"*

The Pope himself (allocution of January 13, 1965) will speak of the "liturgical renewal" as a "new religious pedagogy" that will assume "the place of the central motor in the great movement inscribed in the constitutional principles of the Church," principles renewed by the Council.

Msgr. Dwyer, a member of the *Consilium*[8] on the liturgy and archbishop of Birmingham, recognized the importance of this reform (press conference, October 23, 1967): "It is the liturgy that forms the character, the mentality of men confronted with problems....The liturgical reform is in a sense the key to the *aggiornamento*: Don't deceive yourself; the revolution starts there."[9]

2. Msgr. Bugnini's presentation of the New Mass

At that time, immediately after the Council, I was Superior General of the Congregation of the Fathers of the Holy Ghost, and we had a meeting of the Superiors General at Rome. We had asked Father Bugnini to explain to us what his New Mass was, for this was not at all a small event. Immediately after the Council talk was heard of the Normative Mass, the New Mass, the *Novus Ordo*. What did all this mean? It had not been spoken of at the Council. What had happened? And so we asked Father Bugnini to come and explain himself to the eighty-four Superiors General who were gathered together, amongst whom I was present.

Father Bugnini, with much confidence, explained what the Normative Mass would be: This will be changed, that will be

---

[7] *Open Letter to Confused Catholics* (Angelus Press, 1986), pp.31-32.
[8] The organ created for the application of the Decree on the Liturgy, *Sacrosanctum Concilium,* of Vatican II, created on February 26, 1964, by Pope Paul VI.
[9] Letter to Cardinal Seper, February 26, 1978.

changed and we will put in place another Offertory. We will be able to reduce the communion prayers. We will be able to have several different formats for the beginning of Mass. We will be able to say the Mass in the vernacular tongue. We looked at one another saying to ourselves: "But it's not possible!"

He spoke absolutely, as if there had never been a Mass in the Church before him. He spoke of his Normative Mass as of a new invention.

Personally, I was so stunned that I remained mute, although I generally speak freely when it is a question of opposing those with whom I am not in agreement. I could not utter a word. How could it be possible for this man before me to be entrusted with the entire reform of the Catholic Liturgy, the entire reform of the holy sacrifice of the Mass, of the Sacraments, of the breviary, and of all our prayers? Where are we going? Where is the Church going?

Two Superiors General had the courage to speak out. One of them asked Father Bugnini: "Is this an active participation; is this a bodily participation, that is to say, with vocal prayers, or is it a spiritual participation? In any case, you have spoken so much of the participation of the faithful that it seems you can no longer justify Mass celebrated without the faithful. Your entire Mass has been fabricated around the participation of the faithful. We Benedictines celebrate our Masses without the assistance of the faithful. Does this mean that we must discontinue our private Masses, since we do not have faithful to participate in them?"

I repeat to you exactly what Father Bugnini said. I have it still in my ears, so much did it strike me: "To tell the truth, we didn't think of that," he said!

Afterwards another arose and said: "Reverend Father, you have said that we will suppress this and we will suppress that, that we will replace this thing by that and always by shorter prayers. I have the impression that your new Mass could be said in ten or twelve minutes or at the most a quarter of an hour. This is not reasonable. This is not respectful towards such an act of the Church." Well, this is what he replied: "We can always add something." Is this for real? I heard it myself. If somebody had told me the story, I would perhaps have doubted it, but I heard it myself.[10]

---

[10] Conference to the faithful at Montreal, Canada, 1982 [English version: "The Infiltration of Modernism in the Church," *The Angelus*, March 1992, pp.7-8].

3. Preliminary distinctions for judging the New Mass

If we want to arrive at a judgment about the *Novus Ordo*, we must first refer to the original text as issued by the Congregation for Rites–in Latin. That is the official, authentic version. Then there is the implementation of the *Novus Ordo* by the *Notitiae*. The *Notitiae* is the official publication of the Congregation of Rites directing the application of the *Novus Ordo*. In its prescriptions, there are a multiplicity of details that alter the *Novus Ordo* issued by the Congregation. The third thing to consider is the translations. The *Novus Ordo* was not kept in Latin (I am still speaking of the official versions from the Congregation of Rites, the translations recognized by Rome).

Now, beyond official things, if we consider the usage of it that was made in practice, we arrive at a quasi infinite multiplicity of applications of the new *Ordo*: soon every priest will have his own *ordo*. A distinction can also be made by country: Depending on the country, the *Novus Ordo* was applied more or less strictly.[11]

THE REFORM AND THE LAW OF FAITH[12]

ATTENUATION OF THE THREE PRINCIPAL DOGMAS CONCERNING THE MASS IN THE *NOVUS ORDO*

In order to judge the dogmatic, moral, and spiritual worth of this reform, we must briefly recall the immutable principles of the Catholic Faith concerning the essence of our holy Mass. These propositions are "*de fide divina catholica definita*"–defined truths of Divine and Catholic faith. They are therefore dogmas, such that

---

[11] Spiritual conference, Ecône, October 1, 1979.
[12] According to an adage well known to liturgists, "*Lex orandi, lex credendi*," or "the law of prayer affects the law of faith"; that is to say, the way we pray influences our faith. In his Encyclical *Mediator Dei* on the liturgy, Pius XII explains that this adage, taken from the *Indiculus* of Pope Celestine I (Pope from 422-432, DS 246), does not mean that the liturgy is "a kind of proving ground for the truths to be held of faith, meaning by this that the Church is obliged to declare such a doctrine sound when it is found to have produced fruits of piety and sanctity through the sacred rites of the liturgy, and to reject it otherwise" (§46). It means that "The entire liturgy, therefore, has the Catholic faith for its content, inasmuch as it bears public witness to the faith of the Church" (§47).

someone who did not believe them would by that very fact be outside the Church. The first truth is that "in the Mass a true and real sacrifice is offered to God."[13] We must add that this sacrifice is a propitiatory sacrifice, a point that will be of use when we look at the New Mass.[14] The second is the dogma "The host or the victim is Christ Himself present under the species of bread and wine."[15] The third affirmation is that "The priests, and they alone, are the minsters."[16]

It is obvious that these three fundamental truths are–not to be severe in our judgment of the *Novus Ordo*–at least clearly weakened, and this we can easily prove whether by internal or external factors, that is to say, by an analysis of the *Ordo* itself; also, by what outsiders say about it; and, lastly, by the realities that flow from this reform. But it is especially by the internal proofs, that is to say, by studying the *Novus Ordo* itself, that we reach this conclusion.[17]

Archbishop Lefebvre now illustrates in detail the depreciation of these three dogmas in the *Novus Ordo*.

THE NEW MASS AND THE SACRIFICE

The *Novus Ordo* weakens the notion of sacrifice. The suppression of certain prayers and liturgical gestures hides the sacrificial aspect of the Mass. The churches themselves are no longer centered on the altar.

1. The absence of sacrifice in the liturgy

Basically, there are two parts in the *Novus Ordo*: the Liturgy of the Word and the Liturgy of the Eucharist. The liturgy of the sacrifice is gone. That is why immediately after the quick words of the Consecration the distribution of the Eucharistic bread takes place.

---

[13] *In missa offertur Deo verum et proprium sacrificium.* Cf. Council of Trent, Session 22, Canon 1, DS 1751 (Dz. 948).
[14] The Council of Trent enounces this condemnation: "If anyone says that the sacrifice of the Mass is only one of praise and thanksgiving, or that it is a mere commemoration of the sacrifice consummated on the Cross, but not one of propitiation...: let him be anathema" (Session 22, Canon 3, DS 1753 [Dz. 950]). Propitiation restores man to the Divine friendship (renders God "propitious") by the remission of sins.
[15] *Hostia aut victima est ipse Christus praesens sub speciebus panis et vini.*
[16] *Sacerdotes illique soli sunt ministri.*
[17] Spiritual conference, Ecône, October 26, 1979.

It constitutes a diminution of what is the center of the Mass, of what the sacrifice of the Mass truly is.[18]

2. Suppression of the propitiatory prayers

All the texts that very clearly affirm the propitiatory end, the essential end, of the sacrifice of the Mass have been removed. One or two faint allusions still remain, but that is all. This was done because the propitiatory end is denied by the Protestants.[19]

The prayers that explicitly expressed the idea of propitiation, like those of the Offertory and those pronounced by the priest before communicating, have been suppressed. Likewise, at the end of the Mass, the prayer to the Blessed Trinity, which says "...grant that the sacrifice which I...have offered up in the sight of Thy Majesty may be acceptable to Thee, and through Thy mercy be a propitiation (*propitiabile*–the very word is used!)–for me and for all those for whom it has been offered," has also been suppressed.[20] The expression "sacrifice" is absent from Canon II, attributed to St. Hippolytus.[21]

The diminution of the notion of sacrifice in the new rite is obvious because the term *sacrifice* itself is rarely employed; and when it is employed, it is in a Protestant manner, because the Protestants accept the term *sacrifice* for the Mass but only in the sense of a sacrifice of praise or Eucharistic sacrifice, but certainly not in the sense of a propitiatory sacrifice.[22]

3. A suppression inspired by Protestantism

When you say, "The notion of sacrifice is being lost in the *Novus Ordo*," the innovators respond, "No, look, the word *sacrifice* is still here and there." Indeed, the word *sacrifice* is used a few times....The Protestants also accept the notion of sacrifice in the Mass, but uniquely as a sacrifice of thanksgiving, praise, or adoration, and not as a propitiatory sacrifice, which is essential to the Catholic notion of sacrifice. The Council of Trent wrote entire chapters about this against the Protestants. Thus it is a very serious

---

[18] Spiritual conference, Zaitzkofen, October 1, 1979.
[19] Spiritual conference, Ecône, January 17, 1978.
[20] *Ibid.*, October 26, 1979.
[21] The N.O.M. allows a choice between four "Eucharistic prayers," including one ascribed to St. Hippolytus. *Open Letter to Confused Catholics*, p.21.
[22] Spiritual conference, Ecône, October 26, 1979.

matter to have suppressed all the prayers speaking of propitiatory sacrifice.[23]

The result, unfortunately, of the post-conciliar reforms has been to affect the notion of sacrifice, the notion of the Passion continued in the sacrifice of the Mass. Not that the innovators have denied it outright, but that they do not mention it, with the result that men forget it; they no longer think of it. Certainly, the authors of the new, post-conciliar liturgy have not denied the sacrifice of the Mass, but by the fact that they put so much emphasis on the table, the Eucharistic meal, and by omitting the term sacrifice, or at least by speaking of it only occasionally so that they can claim that they are not unaware of it, people stop believing in the virtue of Calvary.[24]

I could have brought you a book that came out during vacation entitled *Fifteen Bishops Profess the Faith of the Catholic Church*, published by the Cerf Publishing house. Three of the fifteen bishops are cardinals. The worst of the articles is surely the one by the bishop of Arras on the Mass. In the book he writes: "It is said that the sacrifice of the Mass was made to offer satisfaction–that horrible word, *satisfaction*." He asserts that this term originated in a medieval idea that represents God the Father as needing blood for the remission of our sins, as if God were a blood-thirsty executioner who wants to immolate His Son and who wants His Son's Blood.

Yet the Council of Trent clearly affirms that Our Lord offered His life as a propitiation for our sins, hence for satisfaction, which is another term that means the same thing. This approach to understanding Christ's sacrifice is found in St. Paul. If the notion of propitiatory sacrifice is excluded, then there is nothing left to do but cast all St. Paul's epistles into the fire. Consequently, what do these bishops understand of the sacrifice of the Mass?[25]

4. Suppression of the gestures symbolizing the sacrifice.

Moreover, to analyze the new rite, I think that it is necessary to consider not only the texts, but also all the rubrics and the new gestures that are required: the genuflections, the Signs of the Cross,

---

[23] Spiritual conference, Zaitzkofen, October 1, 1979.
[24] Easter retreat, Ecône, April 17, 1984.
[25] Retreat, Ecône, September 22, 1978.

the inclinations…and even the change in the objects.[26] Thus, in the first Canon, all the Signs of the Cross have been suppressed! One day I was celebrating Mass, at the Swiss Carmel, I think. The Carmelites didn't have a new missal. They had an old missal that had been given to them. But the missal had been scrawled all over by the reformers. There was a big red circle over every cross to show that it had been deleted. Likewise, the rubrics mentioning genuflections were crossed through in red. I could see at a single glance the complete transformation of the Canon! I assure you, the first Canon is no longer the Roman Canon.[27] That clearly is not so; everything was changed: no more genuflections, no more Signs of the Cross! Appalling! The Sign of the Cross showed that it indeed concerned the sacrifice of the Cross. Let us not say that these are merely details. These are not details; these are gestures that have meaning and value.[28]

Another example: The grandeur of the sacrifice requires that the altar be made of a noble material and in some way be attached to the ground. From the fourth century, the Church has prescribed the altar stone. Undoubtedly altar stones were already in use, but the pope who prescribed the altar stone for offering the sacrifice only confirmed what probably had been done from the beginning. Well, the altar stone was suppressed. It is no longer obligatory, and now the altar is replaced by a simple table to signify better the meal rather than the sacrifice; and that certainly does not enhance the dignity or sacred character of the Mass, which is a true sacrifice.[29]

The suppression of the altar stone also led to the suppression of the relics of the holy martyrs who were immolated and who shed their blood for Our Lord Jesus Christ, and thus the union of the blood of the martyrs and the Blood of Our Lord expressed by the presence of the saints' relics in the altar stone. The beautiful link

---

[26] Spiritual conference, Ecône, June 25, 1981. The Sacrament is an outward and efficacious sign; it is not a theological treatise. It is thus necessary to consider not only the texts, but also the gestures and postures that contribute to signifying what is occurring.

[27] Among the four Canons left to the celebrant's choice in the new *Ordo*, Canon I is the one that materially most resembles the traditional Canon of the Mass; this has led some to wrongly consider it to be identical to it in substance.

[28] Retreat, Avrillé, October 18, 1989.

[29] Spiritual conference, Zaitzkofen, October 1, 1979.

that exists between the sacrifice of the saints and the sacrifice of Our Lord who offers Himself on the altar is no longer represented. How could they have suppressed these things? It is unbelievable![30] I told Cardinal Seper: "See how the notion of sacrifice is diminished." The Church has always had the sense of sacrifice. I would even say that it is in the nature of man. It is a part of man's nature to offer sacrifices. All sacrifices are offered on a stone, on something solid. And they suppressed the altar stones![31]

The doing away with the altar stone, the introduction of a table covered with a single cloth, the turning of the priest towards the people, the host left on the paten and not on the corporal, the authorization of the use of ordinary bread, vessels made from diverse materials, even the humblest—all these and many other details help to inculcate those present with Protestant notions essentially and gravely opposed to Catholic teaching.[32]

5. The altar cross suppressed or relegated to the side

The crucifixes on the altars have also often been suppressed, or at least moved to the side of the altar. Consequently, there is not even a reminder of the Passion of Our Lord Jesus Christ for something that is the true, real reproduction of Our Lord's sacrifice.[33]

Occasionally finding myself in Spain, I recently went to the mountains to visit the little villages. The first thing I did was to go to the church to see if perhaps in these remote regions of Spain there was still an altar of sacrifice as before. But no, there was nothing. There was no crucifix! But where is the sacrifice? They've suppressed the cross! I looked for the cross, but there was no cross. There was just a bare, meaningless table. That is not the Catholic Faith. The Catholic Faith is the sacrifice of Our Lord Jesus Christ in which we participate and which transforms Christian life—the life of families and societies.[34]

The suppression or displacement of the altar cross betokens a diminution of the idea of sacrifice. The Church requires a crucifix

---

[30] Spiritual conference, Ecône, October 26, 1979.
[31] *Ibid.*, June 25, 1981.
[32] Conference, Florence, February 15, 1975, *A Bishop Speaks*, p.195.
[33] Easter retreat, Ecône, April 17, 1984.
[34] Homily, St-Michel-en-Brenne, April 2, 1989.

on the altar; it must be there precisely because it reminds us of the sacrifice of Calvary.[35]

The innovators no longer see in the Mass a propitiatory sacrifice, but we must always come back to that. We must always put the faithful at the foot of the Cross, before the sacrifice of Our Lord. This must be our recurrent theme. The Mass is a sacrifice. A sacrificial action is effected, and we partake of the Victim. It is not a "sharing of bread"; it is not a "sharing of the word."[36]

People want nothing to do with the Cross of Our Lord Jesus Christ. They want nothing to do with His sacrifice, because His sacrifice reminds us that we must sacrifice ourselves, that to have life we must die to our sins, and men who seek their pleasures and satisfactions cannot stand to see it, hear it, or understand it. They want no part of the Cross. That is why so many crucifixes have disappeared in our day.[37]

6. The Mass celebrated facing the people in the Roman basilicas

The priest turns towards the crucifix for the offering of the sacrifice. Thus the Mass celebrated facing the people takes away this notion of sacrifice. Some argue that at Rome the altars on which the pope celebrates are altars facing the people.[38] That is true, and yet it is not true, because the pope celebrates with his entire chapter, which is behind him. Thus, when the pope would celebrate, he did not turn towards the notables present–all the priests, and cardinals, and his entire court. He turned towards the faithful, but he was at such a distance that his face could scarcely be seen. On all these altars there was a crucifix, candelabra, and other ornamentation that created a separation. And then, he celebrated facing Our Lord Jesus Christ. It was not in order to celebrate Mass facing the

---

[35] Spiritual conference, Ecône, October 26, 1979.
[36] Priests' recollection, Paris, December 13, 1984, *Cor Unum*, p.112.
[37] Homily, Ecône, September 14, 1975.
[38] In Roman basilicas, which were civic buildings originally, the apses are oriented westward. When using them as churches, the Christians celebrated facing east (the symbol of Our Lord, the Sun of Justice), thus facing the people in the nave.

people that he was turned towards the people, but it was because of the orientation[39] of the basilica.[40]

7. The sacrifice of the Mass is no longer visibly signified in the churches

In the beautiful basilicas that our ancestors built, one can see that the altar is truly the heart of the edifice. You have the building's main nave and the transept representing the Cross of Our Lord, and the altar is in the place of Our Lord's heart. Having lost the notion of sacrifice in the Mass, the innovators now create any kind of building for a church. They construct some kind of hall, and a multi-purpose hall at that, suitable for all kinds of events, and there they "do the Eucharist," as they call it. A table can be put anywhere. It isn't necessary to have a building that represents the Cross. It has no meaning at all.

Contrariwise, in the olden days those who built the churches really intended to reproduce the Cross. For them, the sacrifice of the Mass was truly the sacrifice of Our Lord and not only, like now, a "Eucharist."

8. From the disappearance of the Sacrifice to the disappearance of the Sacrament

There are two great realities in the Mass, which are the sacrifice and the Sacrament. These two great realities are realized at the same instant, at the moment when the priest pronounces the words of the consecration of the bread and the wine. When he has finished the words of consecration of the precious Blood, the sacrifice of Our Lord is accomplished, and Our Lord is also there present; the Sacrament of Our Lord is there, too....This mystical separation of the species of bread and wine realizes the sacrifice of the Mass. Thus, these two realities are effected by the words of consecration. They cannot be separated. But that is what the Protestants did; they wanted only the Sacrament with the sacrifice. They have neither the one nor the other, neither the Sacrament nor the sacrifice. And that is the danger of the New Masses. They no longer speak of sacrifice; it seems that they ignore the sacrifice. Now they only

---

[39] In churches properly situated, the priest celebrates facing east.
[40] Spiritual conference, Ecône, October 26, 1979.

speak of the Eucharist, they do a "Eucharist" as if it were only a meal. There is a real risk of their having neither the one nor the other. It is very dangerous. Inasmuch as the sacrifice disappears, the Sacrament also disappears because what is present in the Sacrament is the victim. If there is no more sacrifice, there is no victim.[41]

9. An official document from the Paris chancery

Here is a document from the Centre Jean-Bart, official center of the Archbishopric of Paris; there are incredible statements, for instance *Christ's Eucharist Today* (no out-of-date publication, it is dated March 17, 1973): "Is not the Mass Our Lord's Supper, an invitation to communion?" There is no more mention of sacrifice. Then: "At the heart of the Mass lies a story"....No, it is not a story.

What we are celebrating then is a memorial of our redemption. Memorial, a word which it is essential to understand. It is not a question of commemorating a past event, as though meeting simply in remembrance. Neither is it a question of the renewal of that event. Christ died and rose again once for ever–that can never happen again.

"Can never happen again"? Is not Our Lord able to perform a miracle and repeat for us His sacrifice on Calvary?[42]

Those who hold authority in the Church are gradually making the notion of propitiatory sacrifice disappear, and exalt communion even more than the Real Presence.[43]

THE NEW MASS AND THE REAL PRESENCE

Numerous gestures of the new rite and changes in liturgical furnishings, vessels, and vestments, occult the fundamental dogmas of the Catholic Mass. We have just seen this in the analysis of the New Mass and sacrifice, and we shall find confirmation of it in the study of the New Mass in regard to the Real Presence.

---

[41] Retreat, Brignoles, July 27, 1984.
[42] Conference, Tourcoing, January 30, 1974, *A Bishop Speaks*, pp.174-5. Transubstantiation is a miracle broadly speaking, a miracle being a visible reality, strictly speaking.
[43] Retreat, Avrillé, October 18, 1989.

1. The suppression of the genuflection before the elevation

In the New Mass, the priest, like the Protestants, no longer genuflects before the elevation.[44] For the Protestants, Christ is not made present at the Mass as a result of the words of consecration pronounced by the presider of the ceremony, but as a result of the faithful's belief in conjunction with the celebrant's words. It is because the faithful make an act of faith in the presence of Our Lord that Christ is present in the Eucharist. The idea is gradually spreading among Catholics that it is their belief that causes Our Lord to be present. This is a totally Protestant idea, and it explains why the priest does not genuflect before the elevation. The host is elevated first so that the faithful can make an act of faith, and it is by their act of faith that Our Lord is made present in the host.

This is appalling, because the Real Presence is implicitly denied. The presence of Our Lord in the Eucharist is assimilated to the presence of Our Lord in the community: we are together here, and Our Lord is in our midst. But for some, it would be the same for the Eucharist. Our Lord would be made present by the faithful's act of faith. In that case, it would involve a moral presence and no longer Our Lord's Real Presence. In that case, there would no longer be any need to pronounce the words of consecration. It would be enough to elevate the host to rouse the faith of the assistants, and Our Lord would be present in the host. A nun could do that; anybody could do that; there is no need to have received the Sacrament of Holy Orders.[45]

Now the Real Presence is practically denied even by priests, and perhaps even by bishops, because the marks of adoration of the Blessed Sacrament are no longer given. They rarely genuflect. It is really unimaginable! In the end, they come to believe that the Eucharist is only bread, in remembrance of Our Lord, but not His real Body and Blood, nor His Divinity.[46]

If you do not genuflect before Our Lord, if you do not show respect before the Real Presence of Our Lord Jesus Christ in the Blessed Sacrament, you will end up not believing in it any more.

---

[44] He is speaking about the elevations that take place immediately after the consecration of the precious Body and Blood of Our Lord.
[45] Homily, St-Michel-en-Brenne, April 9, 1989.
[46] Retreat, Avrillé, October 18, 1989.

To stop believing in the Real Presence of Our Lord in the Blessed Sacrament is to go astray from the Church, it is to let go of the Church's Tradition.[47]

2. An heretical conference

Here beneath my eyes, I have the text of a lecture on the Eucharist given by the Dean of the Faculty of Theology at Strasbourg: "Contemporary Thought and the Expression of Eucharistic Faith." This lecture, from the first line to the last, is heretical. There is no longer any question of the Real Presence of Our Lord. The Real Presence, for the one who is Dean of the Faculty of Theology at Strasbourg, is comparable to the presence of a composer of a piece of music, who shows himself in his piece when it is played.[48]

He claims that it is not an efficacious sign. Concerning the presence of Our Lord in the Eucharist, he says: "Someone can be present by a symbolic action that he does not accomplish physically, but which others carry out with creative fidelity to his profound intention. The Bayreuth Festival undoubtedly realizes a presence of Richard Wagner that is superior in intensity to that which recordings or occasional concerts can manifest." Now listen to this: "It is in this last context, it seems to me, that we ought to situate Christ's Eucharistic presence." Hence, by his meaning, Christ's Eucharistic presence would be similar to the presence of a musician who composed a piece of music; the piece is played and the audience experiences the composer's presence on that occasion. And that is what the Eucharistic presence is....It is a rather serious matter, coming as it does from a dean of the Theology Faculty of Strasbourg. And, unfortunately, it would be possible to cite very many examples like this.[49]

He [the Dean of the Strasbourg Faculty] smiles at that Eucharist which is called an "efficacious sign," which is the definition of the Sacrament, of all Sacraments. He says: "That is utterly ridiculous; such terms cannot be used today. In our day they are meaningless."

---

[47] Homily, Lyons, February 8, 1976.
[48] Conference, Rennes, November 1972, *A Bishop Speaks*, p.121.
[49] Conference, Auray, January 1973. Archbishop Lefebvre is citing the same dean as the one mentioned in the preceding citation and in the one that follows.

...Young seminarians still in residence are gradually steeped in error, marked by it.[50]

> In many churches, the Gospels are placed on the altar while the Blessed Sacrament is relegated to a side chapel. This elevation of Holy Scripture at the expense of the Blessed Sacrament increases doubts about faith in the Real Presence of Our Lord in the Eucharist.

3. The Gospels placed on the altars

In the *schema* on the Holy Scriptures,[51] the Scriptures and the Eucharist are put on an equal footing. How can we fail to reflect on all the gospels which will henceforth replace the Eucharist on the high altars of our Churches?[52]

4. The Blessed Sacrament and Sacred Scripture conflated

Let us beware of venerating these two gifts of God—Holy Writ and the Eucharist—in exactly the same way. There is an essential difference between the two. The Spirit of God is only in Scripture *in usu*,[53] while the Spirit of God and of Our Lord, His glorious body, are present *in esse*[54] in the Holy Eucharist. It is to commit an inadmissible confusion to treat the Gospels book with the same veneration as the Eucharist.[55]

> Communion received standing and in the hand accentuates the notions of the Eucharist as "memorial" and "meal." The way in which Our Lord is treated in the Blessed Sacrament shows the lessening of faith in the Divinity of Christ and in the Real Presence.

5. Communion in the hand

If there is a tendency to regard the sacrifice of the Mass as a meal, then it is natural to take Communion in the hand. If it is

---

[50] Conference, Rennes, November 1972, *A Bishop Speaks*, pp.121-22.
[51] The reference is to a schema that was published as *Dei Verbum*, Vatican II's dogmatic constitution on Divine Revelation, on November 18, 1965, at the end of the Council.
[52] "To Remain a Catholic Must One Become a Protestant?" October 11, 1964, *Lettres pastorales et écrits* (Editions Fideliter, 1989), p.193.
[53] In usage.
[54] Substantially, in being.
[55] Ordination retreat, Flavigny, June 1976.

a meal, it is a morsel of bread which is distributed, a memento, a memorial. But when we know that Our Lord is present! When we know who Our Lord is! We cannot indeed know, we have no means of telling! Reflect that all the angels of heaven bow before Our Lord, that at the very name of Jesus every knee is bent whether in heaven, on earth, or in hell. Yet we are afraid to kneel in the presence of Him whose name, if it be but spoken on the Day of Judgment, will bring to their knees all humanity, all the souls in heaven, all the angels, and all in hell.[56]

6. The hosts distributed by anybody

The priests do not even genuflect before the Holy Eucharist. They have no more respect for the Blessed Sacrament. The hosts are distributed by anybody. That cannot be our God whom they treat this way.…The people who treat Our Lord Jesus Christ the way He is treated in Eucharistic ceremonies nowadays are people who do not believe in the Divinity of Our Lord Jesus Christ. It is not possible otherwise.[57]

It was the Council of Trent after all that said that Our Lord is present in the least particles of the Holy Eucharist. What a lack of respect is shown by those who may have particles of the Eucharist on their hands and who return to their places without purifying them![58]

The faithful who truly believe in the Real Presence of Our Lord understand very well that it must be the ministers who distribute Holy Communion, and they absolutely refuse to receive Communion in the hand.[59]

In the holy Mass, the reforms that have been introduced cause the loss of faith in the Real Presence of Our Lord Jesus Christ in the Eucharist. For a Catholic, the reforms are such that it is difficult, if not impossible, for children who have not known what we older Catholics knew before, to believe in the Real Presence of Our Lord Jesus Christ. It is not possible to treat the Blessed Sacrament the way it is treated today and at the same time believe that, in

---

[56] Conference, Tourcoing, January 30, 1974, *A Bishop Speaks*, pp.177-78.
[57] Confirmations sermon, Doué-la-Fontaine, May 19, 1977.
[58] Priests' retreat, Hauterive, August, 1972.
[59] Retreat, Avrillé, October 18, 1989.

the Eucharist, are truly found present the Body, Blood, Soul, and Divinity of Our Lord Jesus Christ.

From the way the priests [and the "extraordinary ministers"] distribute the Holy Eucharist and the way the faithful go and receive Holy Communion without genuflection or any sign of respect, communicate, and return to their places after having received, it does not seem possible that they still believe in the real presence of Our Lord Jesus Christ in the Holy Eucharist.[60]

The New Mass and the Priesthood

> The *Novus Ordo* diminishes the essential difference between the sacerdotal priesthood and the priesthood of the faithful. The *Confiteor* recited by the priest together with the faithful, the distribution of Communion by laymen, who also read the Epistle and sometimes even the Gospel, obscure the essential difference between the ordained priesthood and the priesthood of the people. Archbishop Lefebvre sets forth the theological notions that are useful for understanding how the reform strays from the traditional conception of the priesthood.

1. The participation of the faithful

The priests alone are the ministers of the sacrifice. Now this dogma is being altered by the failure to distinguish between priest and laity. Now the prayers at the beginning of the Mass, for example, are being said in common by the priest and the faithful. The "I" of the celebrant has been replaced by "we." The priest used to recite the *Confiteor* alone, and then the faithful recited it in turn. There was a definite distinction between the priest and the faithful. Now there is only one *Confiteor* recited in common. The priest and the faithful confess their sins in common, and this is done for a few other prayers.[61]

It is written everywhere that the faithful "celebrate"; they are associated with the acts of worship, they read the Epistle and occasionally the Gospel, give out Communion, sometimes preach the homily, which may be replaced by "a dialogue by small groups upon the Word of God," meeting together beforehand to "con-

---

[60] Confirmations sermon, Doué-la-Fontaine, May 19, 1977
[61] Spiritual conference, Ecône, October 26, 1979.

struct" the Sunday celebration. But this is only a first step; for several years we have heard of those responsible for diocesan organizations who have been putting forward propositions of this nature: "It is not the ministers but the assembly who celebrate" (handouts by the National Center for Pastoral Liturgy) or "The assembly is the prime subject of the liturgy"; what matters is not the "functioning of the rites but the image the assembly gives to itself and the relationship the co-celebrants create between themselves."[62, 63]

2. What participation of the faithful means

In his book *The Reform of the Liturgy*, Archbishop Bugnini wrote: "The way opened by the Council is destined to radically change the face of traditional liturgical assemblies in which, by an already multi-secular custom, the liturgical service is accomplished almost exclusively by the clergy. The people attend too often like strangers and mute spectators."[64]

Msgr. Bugnini's leitmotiv was the active participation of the faithful....All the reforms were made in the interest of the active participation of the faithful, as if the faithful had never actively participated in the sacrifice before all these reforms. What constitutes active participation? What does "active" mean? For Msgr. Bugnini, active participation means an outward participation, and not the participation of mind and heart by faith....Yet it is participation by faith that is the real action, spiritual action. It does not involve purely material action. "Active participation" of the faithful–what does it mean?–that the faithful will do the readings? Nowadays even women do the readings, and it is approved....[65]

3. The danger of confounding the priesthood of the laity with that of the priest

Elsewhere Msgr. Bugnini writes: "A lengthy education will be required to make it understood that the liturgy is an action of the entire people of God." Well, that is an error. I do not say that it is formally heretical, but underlying that statement is a heresy, the

---

[62] Fr. Gelineau, architect of the liturgical reform and professor at the Paris Catholic Institute.
[63] *Open Letter to Confused Catholics*, pp.24-25.
[64] Spiritual conference, Ecône, June 12, 1984.
[65] *Ibid.*, October 26, 1979.

idea that the priesthood of the faithful is the same as that of priests, and that everyone is a priest, and that the whole People of God must offer the holy sacrifice.[66]

The priest groups the faithful around himself in such a way that you would think that it is not only the priest who is offering the sacrifice, who is truly the priest, but the faithful, too. Similarly, the faithful distributing the Eucharist, the Eucharistic bread, is harmful to the correct notion of what the priest is. There is a very great danger in these practices, because one risks confounding what is called the priesthood of the faithful with the priesthood conferred by the Sacrament of holy orders.[67]

4. The nature of the sacerdotal priesthood

The grace of the priesthood is a special participation in the grace of Our Lord. You know that there are two graces in Our Lord, according to what theology teaches us. There is the grace of union, called the hypostatic union, that is to say the union of the Divinity with human nature. Human nature is in some way anointed, filled with this grace of union: Christ is truly the Anointed, so that His human nature is filled by the Divinity, as oil seeps into material things. By this grace, Our Lord is consecrated priest from the first instant of His Incarnation. By an extraordinary privilege, the priest participates in this grace of union through the Sacrament of Holy Orders.[68]

Moreover, Our Lord's grace of union is the cause of His sanctifying grace. In the ground of Divinity, so to speak, sanctifying grace blooms like a flower. Thus, Our Lord's soul receives the plenitude of sanctifying grace. Sanctifying grace is thus the fruit of His grace of union. And by baptism, by the Sacraments, the faithful and we, too, participate in the sanctifying grace of Our Lord Jesus Christ.

Thus, it is completely false to say that all the faithful are priests, and that there is no difference between the priesthood of priests and the priesthood of the laity.[69]

---

[66] *Ibid.*, June 12, 1984.
[67] Spiritual conference, Zaitzkofen, October 1, 1979.
[68] The priest participates in it as the instrument of Christ's sacerdotal action.
[69] Retreat, Ecône, September 22, 1978.

5. The nature of the priesthood of the faithful

So why does one speak of the priesthood of the faithful? Baptism dedicates us in some way to the worship of Our Lord Jesus Christ. That is why St. Peter alludes to the priesthood of all Christians.[70] Since we are marked for the worship of God by baptism, we must offer ourselves in oblation. It is in this sense that Christians are priests. The faithful have a priesthood in the sense that they too, in some way, are obliged to offer themselves to God as agreeable victims and so make an act of sacrifice.[71] But they are not vested with the official priesthood of the Church, which enables a man to pronounce the words of consecration and to make Our Lord come down from heaven under the appearances of bread and wine. The faithful say the words of the consecration in vain; nothing happens. So one cannot say that they are priests. There is an essential difference between the priesthood of Christians and that of priests. The two things must not be confused.[72]

Of course, it is affirmed in the Council that there is a difference between the action of the priest and that of the faithful, but in practice, they act as if there were none. Only the priest is a priest. The faithful have no power. The term *priesthood* applied to the faithful is an image to help the faithful offer themselves in union with the offering that takes place in the sacrifice of the Mass. Of course we must offer ourselves to God during the sacrifice of the Mass, but that has nothing to do with the priesthood of the priest, who is truly the "sacrificer," who is truly marked by the sacramental character. This is yet another serious objection.[73]

The New Mass is no longer hierarchical but democratic, so much so that some priests no longer celebrate Mass without some of the faithful attending.

---

[70] I Peter 2:9: "But you are a chosen generation, a kingly priesthood...."
[71] In the Encyclical *Mediator Dei*, Pope Pius XII describes the people's participation in the offering: "...it is based on the fact that the people unite their hearts in praise, impetration, expiation and thanksgiving with prayers or intention of the priest, even of the High Priest himself, so that in the one and same offering of the victim and according to a visible sacerdotal rite, they may be presented to God the Father" (§93).
[72] Retreat, St-Michel-en-Brenne, April 1, 2007.
[73] Spiritual conference, Zaitzkofen, October 1, 1979.

6. The modern error on the need to have the presence of the faithful at Mass

The introduction of the idea that the Mass is not useful or really opportune unless the faithful can participate, is yet another of the misfortunes of our time. It is the revival of a Lutheran teaching against private Masses. For if the Mass is but a meal, there can be no meal without people to share it, obviously. But if the Mass is a sacrifice, then that completely changes the outlook. Then the private Mass has as much value as a "public Mass." It is not a private act; it is a public act.[74]

The sacrifice of Our Lord Jesus Christ offered by the priest has an infinite worth, whether the priest is alone or has a thousand people surrounding him. This is what we believe.[75]

7. A democratic Mass

It is numbers that command from now on in the holy Church. And this is expressed in the Mass precisely because the assembly replaces the priest, to such a point that now many priests no longer want to celebrate holy Mass when there is no assembly. Slowly but surely the Protestant notion of the Mass is being introduced into the holy Catholic Church. And this is consistent with the mentality of modern man–absolutely consistent. For it is the democratic ideal which is the fundamental idea of modern man, that is to say, that the power resides in the assembly, that authority is in the people, in the masses, and not in God. And this is most grave, because we believe that God is all-powerful; we believe that God has all authority; we believe that all authority comes from God: *Omnis potestas a Deo.*[76] We do not believe that authority comes from below. Now, that is the mentality of modern man.

And the New Mass is not less than the expression of this idea that authority is at the base, and no longer in God. This Mass is no longer a hierarchical Mass; it is a democratic Mass. And this is most grave. It is the expression of a *whole new ideology*. The ideology of modern man has been brought into our most sacred rites. And this is what is at present corrupting the entire Church. For by this idea

---

[74] Homily, Ecône, April 6, 1980.
[75] *Ibid.*, June 29, 1976.
[76] Cf. Rom. 13:1.

of power bestowed on the lower rank, in the holy Mass, they are destroying the priesthood.[77]

The New Mass is a sort of hybrid Mass, which is no longer hierarchical; it is democratic, where the assembly takes the place of the priest, and so it is no longer a veritable Mass that affirms the royalty of Our Lord.[78]

THE REFORM AND THE LAW OF PRAYER

A succinct analysis of the "prayers of presentation" and of the Consecration shows what kind of changes were made in the second part of the Mass.

ANALYSIS OF THE "PRAYERS OF PRESENTATION" AND OF THE CONSECRATION IN THE NEW RITE

The Offertory of the New Mass no longer expresses the propitiatory and expiatory end of the sacrifice.

1. A practically non-existent Offertory

In the French *Novus Ordo* the Offertory is practically non-existent; besides which it no longer has this name. The New Sunday Missal speaks of the "prayers of presentation." The formula used reminds one more of a thanksgiving, a thank-you, for the fruits of the earth. To realize this fully, it is sufficient to compare it with the formulas traditionally used by the Church in which clearly appears the propitiatory and expiatory nature of the Sacrifice "which I offer Thee for my innumerable sins, offenses and negligences, for all those here present and for all Christians living and dead, that it may avail for my salvation and theirs for eternal life." Raising the chalice, the priest then says, "We offer Thee, Lord, the chalice of Thy redemption, imploring Thy goodness to accept it like a sweet perfume into the presence of Thy divine Majesty for our salvation and that of the whole world."

What remains of that in the New Mass? This: "Blessed are You, Lord, God of the universe, You who give us this bread, fruit of the earth and work of human hands. We offer it to You; it will become the bread of life," and the same for the wine which will become

---

[77] Homily, Ecône, June 29, 1976, *A Bishop Speaks*, p.245.
[78] *Ibid.*, p.271.

"our spiritual drink." What purpose is served by adding, a little further on: "Wash me of my faults, Lord. Purify me of my sin," and "may our sacrifice today find grace before You"? Which sin? Which sacrifice? What connection can the faithful make between this vague presentation of the offerings and the redemption that he is looking forward to?[79]

2. The substitution of a clear text by enigmatic phrases

I will ask another question: Why substitute for a text that is clear and whose meaning is complete, a series of enigmatic and loosely bound phrases?[80] If a need is found for change, it should be for something better. These incidental phrases which seem to make up for the insufficiency of the "prayers of presentation" remind us of Luther, who was at pains to arrange the changes with caution. He retained as much as possible of the old ceremonies, limiting himself to changing their meaning. The Mass, to a great extent, kept its external appearance; the people found in the churches nearly the same setting, nearly the same rites, with slight changes made to please them, because from then on people were consulted much more than before; they were much more aware of their importance in matters of worship, taking a more active part by means of chant and praying aloud. [81]

These prayers of the Offertory were already several centuries old at the time of the codification of the Mass by St. Pius V.... Since they constituted a rampart against Protestantism, removing them was tantamount to giving up the fortress. They did not exist in that form at the time of St. Gregory the Great. Neither did the Protestant heresies![82]

---

[79] *Open Letter to Confused Catholics*, p.26.
[80] These prayers "are inspired by the beautiful Jewish festive prayers before meals" (Jean-Charles Didier, "On the Mass and Its Celebration," *Esprit et Vie: L'Ami du Clergé*, No.1, January 2, 1975, p.15). Some defenders of the new Offertory are pleased by the separation of the Offertory from the Eucharistic sacrifice: "The formulas for the deposition of the bread and wine are replaced with Biblical formulas in order to avoid confusion with the actual offering made in the Canon" (Charles Lefebvre, "The Decree *Ordine Missae* of the Sacred Congregation of Rites," *L'Année Canonique*, XIV, 1970).
[81] *Open Letter to Confused Catholics*, pp.26-27.
[82] Heresies, in particular those of Protestantism, occasioned liturgical clarifications to protect dogma and to give expression to it in the Church's

During the New Mass, the words of consecration are no longer pronounced in a declaratory manner [**as a statement of fact], but in a purely narrative way, giving the impression of a simple account rather than an action. The distinct separation of the narrative parts from the consecration properly speaking was suppressed.

3. The Consecration: an action or a narration?

Most priests nowadays recite as one continuous passage the principal part of the Canon which begins, "the night before the Passion He took bread in His holy hands," without observing the pause implied by the rubric of the Roman Missal: "Holding with both hands the host between the index finger and the thumb, he pronounces the words of the Consecration in a low but distinct voice and attentively over the host." The tone changes, becomes intimatory, the five words *"Hoc est enim Corpus Meum"* operate the miracle of transubstantiation, as do those that are said for the consecration of the wine. The new Missal asks the celebrant to keep to the narrative tone of voice as if he were indeed proceeding with a memorial.[83]

In our missals is written: *Canon actionis*. Indeed, the Canon is an action. The "canon" of the action means the rule the priest must follows to perform the sacrificial action. Now, they have suppressed almost everything indicative of the action. They have made of it a narrative, which is shown in a number of small but important details, such as joining the essential words of the consecration to the words that precede and follow by eliminating the difference in type size. Before, capital letters were only used for the words of consecration, because the action occurs in these words only. The words encompassing them are a narration. But now the difference in print has been removed. Additionally, the priest is no longer directed to bow while reciting the words of consecration. The priest recites in one go the principal part of the Canon that begins by "Who, the day before He suffered, took bread into His holy and venerable hands...," without marking the pause implied by the rubric in the Roman missal: he does not stop again. This is absolutely contrary

---

prayer. To reject these developments at the very least amounts to suppressing the safeguards against heresies, and indeed to accepting them implicitly.

[83] *Open Letter to Confused Catholics*, pp.27-28.

to the theology of the sacrifice of the Mass. This is thus a very serious objection.

Undoubtedly, were you to say to the reformers, "You no longer accomplish an action," they would retort: That is not true; it is not because we say the words in this way that we do not believe in the action. That is a rash judgment." They always have an answer, but the facts are there.[84]

> In the new rite, three modifications were introduced in the words of consecration. In the consecration of the bread, after "This is My Body,"[85] were added the words: "which was given up for you";[86] in the consecration of the wine, after "For this is the chalice of My Blood, of the new and eternal Testament"[87] the words "The Mystery of Faith" were suppressed.[88] Were these modifications made to bring us closer to the Protestants, who use this form to reproduce as exactly as possible the account of the Last Supper as it appears in Sacred Scripture (I Cor. 11:24)? Lastly, in numerous translations "for many"[89] was replaced by "for all."[90]

4. The addition of the words "*quod pro vobis tradetur*" to the words of Consecration

Another reason that shows us that the *Novus Ordo* was unacceptably modified are the changes made to the words of consecration. I am not speaking of translations for the moment, the translations having accentuated the corruption even more. The words *quod pro vobis tradetur* were added to the consecration of the bread. Why this addition? It does not render the consecration invalid since the Eastern Catholics employ it and have employed it before. Now, it cannot be said that the Eastern Catholics have formulas that are invalid. They are Catholic. But what an idea to go and borrow from the Eastern Rites! We Romans have the most beautiful tradition, a tradition that goes back to St. Peter and St. Paul, the founders of the Church at Rome. We have the most venerable and most widely used liturgy in the entire Church. What purpose is served

---

[84] Spiritual conference, Zaitzkofen, October 1, 1979.
[85] *Hoc est Corpus meum.*
[86] *Quod pro vobis tradetur.*
[87] *Hic est enim calix Sanguinis mei, novi et aeterni Testamenti.*
[88] *Mysterium fidei*: this formula was transferred after the consecration, but no allusion is made to the transubstantiation that was just effected.
[89] *Pro multis.*
[90] *Pro omnibus.*

by destroying our liturgy to take that of small Eastern groups? The Eastern Rite Catholics are respectable, but what an idea to imitate them, when it is rather they who should align themselves with us! The reason for this innovation is certainly ecumenical. One can surmise that it is to bring us closer to the Protestants since Luther also added these same words. Why did he go to the trouble of adding *quod pro vobis tradetur*? Luther did it so that the words would follow the Bible more exactly,[91] and so that it would more closely resemble the narration of the Last Supper. But it is absolutely inadmissible to imitate Luther.[92]

5. A meal or a sacrifice?

For the Protestants, the Last Supper is only a meal, and not a sacrifice. But there was a real sacrifice at the Last Supper: Our Lord separated His Body and Blood, thus prefiguring the sacrifice He was to offer on the Cross. The Protestants deny it and deliberately want to reproduce the narration of the Last Supper only as a commemorative meal....

The Protestant conception is something lifeless because it is only historical: they repeat things that were done in the past. In the Catholic conception, on the contrary, the Mass is truly a sacrifice, the very same one that took place on Calvary.[93]

6. St. Thomas Aquinas rebuts Luther ahead of time

If you study the question of the form[94] of the Eucharist, and thus the words of consecration, in the *Summa Theologica*, you will see that St. Thomas asks why the Church limited the words for the consecration of the bread to "This is My Body." Why weren't the words "which is given up for you" added? He brings up the objection himself. Scripture seems to invite us to say these words: *Quod pro vobis tradetur*. And he answers: it is not the Gospel only that teaches us what is to be done, but Tradition also. We must consider that these words as they were given are traditional, and that they almost certainly come to us from the Apostles. If the sacrifice of Our

---

[91] Cf. I Cor. 11:24.
[92] Spiritual conference, Zaitzkofen
[93] *L'Église infiltrée par le modernisme*, p.85.
[94] "The form of the Sacraments consists of the words said to confect them." Catechism of St. Pius X, Part IV, Ch.1, §1 [French edition].

Lord is truly the heart of the Church, if it has so much importance in the Church, how could it be that Our Lord would not have given directions to His Apostles before His death, at least in the main lines, on the fundamentals of the sacrifice of the Mass?

Of course, the entire liturgy was elaborated over centuries, but it can be said that it was already at least substantially the same, that it was already in its main lines designed by Our Lord Jesus Christ Himself. It cannot be doubted that during the forty days Our Lord lived on earth after His Resurrection that He instructed His disciples, even on questions that may seem mere details, but which have a very great importance.[95]

7. The suppression of the *"mysterium fidei"*

In the words of consecration the clause *"mysterium fidei"* was suppressed, a clause that perhaps goes back to Our Lord Himself, during the forty days spent with His Apostles after the Resurrection.[96]

In this regard, it is interesting to read the reply made by Pope Innocent III to John, Archbishop of Lyons, in 1202, thus at the beginning of the thirteenth century...: "You have asked (indeed) who has added to the form of the words which Christ Himself expressed when He changed the bread and wine into the Body and Blood, that in the Canon of the Mass which the general Church uses, which none of the Evangelists is read to have expressed...." (It seems that the Archbishop of Lyons had written a letter to the Holy Father saying, "It is quite curious that in the form of the Sacrament of the Eucharist, the words do not correspond to any of those recorded by the Evangelists. How is this so?"). So the Pope replies: "In the Canon of the Mass that expression, *"mysterium fidei,"* is found interposed among His words. Surely we find many such things omitted from the words as well as from the deeds of the Lord by the Evangelists, which the Apostles are read to have supplied by word or to have expressed by deed....Therefore, we believe that the form of words, as is found in the Canon, the Apostles received from Christ, and their successors from them...."[97]

---

[95] Spiritual conference, Zaitzkofen, February 7, 1980.
[96] Spiritual conference, Ecône, March 21, 1977.
[97] DS 782 (Dz. 414).

That is what Pope Innocent III upholds, you see: the form employed in the Roman Canon for transubstantiation was received from Christ through the Apostles. This corresponds, moreover, with what the Council of Trent says. It does not say it as explicitly, but it gives it to be understood when it says that in the Roman Canon the prayers go back to Christ and the Apostles.[98] These are therefore venerable words, whence the gravity of altering them and especially of changing them in the translations.[99]

St. Thomas asks whether the words *mysterium fidei* belong to the words spoken by Our Lord. He answers yes, and explains that we are certain of these words through Tradition.[100] We must believe Tradition. That is why we must truly believe that we have the words spoken by Our Lord.[101]

As Dom Pace, a good priest of Turin, explains, Tradition is older than Scripture and more extensive. The Apostles offered the Mass before the Gospels and the Epistles were written. It is recorded in the Acts of the Apostles that they broke bread. The sacrifice was thus offered. So for decades the Apostles offered the holy sacrifice of the Mass, and you may well think that they paid attention to the way it should be celebrated. If there is not more information about the first centuries, it is because the Apostles were obliged to keep it very secret so as not to be taken for cannibals. Our Lord indeed said, "Whoever eats my flesh and drinks my blood..." Some were saying, "It seems that they are sacrificing someone, that they are eating someone's flesh." That is why the Apostles were afraid that the places where they said Mass would be discovered. They were afraid of being pursued and persecuted: hence the discretion of the Gospels and Epistles. In such an atmosphere, the Faith was whispered. From the bishops to those whom they ordained, and from bishop to bishop, the sacred mysteries were conserved with jealous care. That is certain! That is why in the catacombs all the representations are in the form of symbols.[102]

---

[98] "For this [the Canon] consists both of the words of God, and of the traditions of the apostles, and also of pious instructions of the holy Pontiffs" (Council of Trent, Session 22, Chapter 4, Dz. 942).
[99] Spiritual conference, Ecône, February 15, 1979.
[100] *Summa Theologica*, III, Q.78, Art. 3, ad 9.
[101] Spiritual conference, Ecône, July 28, 1987.
[102] Retreat, Ecône, September 22, 1978.

8. The words "for many" translated by "for all" in most languages

As regards the form of the Sacrament of the Eucharist, it is especially the translations that give us pause. The form in Latin as given by the reform still has the words *pro multis*–for many, but the translation in most of the vernacular languages is completely false, because it uses the words *pro omnibus*–for all, which is contrary to what the Church understood from Our Lord when He spoke these words. For, in the application of the Redemption, not everyone is saved: Our Lord came to save all men, but not all men profit from it, for men, by their own fault, do not want to receive the graces of the Redemption. That is why the expression used designates the application of the Redemption, which touches many souls, but not all.[103]

The translations are bad, they are absolutely contrary to what the Catechism of the Council of Trent says, which explains why Our Lord did not say *pro omnibus*, and why in the Mass *pro omnibus* is not said, but *pro multis*.[104] If this Catechism explains the matter in such detail, it is because of its importance, because Our Lord's merits are not applied to all. That is a fact, unfortunately.

---

[103] Spiritual conference, Ecône, March 21, 1977.

[104] "The additional words *for you and for many*, are taken, some from Matthew (26:28), some from Luke (22:20), but were joined together by the Catholic Church under the guidance of the Spirit of God. They serve to declare the fruit and advantage of His Passion. For if we look to its value, we must confess that the Redeemer shed His Blood for the salvation of all; but if we look to the fruit which mankind have received from it, we shall easily find that it pertains not unto all, but to many of the human race. When therefore (Our Lord) said: *For you*, He meant either those who were present, or those chosen from among the Jewish people, such as were, with the exception of Judas, the disciples with whom He was speaking. When He added, *and for many*, He wished to be understood to mean the remainder of the elect from among the Jews or Gentiles. With reason, therefore, were the words *for all* not used, as in this place the fruits of the Passion are alone spoken of, and to the elect only did His Passion bring the fruit of salvation. And this is the purport of the Apostle when he says: *Christ was offered once to exhaust the sins of many* (Heb. 9:28)." Catechism of the Council of Trent (Roman Catholic Books), p.227 [Per a letter from Cardinal Arinze, Prefect of the Congregation for Divine Worship, to the Bishops' Conferences, dated October 16, 2006, henceforth the words "*pro multis*" must be translated as "for many" in vernacular versions of the New Mass.–*Ed.*]

otherwise, there would be no hell if everyone really and truly profited from Our Lord's merits; everyone would go to heaven.[105]

THE DISCARDING OF A SACRED AND UNIVERSAL LANGUAGE

1. The linguistic adaptations may undermine the Faith

It cannot be denied that the Faith comes to us in terms of the wording of liturgical prayer–"*Lex orandi, lex credendi.*" A single language guards the expression of the Faith from the linguistic adaptations of the centuries, and thus the Faith itself. Living languages are changing and shifting.[106]

Living languages evolve, expressions change, meanings change, new words are coined....The danger exists of altering the expression of our Faith.[107]

The study of semantics has developed rapidly in the last ten years or so: it has even been introduced into French language courses in the schools. Semantics investigates changes in the meanings of words, the gradual shift of signification in the passage of time and often over very short periods. Let us make use of this branch of knowledge, therefore, to understand the danger of handing over the deposit of faith to changing ways of speaking. Do you believe that we could have kept intangible, eternal truths free of corruption for two thousand years if they were expressed in languages that are constantly evolving and which differ from one country, and even from one region, to another? Living languages change and fluctuate. If we put the liturgy into any one of them at any time, we will have to be continually adapting according to semantic requirements.[108]

The use of a dead language, a fixed language, was a blessing. If the expressions no longer change, the Faith no longer changes either. It is always expressed definitively in the same terms. Formerly, missals were translated into all languages, but at least there was the

---

[105] Spiritual conference, Ecône, February 15, 1979.
[106] Letter to all the Members of the Congregation of the Holy Ghost on the First Session of Vatican Council II, March 25, 1963, *A Bishop Speaks*, p.13.
[107] March 1986.
[108] *Open Letter to Confused Catholics*, p.34.

Latin text, which did not change. If someone made a faulty translation, he could be corrected: "Watch out! You've translated badly. That is not the way to express our faith." There was at least a solid rule that did not budge, since the language was fixed. This fixity of language was a considerable support for the unity of faith.[109]

2. The use of a universal language strengthened the Catholic communion

We should always remember that we are taking part in an action of the Church, the Catholic Church, and in a prayer that teaches us our Faith, our Catholic Faith. Hence the liturgy, in so far as it keeps its universal character, fashions us for a catholic and universal communion. To the extent that the liturgy is localized and individualized, it loses its universal and catholic dimension, which leaves a profound impression on souls....

It cannot be denied that liturgical actions and that supreme act, the Holy Mass, when expressed in the vernacular tongue only, as in certain Eastern rites, circumscribe the Christian community by the setting of limits. For the peoples of a diaspora they necessitate the presence of local priests if they are to take part in the liturgical rite. Communities are cut off and their members suffer from that isolation. Nor is there any evidence that these communities are more devout and fervent than those who use a universal language incomprehensible to many, but available to all in translation.

A second factor is apparent in those new areas of Christendom which adduce this universality of the Catholic liturgy as proof of the truth of the Catholic Church by contrast with the multiplicity of Protestant rites. This indeed is one of the main bulwarks of the solidarity of Islam, which regards Arabic as the sole language of the Koran, and goes so far as to forbid any translation.[110]

Latin has its importance; and when I was in Africa it was marvelous to see those crowds of Africans of different languages—we sometimes had five or six different tribes who did not understand one another—who could assist at Mass in our churches and sing the

---

[109] March 1986. One can read in *Mediator Dei* of Pope Pius XII: "The use of the Latin language...is a manifest and beautiful sign of unity, as well as an effective antidote for any corruption of doctrinal truth" (§60).
[110] Letter...on the First Session of Vatican Council II, March 25, 1963, *A Bishop Speaks*, pp.12-13.

Latin chants with extraordinary fervor. Go and see them now; they quarrel in the churches because Mass is being said in a language other than theirs, so they are displeased and they want a Mass in their own language. The confusion is total, where before there was perfect unity. That is just one example. You have just heard the Epistle and Gospel read in French–I see no difficulty in that; and if more prayers in French were added, to be said all together, I still see no difficulty. But it still seems to me that the body of the Mass, which runs from the Offertory to the priest's Communion, should remain in a unique language so that all men of all nations can assist together at Mass and can feel united in that unity of faith, in that unity of prayer.[111]

3. The Mass in the vernacular–fruit of rationalism[112]

An example of the penetration of Rationalism in the new liturgy is the fact that its proponents wanted the faithful to be able to understand everything. Rationalism cannot accept something it cannot comprehend: everything must be judged by reason. And of course in the liturgy there are mysterious elements: Latin, the sacred language, the prayers said in a low voice. The priest is turned to the cross and the faithful cannot see what he does. They cannot follow all his gestures. Thus, a certain mystery exists. There is a sacred language.

But even if the faithful do not understand this mystery, the consciousness of the mystery of Our Lord is much more profitable to them than for them to hear the prayers of the Mass read aloud in the vernacular. Firstly, even in the vernacular certain passages are difficult to understand; the truths themselves are difficult to grasp. Then one must take into account the inattention of the mind. People are easily distracted; they listen awhile, focus on one phrase and then lose the train of thought. They cannot follow and understand everything.

---

[111] Homily, Lille, August 29, 1976, *A Bishop Speaks*, p.272.
[112] By *rationalism* we mean the error that consists in judging reality by human reason alone, taking the natural order, accessible to reason, as the supreme principle. The rationalist will thus reject everything that appertains to the supernatural order–mystery, miracles–and will attempt to judge and understand everything according to reason alone.

Prayer is above all a spiritual action, as Our Lord said to the Samaritan woman: "...the true adorers shall adore the Father in spirit and in truth. For the Father also seeketh such to adore him." Prayer is more interior than exterior. If there is exterior prayer, it is in order to favor the interior prayer of the soul, spiritual prayer, the elevation of our soul to God. This is the end that is sought: lift up souls to God.

The current liturgy wearies the soul with its continual noise. There is not a moment of silence. And finally, wearied, the people give it up. They themselves admit that it is tiring to always hear talking. They cannot be recollected for a minute, and they complain.

The error committed in desiring to transform the liturgy is the result of the rationalist spirit that has held sway in our time. They wanted to adapt everything to the modern man who wants to understand everything. Yet everyone knows that the faithful have always had missals where the Latin and the vernacular translation were set side by side. This kind of missal was in use throughout the world, and it was not difficult to follow the Mass. So the reasoning was absurd. But they wanted to adapt things to the spirit of modern man, who does not like mystery. So they destroyed the mystery and banished the sacred—the divine—from the ceremonies.[113]

4. Pope Paul VI decides to abandon Latin

On March 7, 1965, Pope Paul VI declared to the faithful massed in St. Pete's Square: "It is a sacrifice that the Church is making by renouncing Latin, a language that is sacred, beautiful, expressive, elegant. It has sacrificed centuries of tradition and of unity of language for an even greater aspiration towards universality." And on May 4, 1967, this "sacrifice" was accomplished, through the Instruction *Tres Abhinc Annos*, which established the use of the common language for the recitation, aloud, of the Canon of the Mass.

---

[113] *C'est moi l'accusé qui devrais vous juger* (Editions Fideliter, 1994), pp.112-13 [English version: *Against the Heresies* (Kansas City: Angelus Press, 1997), p.106-7].

This "sacrifice" in the mind of Paul VI, seems to have been definitive. He explains himself on this again, on November 26, 1969, while presenting the new rite of the Mass:

> It is no longer Latin, but the current language, that will be the principal language of the Mass. For whoever knows the beauty, the power of the Latin, its aptitude in expressing sacred things, this will certainly be a great sacrifice, to see it replaced by the current language. We are losing the language of the Christian centuries; we are becoming like intruders and outsiders in the literary domain of sacred expression. We are thus losing to a great extent that admirable and incomparable artistic and spiritual richness that is the Gregorian chant. We have reason, to be sure, to feel regret and almost a confusion over this....
>
> [Nevertheless], the response seems banal and prosaic, but it is good, because it is human and apostolic. *The understanding of prayer* is more precious than the decrepit silk garments with which it has been royally adorned. More valuable is the participation of the people, of this people of today that wants *to be spoken to* clearly, in an intelligible manner that it can translate into its secular language. If the noble Latin language cuts us off from children, from the youth, from the world of labor and of business, if it was an opaque screen instead of being a transparent crystal, would we be making a good calculation, we, fishers of souls, by keeping for it the exclusive rights in the language of prayer and of religion?[114]

5. Teaching or worship: the thinking of St. Pius X

The liturgy is not an *instruction* addressed to the people, but the worship directed by the Christian people to God. The catechism is one thing, the liturgy another! It is a question, for the people assembled at the church, not of "being spoken to clearly," but of this people's being able to praise God in the most beautiful, the most sacred, the most solemn manner there is! "To pray to God from beauty"–such was the liturgical maxim of Saint Pius X. How right he was![115]

The understanding of texts is not the last end of prayer, nor is it the sole means of absorbing the soul into prayer, that is, union with God–the aim of prayer. The true object of prayer is God. The soul which attains to God and spiritual union with Him is in

---

[114] *They Have Uncrowned Him* (Angelus Press, 1988), pp.226-27.
[115] *Ibid.*, p.228.

prayer and quenching its thirst at the spring of life. It would thus be contrary to the very end of liturgical action to concentrate so closely on the understanding of the texts as to set up an obstacle to union with God.

On the other hand the simple, untutored but truly Christian soul will attain to union with God, sometimes through the general atmosphere of liturgical action, holiness and quiet of the place, its architectural beauty, the fervor of the Christian community, the nobility and devotion of the celebrant, the symbolic decoration, the fragrance of incense, *etc.* What matter the steps to the altar so long as the soul can raise itself to God and, through the grace of Our Lord, find in Him its heavenly food.

All these considerations in no way diminish the need to seek a better understanding of the liturgical texts and a more perfect sharing in liturgical action. They do, however, lessen the rash and spontaneous desire to seek only one way of such achievement, simply and solely by the use of the vernacular throughout the Mass and the suppression of the universal language of the Church.[116]

TRUTHS HAVE BEEN REMOVED FROM THE PROPER OF THE MASS

> A study by the Benedictine Father Dom Guillou[117] reveals the change in orientation given to the Proper of the New Mass in relation to the traditional Mass. Having become acquainted with it, Archbishop Lefebvre spoke about it on several occasions.

1. The New Mass no longer teaches contempt of the things of this world

In the new missal all the collects and prayers which speak of despising the things of this world for the sake of heavenly things have been changed. What idea inspired those who made these changes? Are the things of heaven not such that we should despise earthly things, which are for us an occasion of sin?[118]

---

[116] Letter...on the First Session of Vatican Council II, March 25, 1963, *A Bishop Speaks*, pp.13-14.
[117] Published in *Fideliter*, No.86, March-April 1992, pp.58-73.
[118] Homily, Mantes-la-Jolie, July 2, 1977.

All the words expressing the spirit of detachment have disappeared: "May we learn to despise what is earthly and love what is heavenly."[119] How often this petition is in our prayers! It is splendid! It is the summary of the spiritual life. What is more beautiful than these words?–to despise the things of earth and love those of heaven. These are St. Paul's own words: "Mind the things that are above, not the things that are upon the earth" (Col. 3:2).[120] What is the reason for these suppressions?[121]

2. The New Mass no longer teaches the spiritual combat

Dom Guillou has done an interesting, very suggestive study that shows that all the collects referring to spiritual combat have been suppressed. Words like *persecutors* and *enemies*[122] have been removed without reason. For example, in the Collect of the Mass for the feast of St. John Capistran[123]: "O God, who...didst enable Thy faithful people to triumph over the enemies of the cross..., grant... that by his intercession we may overcome the snares of our spiritual enemies,"[124] all these terms have been substituted with others from which the notion of combat was eliminated. Likewise in the Secret for the feast of St. Irenaeus,[125] this passage: "...that...Thou wouldst grant peace, and make safe the borders of Christendom against every enemy" was suppressed. The same thing for the Collect: "to overcome heresies by the truth of doctrine," suppressed! Heresy is no longer mentioned. There are no longer pagans, persecutors, enemies, heretics, or those who go astray. Now, what spirit guided those who did this?[126]

It is very sad to have to make the observation, but in all the current prayers, they are striving to eliminate every expression of spiritual combat. There is no more spiritual combat. In all the prayers

---

[119] Cf. Postcommunion of the Mass of the Sacred Heart, the Collect of the Mass of St. Peter Damian (Feb. 23), etc.: *Discamus terrena despicere et amare cælestia.*
[120] *Quæ sursum sunt sapite, quæ sursum sunt quærite.*
[121] Spiritual conference, Ecône, June 25, 1981.
[122] *Persecutores, inimici, hostes.*
[123] March 28th.
[124] *Deus...de crucis inimicis triumphare fecisti: præsta, quæsumus; ut, spiritualium hostium, ejus intercessione, superatis insidiis.*
[125] July 3rd.
[126] Spiritual conference, Ecône, June 25, 1981.

mentioning "combat," "combat against the enemies of our souls," the words have been suppressed, as if there were no more need of spiritual combat. This smacks of Protestantism; the Protestant spirit has penetrated into all the reforms made after the Council.[127]

3. A wave of optimism issued from Vatican II

Dom Guillou cites a text published in the *Documentation Catholique* about the new liturgy: "After the Council, a wave of optimism spread throughout the Church, a stimulating and positive Christianity, the friend of life and earthly values; an intention to make Christianity acceptable, lovable, indulgent, and open, freed from all medieval strictness and of every pessimistic interpretation of men and their mores." As if the Church had always had a pessimistic view of men and their mores. The Church is a good mother who knows us and knows our faults, who knows the reality, and that is why she gives us good counsels.[128]

4. Other truths the New Mass no longer mentions

Everything alluding to miracles or extraordinary events has disappeared from the prayers. The *semper virgo*[129] in numerous instances has also been suppressed. The expression "supreme pontiff" has equally been suppressed because they do not want to hear "supreme" mentioned in our era. In the hymn for the feast of Christ the King, two stanzas that speak of the social reign of Our Lord Jesus Christ have been dropped. One wonders who was responsible for this. Who wanted to change our spirituality?–and this, in the Mass!

The rite for the dead was changed. The word *anima* ("soul") has frequently disappeared from numerous prayers for the dead because with the new philosophies they no longer truly know if there is a real distinction between the soul and the body. So you must not talk about the soul any more. Unbelievable... Devotion to the deceased has disappeared; the reality and purpose of purgatory are no longer understood.[130]

---

[127] Retreat, Brignoles, July 27, 1984.
[128] Spiritual conference, Ecône, June 25, 1981.
[129] "Ever virgin," affirming the perpetual virginity of our Lady.
[130] Spiritual conference, Ecône, June 25, 1981.

5. The Mass for the dead is celebrated less and less frequently

It has to be admitted that now almost no Masses for the dead are offered except for funeral Masses. This is very significant, you see, precisely because Masses for the dead are propitiatory Masses. They call upon God's mercy for the remission of the sins of the souls still in purgatory. This was something Luther could not admit. Moreover, they suppressed the color black for burial Masses. They use the color white or gold because they no longer want to acknowledge purgatory in practice.[131]

For instance, a young priest of the Congregation of the Holy Ghost Fathers, ordained in the diocese two years ago by Bishop Adam, when some friends of his asked him to say a Mass for the repose of the soul of some of his own kinsmen recently deceased, answered: "Oh, no! I do not say Masses for the dead." His friends came back: "Why won't you say Masses for your uncles and aunts who have died just recently?" The young priest, who is now a teacher at the Bouveret school, told them: "Everyone is in heaven. They are all in heaven. So I do not say Masses for the dead." What can this priest be teaching the children of Bouveret?[132]

The Door Opened to Anarchy

1. The New Mass introduced confusion

The New Mass threw everything into total confusion. It opened the doors to a certain freedom, of which clearly everyone takes advantage. One says this Canon, another makes one up; one takes this or that form of confession. The Gospels can be selected according to the circumstances. In short, it is total freedom.

I give you another example: the children's Masses. This is yet another door opened to freedom. What is a "Mass for children"? What is a child? Until what age? What is more, it suffices to have a few children in the assembly to be able to say a children's Mass. You see where they are heading! This freedom leads to innovations, and the result is abuses everywhere. And the children will inevitably become grown-ups. Having been accustomed to having special

---

[131] *Ibid.*, October 26, 1979.
[132] Retreat, Ecône, September 22, 1978.

Masses, when they are told that they are adults, they will retort that they don't understand anything. They will give up the Mass and will no longer practice.[133]

Recently a list of the different authorized Eucharistic prayers was published in all the diocesan weeklies of France. There would be, according to this document signed by the bishops' commission and approved by Rome, ten official Eucharistic prayers that can be used by the priests of France to celebrate holy Mass. Consequently, the priests can choose among these Eucharistic prayers. There is a note that eventually, in different circumstances, the priests are authorized to modify these Eucharistic prayers according to the particular congregations. That is to say, ultimately, that nothing is fixed. A priest can say the Mass as he wants, as he understands it, or, as they say nowadays, according to his "creativity," according to his ideas, his imagination. This is no longer the Catholic Church![134]

2. The rite must not be subject to modification by the priests

The liturgy is a public act. It is the Church's expressed devotion. When we perform liturgical acts...it is the Church who acts through us. We must not transform these acts of public devotion into acts of private devotion. There is a great danger of believing that we can, for example, modify certain things even within the sacrifice of the Mass, prolong our prayers, offer the holy sacrifice of the Mass as if it were an act of private devotion.[135]

3. Is this simply a matter of rare abuses?

When we are answered: "Ah! but you are talking of abuses. Those are the people who do not keep the rule." To my regret, I must answer, unhappily, no. They are not abuses. Look at the little leaflet "Masses for Small Groups and for Particular Groups." It contains rules laid down by the Episcopate, which, consequently, leave the door open to all abuses. That must be so since, for these group masses, there needs be only a reading from the Gospel and the recitation of one of the four Canons–and three more are added

---

[133] Spiritual conference, Ecône, January 1974.
[134] Homily, Geneva, May 15, 1978.
[135] Spiritual conference, Zaitzkofen, February 7, 1980.

ad experimentum–for children! Not to mention that before long, one may legitimately make one's own Canon. As yet, however, we need still say one of the four Canons and one Gospel. All else is open to the choice of the priest who "presides over the assembly." He may begin the Mass as he pleases, say the Offertory as he pleases, and "make up prayers" (that is the wording used).[136]

In the mind of the religious authorities in place, you can make remarks about what they call "abuses"–they call abuses those things pointed out to them here and there: "Ah, but those are just abuses." No, these are not abuses at all; rather they are things accepted by Rome: Communion in the hand, Mass facing the people, no more relics, no more altar stone, a single linen cloth on the altar, no more crucifix...; all these things have been accepted officially by Rome. These are things published in *Notitiæ*.[137]...This has provoked even greater abuses, obviously. But it is not only against abuses that we are reacting, but against the reform itself.[138]

Conclusion

The following fundamental dogmas of the Holy Sacrifice of the Mass are not clearly represented and are even contradicted:
–that the priest is the essential minister of the rite;
–that in the Mass there is a true sacrifice, a sacrificial *action*; that the Victim or Host is Our Lord Jesus Christ Himself, present under the species of bread and wine, with His Body, Blood, Soul and Divinity;
–that this sacrifice is a propitiatory one;
–that the sacrifice and the Sacrament are effected by the words of the consecration alone, and not also by those which either precede or follow them.

It is sufficient to enumerate a few of the novelties in the New Mass to be convinced of the *rapprochement* with the Protestants:
–the altar replaced by a table without an altar stone;

---

[136] "Priests for Tomorrow," March 29, 1973, *A Bishop Speaks*, pp.157-58.
[137] Up to No. 45 (March 1969), *Notitiae* was the journal of the *Consilium* (*Consilium ad Exsequendam Constitutionem de Sacra Liturgia*). From No. 46 (April 1969) onwards, it became the journal of the Sacred Congregation for Divine Worship. From No. 108-109 (August-September 1975) it became the journal for the Sacred Congregation for the Sacraments and Divine Worship.
[138] Spiritual conference, Ecône, January 10, 1983.

–the Mass celebrated facing the people, concelebrated, in a loud voice, and in the vernacular;

–the Mass divided into two distinct parts: Liturgy of the Word and Liturgy of the Eucharist;

–the cheapening of the sacred vessels, the use of leavened bread, distribution of Holy Communion in the hand and by the laity, and even by women;

–the Blessed Sacrament hidden in corners;

–the Epistle read by women;

–Holy Communion brought to the sick by the laity.

All these innovations are authorized.[139]

THE INTENTION BEHIND THE REFORM

THE DEFINITION OF THE *NOVUS ORDO MISSAE*

The *Institutio Generalis* (General Instruction), the official document published in 1969 to introduce the New Mass, contained in its Article 7 a definition of the Mass more Protestant than Catholic. As a result of the opposition its publication aroused, the document was modified the next year, but the texts of the Mass were not changed. Archbishop Lefebvre denounced this Article 7 in which the spirit that had presided over the elaboration of the New Mass was clearly visible.

1. The definition of the Mass in the *Institutio Generalis*[140]

"The Lord's Supper or Mass is the assembly or meeting of the People of God, met together with a priest presiding, to celebrate the Memorial of the Lord."[141] That is the definition.[142] "For this

---

[139] Note on the N.O.M. and the Pope, November 8, 1979, *Cor Unum*, No.4. [English version: *Apologia pro Marcel Lefebvre* (Angelus Press, 1983), II, 369.]

[140] The *Institutio Generalis*, first version, Article 7. On April 3, 1969, Pope Paul VI promulgated simultaneously with the New Order of Mass a General Instruction, the *Institutio Generalis*, which replaced the "General Rubrics" of the Tridentine Missal.

[141] The English version of the entire text of Article 7 is taken from Michael Davies, *Pope Paul's New Mass* (Angelus Press, 1980), p.285.

[142] Even if there was a controversy over the character of the definition of the Mass in Article 7 of the General Instruction, many indications persuade us that it is indeed a definition. The Secretary of the Congregation for Divine Worship, Fr. Bugnini, wrote: "The Fathers reiterated that this 'General

reason the promise of Christ is particularly true of a local congregation of the Church: "Where two or three are gathered in my name, there I am in their midst" (Mt. 18:20). That is how they define the New Mass. This definition is absolutely contrary to Catholic teaching.[143]

2. The new edition of 1970 did not "correct" the rite[144]

Article VII of the instruction which introduces the new rite expressed an already Protestant mentality. The later correction is by no means satisfactory.[145]

In response to a great number of protests and pleading, a foreword was added that makes reference to the notion of sacrifice in

---

Presentation' is not a dogmatic text, but purely and simply an exposition of the norms regulating the Eucharistic celebration; there is no intention to define the Mass, but rather to give a description of the rites" (*Documentation Catholique*, No.1552, December 7, 1969, p.1055). But Paul VI decided the matter: "The new missal is preceded by a 'General Presentation' which is not a simple collection of rubrics, but rather a synthesis of the theological, ascetical, and pastoral principles indispensable for doctrinal understanding as well as for the celebration, catechesis, and pastoral ministry of the Mass" ("The New Roman Missal": Pontifical Letter to the Liturgical Week of Italy, *Documentation Catholique*, No. 1594, October 3, 1971, p.866).

The well-known commentator Fr. Tillard wrote: "In the 1969 text, a remarkable definition..." (Jean-Marie R. Tillard, "The Liturgical Reform and the *Rapprochement* of the Churches," *Liturgia opera divina e umana: Studi sulla riforma liturgica offerti a S.E. Mons. Annibale Bugnini* [Ed. Liturgiche, 1982], p.218). Likewise, Dom Oury speaks of the first edition of Article 7 as "a definition of the Mass...perfectly orthodox" ("Le missel de Paul VI," *Esprit et Vie: L'Ami du clergé*, No. 30, July 23, 1970, p.462).

[143] Spiritual conference, Ecône, January 19, 1982.
[144] After the scandal provoked by the publication of the first version of Article 7, Pope Paul VI ordered its revision. A new version was published in 1970: "In the Mass or Lord's Supper the People of God are called together into one place where the priest presides over them and acts in the person of Christ. They assemble to celebrate the Memorial of the Lord, which is the sacrifice of the Eucharist. Hence the promise of Christ: "Wherever two or three are gathered together in my name, there am I in the midst of them" (Mt. 18:20) applies in a special way to this gathering of the local church. For in the celebration of the Mass whereby the Sacrifice of the Cross is perpetuated, Christ is really present in the very community which has gathered in His name, in the person of His minister and also substantially and continuously under the eucharistic species." [English version: Davies, *Pope Paul's New Mass*, p.287.]
[145] Conference, Florence, February 15, 1975, *A Bishop Speaks*, p.195.

accord with the Council of Trent. The idea of sacrifice is present. Msgr. Benelli said: "Look at the Foreword to the Roman Missal; you will see the sacrifice of the Mass according to the Council of Trent." But in the Mass itself, nothing was changed; everything stayed the same. If they had really wanted to restore the notion of sacrifice to the Mass, it would have been necessary to reintroduce the texts that explicitly express it.[146]

I acknowledge that in the *Proemium*[147] of the 1970 edition, the doctrine of the Council of Trent is to be found expressed materially. But the fact that it was necessary to add a preface clearly shows the incomplete character of the 1969 edition. Moreover, the ensemble of the rituals of the Mass remained as it was in the 1969 edition.[148] It is as if the blue-prints of a house were changed without changing the house itself![149]

3. A purely tactical change

The wording of Article 7 was changed to make it appear less Protestant, but it was not changed fundamentally. Msgr. Bugnini, who was its author, said: "They wanted to make us change something in the definition of the Mass. Some protested against this definition. That is ridiculous. This definition was not at all Protestant." Msgr. Bugnini tried to excuse himself, and he said:[150] "The new definition that was made changes nothing essential."[151]

4. Article 7 was not a work of the Holy Ghost

It is impossible for the Holy Ghost to have inspired the definition of the Mass given in Article 7 of the Constitution, and it is even more amazing that they felt the need to correct it right away,

---

[146] Spiritual conference, Ecône, March 26, 1976.
[147] The Foreword.
[148] Interrogatory at Rome, January 11-12, 1979, in *Itinéraires*, No.233, May 1979, p.147.
[149] Spiritual conference, Ecône, June 24, 1981.
[150] "Since it has been said repeatedly that no doctrinal error was found in the original draft, and that the changes introduced only aimed at cutting short pointless difficulties, one can continue to reference the 1969 wording.
It represents the purest form of the thinking inscribed in the *Institutio Generalis*, beyond "forced" compromises" (Tillard, "The Liturgical Reform and the *Rapprochement* of the Churches," p.233).
[151] March 1986.

which is an acknowledgment of a defect in the Church's most important reality: the holy sacrifice of the Mass.[152]

THE DRAFTERS OF THE *NOVUS ORDO MISSAE*

1. The author of the New Mass

Is the Holy Father in person at the origin of the new Mass, or is it men he appointed–like Msgr. Bugnini at the Congregation for Divine Worship–who exert a considerable influence over him and who were able to put what they wanted in the texts, by compelling him to sign or by imposing on him their point of view.[153]

I do not know whom to blame it on, or if the Pope is responsible for it. What is astounding is that an order of Mass of a Protestant savor, and thus favoring heresy,[154] could have been diffused by the Roman Curia.[155]

2. Monsignor Bugnini's authority

Cardinal Ratzinger wrote to me in his letter of July 20, 1983, "You also know that for the interpretation of the missal, the essential is not what private authors say about it, but only the official documents of the Holy See. The statements of Father Boyer and Msgr. Bugnini to which you allude are only private opinions." It is astounding to see how the Cardinal fails to recognize the authority of Msgr. Bugnini, head of the Commission on the Liturgy, secretary of the combined Congregations for Worship and the Sacraments. Msgr. Bugnini had Paul VI's entire confidence, and replied many times in his name and in the name of the Congregations of which he was the secretary. One can only wonder what the liturgical reform of which he is the mainspring amounts to if it is merely a private work.[156]

---

[152] *Satan's Masterstroke* [French], October 13, 1974, pp.7-8.
[153] Spiritual conference, Ecône, January 1974.
[154] *Favens haeresim*. A theological note assigned to an error that is opposed to a proposition held as certain in theology.
[155] Interrogatory at Rome, *Itinéraires*, No. 233, May 1979, pp.146-47.
[156] Commentary on Cardinal Ratzinger's letter of July 20, 1983, *Fideliter*, No.45, May-June 1985.

3. Monsignor Bugnini's past

The liturgical reform, everyone knows, was brought about by a well-known Father: Father Bugnini, who prepared it long beforehand. As early as 1955, he had the Protestant texts translated by Msgr. Pintonello, general chaplain of the Italian armies (who had spent a lot of time in Germany during the Occupation), because he did not know German. It was Msgr. Pintonello who told me personally that he had translated the Protestant liturgical books for Father Bugnini, who, at that time, was only an insignificant member of a liturgical commission. He was nobody. Afterwards, he was professor of Liturgy at the Lateran. Pope John XXIII made him leave because of his modernism and progressivism. Well, he ended up head [secretary] of the Commission for implementing the liturgical reform. That is, all the same, incredible! I had the opportunity to see for myself the influence Father Bugnini had. One wonders how something like that could happen at Rome.[157]

THE FINALITY OF THE *NOVUS ORDO MISSAE*

Having analyzed the rite of the New Mass and having introduced its principal artisan, we take a look at the goal assigned to the reform.

1. The ecumenical goal of the New Mass.

When a critical textual examination of the liturgical reform and of everything that was changed in the rite is made, it becomes clear that the fundamental purpose is ecumenical. The goal is a false ecumenism that, quite simply, makes us adapt the rites in a Protestant manner, no more and no less.[158]

The liturgical reform is an ecumenical reform made in a Protestant direction with the participation of six Protestant pastors, as the *Documentation Catholique* gave us the proof by publishing a photograph of the Protestant representatives surrounding the Holy Father.[159]

---

[157] *L'Église infiltrée par le modernisme*, p.31.
[158] Spiritual conference, Ecône, January 16, 1975.
[159] Conference, Nantes, October 13, 1985. Number 1562, of May 3, 1970, of the *Documentation Catholique* shows the photograph of the six Protestant pastors (Dr. Georges, Canon Jasper, Dr. Sephard, Dr. Konneth, Dr.

No Protestant official was an accredited member...of the commission charged with the drafting of the new Mass....It is presumptuous to conclude from this fact that "the Protestants had nothing to do with the drafting of the new Anaphoras,"[160] and, still more so, of the New Mass. As far as I know, this commission did not work in a conclave, and Dom Botte[161] cannot state with certainty that, between the meetings, none of his colleagues communicated with the six Protestant "observers"attached *qualitate qua* to the Consilium for liturgical reform, to which the said commission was answerable....Is it possible to imagine that they could have been ignored at the very moment when one of the questions of greatest importance to them was being discussed, since it touches on the sacrificial nature of the Mass?

The active intervention of these observers is corroborated by the declarations of Msgr. W. W. Baum, Executive Director for ecumenical affairs of the American episcopal conference: "They are not simply there as observers, but as consultants as well, and they participate fully in the discussions on Catholic liturgical renewal. It wouldn't mean much if they just listened, but they contributed."[162] Nevertheless, in the highly unlikely case that the so-called "observers" did not collaborate in the drafting of the new Eucharistic prayers (and in the vandalizing of the Roman Canon of which the

---

Smith, and Brother Max Thurian, representing the Ecumenical Council of Churches, the Anglican and Lutheran communities, and the Taizé community) who participated in the Consilium for the implementation of the Constitution on the Liturgy.

[160] *Anaphore* means "offering." It is the usual term for the Eucharistic prayer or Canon of the Mass in the Oriental Rites.

[161] Dom Botte had asserted that "the Protestants had absolutely nothing to do" with the Eucharistic prayers of the new *Ordo* ("Quelques précisions sur les prières eucharistiques," *La Libre Belgique*, September 15, 1976).

[162] *The Detroit News*, June 27, 1967. Msgr. Boudon gives a similar testimony in his account of the eighth session of the Consilium: "We had the pleasure of benefitting, as during the previous session in October 1966, from the active presence of observers delegated by the other Christian Churches. Taking part in our work, they were able to contribute the testimony of their own research and to compare this with our own. The liturgical reform was elaborated in a climate of ecumenism eminently profitable for everyone and, in the long run, for the unity of the Church" ("The Eighth Session of the Consilium on Liturgy" [French], *Documentation Catholique*, No. 1494, May 21, 1967, col.957).

Eucharistic Prayer I[163] is but a skillful counterfeit), it would be necessary to say that their spirit had so influenced the members of the commission that they spontaneously fulfilled the unexpressed wishes of the heretics.[164]

They wanted to draw nearer to the Protestants, not by attracting them towards Catholicism, but conversely by conflating the latter with Protestantism.[165] The reformers of the Mass worked things out so that practically everything that was opposed to Protestantism was suppressed in order, so they claimed, to reach union in prayer, a union which is not unity in belief.[166]

Msgr. Bugnini himself said as much on March 19, 1965, as you can read in *L'Osservatore Romano*...: "We must strip from our Catholic prayers and from the Catholic liturgy everything which can be the shadow of a stumbling block for our separated brethren, that is, for the Protestants." This was on March 19, 1965, thus before all the reforms. Is it possible that we were now going to go and ask the Protestants about the holy sacrifice of the Mass, our Sacraments, all our prayers, our catechism: What do you disagree with? You don't like this, you don't like that... Good, we'll get rid of it.[167]

This is why they changed the formulas of the holy sacrifice of the Mass, as well as those of the Sacraments; they changed the priests' breviary and the calendar. Everything was done to avoid anything that might bother the Protestants. But by dint of asking before each reform what the Protestants think, obviously one ends by eliminating everything that is specifically Catholic, everything that truly recalls our faith in opposition to Protestant errors.[168]

---

[163] The first Canon of the four proposed in the new *Ordo*.
[164] "The New Mass Is of a Protestant Spirit," Reply to Dom Bott published in *La Libre Belgique*, September 25, 1976.
[165] *L'Église infiltrée par le modernisme*, p.84.
[166] Spiritual conference, Ecône, January 16, 1982.
[167] *L'Église infiltrée par le modernisme*, pp.50-51.
[168] *Ibid.*, p.84.

2. The Protestants' own admission

The statements of the Protestants who contributed to this reform candidly and sadly illustrate this truth: "The Protestants no longer see any obstacle to their celebrating the *Novus Ordo*."[169] *L'Église en Alsace*, the bulletin of the diocese of Strasbourg, published this declaration of the Higher Consistory of the Church of the Confession of Augsburg, Alsace, and Lorraine, Protestant Church, on December 8, 1973: "Given the current forms of the Eucharistic celebration in the Catholic Church, and because of contemporary theological convergences, many of the obstacles that could have kept a Protestant from participating in these Eucharistic celebrations seem to be on the way out. Today it should be possible for a Protestant to recognize in the Catholic Eucharistic celebration the Supper instituted by Christ," that is to say, the way in which the Protestants carry out their worship service. In the present circumstances, the new rite allows Protestants to worship with Catholics, because, they say it explicitly further on, "the new Eucharistic prayers being used have the advantage of nuancing the theology of sacrifice we are accustomed to attribute to the Catholics. These prayers invite us to rediscover the evangelical theology of sacrifice,"[170] that is, the Protestant theology of sacrifice.[171]

If I read *Documentation Catholique* or the diocesan papers, I find there, from the Joint Catholic-Lutheran Commission, officially recognized by the Vatican, statements like this:

---

[169] Rome, May 13, 1971. Cf. Max Thurian, *La Croix* of May 30, 1969, cited by Romano Amerio in *Iota Unum: A Study of Changes in the Catholic Church in the 20th Century* (Sarto House, 1996), p.651.

[170] Official Declaration of the Higher Consistory of the Church of the Confession of Augsburg of Alsace and Lorraine, December 8, 1973.

[171] Conference, Mantes-la-Jolie, April 22, 1977. The following declarations might also be mentioned: The new Eucharistic prayers II and IV present "a structure that corresponds to the Lutheran Mass" (F. Schukz, Dossier of the Lutheran Liturgical Conference, May 15, 1972); "The revised Roman liturgy now very closely resembles the Anglican liturgy" (Anglican Archdeacon Bernard C. Pawley, *Rome and Canterbury through Four Centuries*); "The reintroduction of the Mass of St. Pius V is much more than a matter of language: a doctrinal question of the highest importance is at the center of the debates between Catholics and Protestants....Many of our ancestors in the law reformed according to the Word of God preferred to go to the stake rather than hear the type of Mass that Pope Pius V codified against the reform" (Pastor Michel Viot, 1984).

Among the ideas of the Second Vatican Council, we can see gathered together much of what Luther asked for, such as the following: description of the Church as 'the people of God' (a leading idea of the new Canon Law–a democratic, no longer hierarchic, idea), accent on the priesthood of all baptized, the right of the individual to freedom of religion. Other demands of Luther in his time can be considered as being met in the theology and practice of the Church today: use of the common language in the liturgy, possibility of Communion under two species, a renewal of the theology and celebration of the Eucharist.

Quite a statement! Meeting the demands of Luther, who declared himself the resolute and mortal enemy of the Mass and of the pope! To gather together things requested by a blasphemer who said: "I declare that all brothels, murders, thefts, adulteries, are less evil than this abominable Mass!"[172]

3. An inexplicable rapprochement

Now, it is easy to show that the New Mass, as it was formulated by the officially authorized Conciliar Liturgical Commission considered together with the explanation of Msgr. Bugnini, manifests an inexplicable *rapprochement* with the theology and liturgy of the Protestants. The fundamental dogmas of the holy sacrifice of the Mass are not clearly represented and are even contradicted.[173]

Conclusion

1. Tradition and Sacred Scripture: two paths from which one must not stray

When the ensemble of Church authorities, the hierarchy, take a position, might it not be pride that would make us say that we are right and they are wrong? Isn't it an exaggeration, after all, to say that we have the truth? Our having the truth does not depend on us. Where is the truth? The truth is in Revelation. Revelation is manifested to us by Tradition and Sacred Scripture, the two ways through which Revelation is handed down.[174]

---

[172] *Open Letter to Confused Catholics*, p.3.
[173] Note on the N.O.M. and the Pope, November 8, 1979, in *Cor Unum*, No.4. [Davies, *Apologia*, II, 368-69.]
[174] Homily, Zaitzkofen, February 15, 1987.

2. What changes can legitimately be made in a rite?

Undoubtedly, the Pope could have changed certain rites, but rather by emphasizing the three or four fundamental notions of the Mass. So, yes: change for the sake of affirming these fundamental truths more forcefully is possible, but not to make them disappear, not to suppress them–that is impossible.[175]

3. The novelties of the Mass are incompatible with Tradition

We are in this Tradition, so important, so essential, so fundamental, because it continues the expiatory sacrifice of the Old Testament and of the New Testament of Our Lord Jesus Christ, it continues to expiate sins, and it continues the Redemption willed by Our Lord Jesus Christ. We refuse the New Mass because it no longer embodies the spirit of expiation of Our Lord Jesus Christ's Redemption by His Blood. This idea of expiatory sacrifice fades and disappears in this new rite that Paul VI intended to be new. He himself said it: "We are abandoning the old rite to make a new rite."[176]

4. The spirit of novelty is contrary to the traditional principles of the liturgy

The secretary of the Consilium...presented the liturgical reform in this way: "The issue is not simply one of touching up, so

---

[175] Flavigny, August 7, 1972. Ecône Seminary archives. The Council of Trent teaches: "...this power has always been in the Church, that in the administration of the Sacraments, preserving their substance, she may determine or change whatever she may judge to be more expedient for the benefit of those who receive them or for the veneration of the Sacraments, according to the variety of circumstances, times, and places" (Session 21, Ch. 2, DS 1728 [Dz. 931]).This chapter speaks about the practice of Communion under one species, which was introduced very gradually in the Church and not suddenly and in rupture. This statement does not mean that the Sovereign Pontiff has full power to introduce a new liturgy. There is a certain analogy between the domain of liturgy and the domain of dogma, for which "the Holy Spirit was not promised to the successors of Peter that by His revelation they might disclose new doctrine, but that by His help they might guard sacredly the revelation transmitted through the apostles and the deposit of faith, and might faithfully set it forth" (Vatican Council I, *Pastor Aeternus*, DS 3070 [Dz. 1836]).

[176] Spiritual conference, Ecône, September 27, 1986.

to speak, a priceless work of art; in some areas entire rites have to be restructured *ex novo* [from scratch]. Certainly this involves restoring, but ultimately I would almost call it a remaking and, on certain points, a creating anew. Why a work that is so radical? Because the vision of the liturgy the Council has given us is completely diverse from what we had before."[177] That is not in the spirit of Catholic tradition evoked by Dom Gueranger[178]: "The antiquity, the immutability of the formulas of the altar is the first of their qualities."[179]

5. The novelties are human inventions

We are obliged to state very firmly and clearly that the *Novus Ordo Missae* and all the novelties that have been realized after the Second Vatican Council are human creations. Undoubtedly a few vestiges of the old *Ordo* have been retained, but so few! And the instigators of all these upheavals have been pleased to say that it truly is a new Order of Mass, a new liturgy.[180]

Consider Msgr. Bugnini's principles concerning what he calls sound tradition and legitimate development: "It has been said that 'in important matters authentic tradition consists not in restoring what others have done, but in rediscovering the spirit that brought those things into existence and that would do other, completely different things at other times.'"[181] With principles like these, anything goes. It suffices to rediscover the spirit of tradition to do things completely different. He continues:

> "To rediscover the spirit": this requires research and review; a scrupulously careful and diligent determination of what makes up the sacred patrimony so that a valid appraisal may emerge objectively and, as it were, naturally and spontaneously from study, meditation, and prayer....Rediscovery of the spirit, then, and the effort to make the rites speak the language of our own time so that

---

[177] Annibale Bugnini, Press Conference of January 4, 1967: *Notitiae*, I (1967), 39-45. [English version: *Documents on the Liturgy, 1963-1969: Conciliar, Papal, and Curial Texts* (The Liturgical Press, 1982), §437.]

[178] *Institutions liturgiques*, 2nd ed., I, 389.

[179] "The New Mass Is of a Protestant Spirit," *La Libre Belgique*, September 25, 1976.

[180] Homily, Flavigny, June 26, 1984.

[181] A. Bugnini, *The Reform of the Liturgy* 1948-1975 (The Liturgical Press, 1990), p.44.

the men and women of today may understand the language of the rites, which is both mysterious and sacred.....[182]

With principles like that, it is over. They do whatever they like. This is the spirit in which the liberals speak and act. So, standing on these principles, Msgr. Bugnini destroyed the liturgy and practically imposed his reform on Paul VI. I say imposed because Pope Paul VI himself publicly criticized Msgr. Bugnini's reform, in particular the absence of the exorcisms in the new rite of Baptism..., and he also expressed regrets over the changes in the Offertory of the Mass.[183]

6. The avowal of the chief author of the New Mass

This is what Msgr. Bugnini wrote in the chapter of a book he devoted to the principles of liturgical reform: "It is true in fact that the New Mass represents, in relation to the old, a real departure from the past."[184]

"Indeed," he says, "it must be recognized that during the course of the centuries preceding the Second Vatican Council, the Church strove to uphold the tradition of the Roman Rite." He recognizes that the Gregorian reform and that of the Council of Trent were nothing else than official acts of the Church to maintain the Roman Rite in its purity and perfection. And he adds: "After the Council of Trent, the Congregation for Divine Worship was established." He himself quotes and puts in quotation marks the reason for this foundation: "To conserve the tradition of the Roman Rite." And he further specifies: "Indeed, from this foundation to our time, seven volumes of decrees have accumulated, representing five thousand decrees: all were written, all were made to uphold

---

[182] *Ibid.*, pp.44-45.
[183] Spiritual conference, Ecône, June 12, 1984.
[184] Concerning this innovative, anti-traditional attitude of the artisans of the N.O.M., Cardinal Antonelli, a member of the Consilium of which Fr. Bugnini was Secretary, confided: "It is a fundamental disposition, a mind set, a pre-established position, namely, that many of those who influenced the reform...and others, have no love, no veneration, for what was handed down to us....[It was] a negative spirit, unjust and harmful" (quoted in N. Giampetro, *Ferdinando Antonelli e gli sviluppi della riforma liturgica dal 1948 al 1970* [Rome, 1998], p.258).

the Tradition of the Church." This is what Father Bugnini himself states in his posthumously edited book.

He himself wrote that the New Mass constitutes a real departure from the past, and he confirms that the Church, by the thousands of decrees enacted up to the eve of Vatican II, always wanted steadfastly to preserve Tradition. How then, after such an assertion, can one pass to something new? The author explains it to us: "In our era, a cultural, religious, social, and human evolution is taking place such that one no longer wants to keep the things of the past. And that is why it seemed to us necessary to make a rite that is better adapted to the mentality of the modern world."

This is what the author, himself, of the *Novus Ordo Missae* has to say. It is not we who say it; it is he who explicitly and formally wrote it. He no longer pretends, as many have asserted and still repeat, that "Just as there were the Gregorian reform and the Tridentine reform, so also there is the reform of the Second Vatican Council." Bugnini acknowledges that the first two reforms were intended to preserve Tradition, and that the reform that issued from Vatican II is truly a novelty, something new, that it is truly a departure from the past. That is why we cannot accept that today they take away from souls the very thing by which they were nourished for centuries. Souls still need the same sacrifice of Our Lord.[185]

---

[185] Homily, Flavigny, June 26, 1984.

II. Luther's Mass

We have previously seen how the new rite weakened the fundamental dogmas manifested in the Mass celebrated according to the traditional rite. Time and again, Archbishop Lefebvre asserted that this modification tended towards Protestantism. He offered a confirmation of this assertion by his analysis of the Protestant Eucharistic liturgy and notion of priesthood.

Lutheranism and Anglicanism

The Protestants center their worship on man; they suppress the Offertory, change the words of the Consecration, for wrong reasons communicate under both species, and pray in the vernacular tongue. Their reform was established progressively in such wise that the people gradually slid into heresy without really realizing it.

1. Luther's reform

Luther said: "Worship used to be addressed to God in homage; in future it will be addressed to man to console and enlighten him. Sacrifice used to occupy the first place; the sermon now supplants it."[1] According to his reform, the way of saying Mass was laid down. The Introit, the *Gloria*, the Epistle, the Gospel, and the *Sanctus* were kept. A sermon followed, the Offertory and the Canon were abolished. The priest would simply narrate the institution of the Last Supper; he would speak aloud in German the words of the consecration and would give Communion under both kinds....The consecration is to be sung in German. It is in these words:

> Our Lord, in the night in which He was betrayed, took bread and brake it and said, "Take and eat–This is my Body which is given for you: Each time you do this, do it in remembrance of Me." In like manner also He took the cup after supper saying: "Take all of you and drink. This cup is the New Testament in my Blood which is shed for you and for the remission of sins. This do, as often as ye drink this chalice, in remembrance of Me.[2]

---

[1] Msgr. Leon Cristiani, *Du luthéranisme au protestantisme*, p.312.
[2] *Ibid.*, p.317.

Do not these accounts of the evangelical Mass express the feeling we have about the reformed liturgy which followed the Council?[3]

Studying all the details of the new reform of the Mass in particular, one is astounded to find all the reforms that Luther, the Jansenists, and the Council of Pistoia[4] advocated.[5] There is really no difference between the New Mass and the Mass that Luther said in his lifetime. Of course, [in Luther's day], the youth were full of enthusiasm because the Mass was said in German; people understood, it was much more beautiful, more in conformity with the pastoral spirit, *etc*. All the reasons that are given today in favor of the vernacular language were given when Luther translated the rite of Mass. The same things happened: when a host fell during the distribution of Communion, the people were reluctant to touch it because they still reverenced the Holy Eucharist. And one of Luther's disciples who was there said: "Come now, pick it up! Look, pick it up with your hands!" But the people did not want to: there was still respect. Slowly but surely, this respect disappeared. This is also what is happening nowadays.

You can see all the other changes. For example, now they have introduced part of the narrative into the words of consecration. But that is exactly what Luther did, too. Take a look at the book *Lutheranism and Protestantism* by Cristiani, and you will see that all that has been quoted. The book was published in 1910; it does not date from today, so its author could not be thinking of what would be taking place now. Luther changed exactly the same words in the consecration. The only difference is that Luther suppressed

---

[3] Conference, Florence, February 15, 1975, *A Bishop Speaks*, pp.189-202.
[4] The Council of Pistoia was a Jansenist assembly convoked by the Bishop of Pistoia, the decisions of which together with those of the Council of Florence were condemned by Pius VI (Bull *Auctorem Fidei*, August 28, 1794). Pius VI condemned, among others, a proposition of this "synod" for the simple reason that it omitted the word *transubstantiation* (DS 2629), as well as the following proposition: "The proposition asserting that 'it would be against apostolic practice and the plans of God, unless easier ways were prepared for the people to unite their voice with that of the whole Church'; if understood to signify introducing of the use of popular language into the liturgical prayers,–false, rash, disturbing to the order prescribed for the celebration of the mysteries, easily productive of many evils" (DS 2666).
[5] Letter to Cardinal Seper, February 26, 1978.

the "*pro multis/pro omnibus*–for many, for all." I would say that that was better than what is done today, because now they say *pro omnibus* in the vernacular languages, whereas he simply left it out. But as for the rest, it is exactly the same thing. He suppressed "*mysterium fidei*–the mystery of Faith," and he added "*quod pro vobis tradetur*–which will be given up for you" to the form of the consecration of the bread. Well, this is exactly what has come to us from Rome in the *Notitiae*,[6] etc. The same holds true for the suppression of the Offertory, because Luther did not want it to be a sacrifice. He said: "We absolutely refuse to call the Mass a sacrifice. Let us call it a *meal, Eucharistic supper*, or *Eucharist*." These are the very same terms employed nowadays. Internal textual criticism also shows us a veritable absence of Catholic theology on the sacrifice of the Mass and the priesthood. It also betrays an ignorance of pastoral ministry. One might say that these reforms in general are completely contrary to true ministry. The best proof of that is that since these reforms, people have been abandoning religious practice instead of flocking to the churches. The progressivists themselves recognize that religious practice is constantly decreasing.[7]

2. The Anglican reform

In the new *ordo* imposed under Edward VI, the *Confiteor*, translated into the vernacular, was recited at the same time by the celebrant and the faithful, and served as an absolution. The Mass was transformed into a meal or Communion. But even clear-headed bishops eventually accepted the new Prayer Book in order to maintain peace and unity. It is for exactly the same reasons that the post-Conciliar Church wants to impose on us the *Novus Ordo*. The English bishops in the sixteenth century affirmed that the Mass was a "memorial"! A sustained propaganda introduced Lutheran views into the minds of the faithful. Preachers had to be approved by the Government.

During the same period the Pope was only referred to as the "Bishop of Rome." He was no longer the father but the brother of the other bishops and in this instance, the brother of the King of England who had made himself head of the national church.

---

[6] Official review of the Congregation for Divine Worship.
[7] Spiritual conference, Ecône, January 16, 1975.

Cranmer's Prayer Book was composed by mixing parts of the Greek liturgy with parts of Luther's liturgy. How can we not be reminded of Msgr. Bugnini drawing up the so-called Mass of Paul VI with the collaboration of six Protestant "observers" attached as experts to the Consilium for the reform of the liturgy? The Prayer Book begins with these words: "The Supper and Holy Communion, commonly called Mass...," which foreshadows the notorious Article 7 of the *Institutio Generalis* of the New Missal, revived by the Lourdes Eucharistic Congress in 1981: "The Supper of the Lord, otherwise called the Mass." The destruction of the sacred, to which I have already referred, also formed part of the Anglican reform. The words of the Canon were required to be spoken in a loud voice, as happens in the "Eucharists" of the present day.

Tudor England, led by its pastors, slid into heresy without realizing it, by accepting change under the pretext of adapting to historical circumstances of the time. Today the whole of Christendom is in danger of taking the same road.[8]

3. The progressive establishment of the reform

Luther was quite displeased with Zwingli, Melancthon, and the others. They were the hard-liners constantly pushing ahead and going too fast. Luther would say: "No, no, slow down." For the suppression of Latin, for Communion in the hand, for all these things, he would advise: "Easy does it; be careful. There are going to be reactions; go slowly but surely." He knew very well that they had to avoid upsetting the faithful, who would not have followed if he had proceeded too brusquely. Formal heresies were not to be found in the texts because otherwise the Catholics who finally became Protestants would have reacted. He accomplished it very cunningly. And that is exactly what happened to us.[9] I would go so far as to say that Luther was even more prudent and slow in the application of his reforms than the current ecclesiastical authorities were in the application of the new rite of Mass.[10]

Luther does not hesitate to show the liberal spirit which animates him. He writes: "Above all, I amicably beg all those who

---

[8] *Open Letter to Confused Catholics*, pp.134-36.
[9] Spiritual conference, Ecône, June 24, 1981.
[10] *Ibid.*, January 16, 1975.

want to examine or follow the present rules for divine service not to see in them a compulsory law or by them to constrain any conscience. Each one should adopt them when, where and as he pleases. That is required by Christian liberty."[11]

The rite of Paul VI strangely resembles the Lutheran and Anglican rites. A quick survey of these rites suffices to show it. Now we consider what the Mass, the presence of Christ in the host, and the priesthood were for Luther.

THE DENIAL OF THE PROPITIATORY SACRIFICE

Luther pretends that faith saves without works. He denies in consequence the sacrificial act which is the Catholic Mass. For him, the Mass is first and foremost the liturgy of the Word, and secondly communion.

1. Luther denies the sacrificial aspect of the Mass

Luther's second grave doctrinal error follows from the first and is based on his first principle: it is faith or trust that saves, and not works. This is the negation of the sacrificial act which is the essence of the Catholic Mass. For Luther the Mass may be a sacrifice of praise, that is an act of praise and thanksgiving, but certainly not an expiating sacrifice renewing and applying the sacrifice of the Cross. Speaking of the perversions of worship in the monasteries, he said: "The chief element in their worship, the Mass, passes all impiety and all abomination; they make of it a sacrifice and a good work. Were there no other reason for abandoning the habit, leaving the convent, and breaking their vows, that in itself is amply sufficient."[12]

The Mass is a "synaxis," a communion. The Eucharist has been subjected to a triple and lamentable captivity: the laity have been denied the chalice; the notion of transubstantiation, invented by the Thomists, has been imposed as a dogma; and the Mass has been made a sacrifice. Luther here touches on a point of capital importance. He does not hesitate, however. "It is then a manifest and

---

[11] Quoted by Msgr. Cristiani in *From Lutheranism to Protestantism* [French ed.], p.314. Conference, Florence, February 15, 1975, *A Bishop Speaks*, p.193.
[12] Cristiani, *From Lutheranism to Protestantism*, p.258.

impious error," he writes, "to offer or apply the Mass for sins, for reparation, or for the dead. Mass is offered by God to man, not by man to God." ...He believes that the Mass is first and foremost the liturgy of the Word, and secondly a communion.

It is difficult to avoid stupefaction in realizing that the new reform has brought about the same changes, and that in very truth the modern texts given to the faithful no longer speak of sacrifice but of "the liturgy of the Word," of the story of the Last Supper, and of the sharing of bread or of the Eucharist.

Luther suppressed the Offertory; why offer the pure and immaculate host if there is no more sacrifice?[13]

2. According to Luther, the Mass is offered by God to man

Luther wrote: "The Mass is offered by God to man, and not by man to God." You see Luther's impiety: the Mass is offered by God to man and not by man to God. It is clear: he does not accept the propitiatory sacrifice. Luther drew the consequences of this heresy and suppressed the Offertory, which clearly expresses the propitiatory end of the sacrifice. He suppressed most of the Canon and simply kept what he called the narration, the Supper. So one is rather astounded to see that the reform Luther made because of his heresy was repeated in the new *Ordo*, but purportedly without the heresy.[14]

3. The "faith–confidence" of Protestants

Protestants say there is only one sacrifice, that of the Cross, and it is through belief in the sacrifice of the Cross that we draw into ourselves the merits of the Cross, and that we cover our sins. Our sins are merely covered–for they do not believe in an inward renewal.[15]

---

[13] *Open Letter to Confused Catholics*, p.26.
[14] Spiritual conference, Ecône, October 26, 1979.
[15] Conference, Paris, March 29, 1973, *A Bishop Speaks*, p.155. The Protestants do not believe in an interior renewal by grace. According to them, the merits of Christ are imputed to the believer, but he remains a sinner.

For the Protestants, there is no continuation of the Redemption. Our Lord died on the Cross; He redeemed the whole world. It is finished. To be saved, it suffices to have confidence in Our Lord.[16] [For Catholics, on the contrary] it was Our Lord's wish that we should share in the sacrifice of the Cross, that we should receive His merits, that our souls should be washed of their sins by His sacrifice perpetuated by His priests. When, at the Last Supper, He said to them, "Do this in remembrance of me–*hoc facite in meam commemorationem*," Our Lord did not say: tell the story of My supper, call My sacrifice to remembrance. He said: *facite*–make this sacrifice, reproduce this sacrifice, continue My sacrifice; "*hoc facite in meam commemorationem.*" That is the whole difference between the Catholic doctrine we have always been taught and Protestant doctrine. Protestants forget, they do not want to remember that Our Lord said: "*hoc facite*–do this in remembrance of me." They say only "*in meam commemorationem*–in remembrance of me." Those are the words used by those who do not continue the sacrifice of Our Lord Jesus Christ.[17]

THE DENIAL OF TRANSUBSTANTIATION

Luther did not believe in the dogma of transubstantiation. Some of his disciples and other, later Protestants arrived at the denial pure and simple of the Real Presence[18] (Melanchton, Zwingli, *etc.*); whence Communion in the hand and under both species.

Luther concludes with the denial of transubstantiation and the Real Presence as taught by the Catholic Church. For him the bread remains. Hence his disciple Melanchthon,[19] who strongly

---

[16] Conference, Nantes, February 5, 1983.
[17] Mariazell Pilgrimage, September 8, 1975, *A Bishop Speaks*, pp.216-17.
[18] Luther taught *consubstantiation*: the simultaneous presence of the body of Christ and the bread. This affirmation was condemned by the Council of Trent (DS 1652): "If anyone says that in the sacred and holy Sacrament of the Eucharist there remains the substance of bread and wine together with the Body and Blood of Our Lord Jesus Christ, and denies that wonderful and singular conversion of the whole substance of the bread into the body, and of the entire substance of the wine into the blood, the species of the bread and wine only remaining, a change which the Catholic Church most fittingly calls transubstantiation: let him be anathema" (Dz. 884).
[19] Humanist and German "reformer" (1497-1560). An influential professor at Wittenberg as early as 1518, he was strongly influenced by Luther, whose

attacks the adoration of the Blessed Sacrament, says: "Christ instituted the Eucharist as a remembrance of the Passion. To adore it is idolatry."[20] From that follows Communion in the hand and under both species, in effect the denying of the presence of the Body and Blood of Our Lord under each of the two species; logically, the Eucharist must be regarded as incomplete under one species.

There again one may measure the extraordinary similarity between today's reform and that of Luther. All the new authorizations touching the rite of the Eucharist tend to a diminished reverence and neglect in worship: Communion in the hand, its distribution by the laity, even by women; the reduced number of genuflections, which, in the case of many priests, has led to their disappearance; the use of ordinary bread and ordinary vessels; all such reforms are contributing to the denial of the Real Presence as taught by the Catholic Church.[21]

The Denial of a Visible Priesthood

For the Protestants, it is the People of God who celebrate under the presidency of a pastor.

1. Luther: "A curse on pretended priests!"

What does Luther think of the priesthood? In his work on private Masses, he tries to show that the Catholic priesthood is an invention of the devil. To do that he invokes this principle, which henceforward is fundamental:

What is not in Scripture is an addition by Satan. Well, Scripture knows nothing of a visible priesthood. It knows only one priest, one Pontiff, one alone, Christ. With Christ we are all priests. Priesthood is at one and the same time unique and universal. What madness to want to corner it for a few....All hierarchical distinc-

---

theology he more "rationally" systematized. He gave important conferences in theology and was one of the principal authors of the Confession of Augsburg (1530). He attempted to devise a formulation of the Protestant position that would be acceptable to the Catholics. His teaching on the Eucharist ultimately converges with that of Calvin.

[20] Quoted by Cristiani, *From Lutheranism to Protestantism*, p.262.
[21] Conference, Florence, February 15, 1975, *A Bishop Speaks*, pp.195-96.

tions among Christians are worthy of Antichrist....A curse, then, on pretended priests.[22]

In 1520, he wrote his *Manifesto to the Christian Nobility of Germany*, in which he attacks "Romanists" and demands a free Council.

The first barrier erected by the Romanists [is the distinction drawn between clergy and laity]. They have made the discovery [says he] that the Pope, bishops, priests, and monks make up the ecclesiastical estate while princes, lords, artisans, and peasants compose the secular estate. It is a pure invention and a lie. In reality all Christians form part of the ecclesiastical estate and the only difference among them is that of function. When the pope or a bishop anoints, gives the tonsure, ordains, consecrates, or dresses differently from the laity, he may create deceivers or anointed idols, but he can make neither a Christian nor a cleric...all that have been baptized may boast of being consecrated priest, bishop, and pope, even though it may not be fitting for all to exercise that function.[23]

From this doctrine Luther draws conclusions opposed to clerical dress and celibacy. He and his disciples set the example by abandoning celibacy and marrying.

How many of the effects flowing from the reforms of Vatican II resemble Luther's confusions—the abandonment of monastic and clerical dress, the absence of any distinctive character between priest and layman, and the many marriages of priests sanctioned by the Holy See. This egalitarianism will become evident in the granting to laymen of liturgical functions formerly reserved to priests.... [O]rdination is directed to the service of the community, no longer to sacrifice, which alone justifies the Catholic conception of the priesthood.[24]

2. The priesthood of the laity according to Luther

Luther [held that] all Christians are priests; the pastor is only exercising a function in presiding at the Evangelical Mass.[25]

These reflections of Luther on the Eucharistic liturgy and the priesthood show the abyss separating him from Catholicism.

---

[22] Cristiani, *op. cit.*, p.269.
[23] *Ibid*, pp.148-49.
[24] Conference, Florence, February 15, 1975, in *A Bishop Speaks*, pp.193-94.
[25] *Open Letter to Confused Catholics*, p.24.

III. THE CONSEQUENCES OF THE *NOVUS ORDO MISSAE*

The consequences of the liturgical reform in society, in the Church, in the seminaries, on priests, and on spiritual life in general, are extremely grave. When the fundamental truths of our faith are diminished, the supernatural spirit is lost; the spirit of sacrifice is lost; the spirit of oblation is lost.[1]

THE LOSS OF FAITH AND THE SPIRIT OF FAITH

> In January 1974, Archbishop Lefebvre said: "We are not attached to a special rite." His attachment to the rite of St. Pius V, in opposition to that of Pope Paul VI, derived from his attachment to the Catholic Faith, weakened by the liturgical reform.

LITURGY AND FAITH

I would like to show you the profound reasons why we are opposed to the liturgical reform. It is assuredly not for the pleasure of opposing Rome. It is not to make ourselves important or from attachment to a certain non-essential tradition. If we oppose, and if we have opposed to the present day, the liturgical reform, it is for serious reasons, reasons of faith, which condition our entire Catholic life, our spiritual life. So it is not a small matter. The fruits of the New Mass are always the same, always disastrous.[2]

1. Is the liturgy purely a matter of discipline?

Is there really a profound link between our faith and the liturgy? Is the liturgy purely a series of ritual actions, purely formal, which has no profound link with the faith? This is what many progressivists and modernists today would readily claim: It little matters how the liturgy is organized, that is not what is important. For

---

[1] Spiritual conference, Ecône, June 25, 1981.
[2] *Ibid.*, Ecône, January 10, 1983.

them, the liturgy would be merely a purely disciplinary question, having nothing to do with faith or dogma.[3]

2. Why did the Church keep the treasure of the rite of the Mass?

We are not attached to a particular rite, to a particular manner of celebrating Mass, to something ancient because it is ancient, but because it is a matter of faith.[4] You have the Syro-Malabar rite, the Eastern rites, the Greek rite, the Maronite rite. These are all Catholic rites, you understand. These different rites rest upon the same doctrine, the same dogmas, express the same faith–sometimes, I would say, with even more expression, with more sentiment and warmth than the Latin rite, which is the Roman rite.

The Romans were a measured, moderate people. They are not Easterners, and their rite appeals more to reason than to sentiment and the exterior expression of the Faith. But you also have rites like, for example, if I am not mistaken, the Syro-Malabar rite, in which the priest, at the moment of the Consecration, draws a curtain behind him, separating himself thus from the assembly to be as it were in the Holy of Holies of the Old Testament, in which the high-priest entered alone once a year; similarly, the priest enters into the Holy of Holies, too, and finds himself in some way alone with God to offer the sacrifice, and to make God descend upon the altar. Then the curtain is opened and the priest presents the Body of Our Lord to the assembly, and all the faithful kneel in adoration of Our Lord Jesus Christ. It is a different rite. It little matters if they give us different rites, provided that these rites keep the idea of sacrifice that is essential, the Real Presence of Our Lord as Victim, the sacerdotal character of the priest, which is a specific character the faithful do not have.[5]

If the most holy Church has wished to guard throughout the centuries this precious treasure which she has given us of the rite of Holy Mass which was canonized by St. Pius V, it has not been without purpose. It is because this Mass contains *our whole Faith*, the *whole* Catholic Faith: Faith in the Most Holy Trinity, faith in

---

[3] *Ibid.*, Zaitzkofen, February 7, 1980.
[4] *Ibid.*, Ecône, January 1974.
[5] Conference, Sherbrooke, November 11, 1975.

the Divinity of Our Lord Jesus Christ, faith in the Redemption of Our Lord Jesus Christ, faith in the Blood of Our Lord Jesus Christ which flowed for the redemption of our sins, and faith in supernatural grace, which comes to us from the holy sacrifice of the Mass, which comes to us from the Cross, which comes to us through all the Sacraments. This is what we believe. This is what we believe in celebrating the holy sacrifice of the Mass of all time. It is a lesson of faith and at the same time a source of our faith, indispensable for us in this age when our faith is attacked from all sides.[6]

3. The liturgy is not a simple disciplinary measure

The new liturgical reform fosters attitudes that are no longer attitudes of faith. It imposes on us a naturalistic and humanistic cult. Thus, people are afraid to genuflect; they no longer want to show the adoration that is due to God; they want to reduce the sacred to the profane.[7]

In virtue of the adage recognized in the Church for many centuries: *lex orandi, lex credendi*–the law of prayer is the law of faith, if the expression of our faith is significantly altered, going so far as to change the words of consecration, for example, we run the risk of having our faith altered, too. And that is very, very serious. Consequently, the liturgy is not simply a disciplinary law.[8]

4. The rampart of the Faith has been destroyed

The New Mass is not heretical; it is not formally heretical, but it indirectly favors heresy because it creates an atmosphere that does not sufficiently uphold the fundamental truths of the Holy Mass. At present, the rampart of the Faith constituted by the liturgy has been demolished. Why should one be surprised, then, that faith disappears and the people no longer believe in anything and are ignorant of the rudiments of their Faith? It is the logical outcome; it is fatal.[9]

---

[6] Homily, Ecône, June 29, 1976, *A Bishop Speaks*, pp.244-45.
[7] Spiritual conference, Ecône, March, 1974.
[8] Conference, Angers, November 23, 1980.
[9] *Against the Heresies*, p.53.

The Loss of the Sacred

The traditional liturgy conveys the sacred. Inversely, the new liturgy leads to a kind of profanation such that the modern Masses are often bereft of any supernatural savor.

1. Why did the Church have so many ceremonies?

The Church, to which Our Lord bequeathed His ministerial priesthood to accomplish it till the end of time, has carried out the sacrifice of the Mass with love and devotion; it has ordained its prayers, ceremonies, and rites to signify these realities and to preserve our faith in these realities willed and determined by God Himself. The Council of Trent teaches us that (Session 22, Canon 5):

> The nature of man being such that he cannot easily or without some external aids rise to meditation on divine things, the Church, as a good Mother, has established certain practices, such as speaking parts of the Mass quietly and others aloud; and in accordance with the discipline and tradition of the Apostles it has introduced such ceremonies as mystical blessings, lights, incense, ornaments and many kindred things so as, in that way, to signify the majesty of so great a sacrifice, and to raise the souls of the faithful by these outward signs of piety and religion to the contemplation of the great things hidden in this sacrifice.[10]

2. The desecration of the holy mysteries

A kind of desecration has taken place:

- By the adoption of the vernacular language. The suppression of its sacred language, Latin, made the holy Mass in some way profane; it made it something that is no longer truly sacred.
- By the recitation aloud of the translation throughout the entire holy Mass. There are no more moments of silence; there are no more words said in a low voice by the priest. But the Council of Trent alluded to the various prayers of the holy sacrifice of

---

[10] Priests' retreat, Barcelona, March 1971, *A Bishop Speaks*, p.93.

the Mass that are said secretly,[11] inviting meditation on the great mystery taking place.
- By the introduction of a table in place of the altar. For the altar to be considered an altar, it must in principle be made of stone. Sacrifice is offered on a rock. However, the altar stone was suppressed; it is no longer obligatory, and now the altar has been replaced by a simple table.
- By the position of the priest. The Mass facing the people is not conducive to recollection before the great mystery unfolding. The priest himself is distracted by the people he has in front of him, and the people are distracted by the priest, especially if he acts in a quick, disordered, or irreverent manner. At least, when the priest turns his back, his mannerisms are less noticeable. In this, too, there is a lessening of the sacred character of the Mass.
- By the distribution of the Eucharist by the faithful. In my opinion, the distribution of the Eucharist in the hand not only diminishes the sacred character of the Blessed Sacrament, but it has an almost sacrilegious character. It is one of the examples of sacrilege given by St. Thomas. People will say that now the Church allows it, but the Church cannot allow such handling of the Holy Eucharist.
- By the simplification of the celebrant's attire. Now, in most cases, there are no more vestments. The only thing left is an alb (called a Taizé alb) that looks like the one the Taizé Fathers wear, which has a stole sewn onto the alb so that the priest has only one garment to zip on. In a few seconds the priest is dressed, and in a few seconds he is back in his civilian attire. Isn't this also a desecration? The beauty of the vestments also manifests the important and noble character of the Consecration.

Concelebration, too, far from adding to the dignity of the Mass, imparts a very common character to the Mass. The fact that the priests merely extend their hands toward the consecration is un-

---

[11] The Council of Trent is very severe on the subject of the silence to be observed during the Canon: "If anyone says that the rite of the Roman Church, according to which a part of the canon and the words of consecration are pronounced in a low tone, is to be condemned...: let him be anathema" (DS 1759 [Dz. 956]).

worthy of the Holy Eucharist and of the sacrifice. Finally, I would add that the multiplicity of the authorized Canons also detracts from the fixed character of the rite, from the traditional character which the Canon of the Mass had, of which the Council of Trent said that there was nothing so holy or beautiful as the Latin Canon. The multiplicity of Canons has diminished the sacred character of the Canon.

The use of ordinary, leavened bread for the Eucharist is completely contrary to Tradition, to the Church's custom. Why does the Church ask us to use unleavened bread? St. Paul tells us in his letters that it is Our Lord Jesus Christ who is the leaven of the Eucharist. Quite rightly, then, the Church requires that there be no leaven in the bread dough, because it is Our Lord Jesus Christ Himself who represents the leaven of the Eucharist, and who represents the living Eucharistic bread. Hence it is a very beautiful and very significant custom. The use of ordinary, leavened bread once again betrays a lack of comprehension and of application of this beautiful tradition.

Until now, in these considerations of the *Novus Ordo Missae*, I have only mentioned official changes. These are not the inventions of a few priests, but official changes authorized by Rome. So, obviously, I shall not speak about the creativity, of which Rome has spoken, especially Msgr. Bugnini, as if the liturgy should be constantly in evolution, in flux. Let us not speak about that, because it would take us days.[12]

3. An inevitable consequence

Furthermore, it can be said without any exaggeration whatsoever, that the majority of Masses celebrated without altar stones, with common vessels, leavened bread, with the introduction of profane words into the very body of the Canon, *etc.*, are sacrilegious,[13] and they prevent faith by diminishing it. The "desacralization" is such that these Masses can come to lose their supernatural charac-

---

[12] Spiritual conference, October 1, 1979.
[13] *Summa Theologica*, II-II, Q.99, Art. 1: "Therefore whatever pertains to irreverence for sacred things is an injury to God, and comes under the head of sacrilege."

ter, "the mystery of faith," and become no more than acts of natural religion.[14]

4. Masses with no supernatural savor

This is why the modern Masses are often so empty, so flat. The faithful have the impression of watching a sketch, a play, something that is sometimes beautiful and well done, but that no longer has a supernatural savor, a sense of the divine or sacred, which existed before in the ministry of the sacrifice, because they gradually made the Mass into a meal; they banished the sacrifice of the Cross of Our Lord Jesus Christ.[15]

5. A feeling of emptiness

The changes that took place in the Church took away from us all the theology, the divine reality, this presence of Heaven among us; and forced us back, as it were, into time and the midst of men whereas we had been lifted up into eternity, and the good Lord had wanted to come among us to make us partakers even now of eternity by coming into our hearts. These worship meetings more and more resemble human gatherings rather than divine ones. And that is, I think, the fundamental problem that should concern us today. If it is no longer Heaven on our altars, if it is no longer Heaven put in our hearts, then we fall back into time among men. One will speak in vain of "human dignity," of "adult men"; all of that will be empty–empty of meaning, empty of divine reality. That is why Christan civilization can no longer develop, will not be able to develop. And that is why there are no more priestly or religious vocations: because God is no longer present among us.[16]

---

[14] *Open Letter to Confused Catholics*, p.29.
[15] Spiritual conference, Ecône, December 2, 1974.
[16] Homily, Ecône, April 3, 1976.

Assessment of the Effects of the New Mass on the Faith

A study of Archbishop Lefebvre's statements from 1972 to 1983 shows that he soon saw the consequences of the reform, and he did not waver in his speculative judgment of the New Mass: namely, that without being formally heretical, it leads to the loss of the Catholic Faith.

1. Assessment of 1972: a failure acknowledged by the authorities

In France, the C.N.P.L. (*Centre National de Pastorale Liturgique*) admits in its January issue a check on reform. It merely notes an obvious decline in religious practice and the boredom of the faithful confronted with the new liturgy. But it does not point out the most serious aspect, the loss of faith in many believers and priests.[17]

2. Assessment of 1975: the Faith endangered

It is difficult to escape the conclusion that, principles and practice being intimately linked, as the adage *"lex orandi lex credendi"* has it, the fact of imitating Luther's reform in the liturgy of the Mass must infallibly lead to the gradual adoption of the very ideas of Luther. The last six years since the publication of the new *Ordo* afford ample proof of the fact. The consequences of this so-called ecumenical practice are catastrophic, firstly in the domain of faith, and above all in the corruption of the priesthood and the lack of vocations, in the unity of Catholics who, at every level, are divided on this question which concerns them so nearly, and in the relations with Protestants and members of the Orthodox Church.

The Protestant conception of this vital and essential question of the Church's priesthood-sacrifice-Eucharist is wholly contrary to that of the Catholic Church. The Council of Trent did not take place in vain; for four centuries all the documents of the magisterium have referred to it.

Psychologically, pastorally, and theologically it is impossible for Catholics to give up a liturgy which is the true expression and stay of their faith, and adopt new rites conceived by heretics without exposing their faith to the greatest danger. It is not possible to

---

[17] Priests' retreat, Barcelona, April 1972, *A Bishop Speaks*, p.102.

imitate Protestants indefinitely without becoming one. How many of the faithful, how many young priests, how many bishops have lost their faith since these reforms were adopted? One cannot flout nature and faith and escape their vengeance.[18]

3. Assessment of 1981: an unavoidable change of mentality

Has the usage of the N.O.M., the central act of the liturgical reform, had the salutary consequences anticipated, or has it produced the disastrous effects that could be foreseen? To answer this question, it is necessary to know what the liturgical reform consisted in. Ultimately, it consisted in taking a Protestant text while claiming that one did not deny the truths the Protestants deny.

The Protestants, in the beginning, had the the Catholic Mass, and they became Protestants. They denied the fundamental truths of the holy Mass: the propitiatory sacrifice, the distinction between the priesthood of the priests and of the laity, the Real Presence. They denied those things, in virtue of which they instituted a Mass derived from the Catholic Mass, but by expurgating everything that might recall these truths.

Here we are now four centuries later. The modernist liturgists who infiltrated the Church could find nothing better to do than take the Protestant text. And to reassure the Catholics, the reformers said: "We do not deny the truths the Protestants deny, of course, but we are taking the same text because the text has no formally heretical part. These texts, of course, were composed in virtue of the denial of the truths of the Catholic Faith, but they do not deny them explicitly. Therefore, we are not doing something heretical in adopting these texts."

But what will be the result of such an operation? Since the texts were composed by Protestants with the intention of denying these truths, the people who are going to use them will end up denying the truths themselves. That is obvious. For example, in the New Mass, they suppressed everything that could recall that the Mass is not only a narrative, but is truly an action. So, little by little, it goes without saying that by dint of saying a Protestant text, even if it is

---

[18] Conference, Florence, February 15, 1975, *A Bishop Speaks*, p.196.

not formally and of itself heretical, one will end by no longer having Catholic ideas.[19] How could it be otherwise?[20]

4. Assessment of 1982 and 1983: heresy is favored

Ten years ago I wrote these pages entitled "Why We Choose the Mass Codified by St. Pius V." They readily answer the objection made to us: "You are not as you were at the start; you have changed your opinions and your way of acting." Well, I believe that I can repeat this text to you with the same conviction, because for me nothing has changed. At that time I listed the reasons for which we chose this Mass and then those for which we refused the New Mass....In summary, the New Mass was truly the principal means of expressing what I would almost call the modern heresy, or at least something that favors the modern heresy.[21]

It is astonishing to see that the people who regularly attend the New Mass, that is to say, who consent to the reforms, who in some way give it their approbation, who do not resist all these liturgical reforms, gradually take on a Protestant mindset. When they are asked questions about mixed marriages, ecumenism, religious truth, or the possibility of salvation in different religions, they always have false ideas; they no longer possess the Church's doctrine. It is curious to note that, even if they have not been publicly instructed, even if it is not the priest who told them false things, the

---

[19] The Church has always stressed the importance of adequately matching the signs used to the truths to be signified. The Synod of Pistoia affirmed the Real Presence, but was condemned solely for not utilizing the term "transubstantiation." The N.O.M. is thus a rite that is inadequate, at least by defect, to express in its texts and external elements the integral Catholic doctrine on the sacrifice of the Mass. The most important text on this question is by St. Thomas Aquinas (*Summa Theologica*, II-II, Q.93, Art. 1). In this question, he writes that there is a superstitious alteration of worship when there is a discordance between the reality signified and the rite, a discordance to be judged by the words and actions. Further on, he teaches that there is another form of this defect, when the one celebrating the liturgy exercises it according to a form contrary to the form prescribed and customary in the Church. Do we not find this defect in the N.O.M., "created" in contradiction with the traditional liturgical principles of the Church?

[20] Spiritual conference, Ecône, June 24, 1981.

[21] *Ibid.*, January 16, 1982.

mere fact of being in this ambiance of ecumenical liturgy gives them a spirit that is no longer Catholic.[22]

Ask people who have a habit of attending the New Mass if they still believe that the Catholic Church is the only one that possesses the truth given by Our Lord Jesus Christ. No, they think that there is truth in all religions and that, consequently, one can be saved in any religion. They no longer have the notion of the truth of the Church, the notion of the truth of salvation by Our Lord Jesus Christ and not by any other. The result of the disappearance of the Mass of all time is readily observed: people no longer have the Catholic Faith. They no longer believe that one cannot enter heaven except through Our Lord Jesus Christ, that one cannot enter there except by His Cross, by His holy Mass, by baptism, by the Sacraments as they are given by the Church.[23]

The liturgical reform favors heresy. We clearly see people losing the Faith. We clearly see around us, even in our families, that people think like Protestants; they no longer think like Catholics. Hence, slowly but surely these reforms, especially the liturgical reform, make people lose the Faith. That is why we refuse them.[24]

THE LOSS OF THE SPIRIT OF SACRIFICE

One of the effects of the liturgical reform is the loss of the spirit of sacrifice. Self-denial is out; fun is in. Archbishop Lefebvre denounces this new orientation, and recalls why the Church until now has asked the faithful to practice mortification.

1. If there is no more sacrifice of the Mass, there is no more spirit of sacrifice

Catholicism is essentially founded on the Cross. If we no longer have a clear idea of the sacrifice of the Cross, if we lose the notion of the sacrifice of the Mass continuing the sacrifice of the Cross, we are no longer Catholics. It is in this Faith that we find all the resources of grace, in the Cross of Jesus, in His opened heart. It is by

---

[22] *Ibid.*, January 22, 1982.
[23] Conference, Nantes, February 5, 1983.
[24] Spiritual conference, Ecône, March 15, 1983.

contemplating His head crowned with thorns, His pierced hands, that we indeed find all the graces of resurrection, all the graces of redemption of which we are in need. If we suppress the sacrifice of Our Lord Jesus Christ on our altars, if our altars no longer reproduce the sacrifice of the Cross of Jesus, then only a "Eucharist," that is to say a meal, a sharing, a communion, remains. This is no longer the spirit of the Catholic Church. The Catholic Church is essentially founded on the Cross, on the spirit of sacrifice.

And all around us, it must be recognized, the spirit of sacrifice is disappearing. No one wants to practice mortification. One wants to have enjoyment, one wants to make the most of life, even among Catholics. Why? Because the Cross of Our Lord Jesus Christ is no longer there. And if there is no more Cross, then there is no more Catholic Church. This is a matter of considerable gravity. It is a change of direction that took place during the Council.[25]

2. Without the spirit of sacrifice, all of family life suffers

From the fact that since the Council no one wants to speak of the Mass as a sacrifice, the spirit of sacrifice is disappearing; it is no longer understood. We have freedom; life is made to enjoy the good things and the amusements! Everyone should have as many things, and as many pleasures and opportunities to have a good time. But with such an attitude, the very notion of sacrifice is made void. It is the reason why marriages no longer last: why make the sacrifice? If they no longer get along, they separate! The children are a burden; the parents do not want to sacrifice for them so they will not have any; they will kill by abortion these poor innocent children. That is the modern world: no sacrifice.[26]

3. Why did the Church call for the contempt of the things of this world?

Everything that specifies the spirit of detachment from the things of this world—"May we learn to despise what is earthly and love what is heavenly"[27]—has disappeared from our prayers, since the things of earth need no longer be despised. Rather, the things

---

[25] Homily, Ecône, November 1, 1990.
[26] Homily, Rouen, May 1, 1990.
[27] Postcommunion of the Mass of the Sacred Heart, Collect of the Mass of St. Peter Damian, *etc.*: *Discamus terrena despicere et amare cælestia.*

of the world, material goods, must be esteemed. The contempt of the things of the world is inadmissible. Obviously, it is inadmissible if you no longer recognize that the things of this world are an occasion of sin.

These things are not contemptible in and of themselves, but they are for us an occasion of sin. That is because wealth and sensual pleasure make us fall into the sins from which we must detach ourselves. Unfortunately, all these things of the earth, because of the malice in us, attract us to sin. Whence the need for asceticism. So what is the new asceticism?[28]

The good God Himself asks us to use the goods of this world to accomplish our duty of state. Consequently, it is clear that we must use the things of the world. But the disorder introduced into us by original sin makes us seek these goods inordinately, excessively, and leads us away from prayer and from God. What is prayer, after all, but the raising of our souls to God? Many people no longer lift up their soul to God because they are preoccupied by the things of this world. They no longer pray, and they no longer come and unite themselves to the great prayer of Our Lord which is the holy sacrifice of the Mass. They desert the churches because they are taken by the spirit of the world.[29]

Loss of the Sense of Our Lord's Kingship

The Kingship of Our Lord is no longer upheld in the new liturgy. This leads insensibly to indifferentism, the error that consists in putting all religions on the same level. In Africa, India, and Vietnam, elements of the local culture and pagan religion are being incorporated into Catholic liturgy.

1. Christ's kingship is no longer upheld

The new liturgy no longer proclaims Our Lord Jesus Christ's kingship as did the traditional liturgy, with all the consequences that flow from His kingship; namely, that Our Lord must be the King and center of all hearts, and that for salvation it is necessary to

---

[28] Spiritual conference, Ecône, June 25, 1981.
[29] St-Michel-en-Brenne, February 11, 1990.

be a member of His Mystical Body. The new liturgy no longer has the same teachings that were evident in the traditional liturgy. The new liturgy no longer holds up the Cross of Our Lord, the Victim who offered Himself for us.[30]

2. Towards indifferentism

All these profound changes were carried out in an ecumenical spirit that, in its exaggeration, leads to indifferentism in matters of religion, and thus convergence with the error of religious freedom.[31]

The use of this ecumenical Mass leads to the acquisition of a Protestant, indifferentist mentality that puts all the religions on an equal footing, in keeping with the Declaration on Religious Liberty, with its doctrinal foundation in the Rights of Man, a wrongly understood notion of human dignity, condemned by St. Pius X in his letter on the Sillon.[32]

3. "Ecumenical inculturation"

In the countries of the Third World, for instance Africa, India, Vietnam, *etc.*, they introduce elements of the local "civilization" into the liturgy, and practically into the Faith: it is what they call "inculturation." The Faith is corrupted because they introduce these elements into the liturgy. In Africa, the rudiments of pagan culture are inserted into the liturgy, a practice that will lead, quite simply, to a form of voodoo, a religion that is an admixture of paganism and Christianity practiced in countries like Haiti and Brazil. It is already appearing in Africa.

As regards India, I do not know whether you have had an opportunity to read a recent article by Madam Edith Delamare speaking about the demands introduced at Rome by some Christians and priests. They pointed out the danger to which the faith of Catholics is exposed in India because of the incorporation of Hindu ceremonies into the liturgy. Statutes of Buddha have been put in Catholic churches, and they are incensed during Catholic ceremonies. Enough! Is our God still Our Lord Jesus Christ?[33]

---

[30] Spiritual conference, Ecône, January 22, 1982.
[31] Circular letter, January 20, 1978, p.1.
[32] Letter to Pope John Paul II, April 5, 1983.
[33] Conference, Brussels, March 22, 1986.

Last year, I was present at Melbourne during the Eucharistic Congress. At the Congress, they had what were called "kangaroo Masses": they brought Aborigines in from the Australian interior, who performed savage dances at the Congress podium, and in the midst of these dances in which the dancers were half naked, they pronounced the words of the consecration. Doing this in front of these people who do not believe, who are not Christians, who are not Catholics–is this not a scandal? Is not shameful to put Our Lord Jesus Christ in contact with these people who do not believe in anything and with these dances that are positively lewd?[34]

REDUCTION OF THE NUMBER OF MASSES

1. Decrease in religious practice and the number of vocations

Some will claim: "If there are far fewer people in the churches nowadays, that has nothing to do with the liturgy. It results from the ambiant materialism." But even the progressivists themselves acknowledge the correlation. For example, Msgr. Grégoire, Archbishop of Montreal, made a lengthy report on the situation of his diocese. He said explicitly: "We think that the liturgical reform has a great deal to do with the faithful's abandoning the churches." Cardinal Ratzinger recognized the same thing. It is not only we who say it. It is necessary to really deny the obvious to maintain that the liturgy is not involved. The same holds for the lack of vocations and the ruination of the priesthood. The priesthood is essentially linked to the Mass. It is impossible to conceive of sacrifice without the priest, nor of the priest without sacrifice. There is an essential relation between the priest and the sacrifice. Do you believe that all those priests who left the priesthood would have done so if they had not been cut to the quick by the destruction of the sacrifice? Obviously not.[35]

If the Cross of Our Lord disappears, if His Body and Blood are no longer present, men find themselves gathered around an empty

---

[34] Conference, Sainte-Yvette, Montreal, November 16, 1975.
[35] Spiritual conference, Ecône, January 21, 1982.

table. Nothing will unite them any more. And that is what is happening: there is no more life! The people perceive it, and this gives rise to this lassitude, this boredom that is beginning to be expressed everywhere, and the disappearance of vocations, which no longer have any purpose. This leads to the secularization, the profanation of the priest, who no longer finds any purpose, and who experiences a need for people or for some escape. The priest no longer knows what he is, so he approaches people without really knowing what he is supposed to bring them, without knowing the reason for his priesthood. The priest profanes himself, becomes worldly, mingles with people, and finally marries. He finally discovers that, after all, there is no reason why he cannot have a career and celebrate a worship service simply on Sundays... Because of the Protestant conception of the Mass, Jesus Christ eventually leaves the churches which are unfortunately profaned.[36]

2. The lessening of the application of Our Lord's merits

There is a dramatic reduction in the number of Masses today. This is easy to see, taking into account the number of defrocked priests, the decrease in vocations and consequently of ordinations, the number of young priests who no longer celebrate Mass when none of the faithful is present, and by the number of those who concelebrate. Indeed, according to a number of theologians, during a concelebration, there is only one Mass instead of as many as the number of concelebrants. This is the opinion in particular of Cardinal Philippe. He made a study of this subject for the preconciliar central commission of which I was a member. I remember very well having heard him say that concelebration could only be exceptional, because, one Mass being celebrated, there would not be as many Masses as celebrants. So, taking into account all these factors, you see how many fewer Masses there are. If you include the number of invalid Masses, seeing the doubts that can be expressed concerning the validity of numerous Masses, there are even fewer.[37]

---

[36] *Ibid.*, May 31, 1971.
[37] *Ibid.*, December 5, 1974.

3. Why habitual concelebration is so baneful

I am intimately persuaded that concelebration goes against the very end of the Mass.[38] The priest was consecrated individually, personally, as priest to offer the sacrifice of the Mass. It is he himself who is consecrated. There was no massive and global consecration of all the priests. Each of them received the character.[39] The character was given personally and not to the group. That is why the priest is made to offer the holy sacrifice of the Mass individually.

There is no doubt that concelebration lacks the value of the ensemble of Masses that would be celebrated individually. That is not possible: there is only one transubstantiation, and consequently only one sacrifice of the Mass. Why multiply the sacrifices of the Mass if one single transubstantiation is worth all the sacrifices of the Mass? Then there should have been only one Mass in the world after Our Lord, supposing that even that would have been of use... The multiplication of Mass would thus be pointless if ten priests concelebrating accomplish an act worth ten distinct Masses. But that is false, absolutely false. Why would they make us say three Masses at Christmas and All Saints'? That would really be a ridiculous practice.

The Church needs this multiplication of the holy sacrifice of the Mass both for the application of the sacrifice of the Cross and for all the ends of the Mass: adoration, thanksgiving, propitiation, and supplication. All the novelties denote a lack of theology and a failure to define things.[40]

---

[38] Allusion to the declaration of the Rev. Father Guérard des Lauriers on the practice of concelebration: "Renewal or Subversion?"

[39] "The character imprinted on the soul...is a spiritual sign that can never be effaced" (Catechism of St. Pius X [French ed.], Part IV, Ch.1, §3 (Ed. DMM, 1993), p.121). Three Sacraments imprint a character on the soul: baptism, confirmation, and holy orders. According to St. Thomas, "by them we are deputed to the worship of God" (*Summa Theologica*, III, Q.63, Art. 2).

[40] Priests' retreat, Hauterive, August, 1972.

IV. JUDGMENT OF THE REFORM

THE NEW RITE CONDEMNED BY THE CHURCH'S TRADITION

Archbishop Lefebvre adopted the judgment of the New Mass made by Cardinals Ottaviani and Bacci in September 1969. The innovations of the New Mass are absolutely contrary to the teachings of the Councils and of the Popes from St. Pius V to Pius XII. Moreover, Pope Paul VI himself recognized the opposition between the traditional Mass and the new current of thought that issued from Vatican II.

1. The judgment of Cardinals Ottaviani and Bacci

We do not judge intentions, but the facts (and the consequences of the facts, similar, moreover, to those produced in centuries past wherever these reforms were introduced) oblige us to acknowledge with Cardinals Ottaviani and Bacci[1] (*The Ottaviani Intervention: A Short Critical Study of the New Order of Mass* handed to the Holy Father on September 3, 1969) that "the *Novus Ordo Missae*...represents, both as a whole and it its details, a striking departure from the Catholic theology of the Mass as it was formulated in Session 22 of the Council of Trent."[2]

2. A new rite already condemned by several popes and councils

It is a conception more Protestant than Catholic, and it explains all that which has been unduly exalted and all that which has been diminished.

---

[1] Cardinal Stickler wrote on November 27, 2004, on the occasion of a reprint of the *Ottaviani Intervention*: "The analysis of the *Novus Ordo* made by these two Cardinals has lost nothing of its value, nor, unfortunately, of its timeliness....The results of the reform are deemed by many today to have been devastating. It was the merit of Cardinals Ottaviani and Bacci to discover very quickly that the modification of the rites resulted in a fundamental change of doctrine."

[2] Letter to Cardinal Seper, February 26, 1978.

Contrary to the teaching of the Council of Trent in its twenty-second session, contrary to the Encyclical *Mediator Dei* of Pius XII, the role of the faithful in the participation of the Mass has been exaggerated, and the role of the priest, now become a simple president, has been diminished. The importance of the Liturgy of the Word has been exaggerated, and the importance of the propitiatory Sacrifice has been diminished. The meal of the community has been exalted, and the Mass has been laicized, to the detriment of the respect and the faith in the Real Presence by transubstantiation. By the suppression of the sacred language, the rites have been infinitely multiplied. They have been profaned by worldly and pagan additions. False translations have been propagated to the detriment of the true faith and the true piety of the faithful.

And yet the Councils of Florence and Trent had pronounced anathemas against all these changes and they had affirmed that the Canon of our Mass goes back to Apostolic times. The Popes, St. Pius V and Clement VIII, had insisted upon the necessity of avoiding changes and mutations, by perpetually keeping this Roman Rite consecrated by Tradition.

The removal from the Mass of that which is sacred, and its laicization have led to the laicization, in a Protestant manner, of the priesthood.[3]

How can this reform of the Mass be reconciled with the canons of the Council of Trent and the condemnations of the Bull *Auctorem Fidei*[4] of Pius VI?[5]

3. "Tradition condemns them, not I"

I do not set myself up as judge; I am nothing but the echo of a magisterium that is clear, evident, that is in all the books, the papal encyclicals, the conciliar documents—in short, in all the theological books from before the Council. What is being said now is not at all in conformity with this magisterium that was professed for two thousand years. Thus it is the Tradition of the Church, the magisterium of the Church, that condemns them, not I![6]

---

[3] "An Open Letter to the Pope: An Episcopal Manifesto," November 21, 1983, in *The Angelus*, December 1984, p.6.
[4] Bull of August 28, 1794, DS 2600.
[5] Letter to Cardinal Seper, February 26, 1978.
[6] Spiritual conference, Ecône, March 13, 1975.

4. The traditional judgments of the Church regarding the Eucharist are definitive

As for our attitude towards the liturgical reform and the reform of the breviary, we must hold fast to the affirmations of the Council of Trent. I do not see how to reconcile it with the liturgical reform. Yet the Council of Trent is a definitive, dogmatic council, and once the Church has spoken definitively upon certain subjects, another council cannot change these definitions. Otherwise, truth would no longer be possible!

The Faith is something unchangeable. When the Church has presented it authoritatively, one is obliged to believe it without change. Now, if the Council of Trent took care to add anathemas to all the truths concerning the Sacraments and the liturgy, it was not for no reason. How then can one, with the levity that was employed, act as if the Council of Trent no longer existed and say that the Second Vatican Council has the same authority and consequently can change everything? If so, then one could also change our Creed made at the Council of Nicaea, which is even more ancient, because the Second Vatican Council has the same authority and is more important than the Council of Nicaea...We must be firm about these matters, and this is the strongest answer one can make to the liturgical reform: It goes against the absolutely definitive dogmatic definitions of the Council of Trent.[7]

5. An avowal of Pope Paul VI

Here is an interesting little fact that shows what Paul VI thought about changing the Mass....Jean Guitton asked him: "Why wouldn't you accept that at Ecône the priests continue to celebrate the Mass of St. Pius V? They said it before. I do not see why one would deny the old Mass to this seminary. Let them go ahead." Pope Paul VI's reply was very significant. He said: "No, if we allow the Mass of St. Pius V to the Fraternity of Saint Pius X, everything we have gained by the Vatican Council will be ruined."[8] It is, all the same, extraordinary that the Pope sees in the return of the old Mass the ruin of Vatican II. This is an incredible revelation! That's why the liberals are bothered by our saying this Mass, which represents

---

[7] *Ibid.*, March 18, 1977.
[8] Jean Guitton, *Paul VI Secret* (Ed. Desclée De Brower, 1979), pp.158-59.

for them a completely different conception of the Church. The Mass of St. Pius V is not liberal, it is anti-liberal, it is anti-ecumenical, so it cannot correspond to the spirit of Vatican II.[9]

THE VALIDITY OF MASSES SAID ACCORDING TO THE *NOVUS ORDO MISSAE*

The liturgical reform, of Protestant inspiration, contributes to the loss of the Faith in souls. This unintended consequence prompts a certain number of questions: Is the New Mass valid? Is it simply less good than the traditional Mass, or is it bad? Is it permissible to celebrate it or to attend it? As a pastor of souls, Archbishop Lefebvre bases his answers upon the principles of moral theology and canon law.

MATTER AND FORM IN THE SACRAMENT OF THE EUCHARIST

The matter of the Sacraments is the material element used, and the form consists in the words that are pronounced to confect them.

If the Eucharist is to be valid, and so for all the other Sacraments, there must be present the matter, form, and intention necessary for their validity. The pope himself cannot alter that.[10]

1. The matter of the Sacrament of the Eucharist in the New Mass

Do the validly ordained priests who celebrate the New Mass use a valid matter? One can answer yes. The priests employ bread and wine as the Church requires.[11]

2. The words of the consecration of the bread

One can say that the words of the consecration of the bread used in the New Mass are valid because they are used in the Catholic Eastern rites. They also say "*Quod pro vobis tradetur*–Who

---

[9] Homily, Zaitzkofen, February 15, 1987.
[10] Conference, Rennes, November 1972, *A Bishop Speaks*, p.138.
[11] Spiritual conference, Zaitzkofen, October 1, 1979.

is given up for you." Rome has always considered that the Catholic Eastern-Rite Churches have a valid Mass.[12]

3. The words of the consecration of the wine

It is not certain that all the words of the consecration are absolutely necessary for the Real Presence, for when the priest says *"mysterium fidei*–the mystery of faith," it seems that the mystery has already been accomplished at that moment. The priest exclaims before the mystery that has taken place, the great mystery of our faith. The phrase *mysterium fidei* leads us to think that the Real Presence already exists at the moment it is uttered. The majority of theologians think that the Real Presence already exists from the first words of the consecration of the precious Blood. This is not an absolutely definitive argument, but it is still a noteworthy fact.

But the more one examines the liturgical reform, the more one wonders what could have been the authors' intentions. What ideas, what advantages did they hope to gain by changing these words of the sacramental form, which have been said for centuries upon centuries by the Church? Why, then, remove the formula *mysterium fidei*; why alter something in the form?[13]

The Intention of the Priest at Mass

Another question that affects the validity of a Sacrament is the intention of the minister. For a Mass to be valid, the priest must intend to do what the Church does. Since the texts of the New Mass no longer clearly express the intention to offer a sacrifice, and notably a propitiatory sacrifice, can this negate the intention of the minister to the point of rendering the Mass invalid?

1. Can the intention of the minister affect the validity of the Sacrament?

I have spoken of the matter and the form, leaving the intention. The intention, obviously, is something very important and rather difficult to determine because it is not visible. The bread and the wine, we can see. The words can be heard, but the priest's in-

---

[12] *Ibid.*
[13] Spiritual conference, Ecône, March 21, 1977.

tention, obviously, is more difficult to discern....In the old rite, the intention was clearly determined by all the prayers that were said before and after the consecration. There was an ensemble of things throughout the sacrifice of the Mass that determined the priest's intention.[14]

It is by the Offertory that the priest clearly expresses his intention. But that no longer exists in the *Novus Ordo*. The New Mass can thus be valid or invalid depending on the celebrant's intention, while in the old Mass, it is impossible for someone who has the faith not to have the precise intention of offering the sacrifice, and of doing it for the ends set by the Church.[15]

2. The new rite no longer guarantees the celebrant's intention

I had occasion to reread the short study–well-known to you, obviously–*A Short Critical Study of the New Order of Mass*, which was approved by Cardinals Ottaviani and Bacci. There is a note in this study about the words of the consecration that bears rereading, because this has been the subject of many discussions and analyses ever since the introduction of the new *Ordo*. I can tell you that what is there represents what I personally have always considered to be the most exact assessment of the validity or the invalidity of the *Novus Ordo Missae*.

"As they appear in the context of the *Novus Ordo*, the words of Consecration *could* be valid in virtue of the priest's intention. But since their validity no longer comes from the force of the sacramental words themselves (*ex vi verborum*)–or, more precisely, from the meaning (*modus significandi*) the old rite of the Mass gave to the formula–the words of Consecration in the New Order of Mass *could also not be valid*. Will priests in the near future, who receive no traditional formation and who rely on the *Novus Ordo* for the intention of "doing what the Church does," validly consecrate at Mass? One may be allowed to doubt it."[16]

This is what I believe I have always held: there will be more and more invalid Masses because of the formation of young priests

---

[14] Spiritual conference, Zaitzkofen, October 1, 1979.
[15] Spiritual conference, Ecône, February 28, 1975.
[16] *The Ottaviani Intervention*, tr. by Fr. Anthony Cekada (Rockford, Ill.: TAN Books & Publishers, 1992), p.60, n.29.

who will no longer have the right intention of doing what the Church does. To do what the Church does means to do what the Church has always done, what the Church does–I would say, if it could be said–eternally. So these young priests will not intend to do what the Church does because they will not have been taught that the Mass is truly a sacrifice. They will not intend to offer a sacrifice; they will intend to do a Eucharist, a sharing, a communion, a memorial, which has nothing to do with faith in the sacrifice of the Mass. Thus, at that moment, as these badly formed priests no longer have the least intention of doing what the Church does, more and more Masses will be invalid, obviously.[17]

SOME EXAMPLES OF NULLIFIED INTENTIONS

Some priests imbued with modernism may have an idea of the Sacrament that alters their intention to the point of rendering the Sacrament invalid.[18]

1. The modernist conception of a Sacrament

For the modernists, the Sacraments spring from a double need, "for, as we have seen, everything in their system is explained by inner impulses or necessities."[19] But worship must be given a sensible form:

"But for the Modernists the Sacraments are mere symbols or signs, though not devoid of a certain efficacy–an efficacy, they tell us, like that of certain phrases vulgarly described as having "caught on," inasmuch as they have become the vehicle for the diffusion of

---

[17] Spiritual conference, Ecône, February 8, 1979.
[18] A modernist, rationalist priest who does not believe in the supernatural is exposed to lacking the intention of performing the rite instituted by Christ. To him could be applied what was said in the Ritual of the Diocese of Basel about baptism administered by Protestant ministers: "If an adult wanted to convert from heresy to the Catholic Faith, an inquiry should be conscientiously made (in so far as necessary) into his baptism, especially to discover whether, in the sect or place where he received baptism, the true and legitimate matter and form of the Sacrament have been prescribed and preserved, and whether the heretical minister, by whom he was baptized, is known as firmly holding the faith in Christ, the Son of God, or rather as an adherent of rationalism" (translated from the Latin by the editor).
[19] Pope St. Pius X, *Pascendi Dominici Gregis*, on the Doctrine of the Modernists, September 8, 1907, §21.

certain great ideas which strike the public mind. What the phrases are to the ideas, that the Sacraments are to the religious sentiment–that and nothing more. The Modernists would be speaking more clearly were they to affirm that the Sacraments are instituted solely to foster the faith–but this is condemned by the Council of Trent: *If anyone say that these Sacraments are instituted solely to foster the faith, let him be anathema.*"[20]

This idea recurs in the writings of Besret, for example, who was an "expert" at the Council: "It is not the Sacrament that puts the love of God in the world. God's love is at work in all men. The Sacrament is the moment of its public manifestation in the community of disciples....Saying that, in no wise do I mean to deny the efficacious aspect of the signs employed. Man also fulfills himself by his speaking, and that holds true for the Sacraments as it does for the rest of his activity.[21]"[22]

2. Transignification and transfinalization

If [some priests] are asked "Is the Eucharist that you are celebrating that of the Council of Trent?" the reply will be: "No. Much has happened since the days of the Council of Trent. We have Vatican II now. Now it is transignification[23] and transfinalisation.[24] Transubstantiation[25]–the Real Presence of Our Lord, of the Body of our Savior, the physical presence of Our Lord under the species of bread and wine? No, not in these days." Should priests say that to you, the consecration is invalid, for they no longer carry out what the Church defined at the Council of Trent, which is ir-

---

[20] *Ibid.*
[21] Dom Bernard Besret, *De commencement en commencement* (Paris: Ed. du Seuil, 1976), p.176.
[22] July 4, 1984.
[23] *Transignification*: the bread and the wine acquired a new signification, that of the Lord's presence (Arnaud Join-Lambert, Chairman of Pastoral Theology of the Theology Faculty of the University of Fribourg, Switzerland, *La Messe* [Mame, June 2003], p.40).
[24] *Transfinalization*: the bread and the wine acquired a new finality, since their new purpose is to represent the Lord, and no longer to nourish the body as human food (*ibid.*, pp.40-41).
[25] *Transubstantiation*: by the consecration, a change is effected in the substance of the bread and wine, which become the Body and the Blood of Christ, under the accidents of bread and wine. (The accidents are the color, taste, and shape, which are directly apprehended by the senses).

reformable.[26] What the Council of Trent laid down on the Holy Mass and the Eucharist, Christians are bound to believe till the end of time. Terms may be made more explicit, but they cannot be changed; that is an impossibility. Whoever says that he does not accept transubstantiation is anathema, says the Council of Trent, and therefore separated from the Church. One day you may be obliged to ask your priests: "Do you believe in the definitions of the Council of Trent, yes or no? If you no longer believe, your Eucharist is invalid. The Lord is not present."[27]

Conclusion on the validity of Masses

The general Protestant ambiance of the New Mass has the effect that even good priests who say this Mass for ten years risk losing the real intention of doing what the Church does. It is possible that there will be more and more invalid Masses. But it seems to me that it cannot be said absolutely that all the Masses are invalid in principle. The duty to analyze and to judge these problems rightly in accordance with traditional dogmatic and moral theology imposes on us an objectivity as perfect as possible.[28]

ARE ALL THE VALID MASSES GOOD?

In light of all the defects of the liturgical reform, is the New Mass simply less good than the traditional Mass, or can it be called bad?

1. Validity is not enough to make a Mass good

The word *validity* is a snare. For many people unaccustomed to theological and canonical vocabulary, *validity* means good.... That is not what it means! Validity means the presence, the efficacy if you will, of the grace found in the Sacrament. The efficacy of the rite can be preserved even if the ceremony is sacrilegious! A valid Mass can very well be sacrilegious![29]

---

[26] The dogmatic canons of the Council of Trent that define the Church's doctrine on the Eucharist enjoy the privilege of infallibility, because they fulfill the conditions stipulated by the First Vatican Council (Constitution *Pastor Aeternus*, DS 3074 [Dz. 1839]).
[27] Conference, Rennes, November 1972, *A Bishop Speaks*, pp.138-39.
[28] Spiritual conference, Ecône, October 25, 1979.
[29] Conference, Flavigny, June 11, 1988.

2. Is the reformed Mass only less good?

Even though the validity of the Mass cannot be called in question, it is a corrupted Mass. Because it no longer affirms the specifically Catholic truths of the Mass for the sake of pleasing the Protestants, little by little faith in these truths also disappears. That this is so is made plain by the results. That is why it is impossible for me to say that this reform is only bad in a purely accidental, extrinsic way.[30]

We are of the opinion that, having been drafted with the aid of Protestants, there is an ecumenical influence on the reformation of the Mass that imparts a Protestant savor. Little by little the notion of sacrifice has disappeared, particularly the notion of propitiatory sacrifice. The changes that have been made in the Mass make it dangerous, corrupted.[31]

This reformation, deriving as it does from Liberalism and Modernism, is entirely corrupted; it derives from heresy and results in heresy, even if all its acts are not formally heretical. It is therefore impossible for any conscientious and faithful Catholic to espouse this reformation and to submit to it in any way whatsoever.[32]

The facts are there to show us that faith in the essential dogmatic realities of the Mass is being lost....It is relatively easy to do a study of the harmfulness of the New Mass. And such a study does not lead to the conclusion some people reach, sometimes even people close to us, who are self-styled "traditionalists." You hear them say: "The old Mass is better, certainly, but the other is not bad." That is what the Father Abbot of Fontgombault says. He replied to someone who wrote to him explaining that she could no longer be a Benedictine oblate at the monastery because they accept the New Mass. The Father Abbot of Fontgombault replied: "Yes, that is true. I recognize, indeed, that the old Mass is better; but the other is not bad. Thus, for obedience's sake, we say it."[33] You see the conclusion they reach!

---

[30] Spiritual conference, Ecône, June 24, 1981.
[31] Conference, Flavigny, June 11, 1988.
[32] Declaration, November 21, 1974. English version: Michael Davies, *Apologia pro Marcel Lefebvre*, I, 39-40.
[33] Dom Jean Roy, Abbot of Fontgombault, accepted the celebration of the New Mass in 1974.

We absolutely do not agree. We refuse to say that the New Mass is good! The New Mass is not good! If it were good, then tomorrow we would have to start saying it, obviously. If it is good, we must obey. If the Church gives us something good and tells us "You must take it," what reason could there be to say no? Whereas, if we say, "This Mass is corrupted; this Mass is bad; it makes us gradually lose the faith," then we are indeed obliged to refuse it.[34]

BECAUSE OF ITS DEFICIENCIES, THE *NOVUS ORDO MISSAE* CANNOT OBLIGE

LAW AND OBEDIENCE

The reasons for Archbishop Lefebvre's refusal to adopt the reform are based upon the nature of law, the fruits of the New Mass, and the nature of the obedience due to the pope.

1. Under what conditions does a law oblige?

What is a law? What is a decree? What constrains us to obey? A law, Leo XIII says, is an ordinance of reason for the common good, and not for the common woe. This is so obvious that if a law is made to bring about some evil, it is no law, and, as Leo XIII explicitly wrote in his Encyclical *Libertas*,[35] one must not obey it.

Many canon lawyers at Rome say that Msgr. Bugnini's Mass is not law. There was no law imposing the New Mass. It was merely authorized or permitted. Let us go so far as to grant that there was a law. Now, it is clear that the New Mass is in the process of destroying the Church and the Faith. The Archbishop of Montreal, Msgr. Grégoire, in a published letter, was very courageous. He is one of the rare bishops who dared to write a letter in which he decried the evils which the Church of Montreal is suffering. "We are grieved to see the parishes abandoned by a great number of the faithful. We attribute this, in large part, to the liturgical reform." He had the courage to say that.[36]

---

[34] Spiritual conference, Ecône, January 21, 1982.
[35] June 20, 1888.
[36] *L'Église infiltrée par le modernisme*, pp.40-41.

2. A bad law cannot command obedience

One approach to judging the soundness of the liturgical reform is to examine the effects of the law. Even granting that the law was obligatory, a law that produces effects as disastrous as those produced by this liturgical reform should open the eyes of those who apply it and lead them to conclude: "We must stop celebrating this Mass; this cannot go on!" A law is made for the good of the Church and not its harm! Now, we see that it produces absolutely deplorable effects, that is to say, a liberty, a license, in the liturgy and in the application of the Sacraments to the point of disgusting the faithful and causing them to give up the Sacraments and the Mass. Very many of the faithful no longer put a foot in church, very many young people lose the faith, very many vocations are lost, and so on. For what is the use of attending these ceremonies, which are nothing but theater when they are not outright sacrilege? So how can you expect people to continue to believe when they see this theater? And even when it is well done, it is empty, flat, without savor, without the supernatural, without grace. One feels that the Holy Ghost is absent from these ceremonies, which are stories. The New Mass is now a narrative and not an action; it is no longer a sacrifice, but a simple meal. Everything is going in that direction. These effects should already suffice to cause us to suspend the application of the law. One does not enforce a law that is bad, that goes against the goal that must be sought: the good of the Church, its vitality, the supernatural in the Church, the increase of the Mystical Body. Common sense says as much.[37]

3. Have we the right to refuse an order of the pope?

The principles governing obedience are known and are so in conformity with right reason and common sense that one is driven to wonder how intelligent people can make a statement like, "They prefer to be mistaken with the Pope, than to be with the truth against the Pope." That is not what the natural law teaches, nor the Magisterium of the Church. Obedience presupposes an authority which gives an order or issues a law. Human authorities, even those instituted by God, have no authority other than to attain the end apportioned them by God and not to turn away from it. When an authority uses power in opposition to the law for which this power

---

[37] Spiritual conference, Ecône, January 16, 1975.

was given it, such an authority has no right to be obeyed, and one must disobey it. This need to disobey is accepted with regard to a family father who would encourage his daughter to prostitute herself, with regard to the civil authority which would oblige doctors to perform abortions and kill innocent souls, yet people accept in every case the authority of the pope, who is supposedly infallible in his government and in all words. Such an attitude betrays a sad ignorance of history and of the true nature of papal infallibility.

A long time ago St. Paul said to St. Peter that he was "not walking according to the truth of the Gospel" (Gal. 2:14). St. Paul encouraged the faithful not to obey him, St. Paul, if he happened to preach any other gospel than the Gospel that he had already taught them (Gal. 1:8). St. Thomas, when he speaks of fraternal correction, alludes to St. Paul's resistance to St. Peter and he makes the following comment: "To resist openly and in public goes beyond the measure of fraternal correction. St. Paul would not have done it towards St. Peter if he had not in some way been his equal.... We must realize, however, that if there was question of a danger for the faith, the superiors would have to be rebuked by their inferiors, even in public." This is clear from the manner and reason for St. Paul's acting as he did with regard to St. Peter, whose subject he was, in such a way, says the gloss of St. Augustine, "that the very head of the Church showed to superiors that if they ever chanced to leave the straight and narrow path, they should accept to be corrected by their inferiors."[38]

The case evoked by St. Thomas is not merely imaginary, because it took place with regard to John XXII during his life. This pope thought he could state as a personal opinion that the souls of the elect do not enjoy the Beatific Vision until after the Last Judgment. He wrote this opinion down in 1331, and in 1332 he preached a similar opinion with regard to the pains of the damned. He had the intention of putting forward this opinion in a solemn decree. But the very lively action on the part of the Dominicans, above all in Paris, and of the Franciscans, made him renounce this opinion in favor of the traditional opinion defined by his successor, Benedict XII, in 1336.

---

[38] St. Thomas, II-II, Q.33, Art. 4, ad 2.

And here is what Pope Leo XIII said in his Encyclical *Libertas Præstantissimum*, June 20, 1888: "If, then, by any one in authority, something be sanctioned out of conformity with the principles of right reason, and consequently hurtful to the commonwealth, such an enactment can have no binding force of law." And a little further on, he says: "But where the power to command is wanting, or where a law is enacted contrary to reason, or to the eternal law, or to some ordinance of God, obedience is unlawful, lest while obeying man, we become disobedient to God."

Now our disobedience is motivated by the need to keep the Catholic Faith. The orders being given us clearly express that they are being given us in order to oblige us to submit without reserve to the Second Vatican Council, to the post-conciliar reforms, and to the prescriptions of the Holy See, that is to say, to the orientations and acts which are undermining our Faith and destroying the Church. It is impossible for us to do this. To collaborate in the destruction of the Church is to betray the Church and to betray Our Lord Jesus Christ. Now, all the theologians worthy of this name teach that if the pope, by his acts, destroys the Church, we cannot obey him,[39] and he must be respectfully, but publicly, rebuked.[40]

---

[39] On this matter, we can cite St. Robert Bellarmine: "Just as it is licit to resist the Pontiff who attacks the body, it is licit to resist if he attacks souls and destroys the civil order or especially if he tries to destroy the Church. I say that it is licit to resist him by not carrying out his orders or by impeding the execution of his will; nevertheless, it is illicit to judge him, to punish him and to depose him" (*De Summo Pontifice* [Ed. de Paris, 1870], Book II, Ch. 29); Vitoria: "If the pope by his orders or his acts destroys the Church, one can resist him and prevent the execution of his orders" (*Obras de Fransisco de Vitoria*, pp.486-87); Suarez: "If the pope gives an order that is contrary to accepted customs, one must not obey him" (*De Fide*, disputatio X, sectio VI, no.16). It is noteworthy that the theologians cite as a grave fault of the pope against the common good "not to observe what has been universally commanded by the ecumenical councils or by the Apostolic See, especially as regards divine worship if he does not want to observe what concerns the universal worship of the Church" (Cardinal Torquemada, *Summa de Ecclesia* [Venice, 1560], Book IV, Ch.11; to want "to abolish all the ecclesiastical ceremonies that have been confirmed by Apostolic tradition, as Cajetan remarks" (Suarez, *De Caritate*, disputatio XII, sectio I, *Opera Omnia* [Paris, 1858], 12, 733ff).

[40] Circular letter, January 20, 1978, quoted by Archbishop Lefebvre in his statement of March 29, 1988. [English version: *The Angelus*, July 1988, pp.39-40.]

4. The duty to use the liturgical books issued by the authority of the Holy Father

On the contrary, when a reform like that of Pope John XXIII does not affect or diminish our faith, we have the duty to recognize the authority of the Sovereign Pontiff who edicts the book–the new breviary, for example–and we submit even if we have a greater affection for the breviary or missal of St. Pius X....Consequently, we must be on guard against our personal desire or attachment. When books have been issued by the authority of the Holy Father, there is indeed a certain obligation to comply provided that they do not harm our Catholic faith.[41]

WAS IT ACTUALLY THE POPE WHO IMPOSED THE NEW MASS?

There were defects in the form of the publication and the application of the liturgical decrees. The promulgation of these decrees was dubious and the reform was surreptitiously imposed, especially in Spain and Italy.

1. Did Paul VI read the *Institutio Generalis* before signing it?

At the time at which this Normative Mass began to be put into practice, I was so disgusted that we met with some priests and theologians in a small meeting. From it came the "Short Critical Study," which was taken to Cardinal Ottaviani. I presided that small meeting. We said to ourselves: "We must go and find the Cardinals. We cannot allow this to happen without reacting."

So I myself went to find the Secretary of State, Cardinal Cicognani, and I said to him: "Your Eminence, you are not going to allow this to get through, are you? It's not possible. What is this New Mass? It is a revolution in the Church, a revolution in the Liturgy."

Cardinal Cicognani, who was the Secretary of State of Pope Paul VI, placed his head between his hands and said to me: "O, *Monseigneur*, I know well. I am in full agreement with you; but what can I do? Father Bugnini goes into the office of the Holy

---

[41] Spiritual conference, Ecône, March 15, 1983.

Father and makes him sign what he wants." It was the Cardinal Secretary of State who told me this! Therefore the Secretary of State, the number two person in the Church after the Pope himself, was placed in a position of inferiority with respect to Father Bugnini. He could enter into the Pope's office when he wanted and make him sign what he wanted.

This can explain why Pope Paul VI signed texts that he had not read. He told Cardinal Journet that he had done this. Cardinal Journet was a deep thinker, professor at the University of Fribourg in Switzerland, and a great theologian. When Cardinal Journet saw the definition of the Mass in the instruction, which precedes the *Novus Ordo*, he said: "This definition of the Mass is unacceptable; I must go to Rome to see the Pope." He went, and he said: "Holy Father you cannot allow this definition. It is heretical. You cannot leave your signature on a document like this."

The Holy Father replied to him (Cardinal Journet did not tell me himself, but he told someone who repeated it to me): "Well, to tell the truth, I did not read it. I signed it without reading it." Evidently, if Father Bugnini had such an influence on him, it's quite possible. He must have said to the Holy Father: "You can sign it." "But did you look it over carefully." "Yes, you can go ahead and sign it." And he signed.

But this document did not go through the Holy Office. I know this because Cardinal Seper himself told me that he was absent when the *Novus Ordo* was edited and that it did not pass by the Holy Office. Hence it is indeed Father Bugnini who obtained the Pope's signature and who perhaps constrained him. We do not know, but he had without a doubt an extraordinary influence over the Holy Father.

A third fact of which I was myself the witness, with respect to Father Bugnini, is also astonishing. When permission was about to be give for Communion in the hand (what a horrible thing!), I said to myself that I could not sit by without saying anything. I must go and see Cardinal Gut, a Swiss, who was Prefect of the Congregation for Worship. I therefore went to Rome,[42] where Cardinal Gut received me in a very friendly way and immediately said to me: "I'm

---

[42] Archbishop Lefebvre went there in February 1969.

going to make my second-in-charge, Archbishop Antonini, come that he also might hear what you have to say."

As we spoke I said: "Listen, you who are responsible for the Congregation for Worship, are you going to approve this decree which authorizes Communion in the hand? Just think of all the sacrileges it is going to cause. Just think of the lack of respect for the Holy Eucharist that is going to spread throughout the entire Church. You cannot possibly allow such a thing to happen. Already priests are beginning to give Communion in this manner. It must be stopped immediately. And with this New Mass they always take the shortest Canon, that is the second one, which is very short."

At this, Cardinal Gut said to Archbishop Antonini, "See, I told you this would happen and that priests would take the shortest Canon so as to go more quickly and finish the Mass more quickly."

Afterwards Cardinal Gut said to me: "*Monseigneur*, if one were to ask my opinion [when he said "one" he was speaking of the Pope, since nobody was over him except the Pope], but I'm not certain it is asked of me [don't forget that he was Prefect for the Congregation for Worship and was responsible for everything related to worship and to the liturgy!), but if the Pope were to ask for it, I would place myself on my knees, *Monseigneur*, before the Pope and I would say to him: 'Holy Father, do not do this; do not sign this decree.' I would cast myself on my knees, *Monseigneur*. But I do not know that I will be asked. For it is not I who command here."

This I heard with my own ears. He was making allusion to Bugnini, who was the third in the Congregation for Worship. There was first of all Cardinal Gut, then Archbishop Antonini, and then Father Bugnini, President of the Liturgical Commission. You ought to have heard that![43]

2. Defect of form in its publication

I sincerely believe that when the Holy Father approved the new missal, in his mind he was establishing a new rite, but he did not abolish the former rite. It was Msgr. Bugnini who wanted ab-

---

[43] Conference, Montreal, 1982. [English version: "The Church Infiltrated by Modernism" *The Angelus*, March 1992, p.8.]

solutely to suppress the old rite, because he was very well aware that if they did not suppress the old rite, they would never succeed in passing off the new one. In the publication of the law calling for the celebration of the new rite and in its application, there were such defects of form that one can sincerely doubt its validity. In the *Acta Apostolicae Sedis*[44] there were two editions of the same Apostolic Constitution of Pope Paul VI. It was indeed the same Constitution because the date is the same. So there were two different versions of the *A.A.S.* in two different books: a first edition, dated April 3, 1969, and a second, also dated at Rome on April 3, 1969. Thus it is indeed the same Constitution. Now in the same Constitution that is reproduced, an article has been added to it. Who added it? If it were an addendum, it would be necessary to say so explicitly; it should be properly notified and signed again by the Pope. Besides, no one has the right to modify a Constitution except the one who signed it, the Holy Father himself. Therefore an explicit modification of the Constitution by the Pope himself would have been necessary. The article added reads: "We order that the prescriptions of this Constitution go into effect November 30th of this year, the first Sunday of Advent."[45] The implementation of this Constitution was consequently rushed without any explanation; such things are quite simply unheard of in pontifical law![46]

3. How the New Order of Mass was imposed

I had in my hands a very interesting document. It was the reply Msgr. Bugnini made to five thousand Spanish priests who refused the New Mass, which they described as heretical, and protested their desire to continue saying the traditional Mass. Msgr. Bugnini said in essence: "The Pope formally desires that the New Mass be said. You must submit to the will of the Pope and obey him. If you say that the New Mass is heretical, it means the Pope who signed it is heretical. If he is a heretic, he is not pope. Before the gravity of such an attitude, I ask you to reflect and to submit to the Holy Father's desire."

---

[44] Or A.A.S., the official organ of the Vatican in which official acts are published.
[45] *Quae Constitutione hac Nostra praescripsimus vigere incipient a die XXX proximi mensis Novembris hoc anno, id est a Dominica I adventus.*
[46] Spiritual conference, Ecône, January 16, 1975.

It is interesting to note that Msgr. Bugnini did not write: the old Mass is suppressed. No, he simply affirmed that it is a formal desire of the Pope. Unfortunately, all these priests obeyed.[47]

4. Defect of form in its application, contrary to canon law

The Italian Episcopal Conference was forced to apply the Constitution after a month, even though the bishops had legitimately decided to delay its application for two years in order to allow enough time to make the translations and to explain to the faithful the changes being made. They were forced by an unsigned article published in *L'Osservatore Romano* that said: "the Italian Bishops will implement the constitution in a month," while the decision to wait had been made unanimously by the episcopal conference. The application of the Constitution was officially left to the free choice of the episcopal conference according to the Congregation for Worship.

I personally telephoned Msgr. Carli to ask him, "Are you aware of this? I saw this article at Rome." He told me: "Yes, indeed, I am aware of it, but I also telephoned: I don't know how this can happen; it is absolutely inadmissible. Moreover, I just filed an official complaint with the Sacred Congregation of the Rota to request a judgment in this matter, because it is really contrary to the law that was passed." Then he added: "I telephoned the president of the Italian Episcopal Conference in Bologna, Cardinal Poma, who told me that he was uninformed. Then I telephoned the secretary of the episcopal conference, Cardinal Pelegrino of Turin. He gave me the same response." In reality, it was Msgr. Bugnini who came to realize that waiting two years would perhaps cause the Italian bishops to reflect. There would be difficulties in implementing the Constitution, hence it would be better to apply it right away. And they implemented it–always in the Pope's name, obviously. Was the Pope even apprised of this? No one knows. These are all little examples that clearly show that what happened is inadmissible.[48]

---

[47] "Despite the Persecutions: The Epic of the Fraternity," *Fideliter*, September-October 1987, p.72.
[48] Spiritual conference, Ecône, January 16, 1975.

Practical Consequences

> Archbishop Lefebvre proved that it is not permissible to obey a law that imperils the Faith. Moreover, he showed that the reform of the Mass was imposed insidiously. The only thing that remains to be done is to elaborate the consequences. To understand the position of Archbishop Lefebvre in this very delicate matter, one must not be content with a single citation, but rather consider his declarations as a whole. On this particular topic, the date of his writing or speech is of great importance.

1. If the New Mass is valid, may one actively participate in it?

On the subject of the New Mass, let us be rid once and for all of this absurd idea that if the New Mass is valid one may attend it. The Church has always forbidden the faithful to attend the Masses of schismatics and heretics even if they are valid. It is obvious that one cannot participate in sacrilegious Masses, nor in Masses that endanger our faith.[49]

2. Moral judgment of the New Mass

These New Masses cannot be made the object of an obligation for satisfying the precept to attend Mass on Sundays; we must, moreover, apply to them the rules of moral theology and canon law, which are rules of supernatural prudence as regards the participation or attendance at an action that endangers the faith or that may be sacrilegious.[50] That is why we reject this Mass in spite of its validity. And that is why we absolutely refuse to encourage the faithful to go to this Mass. We discourage the faithful from attending these Masses that gradually destroy the faith of both the celebrant and the faithful–that's quite sure.[51]

The New Mass, even when said with piety and respect for the liturgical rules, is subject to the same reservations since it is impregnated with the spirit of Protestantism. It bears within it a poison harmful to the faith.[52] Even if the Mass is valid, even if it is not sacrilegious, and even if it is said in Latin, it was reformed accord-

---

[49] Note on the N.O.M. and the pope, November 8, 1979, in *Cor Unum*, No.4.
[50] *Ibid.*
[51] Conference, Flavigny, June 11, 1988.
[52] *Open Letter to Confused Catholics*, p.29.

ing to Protestant, ecumenical principles. It gradually protestantizes Catholics. It has lost its mystical and supernatural, its royal and hierarchical, character. It no longer has its dogmatic character, which was expressive of our Catholic Faith. It is thus dangerous, especially when practised regularly. It slowly but surely weakens and corrupts the Faith. Therefore one could only attend it rarely and for serious reasons, while striving to avoid anything that would oblige us to make odious concessions like receiving Communion in the hand or standing, or taking part in the readings. Instead, one should read the Mass in the old missal and unite one's heart to the true Masses being offered throughout the world.[53]

It is impossible for any informed and loyal Catholic to embrace this reform or submit to it in any way whatsoever. The only attitude of fidelity to the Church and to Catholic doctrine appropriate for our salvation is a categorical refusal to accept this reformation.[54]

This attitude of vigilance is made necessary by reason of all the scandals we have witnessed within the Church itself. We cannot deny the facts, the writings and speeches which have led to the servitude of the Church of Rome and its annihilation as Mother and Mistress of all the Churches, and which tend to make Protestants of us all. To hold out against these scandals is to live one's faith, keep it free from all contagion, and safeguard the grace in our souls. To offer no resistance is to allow oneself to be poisoned slowly but surely and, all unconsciously, to become Protestants.[55]

3. Acceptance of the 1965 reform, refusal of that of 1969

The whole business was conducted with such cunning, progressively, by stages, from 1965. At first, I was not satisfied with it, but I had accepted a few reforms: fewer genuflections, fewer Signs of the Cross, fewer prayers at the foot of the altar. But noth-

---

[53] Circular letter, January 20, 1978, p.3. Archbishop Lefebvre is here applying Canon 1258, § 2 (1917 Code), which forbids attendance at non-Catholic worship without serious motive "of homage to render or duty of courtesy to fulfill" (funerals, *etc.*). In this case, participation may only be passive (no participation in singing or other liturgical actions).
[54] Declaration of November 21, 1974, reprinted in *A Bishop Speaks*, p.188.
[55] Rome, June 5, 1970, *A Bishop Speaks*, pp.85-86.

ing important altered the very essence of the rite. The Offertory and the Canon were still complete. There was no change in the words of Consecration. Even while trying to oppose these reforms, we followed obedience to the limit. But that was just a stage. Then came the radical reform of 1969. I refused it, and, so as not to be dragged further along, together with the professors, and with Father Guérard des Lauriers, who was with us at the time, and with the seminarians, we decided to return wholly to the old liturgy.[56]

4. The Society of Saint Pius X was not founded in reaction against the New Mass

The New Mass is not the cause of our existence. It did not yet exist when we began: the New Mass was inaugurated in November 1969, and we had been in existence since October. That is not very much longer, but still... It is a fact. The seminary was not founded in reaction against the New Mass. We were against the New Mass, of course, but the seminary was not founded because of it. History willed that the combat be crystallized, synthesized, by the Mass. The focal point could have been something else; it might have been, for example, the Council, or the question of religious liberty, or the question of *Gaudium et Spes*,[57] or other objects: over these points one could have found oneself, I would say, in contradiction, in contention with the Council or with the Pope, with Rome. But everything centered on the Mass, everything was in some way comprised in it.[58]

5. Hypothetical cases

If [an apostolic visitor] coming to Ecône were to speak with the professors and students...and if he were to say, "Tomorrow I shall ask the professors to concelebrate with me at Mass," what would the professors reply? "We cannot accept."... If Msgr. Graber said, "But listen, I would like one of your professors to come, because I need a priest to celebrate the Mass for a feast at the cathedral, but obviously he would have to celebrate the New Mass." What would you do? You would answer, "That is not possible. If it's the old

---

[56] "The Epic of the Fraternity," *Fideliter*, September-October 1987, p.73.
[57] The Pastoral Constitution on the Church in the Modern World, voted December 7, 1965.
[58] Spiritual conference, Ecône, January 16, 1982.

Mass, yes; but if it's the new Mass, no."....If the Pope were to come here and were to ask to concelebrate the New Mass with the professors, what would the professors do?...They would say, "No, not even with the Pope; we cannot concelebrate this new Mass."

They are not going to require us to adopt the New Mass because they know very well that we want no part of it. But they are certainly going to try every angle to say, "Come now, something must be done. You have to accept the liturgy somewhat; you have to say the New Mass at least once a month, for instance, or at least once in a while." If we were to yield to these pressures, we would be obliged to admit that we are giving the faithful a Mass we know to be bad and corrupted. It would be like telling a pharmacist to give his clients poison, but just a little–one pill, for example. The pharmacist would say, "Never! My pharmacy may be closed and I may be put in prison, but I refuse to do it." It is the same thing for us: we do not want to give poison to our faithful.[59]

We are quite saddened to see that some priests have felt bound to accept the New Mass and to say that it is as good as the old Mass, and to have done so, they say, in order to be able to say the old Mass in complete security and in conformity with the bishops' rules. And now, for the sake of being in regulation as regards the old Mass, they have given up the fight against the novelties, especially liturgical novelties....It is to be feared that one day they will be obliged by their bishop to celebrate the New Mass too, to celebrate both Masses, and eventually to concelebrate, to give Communion in the hand, or say the Mass facing the people–things that are repugnant to us.[60]

6. Practical directives

Faithful Catholics must do everything possible to keep the Catholic Faith whole and entire. Therefore they must attend the Mass of all time when they can, even if only once a month; they must actively collaborate in helping faithful priests to celebrate the Mass of all time and to distribute the Sacraments according to the traditional rites and catechisms. Those who are unable to get to these Masses should read their missal on Sundays, in family if pos-

---

[59] Spiritual conference, Zaitzkofen, April 18, 1981.
[60] *Communicantes*, August 1985.

sible, like the Christians in mission lands do, who are visited by a priest just two or three times a year, and sometimes just once! These directives are given so that each one may adopt the line of conduct most favorable to keeping the faith. It goes without saying that the Sunday obligation must be fulfilled when there is a Mass of all time accessible normally.

This is the age of heroism. Isn't it a grace from God to live in these troubled times, which push us to rediscover the Cross of Jesus, His redemptive sacrifice; and to esteem this source of the Church's holiness at its true worth, to restore it to honor, and to better appreciate the grandeur of the priesthood? To understand the Cross of Jesus better is to lift oneself heavenward and to deepen one's understanding of the true Catholic spirituality of sacrifice and the meaning of suffering, penance, humility, and death.[61]

7. Is a fault committed by saying the New Mass or attending it?

The New Mass is scandalous, but not in the sense of a shocking act. It isn't that. Scandal is whatever leads to sin. Well, the New Mass leads to sin against faith, and that is one of the most serious of sins, the most dangerous of sins, because the loss of faith is really estrangement from Revelation, from Our Lord Jesus Christ, and from the Church. One can only conclude that an informed person aware of the danger posed by this Mass and who attended it, would certainly commit at least a venial sin. Why, you will ask, do you not say a serious sin? Because I think that attendance at this Mass once does not constitute a proximate danger. I think that the danger becomes serious and consequently occasion of serious sin by repetition....The sin becomes serious if an informed, aware person goes there regularly anyway, saying to himself that it is all the same to him, he has nothing to fear for his faith, while knowing perfectly well that it is dangerous. He knows it: he has seen for himself that children have lost their faith because they regularly attended the New Mass; he has seen for himself that parents have left the Church. Even so, he still goes. That person is really putting his faith in danger, obviously.[62]

---

[61] Circular letter, January 20, 1978, pp.3-4.
[62] Spiritual conference, Ecône, January 21, 1982.

In order to judge the subjective fault of those who celebrate the New Mass as of those who attend it, we must apply the rules of the discernment of spirits given us in moral and pastoral theology. We (the priests of the Society) must always act as doctors of the soul and not as judges and hangmen. Those who are tempted by this latter course are animated by a bitter spirit and not true zeal for souls. I hope that our young priests will be inspired by the words of St. Pius X in his first encyclical,[63] and by the numerous texts on this subject to be found in such works as *The Soul of the Apostolate*[64] by Dom Chautard, *Christian Perfection and Contemplation* by Garrigou-Lagrange,[65] and *Christ, the Ideal of the Monk*[66] by Dom Marmion.[67]

---

[63] St. Pius X, *E Supremi Apostolatus*, October 4, 1903: "But in order that the desired fruit may be derived from this apostolate and this zeal for teaching, and that Christ may be formed in all, be it remembered, Venerable Brethren, that no means is more efficacious than charity, 'For the Lord is not in the earthquake' (III Kings 19:2). It is vain to hope to attract souls to God by a bitter zeal. On the contrary, harm is done more often than good by taunting men harshly with their faults, and reproving their vices with asperity. True, the Apostle exhorted Timothy: 'Accuse, beseech, rebuke,' but he took care to add: 'with all patience' (II Tim. 4:2)" (§13).

[64] In particular, at the end of Part III: "It refines the purity of his intention."

[65] Fr. Reginald Garrigou-Lagrange, O.P., *Perfection chrétienne et contemplation*, tome II, ch.3, art.4: "The charity of which St. Augustine speaks in the *Canticle of Degrees* (*Enarr. in psalm.* LXXXIII, n.10) and in the *Confessions* (XIII, 8) presupposes that one is ready to die for his brethren, and is inconceivable without this intimate and penetrating knowledge of God which is mystical contemplation." He quotes St. Paul: "But I most gladly will spend and be spent myself for your souls; although loving you more, I be loved less" (II Cor. 12:15).

[66] *Christ, the Ideal of the Monk*, Ch.XVII, 2: "Good zeal knows not this excess; it is not eager to impose its personal conceptions of perfection upon others, nor is it full of the sense of duty accomplished, nor of inconsiderate, violent impulses, but of the love of God, pure, humble, full of sweetness."

[67] Note on the N.O.M. and the Pope, November 8, 1979, in *Cor Unum*, No.4 [Davies, *Apologia*, II, 370-71].

V. THE AUTHORITY OF THE TRADITIONAL RITE

Two considerations spotlight the authority of the so-called Mass of St. Pius V: its origin and the unique privilege it possesses.

THE TRADITIONAL RITE IS OF APOSTOLIC ORIGIN

1. Pope Paul VI acknowledged the antiquity of the traditional Mass

Pope Paul VI himself says in his introduction to the new rite that the Mass we celebrate goes back to St. Gregory the Great.[1] But it can be said that it goes back further than St. Gregory the Great; it goes all the way to the Apostles. The decrees of the Council of Trent say very clearly that the prayers of the Mass, in particular the Canon, probably go back to the Apostles.[2]

The words of the Canon of the Mass are certainly the most venerable of our traditions. According to Dom Pace,[3] it is very likely that during the forty days before His Ascension, Our Lord taught the Apostles at least the words of the Consecration. And it is these precious words that were assiduously preserved in the Latin Church. The most Blessed Virgin received Communion from the hands of St. John after the sacrifice of the Mass was offered. She would never have tolerated that words be spoken that were not identical to those Our Lord had spoken. For years, she attended the sacrifice of the Mass; she received Holy Communion. It is nec-

---

[1] "...[I]nnumerable holy men have abundantly nourished their piety towards God by its readings from Sacred Scripture or by its prayers, whose general arrangement goes back, in essence, to St. Gregory the Great" (Apostolic Constitution *Missale Romanum*, April 3, 1969), §1.

[2] Spiritual conference, Zaitzkofen, February 7, 1980. Cf. Council of Trent, Session 22, Ch. 4 (DS 1745 [Dz. 942]).

[3] An Italian priest of Turin, author of *Pro Missa Traditionali*.

essary to think about all this. And the Apostles were indefectible, they were inspired. All that is Tradition.[4]

2. St. Pius V restored the rite "to the pristine norm of the Holy Fathers"

In the Bull of St. Pius V, which he published at the restoration of the veritable rite of Mass, the Pope says of the commission of Cardinals he had assembled to restore the Mass: "They restored the Missal itself and the ritual to the pristine (original) norm of the Holy Fathers." What does St. Pius V mean by this restoration according to the norm of the Holy Fathers? He is speaking of the Fathers of the first centuries who were our fathers in the Faith. Thus St. Pius V has no intention of establishing a new Mass, but of restoring the Mass according to the principles and the form it had in the first centuries. He desires to restore the Mass that originated with our holy Fathers, *sanctorum Patrum*, our Fathers in faith, our Fathers in Tradition. He wants to restore the holy mysteries that Our Lord Jesus Christ Himself instituted and that our holy Fathers transcribed integrally and with doctrinal precision, in the different prayers that they received either from Our Lord, or from the Apostles, or from the first Fathers.[5]

It is impossible to read without emotion what the Council of Trent has to say about [the traditional rite of Mass]: "As it is meet that holy things should be given holy treatment and as this sacrifice is the most holy of all, the Catholic Church, so that it may be offered and received with due dignity and reverence, instituted centuries ago, the holy Canon, so free from all error that it holds nothing save what breathes holiness and outward devotion and whatsoever lifts to God the minds of those who offer it. It is, indeed, made up of Our Lord's own words, the traditions of the Apostles, and the pious teachings of Sovereign Pontiffs."[6,7]

---

[4] Retreat, Ecône, September 22, 1978.
[5] Spiritual conference, Ecône, September 27, 1986. The prayers of the Roman Canon, for example, are found in the treatise *De Sacramentis* of St. Ambrose (end of the fourth century).
[6] Council of Trent, Session 22, Ch. 4 (DS 1745; Dz. 942); Ch. 5 (DS 1746): "Holy mother Church ...has likewise made use of ceremonies such as mystical blessings, lights, incense, vestments, and many other things of this kind in accordance with apostolic teaching and tradition...."
[7] Conference, Florence, February 15, 1975, *A Bishop Speaks*, p.192.

It is quite understandable that the prayers that were surely composed by the Apostles were carefully preserved by the Christians, by the priests who handed them down faithfully one after the other in order to preserve them. That is why all the texts that speak about the Latin Mass always refer to it as the Mass of Apostolic Tradition.[8]

There are publishing houses in Austria that have made wonderful reproductions of the ancient Sacramentaries. And in these Sacramentaries quite often one finds, sometimes from the Offertory, but in any case from the Canon, the prayers of the Roman rite. These books are wonders of illumination. They have been marvelously photographed with modern methods. And you can see that it is exactly the same Canon as the one we use! All the Signs of the Cross, all the genuflections are identical to what we do. And some of these Sacramentaries date back to the eighth century. And there is not any change. That is what the saints, the popes, all those who followed the Roman rite said for centuries.[9]

3. St. Pius V did not elaborate a new Mass

The so-called Mass of St. Pius V thus is not a new Mass. St. Pius V did not say: "For the sake of conforming ourselves to the spirit of our time, to the spirit of modern man, we are making a Mass that will be called the Mass of Pius V."[10] St. Gregory the Great himself did not invent the Mass we celebrate. He probably acted like the Council of Trent and St. Pius V. He eliminated things that had been added and kept the things that he deemed should be maintained and definitively fixed for the holy sacrifice of the Mass.[11]

We sometimes hear certain discussions between our faithful, who, resolved to hold fast to Tradition, speak of the Mass of John XXIII, the Mass of St. Pius X, the Mass of St. Pius V. In reality, there is no Mass of John XXIII, there is no Mass of St. Pius X, there is no Mass of St. Pius V.[12] "The Mass of St. Pius V" is not a good term to use. One should rather say "the Mass of all time," the

---

[8] Spiritual conference, Ecône, September 14, 1975.
[9] Retreat, Avrillé, October 18, 1989.
[10] Spiritual conference, Ecône, September 14, 1975.
[11] *Ibid.*, Zaitzkofen, February 7, 1980.
[12] *Ibid.*, Ecône, September 27, 1986.

Catholic Mass, for this Mass goes back to St. Gregory the Great and even to the time of the Apostles.[13] Our Mass today is essentially the same as the so-called Mass of John XXIII, of St. Pius X, and of St. Pius V. If there was a reform, this reform aimed precisely at maintaining the forms of the Mass according to our holy Fathers, even the so-called reform of John XXIII, which was not a veritable reform, but which was also desired in order to recover the original form of our holy Mass.[14]

THE PERPETUAL PRIVILEGE OF THE TRIDENTINE RITE

1. The traditional Mass is not prohibited

Some reproach me with faithfulness to the Catholic Mass of immemorial tradition....and never forbidden by Paul VI (that would require an explicit act of legislation emanating from the Pope in person; if any such exists let it be quoted, but not a text surreptitiously introduced between the first and second edition of Pope Paul VI's Apostolic Constitution of April 3, 1969, or falsified in translation).[15]

This Mass [what is called the Rite of St. Pius V] is not forbidden and cannot be forbidden. St. Pius V who, let us repeat, did not invent it but "re-established the Missal in conformity with the ancient rule and the rites of the Holy Fathers," gives us every guarantee in the Bull *Quo Primum*, signed by him on the 14th July 1570: "We have decided and declare that the Superiors, Canons, Chaplains and other priests by whatever title they are known, or Religious of whatsoever Order, may not be obliged to celebrate Mass otherwise than as enjoined by Us. We likewise order and declare that no-one whosoever shall ever at any time be forced or coerced into altering this Missal: and this present Constitution can never be revoked or modified, but shall for ever remain valid and have the force of law....Should anyone venture to [make such

---

[13] *Ibid.*, September 14, 1975.
[14] *Ibid.*, September 27, 1986.
[15] Letter to the *Libre Belgique*, August 21, 1975, *A Bishop Speaks*, p.211.

an alteration], let him understand that he will incur the wrath of Almighty God and of the Blessed Apostles Peter and Paul."[16]

2. The traditional Mass was canonized by the Council of Trent and St. Pius V

The old Mass is a Mass that was canonized by the Council of Trent and by St. Pius V. What is a canonized Mass? When the pope canonizes a saint, he canonizes the saint's virtues and the devotion that should be rendered to him. The canonization of a saint is a disciplinary decree that governs the honor that should be afforded the saint: the worship of *dulia*. The same holds true for the Mass. It was neither Pope St. Pius V nor the Council of Trent that made the Mass. They simply observed that for many centuries–most of the prayers dating back to the Apostolic era–this Mass has shown, by its usage, by the fruits it has produced, by its uninterrupted practice of more than twelve centuries, that it was holy. If St. Pius V canonized this Mass, it was because he thought that it was holy, that it would always bring forth grace, and that it would always build up the Church.[17]

3. The canonization of the traditional Mass can be considered to be infallible

I am convinced that St. Pius V's decree is an infallible act because he relies upon a Council and on the whole of Tradition to confirm the holiness of this Mass. Just as one canonizes a saint, St. Pius V canonized this Mass, and it is for that reason that he was able to grant this indult, this privilege, given to the priests when he said: "We grant and concede in perpetuity that, for the chanting or reading of the Mass in any church whatsoever, this Missal is hereafter to be followed absolutely, without any scruple of conscience or fear of incurring any penalty, judgment, or censure, and may freely and lawfully be used."[18]

---

[16] *Open Letter to Confused Catholics*, p.143.
[17] Spiritual conference, Ecône, January 1974.
[18] *Ibid.*, September 14, 1975.

4. Can a pope annul the Bull *Quo Primum*?

The Bull *Quo Primum*, at least to a certain extent, has all the marks of infallibility. I do not think that a pope can annul it.[19]

5. An objection to the opinion that the Bull cannot be annulled

As regards the impossibility of annulling St. Pius V's Bull *Quo Primum*, I received an objection in a letter from a priest from Geneva who told me: "You invoke St. Pius V's Bull, but look at the Bull he issued for the Breviary. It is exactly the same, and yet St. Pius X indeed changed the Breviary and issued a Bull subsequent to that of St. Pius V." First, it should be said that St. Pius X only renewed and seconded what St. Pius V had done: he practically changed nothing. Besides, if the final formulas are identical within the text, the formulas used for the perpetuity of the Mass of St. Pius V are not the same as those used for the Breviary, or are not used in the same way. That is why it is good periodically to reread St. Pius V's Bull, which is printed at the beginning of all the Roman missals. Reread it. These words are truly convincing. I translate on the spot the Latin that appears in the Bull: The Holy Father says that he concedes [the right] in perpetuity, and that these letters can always (*perpetuo*) be used freely and licitly, that that Masses can be sung or said in any church whatsoever without scruple of conscience or fear of incurring any penalty, contrary command, or censure. He states: "We concede and grant [this] in perpetuity."[20]

He then resumes and expounds his idea. One might say that he was truly a prophet, and that he saw a time in which something would be done against this Mass. One might say that, foreseeing this, he precluded every scruple of conscience to which the priests who would continue to say this Mass might be exposed. No prelate, no administrator, no canon, or chaplain, nor any others will be able to oblige secular priests or the priests of any religious order to celebrate Mass otherwise than as we have decreed, and no one will ever be obliged to change a jot or tittle of this missal. *Neque ad mis-*

---

[19] *Ibid.*, January 19, 1982.
[20] *Etiam perpetuo concedimus et indulgemus.*

sale hoc immutandum a quolibet cogi ac compelli praesentes litterae ullo unquam tempore–never–*ullo unquam tempore.*[21] Why did St. Pius V make such a decision to bind the future? Because he felt that he was supported by the whole of Tradition.

6. The Constitution *Missale Romanum* did not prohibit the Tridentine Mass

Supposing that the Pope could withdraw this perpetual indult, he would have to do it by an equally solemn act. The Apostolic Constitution *Missale Romanum* of the 3rd April 1969 authorizes the so-called Mass of Paul VI, but contains no expressly formulated prohibition of the Tridentine Mass. So much so that Cardinal Ottaviani could say in 1971: "The Tridentine rite has not been abolished as far as I know." Bishop Adam, who claimed at the Plenary Assembly of the Swiss Bishops that the Constitution *Missale Romanum* had forbidden the celebration of the Rite of St. Pius V except by indult, had to retract when he was asked to say in what terms this prohibition had been declared.[22]

7. A priest cannot be censured because he celebrates the traditional Mass

It follows from this that if a priest were censured or even excommunicated on this ground [that is to say, for saying the traditional Mass], the sentence would be absolutely invalid. St. Pius V has canonized this Holy Mass, and a pope cannot remove such a canonization any more than he can revoke that of a saint. We can celebrate it and the faithful can attend it with complete peace of mind, knowing furthermore it is the best way of maintaining their faith.[23]

---

[21] Spiritual conference, Ecône, January 16, 1975.
[22] *Open Letter to Confused Catholics*, p.143-44.
[23] *Ibid.*, p.144.

KEEP THE MASS OF ALL TIME

1. A choice between the appearance of obedience and keeping our faith

Two religions confront each other. We are in a dramatic situation, and it is impossible to avoid a choice; but the choice is not between obedience and disobedience. What is suggested to us, what we are expressly invited to do, what we are persecuted for not doing, is to choose an appearance of obedience.[24]

We have to choose between an appearance, I should say, of disobedience–for the Holy Father cannot ask us to abandon our faith. It is impossible, impossible–the abandonment of our faith! We choose not to abandon our faith, for in that we cannot go wrong. The Church cannot be in error in something it has taught for two thousand years. That is absolutely impossible, and that is why we are attached to this tradition which is expressed in such an admirable and definitive manner, as Pope St. Pius V said so well, in the holy sacrifice of the Mass.[25]

St. Paul exhorted Timothy: "*Depositum custodi*–keep the Faith." Now, this deposit had only been in existence for several decades. And he added: "Hold fast to what you learned from your grandmother Lois in your childhood."[26] Timothy's childhood went back almost to the death of Our Lord Jesus Christ. Consequently, St. Paul even then was telling Timothy: keep what you learned from your grandmother, her catechism and all that the Church taught her. Respect and stay with what you learned from you grandmother. If St. Paul was already saying this at a time when the deposit had

---

[24] *Ibid.*, p.133.
[25] Ordination sermon, Ecône, June 29, 1976, *A Bishop Speaks*, p.248. It should be noted that Archbishop Lefebvre bases his argumentation not on the canonical question, by an examination of the conditions under which the N.O.M. was promulgated, but on the theology of the New Mass, which is no longer an expression of the Catholic Faith, and hence is no longer a law in the profound sense of the term. *The Short Critical Study*, made at Archbishop Lefebvre's instigation, approaches the question from this perspective by concluding that the N.O.M. "represents, both as a whole and in its details, a striking departure from the Catholic theology of the Mass." This is the essential reason for Archbishop Lefebvre's refusal of the New Mass.
[26] *Permane, o Timothee, permane in iis quae didicisti ab avia tua Loïde ab infantia tua* (following II Tim. 1:5).

just been formed, when Revelation was hardly known, how much more so then should we keep what was taught us, what the Church has taught her children for twenty centuries. We cannot separate ourselves from this deposit without separating ourselves from our holy religion.[27]

We believe in Peter, we believe in the successor of Peter! But as Pope Pius IX says well in his dogmatic constitution, the pope has received the Holy Ghost not to make new truths, but to maintain us in the faith of all time. This is the definition of the pope made at the time of the First Vatican Council by Pope Pius IX.[28] And that is why we are persuaded that in maintaining these traditions we are manifesting our love, our docility, our obedience to the Successor of Peter.[29]

We must say no to this wave of neo-modernism and of neo-Protestantism. Nor can we accept one part and reject another; that is not possible because everything holds together. That is why we choose what has always been taught, and we turn a deaf ear to the novelties that are destroying the Church.[30]

2. The legitimacy of our position should not be questioned

We must maintain absolutely our firm opposition and not doubt for an instant the legitimacy of our position. We cannot remain indifferent before the degradation of faith, morals, and the liturgy. That is out of the question![31]

We do not want to separate ourselves from the Church; on the contrary, we want the Church to continue! A Church that breaks with its past is no longer the Catholic Church. There is only one Catholic Church; it is the one that continues Tradition. That is why I do not hesitate to say that you are the Catholic Church!

---

[27] Homily, Lyons, France, February 8, 1976.
[28] "For, the Holy Spirit was not promised to the successors of Peter that by His revelation they might disclose new doctrine, but that by His help they might guard sacredly the revelation transmitted through the apostles and the deposit of faith, and might faithfully set it forth" (Vatican Council I, *Pastor Aeternus*, DS 3070 [Dz. 1836]).
[29] Ordination sermon, Ecône, June 29, 1976, in *A Bishop Speaks*, pp.249-50.
[30] Spiritual conference, Ecône, December 2, 1974.
[31] *Ibid.*, March 13, 1975.

Why? Because you continue what the Church has always done.[32] You will be called schismatics, but you are not schismatics. Those who abandon the traditions of the Church are the schismatics. Those who abandon the faith of the Church, who no longer believe in the Real Presence of Our Lord Jesus Christ, who no longer believe in original sin, who no longer believe in sanctifying grace, who no longer believe in angels or demons–those are the ones who separate themselves from the Church.[33]

3. Keep the Faith through the Mass of all time

What is the means to keep the Catholic Faith? Keep your holy Mass. The Mass is the corner stone of the Church; the Mass is the treasure Our Lord Jesus Christ gave us. *"Hic est calix sanguinis mei, novi et aeterni Testamenti*–This is the chalice of my Blood, of the new and eternal Testament." The Testament of Our Lord Jesus Christ is His Blood shed for the remission of our sins. We hold fast to the Mass, not because it is the Latin rite, but because it explicitly encompasses the truths of the Faith (there are Masses in other rites, but all these rites contain the truths of our Catholic Faith and proclaim them).[34]

We must be attached with all our heart and soul to the holy sacrifice of the Mass because it is in the Mass that we shall truly discover what the love of God has done for us. For if there is a testimony of God's love for us, it is indeed Our Lord Jesus Christ on the cross. What more could Our Lord have done than to immolate Himself on the cross to redeem us from our sins?[35]

We cannot abandon the worship of Our Lord Jesus Christ, and even if this must take place in a rented room like this one, which you have tried to make as fitting as possible, where you gather, there you continue the Catholic Church. That is what St. Athanasius said to those who criticized him because he wanted to maintain the traditions: "You have kept the churches; we have kept the Faith. Keep the churches if you like, but we'll keep the Faith." This is what you are saying by coming to one of these rented rooms: "Keep your churches, since you keep us from truly adoring

---

[32] Homily, Geneva, May 15, 1978.
[33] Homily, Lyons, February 8, 1976.
[34] Homily, Ecône, June 29, 1981.
[35] *Ibid.*, September 14, 1975.

Our Lord Jesus Christ there. We'd rather keep the Faith and continue the Church." In this way you show that you desire to gather around the altar, around the holy sacrifice of the Mass, around the priests who accomplish these liturgical functions as the Church has always done, to safeguard you faith and the faith of your children. This is the greatest service you can render the Church, in the hope that one day you will be able to repopulate your churches, the churches built for this worship and not for a worship that resembles Protestant services.[36]

We desire to keep the Catholic faith with the Catholic Mass, and not with an ecumenical Mass, even if it is valid and not heretical (though it favors heresy).[37]

The only logical stance to adopt for safeguarding the Catholic faith is to keep the Catholic Mass, and this Catholic Mass is contrary to the spirit of the Council; it is contrary to ecumenism, and collegiality, and the liberalism which is found in the Council. Our Mass is a Mass of sacrifice, and there is only one sacrifice that opens to us the gate of heaven: "*Tu devicto mortis aculeo*–by delivering us from the chains of hell, Thou hast led us to heaven by the Cross."[38] The Cross is the way that leads to heaven. Our Lord's sacrifice is the royal road that leads us to eternity. There is no other.[39]

What matters to us is to celebrate the holy sacrifice according to the tradition of our holy Fathers, the Apostles, and those who followed them, who handed down to us this rite, which was restored by St. Pius V, by St. Pius X, and by John XXIII.[40]

4. Fidelity in spite of persecution

I very quickly became convinced that my attachment to the Mass of all time would create difficulties with Rome. And indeed, it is the Mass that they have always pressured us to give up. Msgr. Mamie, in his letter advising me, illegally, of the suppression of the Society, reproached us first and foremost for our unwavering attachment to the old liturgy. In 1976, the emissaries from the Vatican repeated the message: "Say the New Mass and all will be

---

[36] Homily, Lyons, February 8, 1976.
[37] Letter to Cardinal Seper, February 26, 1978.
[38] Free translation of the *Te Deum*.
[39] Homily, Ecône, November 1, 1990.
[40] Spiritual conference, Ecône, September 27, 1986.

well." It was their very insistence on getting me to commit this impiety that confirmed me in my plan to perform the ordinations they wanted to prevent. But, as I stated many times, it is our refusal of the New Mass that brought us, and still brings us, persecution.[41] We regret infinitely, it is an immense pain for us, to think that we are in difficulty with Rome *because of our faith!* How is this possible? It is something that exceeds the imagination, that we should never have been able to imagine, that we should never have been able to believe, especially in our childhood–then when all was uniform, when the whole Church believed in her general unity and held the same Faith, the same Sacraments, the same sacrifice of the Mass, the same catechism. And behold, suddenly all is in division, in chaos.

...Christians are torn apart in their families, in their homes, among their children; they are torn apart in their hearts by this division in the Church, by this new religion now being taught and practised. Priests are dying prematurely, torn apart in their hearts and in their souls at the thought that they no longer know what to do: either to submit to obedience and lose, in a way, the faith of their childhood and of their youth, and renounce the promises which they made at the time of their ordination in taking the Antimodernist Oath; or to have the impression of separating themselves from him who is our father, the Pope, from him who is the representative of St. Peter. What agony for these priests! Many priests have died prematurely of grief. Priests are now hounded from their churches, persecuted, because they say the Mass of all time.[42]

Even if we too must suffer, let us suffer for our faith! We are not the first: how many martyrs before us have suffered to keep the Faith. If we must suffer the moral martyrdom of being, in a way, scorned and rebuked by those who should be our fathers in the Faith, then let us endure this suffering; but above all let us keep the Faith! The good Lord wills it, as does the most Blessed Virgin Mary. The Virgin Mary is our mother. It is because we are of the family of the Virgin Mary that we want to keep the Faith she always professed. Is there, in the Virgin's heart, anything else than the

---

[41] "Despite the Persecutions," *Fideliter*, No. 59, September-October 1987, p.73.
[42] Ordination sermon, Ecône, June 29, 1976, *A Bishop Speaks*, p.248.

name of Our Lord Jesus Christ? We too desire to have in our hearts one name alone, that of Jesus, like the most Blessed Virgin Mary.... We are sure that one day the truth will return. It cannot be otherwise; the good Lord does not abandon His Church.[43]

5. True priests will be formed

That is why we will form true priests, that is to say, priests who will offer the true sacrifice. You will confect a true Eucharist; you will act in such a way that Our Lord is truly on the altar. The desire for this is what brought you to the Society's seminary. The synthesis of your entire formation is the altar, the sacrifice of the Mass.[44]

In my own seminary, I do nothing save reaffirm the truths that the Church has always affirmed. So these young men are attracted by the altar, by the sacrifice of the Mass.[45]

That is why, without any rebellion, bitterness, or resentment, we pursue our work of priestly formation under the guidance of the never-changing Magisterium, convinced as we are that we cannot possibly render a greater service to the Holy Catholic Church, to the Sovereign Pontiff, and to posterity.

That is why we hold firmly to everything that has been consistently taught and practiced by the Church (and codified in books published before the Modernist influence of the Council) concerning faith, morals, divine worship, catechetics, priestly formation, and the institution of the Church, until such time as the true light of tradition dissipates the gloom which obscures the sky of the eternal Rome.

Doing this, with the grace of God, the help of the Virgin Mary, St. Joseph, and St. Pius X, we are certain that we are being faithful to the Catholic and Roman Church, to all of Peter's successors, and of being the *fideles dispensatores mysteriorum Domini Nostri Jesus Christi in Spiritu Sancto*—faithful dispensers of the mysteries of Our Lord Jesus Christ in the Holy Ghost.[46]

---

[43] Homily, Geneva, May 15, 1978.
[44] Spiritual conference, Ecône, March 30, 1971.
[45] Pilgrimage to Mariazell, September 8, 1975, *A Bishop Speaks*, p.219.
[46] Declaration, November 21, 1974, in *Apologia pro Marcel Lefebvre*, I, 40. Cf. I Cor. 4:1: "Let a man so account of us as of the ministers of Christ, and the dispensers of the mysteries of God."

6. Let the seminarians become holy priests

I beseech you to pray fervently for all these young seminarians who come to place themselves under the protection and guidance of this seminary of Ecône, that they may understand these things, that they may become holy priests, true priests, the priest you need; priests who will speak to you of God, eternity, and the salvation of your souls. That is what you are looking for and what you need, and that is what we hope to give you by our seminarians of Ecône. I beseech you to pray for them: they will almost need nothing short of heroism to continue along their way, and I hope that they will be capable of it, with the help of your prayers![47]

GENERAL CONCLUSION

The truths of the Catholic Faith regarding the holy sacrifice of the Mass were not mere abstract notions for Archbishop Lefebvre; rather, they were vital principles; he had made them the center of his life. It was thus that he lived his episcopal motto: *Et nos credidimus caritati*—We have believed the charity, which God hath to us" (I Jn. 4:16). Every Christian soul must experience the same attachment for the holy sacrifice of the Mass. From our faith in the infinite love of God that is at work on the altar springs our love for the Eucharist.

The presence of Christ under the Eucharistic species is indeed a proof of the charity which God has towards us. It is a presence that He wanted to be as real, as total, as possible: the corporal, substantial presence of Our Lord Jesus Christ; not in one place only, at a given time, but perpetuated through all the ages and throughout the whole world, henceforth accessible to everyone who approaches the tabernacle. O splendid nearness of the love of God! Without this presence, to whom should we go?[48]

> Imagine a Christian life without the Eucharist! What would we be without Our Lord Jesus Christ, without this extraordinary gift God has made us? How we should be orphans, how we

---

[47] Homily, Garges-lès-Gonesse, February 11, 1973.
[48] Cf. Jn. 6:68.

should feel alone, a little abandoned by the good Lord! But with the Eucharist, when we need to speak to Him, to see Him, to tell Him that we love Him; when we need some special help, we can go to our sanctuaries, kneel before Our Lord Jesus Christ, perhaps alone, alone before the Blessed Sacrament. Surely it has happened to you, while kneeling before the Blessed Sacrament, to say to the good Lord: "Come to my aid, help me, I'm in trouble, I'm sorely tried. Come to the aid of my family, help my children!" And when you went away, you left the church relieved. And you have been, too, I am sure, after every Sunday Mass. How many times it has happened to us as priests to assist the dying. How often we have brought Communion to the sick. What a joy it was for these suffering souls to receive their God from the hands of their priest, who came to give them Holy Communion. What a consolation. What a source of courage for them. Our Lord Jesus Christ by this Sacrament has worked an extraordinary miracle of His love![49]

One of our great consolations in participating in the holy sacrifice of the Mass is the proximity of Our Lord. His presence, so near, ravishes us. But the goodness of Our Lord towards us does not stop there. Indeed, at the Mass, Christ does not content Himself with becoming present among us. He acts. At the altar, this same Christ renews the supreme act of charity that crowned His terrestrial existence: the gift of His life as a Victim of expiation in the place of sinners. "This is the greatest love a man can show, that he should lay down his life for his friends" (Jn. 15:13). On the altar, Christ delivers Himself as Victim for the sacrifice of praise and expiation offered to His Father. There He loves us unto the end (Jn. 13:1). There He also loves us until the end of time, since every day this infinite love is in act upon our altars. Such is the immense reality before which dogma places us when it affirms that the Mass is the renewal of the sacrifice of the Cross, a reality of the utmost importance for a Christian's faith, and which becomes the heart of his prayer:

> It is obvious that the great prayer of the Church is the holy sacrifice of the Mass, as the great prayer of Our Lord Jesus Christ was His Calvary. On the cross He offered His greatest prayer, and the holy sacrifice of the Mass is the Church's great prayer, to which the Church requires that all the faithful unite themselves intimately,

---

[49] Homily, Ecône, June 17, 1976.

profoundly, adoring God, adoring Our Lord Jesus Christ, adoring the Creator, adoring the Redeemer. What a magnificent prayer Jesus transmitted to the Church.[50]

A more particular aspect of the sacrificial character of the Mass leads us to the summit of love that is the Cross, which the Mass perpetuates: the propitiatory finality of the holy sacrifice of the Mass. The death of Our Lord was an expiatory, and thus propitiatory, sacrifice. St. Paul says this explicitly: "Being justified freely by His grace, through the redemption, that is in Christ Jesus, whom God hath proposed to be a propitiation, through faith in His blood, to the shewing of His justice, for the remission of former sins, through the forbearance of God, for the shewing of His justice in this time; that He Himself may be just, and the justifier of him, who is of the faith of Jesus Christ" (Rom. 3: 24-25). The sacrifice of the Mass re-presenting Our Lord's sacrifice, consequently has a propitiatory dimension:

> The entire liturgy, which is the Church's great prayer, invites us to consider Jesus on the cross as Victim, the spotless Lamb, immolated for our sins, the Savior and Redeemer who redeemed us at the price of His blood.[51] This is fundamental for us; it is the essential difference that separates us from Protestantism, for we believe that the sacrifice of the Mass is a propitiatory sacrifice, ...even now: it is the same sacrifice as the one offered on Calvary which continues. Consequently, every time a sacrifice of the Mass is offered, sins are remitted, and graces of sanctification are spread throughout the whole world.[52]

Real Presence, sacrificial action, propitiation for our sins: these three truths of our Catholic Faith had become for Archbishop Lefebvre living realities, the source of his piety as well as his ministry. They were also the cause of his deepest sorrow, when he saw these same realities, so full of love, challenged by the liturgical reform of 1969. Suddenly, the substantial presence of Christ under the Eucharistic species was relativized, because it was put somewhat on the same plane as the purely moral presence of Christ through His word. Soon, moreover, genuflections disappeared, and the very

---

[50] *Ibid.*, February 2, 1982.
[51] Retreat, Le Barroux, August 1985.
[52] Conference, Mantes-la-Jolie, April 22, 1977.

word transubstantiation seemed to be banished from ecclesiastical vocabulary. Similarly, the rite created by Paul VI made the notion of supper outweigh that of sacrifice, and the new missal only spoke of the "narrative of the Institution" where the Church had always seen a properly sacrificial action. Lastly, no more mention was made of propitiation.

In a matter of months, the beautiful realities of the Eucharistic faith, magnificently expressed in the Church's ancient rite, were discarded, abandoned. They were no longer the focal point of the new rite. In all truth, the founder of Ecône could write:

> The following fundamental dogmas of the holy sacrifice of the Mass are not clearly represented and are even contradicted: that in the Mass there is a true sacrifice, a sacrificial *action*; that the Victim or Host is Our Lord Jesus Christ Himself, present under the species of bread and wine, with His Body, Blood, Soul, and Divinity; that this sacrifice is a propitiatory one; that the Sacrifice and the Sacrament are effected by the words of the consecration alone, and not also by those which either precede or follow them; that the priest is the only minister.

From this Archbishop Lefebvre was convinced that a *rapprochement* with Protestantism was the aim, a conclusion corroborated by numerous modifications that taken individually might appear secondary:

> It is sufficient to enumerate a few of the novelties in the New Mass to be convinced of the *rapprochement* with the Protestants: the altar replaced by a table without an altar stone; the Mass celebrated facing the people, concelebrated, in a loud voice, and in the vernacular; the Mass divided into two distinct parts: the Liturgy of the Word and the Liturgy of the Eucharist; the cheapening of the sacred vessels, the use of leavened bread, distribution of Holy Communion in the hand, and by the laity, and even by women; the Blessed Sacrament hidden in corners; the Epistle read by women; Holy Communion brought to the sick by the laity. All these innovations are authorized.[53]

The consequences of such an upheaval were not long in coming: declining worship of the Blessed Sacrament followed by a loss

---

[53] Note on the N.O.M. and the Pope, 8 November 1979, in *Cor Unum*, No. 4 [English: Davies, *Apologia*, II, 369].

of faith in the Real Presence; a forsaking of the sacrificial dimension of the Christian life, and, finally, of the Christian life itself; dramatic relativization of sin, with everyone proclaiming for himself the right to be supreme arbiter of good and evil. In a word, relativism entered the Church of God! Love was no longer loved, and soon our churches emptied...

After years of uncertainty and often of chaos, Truth seems to be timidly reclaiming some of its rights. Here and there Eucharistic adoration flourishes, while for the first time, in 2003, a papal encyclical attempted to rehabilitate the notion of sacrifice. But the words, however important they may be, are not enough. What matters first and foremost is is to make the great realities of God's love for us come to life again with that life they always used to have in the Church's immemorial rite. The pastor in Archbishop Lefebvre understood this immediately. That is why he always refused–as did his priests after him–celebration of the Mass according to the rite created by Paul VI, instead holding fast to the integral Roman missal codified by St. Pius V, a precious treasure so deeply rooted in the bi-millennial tradition of the Church.

Isn't it in the vivifying contact with the holy sacrifice of the Mass that man responds to the infinite charity of God? Incorporated in Christ and purified by Him, man unites himself to the divine Victim in the gift that He makes of Himself to the Father, and thus becomes an offering of an agreeable odor to God:

> The sacrifice of the Mass is an oblation, and this oblation should be the model of our own self-offering. Our life must be an oblation to God through Our Lord Jesus Christ, *per Dominum nostrum Jesum Christum*, always through Our Lord Jesus Christ, in union with the oblation of Our Lord Jesus Christ. There is no other way to attain the beatific vision, to attain beatitude, to attain our last end which is Our Lord Jesus Christ. Whence the importance of the sacrifice of the Mass, and the importance of true sacrifice.[54]

Our Lord pours forth His graces on men especially through the holy sacrifice of the Mass. Archbishop Lefebvre, as a true missionary, greatly desired that all men to respond in their turn to this

---

[54] Spiritual conference, Ecône, March 10, 1989.

Divine love by intimately uniting themselves to the sacrifice of the altar:

> God desired to divinize us, to communicate to us the immense charity with which He has burned for all eternity. He desired to communicate it to us, and He did so by an extraordinary display, by His cross, by His death, by His blood shed. He desired that men chosen by Him should continue this sacrifice in order to give His Divine life to souls, to cure them of their faults and sins, to communicate to them His own life so that one day this life might glorify them and these souls might be glorified with Him in eternity. That is the work of God.....He communicates Himself to us as Victim so that we, too, might offer our lives with His, and that we might thus participate not only in our redemption, but in the redemption of souls. This Divine plan, this Divine thought that made the world is an extraordinary thing. We stand in awe of the great mystery that the good God has realized here below.[55]

To make God's love for us known and to elicit our love for God in return was the motive of Archbishop Lefebvre's works. His attachment to the holy sacrifice of the Mass and to the Catholic priesthood had no other purpose. In one of history's most troubled times, in which so many churchmen, lured by a false modernity, came to lose the sense of these tremendous realities, the former Archbishop of Dakar took his stand for the greater good of the Church. May future generations draw abundantly from his teaching so that they may nourish their souls and taste these realities "of all time," which he knew so well how to put within the reach of all.

---

[55] Homily, Ecône, June 29, 1982.

APPENDICES

THE INDULT MASS

By the Decree *Quattuor Abhinc Annos* of October 3, 1984, the Congregation for Divine Worship gave bishops the faculty to grant an indult for the celebration of Mass according to the 1962 Missal, provided that certain conditions be respected. The first one required that the celebrant and the faithful hearing the Mass "in no way share the positions of those who call in question the legitimacy and doctrinal exactitude of the Roman Missal promulgated by Pope Paul VI in 1970." If such an indult was in some way able to gladden Archbishop Lefebvre, he nonetheless pointed out its limitations. As formulated, the first condition imposed a complete acceptance of the new rite, and, by so doing, forbade those who would avail themselves of it from pointing out its intrinsic defects. Presented in this way, the indult contained an inherent ambiguity that could easily be used by the ecclesiastical authorities to induce its beneficiaries to the celebration of the *Novus Ordo Missae*.

Cardinal Ratzinger's letter implies that the Holy Father may be getting ready to authorize by decree the official public celebration of the Tridentine rite. But the religious authorities would only grant this freedom on condition that the traditional Mass not be celebrated out of contempt for the new rite. They would require priests to say the New Mass at least once in a while. It is difficult not to descry in the arrangement of the conditions a maneuver destined to put pressure on traditional priests to convince them to celebrate the New Mass.[1]

Availing ourselves of the Indult is tantamount to putting ourselves into a state of contradiction because at the same time that Rome gives the Fraternity of Saint Peter, for example, or Le Barroux Abbey and other groups authorization to say the Mass of all time, they also require young priests to sign a profession of faith in which the spirit of the Council must be accepted. It is a contradiction: the spirit of the Council is embodied in the New Mass. How is it possible to desire to preserve the Mass of all time while accepting the spirit that destroys the Mass of all time? It is completely contradictory. One day, very gently, they will oblige those who have been

---

[1] Manuscript note, 1983, Ecône Seminary archives.

granted the use of the Tridentine Mass, the Mass of all time, also to accept the New Mass. And they will tell them that it is simply a matter of squaring themselves with what they have signed, since they signed a statement that they accepted the spirit of the Council and its reforms. You cannot put yourself thus into an unbelievable, irrational contradiction. It is a very uncomfortable situation. This is what has created the difficulty for these groups that have signed it and that currently find themselves in a kind of impasse.[2]

The Fruits of the Indult

From one standpoint (*sous un certain aspect*), Archbishop Lefebvre deemed the effect of this indult to be positive. Besides being a tacit avowal of the weakness of the new rite, which had been unable to supplant the former, it also gave the faithful to understand that the pope no longer opposed the traditional rite. But it also had, alas! more negative fruits. Several priests and laymen abandoned the doctrinal reasons for their refusal of the missal promulgated by Pope Paul VI, and their attachment to the rite revised by St. Pius V was reduced to a subjective and sentimental dimension.

1) First remark. Major precautions to safeguard the permanence of the New Mass. Whoever can say the old Mass must accept the new: bishop's authorization, protection of the parishes.

2) The precautions certify the weakness of the New Mass against the old.

3) The opportunity afforded some priests of saying the traditional Mass proves that some priests and faithful want the old Mass.

The motives adduced and the wording of the Decree reveal a frame of mind that is more political and diplomatic than supernatural.[3]

I had occasion to say, at first, that the indult has been beneficial to us, whatever the conditions, because many people concluded that the Pope was no longer against the celebration of the old Mass, and that, consequently, they could go to it, and that disobedience in going to the traditional Mass [false, moreover] was no longer an

---

[2] Homily, Friedrichshafen, April 29, 1990.
[3] Manuscript notes, 1983, Ecône Seminary archives.

issue. Very many people thus joined us, and we have observed, in general, a rather considerable increase of the faithful coming to our centers. That was an initial positive result that pleased us.

But another result, unfortunate and disagreeable, was that a certain number of priests thought they had to accept the conditions of the indult in order to regularly celebrate the old Mass, and with the approval of their bishop. That has given rise to some fairly serious problems, since they have been obliged to consider the New Mass as good as the old Mass, which we have always refused, and which we have always opposed because we esteem that the New Mass is dangerous, and thus bad, because it was made in an ecumenical spirit. It diminishes the faith of Catholics and ends by giving them a Protestant mentality.

We are very sorry to see that some priests have consented to say that the new Mass is as good as the old Mass, so as to be able to say, so they say, the old Mass in all security and in conformity with the bishops' regulations....And now, supposedly for the sake of following the rules regarding the old Mass, they have given up the fight against novelties, particularly liturgical novelties....

I was surprised to read in the *Una Voce* brochure that was given to me at Ottawa the position they have taken. It is a very ambiguous position and not in accord with the one we defend and which the traditionalists have always defended. They accept both the legitimacy and the orthodoxy of the New Mass, which we refuse to affirm. We do not say that the New Mass is heretical or that it is invalid, but we refuse to say that it is legitimate or that it is perfectly orthodox.[4]

Among traditionalists, you have some who are attached to Tradition the way people are attached to folklore: for example, they like the sung Mass; they like the Mass in Latin, because when they were young they were used to that Mass. They like Latin and Gregorian chant. So for them, as soon as the Mass is said in Latin, whether it is the traditional Mass or the New Mass, all the problems are resolved. Those people are quite content with the indult solution from Rome.[5]

---

[4] *Communicantes*, August 1985.
[5] Spiritual conference, Ecône, January 14, 1986.

Attendance at Mass Conceded by Indult

Considering the dangers of liturgical relativism contained in the first clause of the indult as soon as it was issued, Archbishop Lefebvre advised priests and faithful already habitually benefiting from the traditional Mass not to avail themselves of the indult.

In general, we advise the faithful against going to the Masses of the priests who have given up the fight against the New Mass. It is to be feared that one day they will be obliged by their bishop to celebrate the New Mass also, to celebrate both Masses, and eventually to concelebrate, to agree to give Communion in the hand or to say the Mass facing the people–things which are absolutely repugnant to us, and, consequently, we advise traditionalists against going to the Masses of these priests....As for us, we always give the same instruction: we think that one must not go to these Masses because it is dangerous to affirm that the new Mass is as good as the old. Gradually, the priests who accept the indult's conditions will have the same tendencies as those who say the New Mass, and one day, perhaps, they will say it themselves and will draw our traditionalists towards the New Mass.[6]

---

[6] *Communicantes*, August 1985.

Lexicon of a Few Difficult Words

Acta Apostolicæ Sedis (**or *A.A.S.***): *The Acts of the Apostolic See*, the official publication of the Holy See since the time of St. Pius X.

Adage: A popular old saying that is easy to remember and imparts a rule of moral conduct.

Aggiornamento: The adaptation of the Church to the evolution of the modern world. It was a term used by Pope John XXIII to characterize the paradigm shift he intended to promote, notably thanks to the Second Vatican Council.

Anathema: A solemn excommunication declared against heretics and enemies of the Faith.

Bull: An official papal document or writing, usually containing a general constitution.

Canon: A law or rule concerning the faith or discipline of the Church.

Censure: Doctrinal judgment by which the Church stigmatizes certain teachings detrimental to faith or morals.

Consilium: The organ created on February 26, 1964, by Pope Paul VI for implementing the Second Vatican Council's decree on the liturgy (*Sacrosanctum Concilium*).

Apostolic Constitutions (The): A collection of writings composed at the end of the fourth century in Syria relating to Christian life, ecclesiastical discipline, and liturgical prescriptions.

Dulia: Worship given to angels and saints to obtain their intercession.

Eucharist: The sacrament which, by transubstantiation, contains really and substantially the body, blood, soul and divinity of Jesus Christ our Lord under the species of bread and wine, to be our spiritual food.

Eucharistic: Said of an action or prayer offered to give God thanks for His benefits.

Extrinsic: Not contained in or belonging to a body; unessential.

Favens hæresim: "Favoring heresy"; a theological censure of an error held in opposition to a theologically certain proposition.

Gratia sanans: Grace considered in its aspect of curing the wounds inflicted by sin.

Gratia elevans: Grace considered in its aspect of elevating the receiver into the supernatural order of being and activity.

Impetratory: Said of an action or prayer that obtains necessary graces by asking for them.

Latria: The highest kind of worship, that paid to God only.

Licit: In accordance with the laws promulgated by the Church, or with the rules governing the liturgy.

Normative: Relating to or establishing a norm or standard of usage. The so-called "normative" Mass, the immediate predecessor of the *novus ordo missae*, was presented in 1967 to a group of cardinals and bishops by Fr. Bugnini, secretary of the *Concilium*, with the intention of gathering their impressions.

Propitiatory: That which renders God favorably disposed to us, and thus procures for us the pardon of our sins.

Rite: An entire liturgy, *e.g.* the Roman rite. The liturgy comprises the ceremonies, actions, and language.

Rota: The ordinary tribunal or court of the Roman Curia; it also serves as a court of appeal for all diocesan courts of the world.

Satisfaction: Reparation of the insult given to God by sin.

Theodicy: The part of philosophy (metaphysics) having for its object God and His attributes; also called natural theology.

Transubstantiation: The changing of the substance of bread and wine into the substance of the Body and Blood of our Lord Jesus Christ, under the appearances of bread and wine. The appearances or accidents are the quantity and sensible qualities of bread and wine, such as form, color, and taste.

Tridentine: Of or pertaining to the city, Trent, of Italy, or the ecumenical Council of Trent.

Brief Biographies

In his conferences and allocutions, Archbishop Lefebvre sometimes refers to certain little-known contemporary religious figures, which can render his allusions somewhat difficult to understand. The following biographical notes are not intended to be exhaustive presentations of their subjects, but rather to succinctly provide the details that will enable the reader to situate the person Archbishop Lefebvre speaks about, but only in the context of his speech.

Antonelli, Giuseppe Ferdinando Cardinal (1896-1993): Franciscan, secretary of the conciliar Commission on the Liturgy, member of the Consilium, secretary of the Congregation for Divine Worship in 1965, secretary of the Congregation for the Causes of Saints in 1969, cardinal in 1973, he left numerous writings on the unfolding of the liturgical reform which betray a certain dissatisfaction, especially with regard to the methods employed by Fr. Annibale Bugnini.

Adam, Bishop Nestor (1903-1990): Bishop of Sion (the Valais, Switzerland) from 1952-1977, traditionalist, a friend of Archbishop Lefebvre, he agreed to the opening by the latter of a seminary in his diocese, at Ecône. Shortly thereafter he distanced himself from Archbishop Lefebvre.

Bacci, Antonio Cardinal (1865-1971): a Latin specialist, appointed cardinal in 1960, a traditionalist, he wrote a foreword for a book by Tito Casini that was very critical of the liturgical reform, *The Torn Tunic* (Rome, 1967); he then cosigned with Cardinal Ottaviani the letter presenting *The Ottaviani Intervention: A Short Critical Study of the New Order of Mass* (1969).

Benelli, Giovanni Cardinal (1921-1982): substitute for the Secretary of State from 1967-77 (before being created cardinal and archbishop of Florence) and close collaborator with Pope Paul VI, he was in the thick of the "Lefebvre affair" during the years 1973-77, and made history by his letter to Archbishop

Lefebvre of June 25, 1976, in which he demanded a "true fidelity to the *conciliar* Church."

Besret, Dom Bernard (b. 1935): Cistercian, assistant to the Abbot General of the Order (1963-64) then prior of Boquen Abbey (1964-69), afterward he noisily left the religious life and the priesthood.

Boyer, Fr. Charles (1884-1980): Jesuit, professor at the Gregorian University of Rome and consultant for several Roman Congregations, at the time of Vatican II he became a specialist on ecumenism.

Botte, Dom Bernard (1893-1980): Benedictine of Mont-César Abbey (Belgium), a specialist on liturgy, member of the *Consilium*, he was in charge of the group tasked with reforming the Rite of Ordination, and collaborated with the group tasked with drafting the new Eucharistic prayers.

Bugnini, Msgr. Annibale (1912-1982): Lazarist, secretary of the *Consilium* in 1964, secretary of the Congregation for Divine Worship in 1969, elevated to the episcopacy in 1972, he was the leader and driving force of the liturgical reform. Having fallen into disgrace, he was named Apostolic Pro-nuncio to Iran (1976). In a posthumously published book, *La Riforma Liturgica*, he recounted the development of the reform from his viewpoint, strongly emphasizing Paul VI's involvement.

Carli, H. E. Luigi (1914-86): Bishop of Segni (Italy) from 1957-71, then Archbishop of Gaeta, of a very traditional spirit, he fought along side Archbishop Lefebvre in the *Coetus Internationalis Patrum* during the Second Vatican Council, though without following him afterwards.

Chautard, Dom Jean-Baptiste (1858-1935): Trappist, Abbot of the Chambarand Monastery (1897) then of Sept-Fons (1899), he wrote the celebrated work of spirituality *The Soul of the Apostolate*, which St. Pius X highly recommended.

Cristiani, Msgr. Leon (1879-1971): theologian and historian, dean of the Lyons Catholic Faculty of Letters, he specialized in the study of the sixteenth century, notably Luther.

Davies, Michael (1936-2004): English religious historian of Welsh origin, he was a prolific writer, notably about the current religious crisis. Archbishop Lefebvre would often quote *Cranmer's Godly Order*, a work Davies published in 1976.

Delamare, Edith (1921-93): Journalist, she was the religion columnist for the French weekly *Rivarol* from 1954-89, and proved to be very sympathetic to Archbishop Lefebvre's combat.

Dhanis, Edouard (1902-78): Jesuit, rector of the Gregorian University of Rome, member of the International Theological Commission, consultant of the Congregation for the Doctrine of the Faith, he was sent on June 27, 1976, to Archbishop Lefebvre bearing a letter from Bishop Benelli trying to persuade him either to concelebrate with him in the new rite, or to not proceed to the scheduled ordinations. Archbishop Lefebvre did not adopt either of these two suggestions. In 1977, at the request of Pope Paul VI, Dhanis participated in some doctrinal discussions with Archbishop Lefebvre.

Froget, Rev. Fr. Barthélémy (1843-1905): Dominican, author of a book of spiritual theology of Thomist inspiration, *The Indwelling of the Holy Ghost in the Souls of the Just* (1898).

Garrigou-Lagrange, Rev. Fr. Reginald (1877-1964): Dominican, professor of philosophy, dogma, and mystical theology at the Angelicum University at Rome, he published numerous works of speculative and mystical theology of Thomistic inspiration, notably *The Three Ages of the Interior Life*, *Christian Perfection and Contemplation*, *Divine Providence and Trust in God*, and *The Love of God and the Cross of Christ*.

Gelineau, Rev. Fr. Joseph (b. 1920): Jesuit, liturgical specialist, he was the author of the translation of the psalter for the Jerusalem

Bible and the creator of numerous French hymns during the years 1950-1970.

Graber, H. E. Rudolf (1903-92): Bishop of Regensburg (Germany) from 1962-81, traditionalist, he fought along side Archbishop Lefebvre in the *Coetus Internationalis Patrum* during the Second Vatican Council. In 1973 he published a book (published the same year in French) very critical of the post-conciliar period, *Athanasius and the Church of Our Time*, but did not follow Archbishop Lefebvre in his combat, notably on the question of fidelity to the traditional Mass.

Grégoire, H. E. Paul (1911-93): Auxiliary Bishop of Montreal in 1961, Archbishop of Montreal from 1968-90, Cardinal in 1988.

Guérard des Lauriers, Rev. Fr. Michel-Louis (1898-1988): Dominican, professor of theology at the Roman University of the Lateran, he was one of the writers of the *Short Critical Study of the New Order of Mass*, taught at the Seminary at Ecône, then evolved towards sedevacantism (the "Cassiciacum Thesis"). In 1981, he had himself secretly consecrated bishop by H. E. Ngô Dinh Thuc, former Archbishop of Hué (Vietnam).

Gueranger, Dom Prosper (1805-75): Benedictine, Abbot of Solesmes, restorer of the Benedictine Order in France, propagator of the Roman liturgy, he is often called "the Doctor of the liturgy" because of his magisterial work *The Liturgical Institutions*.

Guillou, Dom Edouard (1911-91): Benedictine of the Abbey of the Source (Paris), he was the liturgical editor of the traditional bulletin *Nouvelles de Chrétienté*, became professor at the Seminary at Ecône, then founded the FSSPX priory at Nice, France.

Guitton, Jean (1901-99): French philosopher and member of the Academy Française, he was a close friend of Pope Paul VI (about whom he published two books: *Conversations with*

Paul VI and *Paul VI Secret*), and was appointed "mediator" by a French court between Cardinal Marty and Msgr. Ducaud-Bourget after the occupation of St. Nicholas du Chardonnet Church (Paris) in 1977.

Journet, Charles Cardinal (1891-1975): theologian, named cardinal in 1965, friend of Pope Paul VI, somewhat traditional, he was consulted by Archbishop Lefebvre before the foundation of the seminary at Ecône, but distanced himself from the Archbishop in 1973.

Mamie, H. E. Pierre (b. 1920): Bishop of Lausanne, Geneva, and Fribourg from 1970-95, on December 29, 1970, he succeeded Msgr. François Charrière, the friend of Archbishop Lefebvre who had erected the Society of St. Pius X in his diocese on November 1, 1970. Hostile towards this foundation, on May 6, 1975, Bishop Mamie withdrew the authorization given by his predecessor, thus (illicitly) depriving the Priestly Society of Saint Pius X of its canonical existence.

Marmion, Dom Columba (1858-1923): Benedictine, Abbot of Maredsous (Belgium), he published three volumes of his spiritual conferences, imbued with scriptural and Thomistic inspiration, which enjoyed an extraordinary success: *Christ, the Life of the Soul* (1918), *Christ in His Mysteries* (1919), and *Christ, the Ideal of the Monk* (1922). He was beatified by Pope John Paul II.

Ottaviani, Alfredo Cardinal (1890-1979): Cardinal in 1953, secretary of the Holy Office from 1959-66, the pro-prefect of the Congregation for the Doctrine of the Faith from 1966-68, eminent representative of the traditional spirit of the Roman Curia, he cosigned with Cardinal Bacci the letter accompanying the *Short Critical Study of the New Order of Mass* (1969).

Pace, Dom Giuseppe (1911-2000): Salesian at Turin (Italy), firmly attached to the traditional Mass, he is the author of numerous works, notably the book *Pro Missa Traditionali*.

Parsch, Dom Pius (1884-1954): Augustinian Canon of Klosterneuburg (Austria), one of the principal actors of the liturgical movement between the world wars (the review *Bibel und Liturgie*), he published a *Guide to the Liturgical Year*.

Philippe, Paul Cardinal (1905-84): Dominican, professor of theology at the Angelicum University at Rome and at Saulchoir (the Dominicans' school of theology at Paris), he was secretary of the Congregation for Religious from 1959-67, secretary of the Congregation for the Doctrine of the Faith from 1967-73, and finally Cardinal Prefect of the Congregation for the Oriental Churches in 1973.

Pie, Louis-Édouard Cardinal (1815-80): Bishop of Poitiers from 1849-80, member of the "Deputation" of the Faith at the First Vatican Council, cardinal in 1879, he preached a solidly theological and ardently anti-liberal doctrine.

Seper, Franjo Cardinal (1905-81): Archbishop of Zagreb (Croatia) in 1960, cardinal in 1965, prefect of the Congregation for the Doctrine of the Faith from 1968-81, it was his duty to examine the *Novus Ordo Missae* at the time of its promulgation, then the *Short Critical Study of the New Order of Mass*, and finally he had to handle the "Lefebvre case."

Stickler, Alfons Maria Cardinal (1910-2007): Salesian, prefect of the Vatican Library in 1983, cardinal in 1985, traditional, he always remained faithful to the Tridentine Mass and on several occasions publicly manifested his esteem for the traditional Mass.

INDEX

The letter *n* following a page number indicates that the information is located in a footnote.

A

ablutions, prayers during, 162-163
Adam, Bishop Nestor, 292
adoration, nature of, 82-83
Agnus Dei (prayer), 141-142
Alleluia, 25-26
altar, 16-17, 55-56, 189-192, 248
Ambrose, Saint, 163
anarchy, and *Novus Ordo Missae*, 219-221
Andrew, Saint, and preaching, 35
angels, 81-82
Anglicanism, 235-239
Antonelli, Giuseppe Ferdinando Cardinal, 233*n*
Antonini, Archbishop, 277
Arabic, use of in Islam, 212
asceticism, 256
attendance, at *Novus Ordo Missae*, 280-285
Aufer a Nobis (prayer), 14-16
Augustine, Saint, 49, 150, 273

B

Bacci, Antonio Cardinal, 261, 266
Baptism, 46
Baum, Msgr. W.W., 227
Beatitudes, 100-102
Benediction, final, 167
Benelli, Giovanni Cardinal, 224
Besret, Dom Bernard, 268
Blessed Sacrament.
 See Holy Eucharist
Blessed Trinity
 invocation of, 165-166
 Kyrie and, 18-19

mystery of, 9-10
Sign of the Cross and, 3-4
See also Holy Ghost
Blessed Virgin Mary
 communion with, 91-94
 Holy Communion and, 149
 priests and, 110-111
 sacrifice and, 70
blessing, of the water, 60-61
Bossuet, Jacques Bénigne, 97-98
Botte, Dom Bernard, 227
Boyer, Fr. Charles, 225
Bugnini, Msgr. Annibale
 as drafter of *Novus Ordo Missae*, 225-226
 ecumenism and, 228
 and imposition of *Novus Ordo Missae*, 275-279
 inculturation and, 65
 Institutio Generalis and, 224
 liturgical principles of, 232-234
 Normative Mass and, 183-185
 and participation
  of faithful, 199-200
burial Mass, 219

C

Canon of the Mass, 26, 78-123, 249
Caritatis Studium (Leo XIII), 52
Carli, H. E. Luigi, 279
Catechism of the Council of Trent
 Credo and, 41
 daily Communion and, 134
 eternal life and, 47-48
 Holy Eucharist and, 159-160
 pro multis issue and, 210
 and sacrifice of Cross, 54-55
 and words of Consecration, 104
Cecilia, Saint, 120
celibacy, reason for, 111
Centre Jean-Bart, 193
chalice, offering of, 62-66

chapel, meaning of, 65
charity
  as internal law of God, 145-146
  virtue of, 16, 134-135
Chautard, Dom Jean-Baptiste, 285
children's Masses, 219-220
Christian Perfection and Contemplation (Garrigou-Lagrange), 285
Christ, the Ideal of the Monk (Marmion), 285
Church, belief in and Creed, 45-46
Church militant, 118-120
Church suffering, 116-118
Church triumphant, 90-94
Cicognani, Cardinal, 275
civilization, source of, 64-66, 161
Collect, 22-23, 163
Communicantes (prayer), 90-94
Communion, in the hand, 196-198
Communion of the Mass, 125-173
compunction, definition of, 13
concelebration, 248-249, 260
Confiteor, 10-13, 152-155
Consecration, words of, 102-111, 203-211, 265
contempt, for things of world, 216-217
Council of Ephesus, 55
Council of Pistoia, 236
Council of Trent
  Canon of the Mass and, 26
  ceremonies and, 247-248
  liturgical reform and, 263
  and Mass as sacrifice, 55, 97
  propitiation and, 117, 188
  Sacraments and, 268-269
  traditional rite of Mass and, 286-287, 290
Credo, 35-50
Cristiani, Msgr. Leon, 236
Cross, sacrifice of, 54-55
crucifixes, in *Novus Ordo Missae*, 190-192
Crucifixion, 7-9, 41-43
Curé of Ars, 142

D

Davies, Michael, 222*n*, 223*n*
dead, Mass for, 219
Debout, Jacques, 137-138
Delamare, Madam Edith, 257
democratic Mass, 202-203
detachment, spirit of, 255-256
Deus, Qui Humanae Substantiae (prayer), 60-61
Domine Jesu Christe (prayer), 144-147
Domine, Non Sum Dignus (prayer), 148-149
dulia (worship), definition of, 290
Dwyer, Msgr., 183

E

Eastern Catholics, 206-207
Ecce Agnus Dei (prayer), 155-156
ecumenism, 226-230, 256-258
Epistle, 24-25
eternal life. *See* life everlasting
eternity, concept of, 47, 79-80
Eucharist. *See* Holy Eucharist

F

faithful, Communion of, 156-158
Faith, Law of, and liturgical reform, 185-203
faith, loss of and *Novus Ordo Missae*, 244-254
Fifteen Bishops Profess the Faith of the Catholic Church, 188
Final Benediction, 167
Fontgombault, church at, 118
Francis Xavier, Saint, and preaching, 35
Froget, Fr. Barthélemy, 71

G

Galatians, Epistle to, 31-32

Index

321

Garrigou-Lagrange, Fr. Reginald, 47, 102, 285
Gelineau, Fr. Joseph, 199*n*
genuflection, suppression of, 194-195
gestures. *See* rubrics
Gloria, 18-22
Gloria Patri, inclination at, 9-10
God
  and *Credo*, 37-39
  description of, 79-80
  and *Pater Noster*, 125-138
Gospel readings, 29-32
Gospels, in *Novus Ordo Missae*, 196
Graber, H. E. Rudolf, 282-283
Gradual, 25-26
Grégoire, H. E. Paul, 258, 271
Gueranger, Dom Prosper, 232
Guérard des Lauriers, Fr. Michel-Louis, 282
Guide to the Liturgical Year (Parsch), 23
Guillou, Dom Édouard, 216-219
Guitton, Jean, 263
Gut, Cardinal, 276-277

H

Haec Commixtio (prayer), 140-141
Hanc Igitur (prayer), 94-96
Holy Communion. *See* Holy Eucharist
Holy Eucharist
  and Communion in hand, 196-198
  and Council of Trent, 97
  and daily Communion, 134
  effects of, 147-148, 162-163
  fruits of, 159-161
  matter and form in, 264-265
  and *Novus Ordo Missae*, 192-193, 196-197, 248, 249
  and offering, 56-58
  as pledge of everlasting life, 140-141
  preparation for, 152-155

Holy Ghost
  and *Credo*, 44-45
  and *Veni, Sanctificator*, 70-71
  See also Trinity
Holy Trinity. *See* Blessed Trinity
host, offering of, 58-60
humility, virtue of, 14-16, 119-120

I

Incarnation, in teaching of Thomas Aquinas, 39
incensement, 72
inculturation, 65, 257-258
indifferentism, 256-258
Indult Mass, 305-308
The Indwelling of the Holy Spirit in the Souls of the Just according to the Teaching of St. Thomas Aquinas (Froget), 71
Innocent III, Pope, 208-209
In Spiritu Humilitatis (prayer), 66-70
Institutio Generalis, 222-225, 275-278
Introibo ad Altare Dei (antiphon), 4-5
Introit, 17-19
Islam, and use of Arabic, 212
Ite, Missa Est, 164-165

J

Jesus Christ
  Crucifixion of, 7-9, 41-43
  and *Gloria*, 18-22
  Incarnation of, 39
  meditation on life of, 29-30
  Resurrection of, 43-44
  and sacrifice of Cross, 54-55
  as sign of contradiction, 6-7
  victimhood of, 155-156
  See also reign of Christ the King
John, Archbishop of Lyons, 208-209
John XXIII, 183, 226

Joint Catholic-Lutheran
    Commission, 229-230
Journet, Charles Cardinal, 276
Judica Me (Psalm), 5-9
Justin, Saint, 128

K

Kingship of Christ. *See* reign of
    Christ the King
kissing the altar, 16-17, 55-56
kneeling, for Communion, 157-158
Kyrie, 18-19

L

laity, role of, 198-200, 243
Last Gospel, 167-173
Latin Mass. *See* traditional
    rite of Mass
Latin, use of, 181-182, 211-216,
    247
Lavabo (Psalm 25), 72-74
law, and obedience, 271-275
Law of Faith, and liturgical reform,
    185-203
Law of Prayer, and liturgical reform,
    203-222
legitimacy, of opposition to
    Novus Ordo Missae, 294-295
L'Église en Alsace (bulletin of
    diocese of Strasbourg), 229
Leo XIII
    and *Caritatis Studium*, 52
    and *Libertas Praestantissimum*,
    271, 274
Lessius, Ven. Leonard, 128-129
Lex orandi, lex credendi (law of
    prayer affects law of faith),
    185*n*, 211, 246, 251
Libera Nos (prayer), 137-138
Libertas Praestantissimum (Leo XIII),
    271, 274
life everlasting, belief in and *Credo*,
    46-50

liturgical reform
    Anglicanism and, 237-238
    basis for, 177-179
    Council of Trent and, 263
    intention behind, 222-234
    Law of Faith and, 185-203
    Law of Prayer and, 203-222
    of Luther, 235-243
    of Msgr. Bugnini, 183-185
    principles of, 179-183
Lutheranism, 235-239
Lutheranism and Protestantism
    (Cristiani), 236
Luther, Martin
    demands of, 230
    liturgical reform and, 235-243
    words of Consecration and,
    207-208

M

Mamie, H. E. Pierre, 296
Marmion, Dom Columba, 13, 285
marriage, sacrament of, 88-90
Mary. *See* Blessed Virgin Mary
"Masses for Small Groups and for
    Particular Groups," 220-221
Masses, reduction in number of,
    258-260
Mass for the dead, 219
Mass of St. Pius V. *See* traditional
    rite of Mass
Melanchthon, 241-242
Memento, of the dead, 116-118
Memento, of the living, 88-90
Missale Romanum (Apostolic
    Constitution), 292
Modernism, and concept of
    Sacrament, 267-268
Montfort, Saint Louis-Marie
    Grignion de, 35
Munda Cor Meum (prayer), 27-29
Mysterium Fidei (Mystery of Faith),
    107-109, 208-209, 265

N

New Mass. *See Novus Ordo Missae*
New order of Mass. *See Novus Ordo Missae*
Nobis Quoque Peccatoribus (prayer), 118-120
Normative Mass, 183-185
Novus Ordo Missae
    anarchy and, 219-221
    assessment of, 251-254
    attendance at, 280-285
    condemnation of by Tradition, 261-264
    Consecration in, 203-211
    definition of, 222-225
    ecumenism and, 226-230
    Latin and, 211-216
    loss of faith and, 244-254
    Msgr. Bugnini as drafter of, 225-226
    number of Masses and, 258-260
    Paul VI and, 233, 275-279
    "Prayers of Presentation" in, 203-211
    priesthood and, 198-203
    and Proper of the Mass, 216-219
    propitiation and, 190-192
    Protestantism and, 226-230, 302
    and question of obligation, 271-285
    Real Presence and, 193-198
    sacrifice and, 185-193
    and spirit of sacrifice, 254-256
    validity of, 264-271

O

obedience
    appearance of, 293-294
    and law, 271-275
oblation, prayer of, 94-96
obligation, and *Novus Ordo Missae*, 271-285

Offerimus Tibi, Domine (prayer), 62-66
offering
    of chalice, 62-66
    of the host, 58-60
    preparation of, 56-58
Offering of the Mass, 112-115
Offertory, 52-55, 58-60, 203-211
Oramus Te (prayer), 16-17
Orate, Fratres (prayer), 76-77
Ottaviani, Alfredo Cardinal, 261, 266, 292
The Ottaviani Intervention: A Short Critical Study of the New Order of Mass (Ottaviani and Bacci), 261
Our Lord. *See* Jesus Christ

P

Pace, Dom Giuseppe, 209, 286
Parsch, Dom Pius, 23
Pater Noster, 125-138
Paul, Saint
    epistles of, 24-25
    and Epistle to Galatians, 31-32
    obedience and, 273, 293-294
    and preaching, 33-35
    and propitiation, 188
Paul VI, Pope
    Latin and, 214-215
    and liturgical reform, 179-180
    Novus Ordo Missae and, 233, 275-279
    traditional rite of Mass and, 286-287
    Vatican II and, 263
Pax Domini Sit Semper Vobiscum (prayer), 138-139
peace, prayer for, 138-139, 142-143
Pelegrino, Cardinal, 279
Perceptio Corporis Tui (prayer), 147-148
Peter, Saint, 35, 273
Philippe, Paul Cardinal, 259
Pie, Louis-Édouard Cardinal, 132

Pintonello, Msgr., 226
Pio, Saint Padre, 142
Pius V, Saint, 289-292
Pius XII, Pope, 178, 182-183
Pius X, Saint
    and Christian civilization, 65-66
    and daily Communion, 134
    and liturgical reform, 182
    liturgy and, 215-216
Poma, Cardinal, 279
pope, and obedience, 272-275
Postcommunion Collect, 163
Prayer, Law of, and liturgical reform, 203-222
preaching. *See* sermon
Precious Blood, drinking of, 152
Preface, 78-83
priest
    Communion of, 150
    and drinking of Precious Blood, 152
    formation of, 298-299
    intention of at Mass, 265-269
    role of, 54
    Thanksgiving of, 151
priesthood
    denial of, 242-243
    in *Novus Ordo Missae*, 198-203
private Mass, 202-203
pro multis issue, 210
Proper of the Mass, and *Novus Ordo Missae*, 216-219
propitiation
    and Council of Trent, 117
    denial of, 239-241
    and *Novus Ordo Missae*, 187-188, 190-192
    and sacrifice of the Mass, 59-60
Protestantism
    and *Novus Ordo Missae*, 226-230, 302
    propitiation and, 187-188
Psalm 25, 72-74
public Mass, 202-203

Q

Quam Oblationem (prayer), 96-102
Quattuor Abhinc Annos (decree), 305
Quo Primum (St. Pius V), 289-292

R

rationalism, 213
Ratzinger, Joseph Cardinal, 225, 258
Real Presence, dogma of, and *Novus Ordo Missae*, 193-198
The Reform of the Liturgy (Bugnini), 199-200
reign of Christ the King, 131-134, 256-258
relics, in altars, 17
religion, virtue of, 52-53
Resurrection, of Our Lord, 43-44
Revelation, and Tradition/Sacred Scripture, 230
Roy, Dom Jean, 270
rubrics, in *Novus Ordo Missae*, 188-190, 194-195

S

Sacrament, concept of, 267-269
sacred, loss of, 247-250
Sacred Scripture
    in *Novus Ordo Missae*, 196
    and Tradition, 230-231
sacrifice
    in Christian life, 67-70
    and *Novus Ordo Missae*, 185-193, 254-256
    and Offertory, 52-55
    as source of salvation, 69-70
sacrifice of the Cross, 54-55
saints, communion with, 90-94
salvation
    Mass as source of, 62-64
    suffering and, 69-70
Sanctus (prayer), 83-84
Secret, 77-78
Seper, Franjo Cardinal, 276

Index

sermon, 32-35
Sermon on the Mount, 100-102
Sign of the Cross
   and Blessed Trinity, 3-4
   in *Novus Ordo Missae*, 189
   over host and chalice, 100-102, 113-114
   silent recitation, of prayers at Canon, 84-86
Sillon movement, 65-66
simplicity, of children, 154-155
sinner, man as, 11-13
social reign, of Christ the King. *See* reign of Christ the King
Society of Saint Pius X, 282
The Soul of the Apostolate (Chautard), 285
spirit of sacrifice, loss of, 254-256
spiritual combat, 217-218
Stephen, Saint, and preaching, 34-35
Stickler, Alfons Maria Cardinal, 261*n*
Supplices (prayer), 115-116
Supra Quae (prayer), 114-115
Sursum Corda (introduction of the Preface), 78-80
Suscipe, Sancta Trinitas (prayer), 74, 75-76
Suscipe, Sancte Pater (prayer), 58-60
Syro-Malabar rite, 245

T

Te Igitur (prayer), 86-87
Thanksgiving, after Communion, 158-161
Thanksgiving, of priest, 151
The Ottaviani Intervention: A Short Critical Study of the New Order of Mass (Ottaviani and Bacci), 266
Thomas Aquinas, Saint
   adoration and, 82-83
   angels and, 81-82
   charity and, 145-146
   Holy Eucharist and, 159-160
   humility and, 14-16, 119-120
   Incarnation and, 39
   and man as sinner, 12
   obedience and, 273
   sacrifice and, 54
   wisdom and, 136
   words of Consecration and, 105, 207-208, 209
"The Three Against the Other" (Debout), 137-138
time, concept of, 47, 79-80
Tract, 25-26
Tradition
   and condemnation of *Novus Ordo Missae*, 261-264
   Revelation and, 230
   Sacred Scripture and, 230-231
traditional rite of Mass
   apostolic origin of, 286-289
   perpetual privilege of, 289-292
transfinalization, 268-269
transignification, 268-269
transubstantiation, 241-242, 268-269
Tres Abhinc Annos (Paul VI), 214
Tridentine rite of Mass. *See* traditional rite of Mass
Trinity. *See* Blessed Trinity

U

Una Voce (organization), 307
Undes et Memores (prayer), 112-114

V

validity, of *Novus Ordo Missae*, 264-271
Veni, Sanctificator (prayer), 70-71
vernacular, use of, 181-182, 211-216
vestments, 248
vocations, 258-259

W

water, blessing of, 60-61
water, mixed with wine, 62